A personal narrative of political experiences

ROBERT M. LA FOLLETTE, 1922
From a photograph by John Glander

A personal narrative
of political experiences
by Robert M. La Follette

La Follette's
Autobiography

with a foreword by Allan Nevins

Madison, 1960

The University of Wisconsin Press

100593

.

published by

The University of Wisconsin Press

430 Sterling Court, Madison 6, Wisconsin

Copyright 1911, 1913, by Robert M. La Follette
Copyright renewed. New edition copyright © 1960
by the Regents of the University of Wisconsin

Printed in the United States of America

Foreword

For an understanding of Bossism, Reform, and Progressivism as they were known in the United States between 1890 and 1912, this book is the most illuminating as well as the most interesting work in existence. It carries us into the very heart of Progressive sentiment and principle. It is astonishing that the autobiography of so magnetic and powerful a leader as Robert Marion La Follette, almost worshipped by millions and deeply distrusted by millions more, should have gone out of print for so many years. Its republication is a service to all who can profit from a record of one of the most significant upheavals of the past generation, from a remarkably honest piece of self-portraiture, and from an eventful story told with fiery energy.

The upheaval, which followed Populism and preceded the New Deal, had a quality all its own. In the stormy period here covered many men thought with La Follette that greedy business interests were fast gaining control of the land through the servants they placed in state governments and the Senate; and with varying degrees of fervor reformers fought their way to the helm in one state after another—Dolliver and Cummins in Iowa, Bristow in Kansas, George W. Norris in Nebraska, Beveridge in Indiana, U'Ren in Oregon, Hughes in New York—to combat these interests. All of them kept their eyes on La Follette and Wisconsin as models, or at least inspiration. Part of the spirit of Progressivism was a deep faith in democracy. In the words of Stephen A. Douglas, "Let the voice of the people rule." La Follette wrote of the year 1900: "I had then, and have had ever since, absolute confidence in the people." Part of the spirit was a crusading belligerence. La Follette likes to use the word "battleground." On one battleground he spoke forty-eight days in succession, and "I averaged eight and one quarter hours a day on the platform." Part of the spirit was pride in the fact that people were being educated by the battles. Not only were reforms won; the voters were meanwhile being made better citizens.

And the reforms were important. Particularly in Wisconsin did they comprise a whole new charter of self-government before La Follette carried his Progressivism to the Senate. Sometimes they were a little disappointing, like the direct primary; sometimes they turned out to be somewhat ineffectual, like the corrupt practises legislation. But the civil service reforms shut out the spoils system; the registration of lobbyists brought pressures into the open; tax equalization helped the poor man, while the inheritance tax and income tax provided fuller public revenues; the regulation of utilities stopped overcharges; legislation protecting the right to join unions gave the worker a squarer deal; the pure food legislation safeguarded health; the development of the schools and the state university meant a better-informed electorate and more use of experts in government. All the while La Follette remained mindful of his central goal. "The supreme issue," he wrote, "involving all others, is the encroachment of the powerful few upon the rights of the many." It was to carry his fight against such encroachment into the national sphere that in 1905 he left Madison, his work there fairly done, and went to Washington.

There at first he found himself, in his phrase, "alone in the Senate"; for the Senate is what a Washington correspondent has called it, the "citadel," and resents outsiders who would storm it. Dramatic as are the early chapters of La Follette's book on his contest with Senator John C. Spooner's machine, on Senator Philetus Sawyer's brazen attempt to bribe him, and on his ten years' battle with the Wisconsin bosses, the later chapters on his duels with Aldrich and others of the Old Guard in the national capital are even better. The pages which relate how Dolliver, Borah, Bourne, and others came to his side, and the description of the culminating battle against the Payne-Aldrich Tariff are magnificent. Of especial interest are the characterizations of public figures ranging from Uncle Joe Cannon to President Roosevelt. La Follette concedes that T. R. was "the keenest and ablest interpreter of what I would call the superficial public sentiment of a given time," but denies his possession of any insight into the deeper convictions of the people. Of special interest, too, is La Follette's stern insistence that any compromise which involves principle is wrong. T. R. always thought a half-loaf better than no bread. Not so, retorts La Follette. "Half a loaf as a rule dulls the appetite, and destroys the keenness of interest in attaining the full loaf. A half-way measure . . . is certain to weaken, disappoint, and dissipate public interest."

In brief, La Follette agreed with John Morley, who said: "It makes all the difference in the world whether we put Truth in the first place, or in second place."   •

Beyond its account of a great and stirring movement, beyond its recital of dramatic episodes, this book has enduring value in its honesty as a piece of self-portraiture. The author is perfectly frank about his relative conservatism during his six early years in Congress, 1885-1891. "I knew next to nothing about the underlying forces," he writes. He helped frame the McKinley Tariff, not realizing that most of the information that was fed him "consisted of the loose statements of interested men." He is frank also in letting us see that his abandonment by the party bosses when disaster overtook him in the Wisconsin elections of 1890 did much to estrange him from them. Sawyer's effort at bribery, the boss actually opening his pocketbook to take a roll of bills in his hand, completed La Follette's disillusionment. Fighting down an impulse to throttle the old man, the young attorney staggered out of the hotel perceiving at last "the extremes to which this power that Sawyer represented would go to secure the results it was after." Yet La Follette was then thirty-six. A certain political simplicity, a naive acceptance of the status quo, characterized him until the "terrible shock" of Sawyer's approach, and the "awful ordeal" of the ensuing winter when old associates treated him as an outcast. This early naivete made his subsequent anger all the fiercer, his resolution all the sterner.

Clearly illustrated in this book are all La Follette's traits. He had the tendency toward stout dissent that had been manifest in Roger Williams, John Woolman, and James G. Birney; dissent not for its own sake, but the sake of principle. He had the frontier self-confidence of Andrew Jackson, and some of the same aggressiveness. No reverse discouraged him. He was as intense as William Leggett, or Garrison. He speaks here of the lack of any humor in one of Garfield's speeches which he heard; but being intense, he also was humorless, at least in public. His certainty that he was in the right, and that what was right must be unflinchingly asserted, sometimes made him a little arrogant—or, as Woodrow Wilson put it, "wilful." His hostility toward the corrupt alliance of business and politics led him to underrate some of the difficulties which struggling businessmen faced; the railroad rebate system, for example, was largely a product of cutthroat competition in the absence of firm law, and nobody was happier to be rid of it than clearsighted railroad men. He was not without prejudice in foreign affairs, and failed to do justice to the constructive aspects of colonial regimes. But in general how just he was, how fearless, how tireless in his crusades, how great and noble a fighter for democracy; and how much he did to promote a movement not only purgative, but constructive!

His friends always recognized his high purposes. William Allen White declared that he was a modern Savonarola, an apostle of revolution, "a nice, decent, and dangerous revolution that will take a long trek toward economic justice." His enemies grudgingly admitted his achievements. "Even those who disagree most strongly with La Follette," said the Detroit *News* during the bitter campaign of 1924, "admit his honesty, his loyalty and his courage."

It is unfortunate that La Follette, who repeatedly injured his health by overwork, was not spared time to bring this story down from 1912 to 1925. He could have told with equal force of his battle against A. Mitchell Palmer's "red raids"; of his leadership in the movement to expel Truman H. Newberry from the Senate for excessive political expenditures; of his championship of the depressed Western farmers in the early 1920's; of his service in turning the spotlight on Teapot Dome and other abuses under Harding; of his share in rescuing Muscle Shoals; and of his sustained struggle against the infiltration of government by selfish public utility interests, oil interests, the ship subsidy interests, and other grasping business interests. He remained a fighting radical to the end; and as Senator Couzens wrote the conservative Vandenberg, "Even Christ was a radical." The story of these later years has been admirably related in the biography* by his widow and daughter. That work, and this book, deserve a careful reading by conscientious citizens; for the battle La Follette led still goes on, and the lessons he instilled still need pondering.

ALLAN NEVINS.

June, 1960.

Robert M. La Follette by Belle Case La Follette and Fola La Follette (Macmillan, two volumes, 1953).

Introduction

In the preparation of this narrative I have no literary intent whatsoever. I am not writing for the sake of writing, nor for the mere purpose of relating the events of my political life. I have not yet reached the secluded age when a man writes his life story for the enjoyment the exercise gives him.

Every line of this autobiography is written for the express purpose of exhibiting the struggle for a more representative government which is going forward in this country, and to cheer on the fighters for that cause. Most of these chapters were written at Washington between the close of one important Congressional struggle and the opening of another. The final chapters were written after the National Convention and before the presidential election of 1912. Thus the entire narrative may be said to have been written from the field.

We have long rested comfortably in this country upon the assumption that because our form of government was democratic, it was therefore automatically producing democratic results. Now, there is nothing mysteriously potent about the forms and names of democratic institutions that should make them self-operative. Tyranny and oppression are just as possible under democratic forms as under any other. We are slow to realize that democracy is a life; and involves continual struggle. It is only as those of every generation who love democracy resist with all their might the encroachments of its enemies that the ideals of representative government can even be nearly approximated.

The essence of the Progressive movement, as I see it, lies in its purpose to uphold the fundamental principles of representative government. It expresses the hopes and desires of millions of common men and women who are willing to fight for their ideals, to take defeat if necessary, and still go on fighting.

Fortunes of birth, temperament and political environment have thrown me into this struggle, and have made me in some degree a pioneer in the Progressive movement. I am therefore writing my own story in these pages because I believe this to be the best means of mapping out the whole field of conflict and exposing the real character of the enemy.

I shall give as faithful an account as I know how of political events in which I have participated and I shall characterize the strong men whom I have known, and especially I shall endeavor to present those underlying motives and forces which are often undiscerned in American politics.

I believe that most thoughtful readers, perplexed by the conditions which confront the country, will find that they have been meeting in various guises the same problems that I have had to meet, and that their minds have consequently been traveling along much the same lines as mine, and toward much the same conclusions. I trust this book may be the means of causing many men to think as one—and to fight as one.

It is a pleasure to express my grateful appreciation of the valuable assistance which Mr. Ray Stannard Baker has given me in the revision of the manuscript for this work and of the helpful suggestions of Professor John R. Commons and his verification of the statistical and economic data.

ROBERT M. LA FOLLETTE

Washington, D. C.,
October 1, 1912.

Contents

A personal narrative of political experiences

Chapter 1

Political Beginnings

Few young men who entered public life thirty years ago had any wide outlook upon affairs, or any general political ideas. They were drawn into politics just as other men were drawn into the professions or the arts, or into business, because it suited their tastes and ambitions. Often the commonest reasons and the most immediate necessities commanded them, and clear understanding, strong convictions, and deep purposes were developed only as they were compelled to face the real problems and meet the real temptations of the public service.

My own political experiences began in the summer of 1880 when I determined to become a candidate for district attorney of Dane County, Wisconsin, and it resulted almost immediately in the first of many struggles with the political boss and the political machine which then controlled, absolutely, the affairs of the State of Wisconsin. I was twenty-five years old that summer. A year previously, in June, 1879, I had been graduated from the University of Wisconsin, and after five months' study of the law, part of the time in the office of R. M. Bashford, and part of the time in the university law school, I had been admitted to the bar, in February, 1880.

I was as poverty-stricken a young lawyer as ever hung his shingle to the wind. I had no money at all. My single term at the university law school had been rendered possible only through the consideration of the faculty in making an extraordinary exception in my case, and permitting me to enter without paying the usual matriculation fee. I had no money—but as fine an assortment of obligations and ambitions as any young man ever had. I had my mother and sister to support, as I had supported them partially all through my college course—and finally, I had become engaged to be married.

To an impecunious young lawyer almost without clients (the district attorneyship of Dane County, paying at that time the munificent salary of $800 a year with an allowance of $50 for expenses, seemed like a golden opportunity. Though it appeared immeasurably difficult of attainment, I determined to make for it with all my strength. What I wanted was an opportunity to work—to practise my profession—and to make a living. I knew that trial work would appeal to me, and I believed I could try criminal cases successfully.)

I had an old horse which I had used during my university course in riding out to a district school I had taught to aid in paying my way, and borrowing a buggy and harness from Ben Miner, a friend and supporter, I now began driving through the country and talking with the farmers about my candidacy.

It was harvest time and I remember how I often tied my horse, climbed the fences, and found the farmer and his men in the fields.

"Ain't you over-young?" was the objection chiefly raised.

I was small of stature and thin—at that time. I weighed only one hundred and twenty pounds—and I looked even younger than I really was. Nor was I then in good health.

Throughout my university course I had been compelled to do much outside work. Besides teaching school I had become proprietor of the *University Press,* then the only college paper, burdening myself with debt in the purchase. It was published bi-monthly, and I not only did the editorial work but made up the forms and hustled for advertisements and subscriptions. Under the strain of all these tasks, added to my regular college work, my health, naturally robust, gave way, and for four or five years I went down under the load at the end of every term of court. A marked physical change came to me later and I have grown stronger and stronger with the years.

But there were a number of things that helped me in my canvass for the nomination. I was born in Primrose Township, Dane County, only twenty miles from Madison, where my father, a Kentuckian by birth, had been a pioneer settler from Indiana. I knew farm ways and farm life, and many of the people who were not acquainted with me personally knew well from what family I came—and that it was an honest family. The people of the county were a mixture of New Englanders, Norwegians and Germans. I had been raised among the Norwegians and understood the language fairly well, though I could speak it only a little—but even that little helped me.

4

I also had something of a claim to recognition on my own account. In my last year as a student I had been chosen, after preliminary tests, to represent the university in the state collegiate oratorical contest. I had won the prize at Beloit with an oration on the character of Shakespeare's "Iago" and then I had been chosen to represent Wisconsin in the interstate contest at Iowa City, Iowa. This I also won, and when I returned to Madison, university feeling ran to so high a pitch that the students met me at the train and drew the carriage up the hill to the university where I was formally welcomed; and that evening I was given a reception in the state-house at which there were speeches by William F. Vilas, the foremost citizen of Wisconsin and afterward United States Senator, by members of the university faculty, and others. All of this, of course, had been reported in the newspapers, especially the Madison newspapers, so that when I went among the farmers, I found that they were able to place me at once.

Thus, while they considered me too young and inexperienced, I made a good many friends—men who began to believe in me then, and have been my warm supporters ever since.

Another thing helped me substantially in my canvass. Many of the farmers were disgusted with the record of inefficient service in the district attorney's office in the recent past, which had required the employment of extra counsel in trying cases. I promised them with confidence that I would do all the work myself and that there should be no extra fees to meet.

Up to this point everything had been clear sailing. I was asking the people for an office of public service which they had the full power to give me; but I had not learned the very first principles of the political game as it was then played—indeed, as it is still played in a greater part of this country. I knew practically nothing about politics or political organization, never at that time having so much as attended a caucus or convention.

The Boss of Dane County was Colonel E. W. Keyes, the postmaster of Madison. He was rarely spoken of as the "Colonel" or "Mr. Keyes," but always then and for many years afterward simply as "the Boss." He had been for a long time the boss of the whole state but stronger men were then coming into the field and he was content to exercise his sway over Dane and neighboring counties. He was a very sharp, brusque, dominating man, energetic in his movements, and not then very young. A Bismarck type of man, he had fine abilities, and if he used the methods of force and of bulldozery toward those who opposed him, he was often generous to those who supported him. And he was big enough to give excellent public service in the office which he held for so many years. He was a good representative of old-time politics: the politics of force and secret management. He was absolute dictator in his own territory; he could make candidates, and he could unmake political office-holders. He fought me for twenty years.

I cannot now remember just how long I had been at my canvass before the Boss called me to account. My recollection is that I went in one day to the post-office to get my mail. He had probably directed his clerks to watch for me, and I was told that the postmaster wished to see me. I had known him, of course, when a student in the university; he was one of the men who had spoken at the reception when I returned from the oratorical contest. I went to him therefore with great friendliness; but I found him in quite a different mood. He burst out upon me with the evident purpose of frightening me at once out of all my political ambitions.

"You are fooling away your time, sir!" he exclaimed roughly.

He told me I was wasting my money, that I had better go to work, that I had not learned the first lesson in politics. He told me who the next district attorney of Dane County would be—and it was not La Follette!

Boss Keyes did not know it, but opposition of that sort was the best service he could have rendered me. It stirred all the fight I had in me.

"I intend," I said, "to go on with this canvass; and I intend to be elected district attorney of Dane County."

I set my face, and as soon as I left him I began to work more furiously than ever before. I kept asking myself what business Keyes or any other man had to question my right of going out among the voters of Dane County, and saying what I pleased to them. And what had Keyes more than any other voter to do with the disposal of the district attorneyship?

I remember having had a similar overmastering sense of anger and wrong and injustice in my early days in the university—and it led to a rather amusing incident—my first experience as an Insurgent. Speakers, I recall, were to be chosen by the students for some public occasion. At that time college life was dominated by two secret fraternities; they controlled the student meetings, and directed the elections. Most of the students, of whom I was one, were outsiders, or "scrubs," having little or nothing to say about the conduct of college affairs; and I was one of the greenest of all the "plebs"—a boy right from the farm. Well, the fraternities made their slate and put it through. That night I visited every nonfraternity man in the university, and after several days' hard work we organized a sort of anti-secret society of some two hundred members. Then we called a new meeting. The whole student body was there, including the fraternity men. We reconsidered the action of the previous meeting and had an honest and open election.

The same sort of feeling which dominated me in that boyish fight now drove me into a more vigorous struggle in Dane County. I traveled by day and by night, I stayed at farm-houses, I interviewed every voter in the county whom I could reach. The Boss was active, too, but he was so secure in his undisputed supremacy and I was so young and inexperienced that he did not take me seriously nor realize until afterward how thoroughly my work was done. He was dependent upon his organization made up of men, most of whom hoped sooner or later to get something from the state or county—some little office or job. But I had gone behind all this organization and reached the voters themselves. Whatever success I have attained in politics since then has been attained by these simple and direct means—and not otherwise.

There were five candidates at the convention. Quite unexpectedly, between the ballots, a Norwegian named Eli Pederson, a neighbor of ours, who had known and worked for my father and who called me "our boy," made a telling speech in my behalf. I can see him now—a big, black-headed, black-eyed man with a powerful frame, standing there in the convention. He was a fine type of man, a natural-born leader of his community, and he spoke as one having authority. It was to him, I think, that at the crisis I owed my nomination, which came on the fifth ballot.

This failure of his well-oiled machine astonished the Boss beyond measure, and my fight for the nomination was nothing as compared with the fight for election. Then, as now, the Boss was quite willing to support the candidate of the opposite party rather than to have his own authority questioned or defied. But the university boys, who were my strong friends and supporters, went out and worked tooth and nail for me all over the county—without regard to politics—and I was elected by the narrow majority of ninety-three votes. In January, 1881, I was sworn in as district attorney of Dane County.

As I look back upon it, politics was very different then from now. In these days fundamental issues and policies are being widely and earnestly discussed, but at that time the country was in a state of political lethargy. The excitement and fervor which accompanied the war had exhausted itself, reconstruction had been completed, and specie payment resumed. The people had turned their attention almost wholly to business affairs. The West was to be settled, railroads constructed, towns founded, manufacturing industries built up, and money accumulated. In short, it was a time of expansion, and of great material prosperity.

But the war and the troubled years which followed it had left at least one important political legacy—one of the most powerful and unified party organizations that ever existed, I suppose, anywhere in the world. I mean the Republican party. We may never see its like again in this country. I had fought a desperate war for a great and righteous cause. It had behind it the passionate enthusiasm of a whole generation of men. It was the party of Lincoln and Grant and Sherman. I remember well the character of the ordinary political speeches of those years. Even well down into the eighties they all looked backward to fading glories, they waved the flag of freedom, they abused the South, they stirred the war memories of the old soldiers who were then everywhere dominant in the North. Of this old type of orator I remember to have heard Zach Chandler of Michigan, a great figure in those days—a sort of old Roman, of powerful and rugged personality, whose sarcastic flings at the Democratic party were accepted as the most persuasive of political argumentation.

This unreasoning loyalty to party which was a product of the war drew thousands of young men like myself into its ranks with the conviction that this was the party of patriotism. It is a notable sign of robust political health in these days that every young man must have his conclusive reasons for voting the Republican or the Democratic ticket; old party names have lost much of their persuasiveness: men must think for themselves—and in that fact lies the great hope for the future of the nation.

Garfield was the first leader to impress me—as I think he impressed many men of the younger generation—as facing forward instead of backward. He glorified the party, it is true, but he saw something of the the work that needed to be done. I was greatly impressed with Garfield: I heard him at Madison in the summer after I was graduated. He was a very handsome man, of fine presence, dignity and power; splendid diction and a rather lofty eloquence. I do not remember a suggestion of humor. His address at Madison at that time was a review of the birth and services of the Republican party. I do not recall that he talked about the tariff;

8

he was not a high tariff man, and even in those days urged lower duties and freer trade. I remember he impressed me more as a statesman and less as a politician than any of the men I had heard up to that time.

But if the old party and the thrill of the old party slogans were still dominant, the issues of the new generation were beginning to make themselves felt. Already there had been severe local political storms. Sporadic new movements began forming soon after reconstruction: the great dark problems of corporations and trusts and financial power were appearing on the horizon. As far back as 1872 there had been a Liberal Republican party organized to ask for civil service reform, and later, a Labor party was organized to agitate the problems of capital and labor, the control of banks and railroads, and the disposal of public lands. In 1876 the Greenback party came into the field and rose to much prominence on a radical platform.

In the State of Wisconsin the Progressive movement expressed itself in the rise to power of the Patrons of Husbandry. The Grange movement swept four or five middle western states, expressing vigorously the first powerful revolt against the rise of monopolies, the arrogance of railroads and the waste and robbery of the public lands. Those hard-headed old pioneers from New England and from northern Europe who thought as they plowed, went far toward roughing out the doctrine in regard to railroad control which the country has since adopted. At that time there was no settled policy, no established laws, but their reasoning was as direct and simple as their lives. It was plain to them that the railroad was only another form of highway. They knew that for the purposes of a highway, the public could enter upon and take a part of their farms. If, then, the right of passage through the country came from the people, the people should afterward have the right to control the use of the highway. It was this simple reasoning which was subsequently adopted by legislatures and courts.

As a boy on the farm in Primrose Township I heard and felt this movement of the Grangers swirling about me; and I felt the indignation which it expressed in such a way that I suppose I have never fully lost the effect of that early impression. It was a time, indeed, of a good deal of intellectual activity and awakening. Minds long fixed upon the slavery question were turning to new affairs; newspapers grew more numerous and books were cheaper. I remember when I was a boy a dog-eared copy of one of Henry

George's early books got into our neighborhood. It was owned by a blacksmith, named Dixon, a somewhat unusual man—a big powerful fellow, who was a good deal of a reader and thinker. He had taken an interest in me and he urged me to read Henry George's book. I knew nothing of public questions, but I read the book.

In Wisconsin the Granger movement went so far as to cause a political revolution and the election in 1874 of a Democratic governor. A just and comprehensive law for regulating the railroads was passed and a strong railroad commission was instituted. It was then, indeed, that the railroads began to dominate politics for the first time in this country. They saw that they must either accept control by the state or control the state. They adopted the latter course; they began right there to corrupt Wisconsin—indeed to corrupt all the states of the Middle West. And as usual they were served by the cleverest lawyers and writers that money could hire. They asserted that the panic of 1873 was caused by the Granger agitation and that capital was being driven from the state by popular clamor. To these arguments they added open threats and defiance of the law. On April 28, 1874, Alexander Mitchell, President of the Chicago, Milwaukee and St. Paul Railroad Company, wrote a letter to Governor Taylor in which he asserted directly that his company would disregard the state law. These are his words:

"Being fully conscious that the enforcement of this law will ruin the property of the company and feeling assured of the correctness of the opinions of the eminent counsel who have examined the question, the directors feel compelled *to disregard the provisions of the law* so far as it fixes a tariff of rates for the company until the courts have finally passed upon the question of its validity."

A more brazen defiance of law could scarcely be conceived. The railroads looked to the courts for final protection, but the law which they thus defied was not only sustained by the Supreme Court of Wisconsin, but by the Supreme Court of the United States.

But the railroads did not intend to submit to control, courts or no courts, and by fallacious argument, by threats, by bribery, by political manipulation, they were able to force the legislature to repeal the law which the Supreme Court had sustained. By that assault upon free government in Wisconsin and in other middle western states the reasonable control of corporations was delayed in this country for many years.

10

From that moment in the seventies—excepting once, and then only for a period of two years when the agricultural and dairy interests defeated the corporations, and elected William D. Hoard governor—until my fight was finally successful, Wisconsin was a corrupted state, governed not by the people but by a group of private and corporate interests. They secured control of the old Republican party organization—the party with the splendid history —and while its orators outwardly dwelt upon the glories of the past and inspired the people with the fervor of patriotic loyalty, these corporation interests were bribing, bossing and thieving within. The machine organization of the Democratic party was as subservient to the railroads and other corporations as the Republican machine, and mastery of legislation was thus rendered complete through all these years.

I never shall forget the speech I heard the old Chief Justice of Wisconsin, Edward G. Ryan, make to the graduating class at Madison in June, 1873, just before I entered the university. He was one of the most remarkable men who ever served at the Wisconsin bar or filled a judicial chair: an Irishman by birth with a fine legal education. Of an erratic, impulsive and passionate temperament, in his decisions he was as cold and judicial as any judge who ever sat on the Bench. It was he who had written the epoch-making decision sustaining the Granger law which in no small measure laid the foundation for judicial action in this country upon the control of corporations. I remember his bowed figure, his fine, almost feminine features, his wavy auburn hair, and the luminous impressive eyes which glowed as the old man talked there in the Assembly Chamber to the graduating students. His voice shook with emotion and his prophetic words, which I have never forgotten, conveyed powerfully the feeling of many thoughtful men of that time. I have used them in scores of speeches in my campaigns. Said he:

"There is looming up a new and dark power. I cannot dwell upon the signs and shocking omens of its advent. The accumulation of individual wealth seems to be greater than it ever has been since the downfall of the Roman Empire. The enterprises of the country are aggregating vast corporate combinations of unexampled capital, boldly marching, not for economic conquests only, but for political power. For the first time really in our politics money is taking the field as an organized power. . . . Already, here at home, one great corporation has trifled with the sovereign power, and insulted the state. There is grave fear that it, and its great rival, have confederated to make partition of the state and share it as spoils. . . . The question will arise, and arise in your day, though perhaps not fully in mine, 'Which shall rule—wealth or man; which shall lead—money or intellect; who shall fill public stations—educated and patriotic free men, or the feudal serfs of corporate capital?' "

It was this power, though I did not know it then, nor indeed fully until years later, that spoke through the voice of Boss Keyes when he attempted to deny my right to appear before the people of Dane County as a candidate for district attorney. It was this power which held together and directed the county machine, the state machine, the national machine, of both the old parties. Of course, the Boss and the machine had nothing against me personally. All it wanted was the acceptance of its authority and leadership: what it feared and hated was independence and freedom. I could have made terms with Keyes and with the state bosses of Wisconsin at any time during my years of struggle with them and secured personal advancement with ease and profit to myself, but I would have had to surrender the principles and abandon the issues for which I was contending, and this I would not do.

In refusing to acknowledge the authority of Boss Keyes at the outset I was merely expressing a common and widespread, though largely unconscious, spirit of revolt among the people—a movement of the new generation toward more democracy in human relationships. No one had thought it out in sharply defined terms, but nearly every one felt it. It grew out of the intellectual awakening of which I have already spoken, the very centre and inspirational point of which in Wisconsin was then, and has been ever since, the university at Madison.

It is difficult, indeed, to overestimate the part which the university has played in the Wisconsin revolution. For myself, I owe what I am and what I have done largely to the inspiration I received while there. It was not so much the actual courses of study which I pursued; it was rather the spirit of the institution—a high spirit of earnest endeavor, a spirit of fresh interest in new things, and beyond all else a sense that somehow the state and the university were intimately related, and that they should be of mutual service.

The guiding spirit of my time, and the man to whom Wisconsin owes a debt greater than it can ever pay, was its President, John Bascom.

I never saw Ralph Waldo Emerson, but I should say that John Bascom was a man of much his type, both in appearance and in character. He was the embodiment of moral force and moral enthusiasm; and he was in advance of his time in feeling the new social forces and in emphasizing the new social responsibilities. His addresses to the students on Sunday afternoons, together with his work in the classroom, were among the most important influences in my early life. It was his teaching, iterated and reiterated, of the obligation of both the university and the students to the mother state that may be said to have originated the Wisconsin idea in education. He was forever telling us what the state was doing for us and urging our return obligation not to use our education wholly for our own selfish benefit, but to return some service to the state. That teaching animated and inspired hundreds of students who sat under John Bascom. The present President of the university, Charles R. Van Hise, a classmate of mine, was one of the men who has nobly handed down the tradition and continued the teaching of John Bascom.

In those days we did not so much get correct political and economic views, for there was then little teaching of sociology or political economy worthy the name, but what we somehow did get, and largely from Bascom, was a *proper attitude toward public affairs.* And when all is said, this attitude is more important than any definite views a man may hold. Years afterward, when I was Governor of Wisconsin, John Bascom came to visit us at the executive residence in Madison, and I treasure the words he said to me about my new work:

"Robert," he said, "you will doubtless make mistakes of judgment as governor, but never mind the political mistakes so long as you make no ethical mistakes."

John Bascom lived to be eighty-four years old, dying last fall, 1911, at his home at Williamstown, Massachusetts. Up to the last his mind was clear and his interest in the progress of humanity as keen as ever. In his later years he divided his time between his garden and his books—a serene and beautiful old age. His occasional letters and his writings were always a source of inspiration to me.

In all my fights in Wisconsin, the university and the students have always stood firmly behind me. In a high sense the university has been the repository of progressive ideas: it has always enjoyed both free thought and free speech. When the test came years ago the university met it boldly where some other institutions faltered or failed. The declaration of freedom was made by the Board of Regents in 1894 when Dr. Richard T. Ely was tried for economic heresy:

"We cannot for a moment believe that knowledge has reached its final goal or that the present constitution of society is perfect. . . . In all lines of investigation . . . the investigator should be absolutely free to follow the paths of truth wherever they may lead. Whatever may be the limitations which trammel inquiry elsewhere, we believe the great State of Wisconsin should ever encourage that continual and fearless sifting and winnowing by which alone the truth can be found."

This declaration of freedom was framed by Herbert W. Chynoweth, then a member of the board, now deceased, and it was incorporated as a plank in the last Republican state platform as a pledge of the party to sustain the academic freedom of the university. It has also been inscribed on a monument erected by a recent graduating class.

In no state of the Union are the relationships between the university and the people of the state so intimate and so mutually helpful as in Wisconsin. We believe there that the purpose of the university is to serve the people, and every effort is made through correspondence courses, special courses, housekeepers' conferences, farmers' institutes, experimental stations and the like to bring every resident of the state under the broadening and inspiring influence of a faculty of trained men. At the same time the highest standards of education in the arts and in the professions are maintained in the university itself.

In other ways the influence of the university has been profound. While I was governor, I sought the constant advice and service of the trained men of the institution in meeting the difficult problems which confronted the state. Many times when harassed by the conditions which confronted me, I have called in for conference President Van Hise, Dr. Ely, Professor Commons, Dr. Reinsch and others.

During my terms as governor I did my best to build up and encourage the spirit which John Bascom in his time had expressed, by the appointment of strong trustees—the sort of men who would understand what the university should do and be. When I became governor the university graduates were not numerically strong on the Board of Regents; when I resigned, the alumni had at least their full representation, and I had also strengthened the board by the appointment of a woman member—the first ever appointed in Wisconsin.

14

I made it a further policy, in order to bring all the reserves of knowledge and inspiration of the university more fully to the service of the people, to appoint experts from the university wherever possible upon the important boards of the state—the civil service commission, the railroad commission and so on—a relationship which the university has always encouraged and by which the state has greatly profited. Many of the university staff are now in state service, and a bureau of investigation and research established as a legislative reference library conducted by Charles McCarthy, a man of marked originality and power, has proved of the greatest assistance to the legislature in furnishing the latest and best thought of the advanced students of government in this and other countries. He has built up an institution in Wisconsin that is a model which the Federal Government and ultimately every state in the Union will follow.

During the last session of the legislature a Saturday lunch club was organized, at which the governor, and some of the state officers and legislators regularly meet the university professors—Van Hise, Ross, Reinsch, Commons, Ely, Scott, Meyer, McCarthy and others —to discuss the problems of the state. Such meetings as these are a tremendous force in bringing about intelligent democratic government: they are very different from the old-time secret, back-room conferences of bosses which once controlled Wisconsin in the interest of private corporations. It is not, indeed, surprising that Dr. Eliot of Harvard, after an examination of the work done at Madison should have called Wisconsin "the leading State University," for in every possible way it has endeavored to make itself a great democratic institution—a place of free thought, free investigation, free speech, and of constant and unremitting service to the people who give it life.

I have endeavored thus to exhibit some of the underlying causes of the progressive spirit in Wisconsin, and I cannot leave the subject without speaking of one other influence which impressed me.

In the campaign of 1876, Robert G. Ingersoll came to Madison to speak. I had heard of him for years; when I was a boy on the farm a relative of ours had testified in a case in which Ingersoll had appeared as an attorney and he had told the glowing stories of the plea that Ingersoll had made. Then, in the spring of 1876, Ingersoll delivered the Memorial Day address at Indianapolis. It was widely published shortly after it was delivered and it startled and enthralled the whole country. I remember that it was printed on a poster as large as a door and hung in the post-office at Madison. I can scarcely convey now, or even understand, the emotional effect the reading of it produced upon me. Oblivious of my surroundings, I read it with tears streaming down my face. It began, I remember:

"The past rises before me like a dream. Again we are in the great struggle for national life. We hear the sounds of preparation —the music of boisterous drums—the silver voices of heroic bugles. We see the pale cheeks of women and the flushed faces of men; and in those assemblages we see all the dead whose dust we have covered with flowers."

I was fairly entranced. He pictured the recruiting of the troops, the husbands and fathers with their families on the last evening, the lover under the trees and the stars; then the beat of drums, the waving flags, the marching away; the wife at the turn of the lane holds her baby aloft in her arms—a wave of the hand and he has gone; then you see him again in the heat of the charge. It was wonderful how it seized upon my youthful imagination.

When he came to Madison I crowded myself into the assembly chamber to hear him: I would not have missed it for every worldly thing I possessed. And he did not disappoint me.

A large handsome man of perfect build, with a face as round as a child's and a compelling smile—all the arts of the old-time oratory were his in high degree. He was witty, he was droll, he was eloquent: he was as full of sentiment as an old violin. Often, while speaking, he would pause, break into a smile, and the audience, in anticipation of what was to come, would follow him in irresistible peals of laughter. I cannot remember much that he said, but the impression he made upon me was indelible.

After that I got Ingersoll's books and never afterward lost an opportunity to hear him speak. He was the greatest orator, I think, that I have ever heard; and the greatest of his lectures, I have always thought, was the one on Shakespeare.

Ingersoll had a tremendous influence upon me, as indeed he had upon many young men of that time. It was not that he changed my beliefs, but that he liberated my mind. Freedom was what he preached: he wanted the shackles off everywhere. He wanted men to think boldly about all things: he demanded intellectual and moral courage. He wanted men to follow wherever truth might lead them. He was a rare, bold, heroic figure.

I have departed somewhat from my direct narrative, but it has seemed necessary to show some of the conditions and influences which have resulted in the spread of the Progressive movement in Wisconsin and elsewhere.

I was sworn in as district attorney of Dane County in January, 1881. I was not yet twenty-six, and, besides the defense of a tramp charged with assault with intent to kill, a few collection cases, and two civil cases in the circuit court, I had had little actual trial experience. I never worked harder in my life than I did during the next two years: I worked almost day and night. I liked it, it suited my talents, and from the first I was successful with most of my cases. I kept my word to the farmers literally: although I often had to meet the foremost lawyers in southern Wisconsin—men like William F. Vilas—no legal assistance was ever employed in my office or to aid in the trial of a case while I was district attorney. I did all the work alone. At the end of two years' service, so well satisfied were the people with my administration that the Boss did not even oppose my renomination and I was the only man on the Republican county ticket who was reelected. I ran over 2,000 votes ahead of my ticket.

During my service as district attorney I began to see some further aspects of boss rule and misrepresentative government, although I had little idea then what it all meant. It was a common practice for men caught in the criminal net, or the friends of those men, not to go forward honestly and try their cases in the public tribunal, but repair to the boss and thus bring underhanded and secret influence to bear in blocking the wheels of justice. And why shouldn't they? The influence of the boss was all-powerful in the election or appointment of sheriffs, police, constables, usually the district attorney, and even judges. With their official life in some measure dependent upon the Boss, a mere nod or a request might easily change the whole course of justice; and there are few criminals who cannot muster some influence with a boss, whose secret of power lies in the personal loyalty of those upon whom he has conferred special benefits.

I began to feel this pressure in all sorts of cases: they did not attempt to reach me directly, knowing that I had defied the Boss in my election, but it came about in the curious ways in which witnesses faded out of the reach of the sheriff's office, in the disagreement of juries, and the like. I remember one case of adultery in which the parties brought powerful influence to bear, defeating my attempts at prosecution. Finally I was taken sick and had to go to bed. Keyes seized eagerly upon the opportunity and used his influence to compel the dismissal of the case against the defendant. I heard of it, and, although too weak to walk, I had myself rolled in a blanket and driven to the courthouse. I entered my appearance and asserted my official authority against having the case dismissed. There was a good deal of a fight, I remember, and I was threatened with being sent to jail for contempt. But I finally secured a postponement and afterward convicted my man.

Under such conditions, it may well be imagined, any man inside the political ring, or a man with great political influence, could escape punishment for almost any offense except, perhaps, a capital crime. I early determined that I would make absolutely no distinctions between men in the administration of justice, and I soon had a very severe test, in which I had to meet the influence of the system which then prevailed. Sanderson, chairman of the Republican State Central Committee, came to Madison at the organization of the legislature, got to gambling and drinking and went to bed in a state of intoxication. Feeling some one trying to take his money, he aroused himself enough to make an outcry, and the next morning the story was all over town. It came up to me and in the regular course of my duty I went to the hotel to get Sanderson to make a complaint. He was insulting; told me it was none of my business, and that if I knew where my political interests lay, I better keep d—— quiet. I told him plainly that we did not permit such things to happen in Madison without prosecution and that I should require him to swear out a warrant. As soon as I left he set the wheels to moving, and before I could get the papers made out a number of friends came to me advising me that it would defeat me for reelection if I made trouble for so important a person. Sanderson got out of Madison by the first train and tried to get out of the state, but I caught him with a subpoena at Milwaukee. I also got the fellow who was charged with taking the money; but the pressure on the witnesses was so great that I could not convict him. However, the purpose of the prosecution—to make the law supreme in Dane County—was well served; and instead of injuring my chances for reelection, the case decidedly helped me.

I do not think, as I look back on my record as district attorney, that I should make as good a prosecutor now as I was then. I saw just two things then: the law and the individual criminal. I believe I broke the record for convictions in Dane County. I worked the sheriff half to death. If there was evidence anywhere to be obtained in my cases I got it, regardless of work or expense. I even sent one sheriff to England. Since then I have come to have a little different point of view regarding crime. I see that the individual criminal is not always wholly to blame; that many crimes grow directly out of the sins and injustices of society.

During the four years I served as district attorney I had practically nothing to do with politics; I made as good a campaign as I knew how for reelection, but I knew nothing and cared nothing for the political organizations of the county and state. I put my whole force into my work as district attorney and thought of nothing else. It was a keen joy to prepare the cases and present them in perfect order before the court. When it became known that a crime had been committed I tried always to be first on the ground myself, interview all the witnesses and see all the surroundings in person. It is facts that settle cases; the law is always the same. And this rule applies to things of larger importance than criminal cases. Facts count high everywhere. Whether the matter in hand is railroad legislation or the tariff, it is always a question of digging out the facts upon which to base your case. In no other one thing does a public man more surely indicate his quality than in his ability to master actual conditions and set them forth with clearness. Neither laws, nor opinions, nor even constitutions, will finally convince people: it is only the concrete facts of concrete cases.

The first and rather surprising suggestion made to me to become a candidate for Congress came about in this way.

Samuel A. Harper and I were classmates and chums in the university. Some time in his sophomore year, while wrestling, he injured his knee so severely that he had to leave the university. He taught school for a time, then studied law, and in 1884, while I was finishing my last year's service as district attorney, he came to visit me in Madison. He was full of imagination and the spirit of youth; six feet tall, lithe and athletic; eyes bright and black; hair in ringlets. He was a handsome and brilliant fellow—a charmer of men. He possessed the most unerring political judgment of any one I have ever known. Dear fellow! Our lives were knit together in a way that rarely comes to men. He became my law partner in 1886, and was my closest friend and most trusted adviser until his death in 1898.

Sam remained with me for several weeks and we talked as such friends will. One night he said:

"Bob, why don't you go to Congress? You can go to Congress just as well as not. You have the opportunity of a public career, and you have the stuff in you."

With inimitable spirit he developed his plan:

19

"There are five counties in this district," he said. "The two big counties, Dane and Grant, outnumber all the others in voting population. Now I live in Grant and you live in Dane. I'll carry Grant for you and you carry Dane for yourself. They will control the convention—and you go to Congress."

Well, we talked it over. It got into my head. It seemed feasible. Neither Sam nor I ever thought of going to the Boss; indeed, I do not think we consulted any one but ourselves until after I decided to run.

The situation was favorable. In the previous Congressional convention, Geo. C. Hazelton who had served the district three terms, was a candidate for renomination. Boss Keyes, who was also a candidate, withdrew from the convention and was nominated by his followers in a separate convention. This three-cornered fight resulted in the election of the Democratic candidate, Burr Jones, of Madison, and left much bitterness among the Republicans of the district. Keyes's enmity toward me naturally made the Hazelton supporters friendly to me. It was also important to have a candidate from Dane County, as Jones had made a good record and was likely to run ahead of his ticket.

Sam and I started out on the campaign as though it were some fine game, and with great enjoyment of the prospect. By this time I was thoroughly well acquainted in Dane County. Besides my service as district attorney I had built up such a good civil-law practice that in the year 1885 I had more civil cases on the calendar than any other lawyer in Madison. All this served to give me an assured place with the people. Well, I conducted my canvass among the farmers very much as I had gone about it four years before. It was the general feeling, I knew, that I had made good as district attorney and I argued that I could and would serve the people just as faithfully as Congressman. I found I had many friends among Democrats as well as among Republicans.

It was not long before the machine found out what I was doing. The so-called "Madison ring," which controlled that Congressional district, was composed of Keyes, Phil Spooner, a brother of John C. Spooner, Oakley, United States Marshal, and Willet Main, a brother-in-law of John C. Spooner, who was deputy-marshal. As I was on my way home one day, Phil Spooner stopped me and said:

"What is this I hear about your running for Congress?"

I told him my purpose.

"Do you expect to be nominated?"

I told him I did.

"Don't you know," he said, "that there hasn't been a Congressman nominated for fifteen years who hasn't had our support? Why haven't you consulted Keyes and Oakley and me?"

I said: "I know of no reason why I should consult you. I've been out in the country consulting the people, and I'm going to consult a good many more."

"Well, young man," he said, "you can't go to Congress."

I said: "I think I can; anyhow I'm going to try."

They gave me a hard fight. They hired most of the teams in Madison and covered the country districts. There was no influence they did not use; no wires they did not pull. But I carried the caucuses against them and elected my delegates. The very night that I got the final returns from Dane County I received a telegram from Sam Harper saying that he had carried the last caucuses that settled Grant. That meant that I had won. Sam had not been out of his buggy for thirty days.

We never went into the other counties in the district at all, although the university men, who were then, as always, my warm supporters, did what they could for me there.

I cannot refrain here from speaking of another individual influence which was helpful to me in my campaign. Among the notable men of southern Wisconsin was General George E. Bryant, a gallant soldier who had commanded a Wisconsin regiment in the war and who had been probate judge of Dane County. He was long an intimate friend of General Grant, and one of the 306 delegates who stood out in the national convention for a third term for Grant in the presidency. He came from a fine old New England family, and he was a wise man, a good lawyer and judge. General Bryant had been a Hazelton supporter, and was a potent influence in my behalf among the old soldiers who were then an important element in the electorate. When I was elected governor he became chairman of the State Central Committee, and he fought with me through all my campaigns. During his last illness, when he thought he would not see me again, he addressed this brief note to me, which I treasure highly:

DEAR BOB: Next to my own two boys, I loved you and Sam Harper better than any one else in the world.

GEN'L.

The convention was held at Dodgeville, and, although the old crowd was there in force, I was nominated on the first ballot. They tried to beat me at the polls by throwing support to the Demo-crats—and they had behind them the influence of the railroads—but I was elected by 400 votes.

My second term as district attorney closed on January 1, 1885. I continued my law practice until Congress met in the fall of that year. At the time of my election I had never been farther east than Chicago, and when I arrived in Washington I found myself the youngest member of Congress. I was twenty-nine years old.

Chapter II

In the House of Representatives

Having thus been elected to Congress, in November, 1884, I began to realize keenly how ill-prepared I was to meet with intelligence any important national question. My service as district attorney during the preceding four years had absorbed my energies to the exclusion of everything else; in trying to do that work thoroughly well, and to keep my promise to employ no legal assistance in the trial of cases, I found I had little time to devote to political or legislative affairs.

For these reasons I resolved to go to Washington in January, 1885. The 49th Congress, to which I had been elected, did not meet until December, but I hoped that by attending the closing session of the 48th Congress, I might learn something of the great national questions then under consideration.

I shall never forget the journey from Madison to Washington. I came by way of Harper's Ferry and I saw the old battlefields and the prison where John Brown had been confined. The first sight of the Capitol stirred me deeply. I recall distinctly how I thought of Jefferson and Hamilton and Webster and Clay and Lincoln, and I had visions of public service which I would hardly dare now to confess. I was very young then, you see. Before breakfast, on my first morning in Washington, I went into Lincoln Park and stood with my hat off before Ball's statue of Lincoln. I know that critics have found fault with it as a work of art, but I cannot forget how it moved me that first morning in Washington. There stood Lincoln holding in one hand the Proclamation of Emancipation, the other extended over the head of a kneeling negro from whose wrists the shackles had just parted! That moment and the day I spent at Mount Vernon were experiences which I shall never forget.

I attended the sessions of the House as faithfully as though I were a member. I studied the rules, followed every debate, read the *Congressional Record* each day. When there was an all-night session I remained all night. It was soon known that I was the youngest member of the House, and this decidedly helped me in getting acquainted.

Carlisle was then Speaker: he was a striking figure. A near view of his face was disappointing; it was almost colorless and his eye was as dull as lead, but, seen from the floor of the House, his great slow-moving figure and his strong head were indeed striking. He possessed something of the Southern courtesy of manner and there was a peculiar steady quality of the voice that suggested not only a reserve of power but absolute impersonality in the decision of questions. I have never known his superior as a presiding officer.

Many other notable figures were then playing their parts upon the national stage. Arthur was in the White House, and Blaine was still a great party leader. In the Senate, where I sometimes occupied a seat in the gallery, were Edmunds, Hoar, Sherman, Evarts, Allison and Ingalls. In the House, the leaders were Tom Reed, McKinley, the brilliant Ben Butterworth and Joe Cannon. Cannon had not then earned the title of "uncle"; he was a rough and rugged man of fifty years of age, a hardy off-hand debater. On the Democratic side were Carlisle, Randall, Mills and Holman of Indiana. Holman was always objecting—the watch-dog of the treasury. During the daytime I heard these men discussing the important issues of the time; many of the nights I spent in the Congressional library, eagerly reading political history. I wanted to get hold of fundamental principles and the reasons underlying current issues. I also read many speeches—Lincoln and Douglas, and the Elliot debates.

I remained in Washington until after the inauguration of Cleveland. I saw Cleveland and Arthur sitting side by side in the Senate chamber on March 4th. My first impression of Cleveland was extremely unfavorable. The contrast with Arthur, who was a fine handsome figure, was very striking. Cleveland's coarse face, his heavy, inert body, his great shapeless hands, confirmed in my mind the attacks made upon him during the campaign. And he was a Democrat!—and I a Republican at a time when party feeling was singularly intense. Later I came to entertain a great respect for Cleveland, to admire the courage and conscientiousness of his character.

In December I moved to Washington with my family, which then consisted of Mrs. La Follette and our little girl Fola.

A new Congressman finds himself at once irresistibly drawn into various groups and alignments. No sooner was I on the ground than I began to feel the influence of Senator Philetus Sawyer, then the leader of the Republican party in Wisconsin. Owing to the fact that I had been elected to Congress without the assistance of the organization—indeed, in defiance of it—I knew next to nothing about the underlying forces which at that time controlled, and in large measure still control, party machinery. A very small coterie of men then dominated the politics of Wisconsin and the two great leaders were Senator Sawyer and Henry C. Payne, who afterward became a member of Roosevelt's cabinet.

Sawyer was a man of striking individuality and of much native force. He was a typical lumberman, equipped with great physical strength and a shrewd, active mind. He had tramped the forests, cruised timber, slept in the snow, built saw mills—and by his own efforts had made several million dollars. So unlearned was he that it was jokingly said that he signed his name "P. Sawyer" because he could not spell Philetus. He was nevertheless a man of ability, and a shrewd counselor in the prevailing political methods. He believed in getting all he could for himself and his associates whenever and wherever possible. I always thought that Sawyer's methods did not violate his conscience; he regarded money as properly the chief influence in politics. Whenever it was necessary, I believe that he bought men as he bought sawlogs. He assumed that every man in politics was serving, first of all, his own personal interests —else why should he be in politics? He believed quite simply that railroad corporations and lumber companies, as benefactors of the country, should be given unlimited grants of public lands, allowed to charge all the traffic could bear, and that anything that interfered with the profits of business was akin to treason.

I had not been long in Washington before Sawyer invited me to go with him to call on the President. I can remember just how he looked climbing into his carriage—a short, thick-set, squatty figure of a man with a big head set on square shoulders and a short neck—stubby everywhere. I remember he talked to me in a kindly, fatherly manner—very matter-of-fact—looking at me from time to time with a shrewd squint in his eye. He had no humor, but much of what has been called "horse sense." His talk was jerky and illiterate; he never made a speech in his life.

We called on President Cleveland and on all the cabinet officers. His form of introduction was exactly the same at each place we stopped. He was not quite sure, always, of my name; "Follette" he called me. He would say:

"This young man we think a great deal of; we think he is going to amount to something. I want you to be fair to him. I'd like him to get all that is coming to him in his district. I hope you will treat him right when he has any business in your department."

As we drove away from our last call, Sawyer asked me if I had in mind any particular committee in the House upon which I desired to serve. I told him I had thought it over and I wanted to go on some committee where I could make use of my legal knowledge. I could not hope to be assigned to the great Committee on Judiciary, so I told him that I should like to go on the Committee on Public Lands. I innocently explained that many land grant forfeitures were pending and I should enjoy grappling with the legal questions which they presented. Sawyer looked at me benignly and said:

"Just leave that to me; don't say another word about it to anybody. I know Carlisle; served with him in the House. Just let me take care of that for you."

I was very grateful, and confided in his promises. But when Carlisle announced the committees I was astonished to find that Stephenson—now a Senator from Wisconsin—was appointed to the Committee on Public Lands and that I had been assigned to a place on the Committee on Indian Affairs. Sawyer came to me promptly and told me that he could not secure my appointment to Public Lands, but he was sure I would enjoy my work on Indian Affairs. There was a reason for putting me on this committee, and not upon Public Lands, which I did not appreciate until later. I had been quite too frank in expressing an interest in land grant forfeitures. It did not occur to the Senator that I might develop "foolishly sentimental" ideas against robbing Indian reservations of the pine timber in which they were very rich.

I was disappointed, but so eager to get to work at something definite that I went out immediately and invested quite a little money in second-hand books on Indians. I also had all the treaties and documents relating to Indians sent to my rooms. It made quite a library. I studied these books diligently, nor was it long before I began to feel a good deal of sympathy with the Indians. Years afterward, when I was on the Committee on Indian Affairs of the Senate, an old Indian chief who had come to Washington to plead for the interests of his people paid me one of the most amusing compliments I ever received. Quay of Pennsylvania, though a cold-blooded politician, was one of the best friends the Indians ever had in Congress. Having Indian blood in his veins he invariably opposed legislation which was unjust to the Indians. Well, this old chief came to see me and I helped him all I could. Afterward, in trying to give me the highest measure of praise he could bestow, he said:

"La Follette—him all same Quay."

I soon found out why Sawyer had secured my appointment to the Committee on Indian Affairs. It was the first illuminating glimpse I had of the inside methods of political organization. Wellborn of Texas was then chairman of this committee. He strongly resembled Stephen A. Douglas, was an able man and a real orator. Cleveland appointed him federal judge in California where he has made a fine record. He is to-day one of the strong men of the state. We have never lost the touch of friendship since our service together in the House.

Wellborn appointed me a sub-committee of one to consider a bill introduced by Guenther of Oshkosh to sell the pine timber from the Menominee Indian Reservation in Wisconsin. Guenther represented Sawyer's Congressional district. When I began to study the bill more closely, it seemed to me to offer unlimited opportunities for stealing the timber from the Indians. I concluded to consult J. D. C. Atkins, the Commissioner of Indian Affairs, about it. He read the bill through; then he looked at me over his glasses and said:

"Mr. La Follette, I think this is a little the worst Indian bill I ever saw."

"Will you write me a letter as Commissioner, saying so?" I asked.

In due time I got his letter and a few days later Guenther came to me and said:

"Bob, why don't you report that bill out?"

I told him it was a bad bill and that I should report it adversely.

"Oh, don't do that," he said; "I know nothing about the bill. Sawyer asked me to introduce it, and he introduced one exactly like it in the Senate. He has passed his bill over there, and he wants me to get the House bill favorably reported and on the calendar by the time his bill comes over."

When I insisted that I would not report it favorably, that ended it and the bill died in Committee. Sawyer never spoke to me about the affair.

I was very soon to meet this question of political self-seeking in another form. My first speech in Congress was made on April 22,

1886. It was on the so-called "pork-barrel" bill for river and harbor appropriations. I was then, as I am now, heartily in favor of generous expenditures of national funds for waterways and harbors, but the scramble for unwarranted appropriations was then and is now not short of scandalous.

The bill called for $15,000,000, the largest amount at that time ever appropriated. It ignored the recommendations of the government engineers that sixty-three improvements already begun should be completed, and provided for completing only five of these unfinished improvements. This recommendation was ignored in order to use the funds to project over one hundred new improvements started to satisfy the demands of members for some of the "pork." I argued that if the sums necessary to complete unfinished work were used to inaugurate new improvements, then the next Congress would be compelled to set aside still larger appropriations merely to keep pace with the destruction resulting from the action of the elements upon the uncompleted improvements.

I argued that Congressmen should not contend as rivals for these appropriations, each seeking all he could get as a grab for his district, but that they should regard the river and harbor bill as a great national measure.

"I believe that the tendency of such legislation is to debauch the country and dull the moral instincts of the American Congress."

I went on further to say, "There is but one right course. Not one dollar of this money belongs to any state, any district, any locality. It all belongs to the United States, and whatever is appropriated with any other view is a misappropriation of public funds. I might use a severer term. No man can shirk the responsibility. . . . He cannot say, 'My constituents want this money, and I will therefore vote for it, though I do not approve of the measure.' The money is neither his nor theirs. So far as this money is concerned, when by his vote he takes it from the treasury, he becomes, in a liberal use of the word, a trustee of the money, and he is bound to expend it for the benefit of national commerce."

I knew that the bill would pass, as it did, but I felt that I ought at least to express my convictions upon the subject. I did not oppose the bill; I opposed the policy.

This little speech — it does not seem of much importance to me now—was commented on, not only in Wisconsin, but by the press of the country. The New York *Tribune,* the New York *Sun* and other papers gave it favorable editorial notice. This helped me in my district and aided in the contest for renomination.

The opposition of Boss Keyes and the old-time politicians of each of the counties of the district in my first nomination and election, warned me of the enemy I would have to meet in the convention of 1886. If I ever expected to serve more than one term in the House of Representatives, I knew I had to fight for that privilege. It had seemed to me in the very beginning that a public official should deal directly with the people whom he was to serve. I did not go to Boss Keyes for the office of district attorney. The district attorney was not employed by Keyes, but by the people. The office was not his to bestow; it was theirs. It was the same in my first fight for Congress. After I had won the nomination and election, it gave me still greater confidence in the people. But while the district attorney did his work in the county where the voters could see how they were being served, Washington was a long way off. How were the people to know about the proceedings of Congress and the work of their Congressman?

I thought it all over. It was clear to me that the only way to beat boss and ring rule was to keep the people thoroughly informed. Machine control is based upon misrepresentation and ignorance. Democracy is based upon knowledge. It is of first importance that the people shall know about their government and the work of their public servants. "Ye shall know the truth, and the truth shall make you free." This I have always believed vital to self government.

Immediately following my election to Congress I worked out a complete plan for keeping my constituents informed on public issues and the record of my services in Congress; it is the system I have used in constantly widening circles ever since.

There were five counties in my district, La Fayette, Grant, Green, Dane, and Iowa. I secured from the county clerks' offices a complete list of all the voters who had voted in the last election.

I had the names written on large sheets, one township, sometimes two, to a sheet. Then I sent the sheets to a friend in each county who filled in all the information he could, indicating especially the strong men in each community—those who were leaders of sentiment. To this information I added the results of my own acquaintance in the district. This gave me a complete descriptive poll list of my district.

When some Congressman made a speech on sound money—Reed or Carlisle—I would get the necessary number of copies of that speech, and send them to those interested in the money question. When the Oleomargarine bill, the Interstate Commerce bill, and other important legislation was pending, I sent out speeches covering the debates thoroughly. In this way I suppose I sent out hundreds of thousands of speeches, my own and others.

It is not generally known that Congressional speeches, reprinted from the *Record* for distribution, must be paid for by the Congressman or Senator ordering them at a cost equal to that of any first-class printing establishment. The size of the bills I paid the government printing office for many years was one of the reasons why I found myself so poor when I left Congress. A Congressman in those days received only five thousand dollars a year, and no secretarial or clerk hire whatever unless he chanced to be chairman of a committee. The result was that the bulk of the actual mechanical work of keeping up all this correspondence and pamphleteering fell upon Mrs. La Follette and myself. Occasionally we indulged in the extravagance of hiring a stenographer for a few weeks, but as a rule, while I was engaged in my Congressional duties, Mrs. La Follette worked until the late hours, writing letters, addressing envelopes and sending away stacks of speeches. We do not look upon those days with any self pity. We were both young and vigorous and they were among the happiest and most hopeful years we ever spent. We gave ourselves comparatively few amusements, but those that we did take, we enjoyed supremely. Our interest in the drama has always been keen, and I remember that whenever Booth and Barrett came to play in Baltimore—they never came to Washington owing to Booth's aversion to the scene of the tragedy with which his brother was connected—Mrs. La Follette and I threw discretion utterly to the winds, and went over to every evening performance while their engagement lasted.

The task of building up and maintaining an intelligent interest in public affairs in my district and afterward in the state, was no easy one. But it was the only way for me, and I am still convinced that it is the best way. Of one thing I am more and more convinced with the passage of the years—and that is, the serious interest of our people in government, and their willingness to give their thought to subjects which are really vital and upon which facts, not mere opinions, are set forth, even though the presentation may be forbidding. Get and keep a dozen or more of the leading men in a community interested in, and well informed upon any public question and you have laid firmly the foundations of democratic government.

Never in my political life have I derived benefit from the two sources of power by which machine politics chiefly thrives—I mean patronage, the control of appointments to office, and the use of large sums of money in organization. During my fight in Wisconsin the old machine used its power of dispensing patronage to the utmost against me. When I became governor I appointed supporters of the Progressive movement to offices whenever there were appointments to make. These men did all in their power for the success of our campaigns. But such service is always criticized by the opposition, and discounted by the public because of the self interest of the officials, and does about as much harm as good. As soon as I had the legislature with me in 1905, I secured the passage of the strongest Civil Service law that could be framed, wiping out the whole system of spoils in state offices. To-day there is less patronage-mongering in Wisconsin than in any other state in the Union. As for federal patronage, I have had very little to dispense —nor have I needed any. When Mr. Taft, soon after he became President, began withholding patronage from the Insurgents, with the idea, I suppose, of disciplining them, I stated my own views and the position of the Insurgents editorially in *La Follette's Magazine,* as follows:

It is well to have this patronage matter understood. The support of the Progressives for progressive legislation will be given without reference to patronage or favors of any sort. That support will be accorded on conviction. And it is idle for the President to presume that he can secure adherence from the Progressive ranks for any policies, or support for any legislation reactionary in its character for the sole purpose of party solidarity.

If you are going direct to the people, you have no need of patronage. Moreover, you have no need of organization in the complicated way in which politics has been organized in the past, nor of the use of large sums of money. The only organization through which I have attained whatever success it has been my lot to win has consisted of a clerical force to send out literature and speeches, and a manager to arrange speaking campaigns. The money for the campaigns which I have conducted—and there has never been much of it—has been supplied, not by business organizations, but by men who were sincerely interested in the cause.

In general it can be said of all the group known as Insurgents or Progressives that they have won their victories without complicated organization, without patronage, often without newspaper support and with the use of very little money. Nothing could show more conclusively that they represent a popular feeling so deep that it cannot be influenced by machine methods.

At the end of my first two years in Congress, I was renominated, overcoming all opposition, and carried my district, which had given me only 400 plurality in 1884, by more than 3,500; and the third time, in 1888, I was elected by a majority of nearly 3,000.

As time passed the more familiar I became with the inner affairs of Congress, the more plainly I saw the constant crowding in of private interests, seeking benefits. I soon had another very illuminating experience.

A voluminous bill was before the Committee on Indian Affairs providing for the opening for settlement of 11,000,000 acres of the Sioux Indian Reservation in Dakota. As it was being read in committee, we came to a provision to ratify an agreement made by the Chicago, Milwaukee and St. Paul and Chicago and Northwestern railroads with the Indians for rights of way through the reservation. My previous study of documents on Indian Affairs here became useful. I discovered that in addition to the rights of way, one company was given the exclusive right to acquire 715 acres, and the other 828 acres of land, ostensibly for "terminal facilities," and that each road was to have at intervals of every ten miles an additional 160 acres of land, presumably for "station privileges." I stopped the reading at this point.

"This looks to me like a town site job," I said. "I cannot see why these railroads should have so much more land than is necessary to use directly in connection with their business as common carriers."

I had no sooner uttered these words than the member of the committee sitting upon my right nudged me and whispered, "Bob, you don't want to interfere with that provision. *Those are your home corporations.*"

But I did interfere and had the paragraphs laid over and we adjourned the session of the committee at twelve o'clock to attend the meeting of the House. I had not been in my seat half an hour when a page announced that Senator Sawyer wanted to see me. I found him waiting for me near the cloakroom. We sat on a settee and talked of general matters for some time. As the Senator rose to go he said, apparently as an afterthought:

"Oh, say, La Follette, your committee will have coming up before long the Sioux Indian bill. There is a provision in it for our folks up in Wisconsin, the Northwestern and St. Paul railroads. I wish you'd look after it."

"Senator Sawyer," I said, "we have already reached that provision in the bill, and I am preparing an amendment to it. I don't think it's right."

"Is that so," said the Senator, in apparent surprise. "Come and sit down and let's talk it over."

We argued for an hour, Sawyer presenting every point in favor of granting the railroads the prior right to acquire all the land they wanted. This was the first time Sawyer had directly and personally attempted to influence me in a matter of legislation. I was respectful to him, but could not yield to his view. I told him that I thought it right to permit the railroads to acquire the land necessary for rights of way, yards, tracks, sidings, depots, shops, roundhouses, and indeed, all they needed solely for transportation purposes, and should favor such a provision. But as framed, the provision plainly allowed them to get prior and exclusive rights to much more land for town site and other speculative uses; that besides they were not required to build their lines within any definite time, and might hold the land to the exclusion of all others indefinitely, without turning a sod or laying a rail; that it was unjust to the Indians and the public, and I could not support it. He was not ill tempered, and said he would see me again about it.

Forty-eight hours later Henry C. Payne arrived in Washington. He was Secretary of the Republican State Central Committee, political manager of the Wisconsin machine, lobbyist for the St. Paul Railroad and the Beef Trust, and had the backing of the important corporate interests of the state. Obviously he had been summoned to Washington by Sawyer.

Everybody was taught to believe that Payne had some occult and mysterious power as a political manager, and that when he said a thing would happen in politics or legislation, it always did happen. He was a perfect ideal of that union of private business and politics that carried on its face apparent devotion to the public interest. A fine head and figure, meditative, introspective eyes, a quiet, clear-cut, convincing way of stating his views, he was certainly the most accomplished railroad lobbyist I ever knew. His intimate friendship and business relation with the Chairman of the Democratic State Central Committee in Wisconsin came to be one of the best-known amenities in the politics of the day in that state. It was said that there was a well-worn pathway between the back doors of their private offices.

Well, Sawyer and Payne came to see me night after night for a week or more. Payne was rather stiff and harsh, but Sawyer was fatherly—much like a parent reasoning with a wayward child.

Nils P. Haugen, Congressman from the tenth district, occupied a seat near me. One day he said:

"I want to tell you something. I saw Payne last night at the Ebbitt House, and he went for you. He said 'La Follette is a crank; if he thinks he can buck a railroad company with 5,000 miles of line, he'll find out his mistake. We'll take care of him when the time comes.' "

Payne was as good as his word. He fought me ever afterward.

But I got my amendment through allowing the railroad to acquire the necessary right of way, twenty acres of land for stations, and only such additional land as the Secretary of the Interior should find to be a necessary aid to transportation, prohibiting the use or sale of any of said lands for town site or other purposes, and providing that each of said roads should within three years locate, construct, and operate their lines or forfeit the lands so acquired to the government.

I felt even then, and learned far better afterward, what it meant to oppose my own party organization; but when party leaders work for corporations and railroad control, when they do not represent the people, what other course is open for a man who believes in democratic government? I believed then, as I believe now, that the only salvation for the Republican party lies in purging itself wholly from the influence of financial interests. It is for this, indeed, that the group of men called Insurgents have been fighting—and it is this that they will contend for to the end. I here maintain with all the force I possess that it is only as the Republican party adopts the position maintained to-day by the Progressives that it can live to serve the country as a party organization.

Two of the incidents which I have related as examples showing how private interests sought advantages in Congress involve the Wisconsin organization. But Wisconsin was no whit worse than other states. While Sawyer and Payne were getting things for their "home corporations" Quay was getting things for *his* and Aldrich for *his*, and Gorman for *his* corporations. And they all traded back and forth, Sawyer helping Aldrich and Quay in getting what they wanted, and they helping him to get what *he* wanted. At first I saw only sporadic cases, such as I have mentioned, and it was some time before I learned how thoroughly all these interests worked together, each serving the other.

It was in my second term that I crossed the trail of the national organizations of both parties meddling in legislation for corporate interests. In the session before the presidential campaign of 1888 an effort was made to pass the Nicaraguan Canal bill. Congressman Haugen and I had been active in opposing this bill. One day we received an invitation to visit Senator Sawyer in his committee room at the Senate end of the capitol, and did so. When we arrived we found Senator Sawyer and the famous Colonel William W. Dudley alone together. Dudley was Chairman of the executive committee of the National Republican Committee. He was a most genial man personally, a brave soldier of the Civil War, who left a leg at Gettysburg. But he was an old-school politician—and practical. It was in the following campaign that the Colonel acquired the title of "Blocks-of-five Dudley," through the publication of a letter to an Indiana follower giving minute instructions as to how voters should be rounded up, watched by faithful lieutenants and voted in "blocks of five."

When we entered the room, Sawyer said:

"I have called you boys over here to talk with you about the Nicaraguan Canal bill. I hear you are ag'in it. Now that bill is all right, and ought to pass. Dudley here knows all about it. Dudley, you tell the boys about it."

Colonel Dudley argued that it was very essential that the measure then on the House calendar should pass before the adjournment of the session. Not meeting with any favorable response from Haugen and myself, he finally appealed to us in the interests of the Republican party, and stated that if the bill was permitted to pass before the adjournment of Congress, the parties interested in the canal would contribute one hundred thousand dollars to the Republican campaign fund. Having understood that Phil Thompson, a prominent Democrat and an ex-Representative, who had the privilege of the floor, was active in behalf of the same measure, I asked Dudley what the Democrats expected if the bill passed, and he frankly admitted that there would be a similar amount contributed to the Democratic National Committee. I jokingly suggested that if the Democrats were to receive a like contribution, one would offset the other. Dudley replied in the same vein, that Republicans had a lot more sense than Democrats in spending their campaign funds, and then proceeded seriously to explain that a plan was afoot by which the Republicans hoped to carry Delaware; that in Delaware at that time only persons owning real estate could vote, and that it was proposed to use this fund, or a part of the fund, to buy a tract of swamp land, and parcel it out among the laboring men so as to qualify them as voters. We stated that it was a matter of principle with us, and that we should not withdraw our opposition to the bill.

The bill did not pass at that session. It did pass with some amendment in 1889.

A striking incident which occurred near the end of my service in Congress, vividly illustrated the relationship between private interests in various parts of the country in seeking legislation for special privilege.

A Ship Subsidy bill was pending in the House, so sweeping in its provisions, that as one of its opponents somewhat extravagantly said, it would "subsidize every fishing smack in New England waters." It was a flagrant effort on the part of private interests to get into the public treasury. The Democrats were generally opposed to the measure. The Republicans were then in control of the House and generally supported it. I was opposed to it, because it granted a privilege to private interests. Therefore I began to canvass among my Republican friends to see if I could not persuade enough of them to join in voting with the Democrats to defeat the bill. These first tests of strength came a few days before the close of the session, about two o'clock in the morning. Enough Republicans voted with the Democrats to defeat it by a narrow margin of five votes. While the clerk recapitulates the roll call on a close vote, effort is often made to get enough members to change their votes to reverse the result. There was great bustling about by the leading supporters of the measure, seeking out members who might be induced to change their votes. I saw what was afoot. Myron McCord was a Republican member of the Wisconsin delegation, with whom I had discussed the measure and who had voted against the bill. Suddenly I saw a group of members coming out of the cloak room, urging, almost pushing McCord down the aisle. He called out, "Mr. Speaker—Mr. Speaker." Obviously he was about to change his vote.

There was confusion everywhere—the same thing going on in different parts of the House. Without at all reckoning the consequences, I jumped from my seat, slipped through the crowd, and seizing McCord by his collar, jerked him suddenly backward. Taken by surprise, unprepared for the pull, he nearly lost his feet, and I kept him going until I had him back in the cloakroom.

"Tell me, Myron," I said, "what do you mean? Why are you trying to change your vote? You promised to vote against the bill."

He did not resent what I had done. He was ashamed, and said:

"Bob, I've got to change my vote. Sawyer has just sent a page over here and insists on my voting for the bill. I've got to do it. He has loaned me money; he has a mortgage on everything I possess. And he is on his way over here now. He seems to have a personal interest in the passage of the bill."

He was much agitated.

"Myron," I said, "here is your hat and coat. Get off the floor as quickly as you can."

I went with him out of the door leading from the House floor into the corridor back of the Speaker's desk. As I returned and was passing up the centre aisle, whom should I see but Senator Sawyer hurrying down the aisle to meet me. He was white with rage. He came directly at me, and jabbing me in the chest with the ends of his stubby fingers, said (I remember his exact words):

"Young man, young man, what are you doing? You are a bolter. The Republican platform promises this legislation. You are a bolter, sir; you are a bolter."

I was furious. I revolted at the whole thing.

"Senator Sawyer," I said, "you can't tell me how to vote on any question. You've no business on this floor seeking to influence legislation. You are violating the rules. You get out of here, or I will call the Speaker's attention to you."

I turned toward the Speaker's desk. He knew I would do what I said, and left the floor immediately without another word. And the House bill was beaten and a substitute measure passed.

A day or two later I chanced to meet Sawyer in the corridor of the capitol. He stopped me and apologized, saying, "I am sorry for what I said the other night. You were right and I was wrong. You have a perfect right to vote as you please." I met him a number of times after that before finally leaving Washington, and he was as cordial toward me as ever.

In those days a Congressman was obliged to spend even more time than now in departmental matters, especially pensions, which are now covered by general laws. At that time the pressure was tremendous and a Congressman with many old soldiers in his district was kept busy examining testimony and untangling their records. During most of my service in Congress I spent from a quarter to a third of my time following up pension cases. This did not relate to private pensions, but to the work of investigation at the Pension Office, where the methods were not so systematized as now.

I recall one interesting case. An old man, by the name of Joseph Wood, living in Madison, very poor, had a claim pending for an injury received at Pittsburg Landing. His case had been repeatedly rejected because the records of the War Department showed that his regiment had not arrived at Pittsburg Landing until forty-eight hours after the claimant swore he had been injured. On going through his papers I found the affidavits of his captain and twenty-five other soldiers all swearing to the facts as stated by him. I was sure these twenty-six men had not committed perjury. I went to the War Department, thinking there might have been a clerical error in copying, but the record was just as reported at the Pension Office.

Finding that the 77th Ohio, in which Wood had served, was brigaded with the army which General Sherman commanded, I wrote to Sherman. He replied, in substance, "See my memoirs, page so-and-so." The date there agreed with the one given by the claimant. I went back to the War Department and said, "General Sherman knows when the 77th Ohio reached Pittsburg Landing." The records were taken to the Secretary of War. He said they could not be changed even on the authority of General Sherman's memoirs. I seemed up against it, when it flashed across my mind that the document looked too new to be the original record. Upon inquiry, I found this was true. The old worn records had been stored away years before. Some one was detailed to examine them, and sure enough, there had been a mistake in copying. General Sherman and my old soldier friend were right. Thirty-six hundred dollars back pension brought comfort to that old man and his wife.

It seems to me now, as I look back upon those years, that most of the lawmakers and indeed most of the public, looked upon Congress and the government as a means of getting some sort of advantage for themselves or for their home towns or home states. River and harbor improvements without merit, public buildings without limit, raids upon the public lands and forests, subsidies and tariffs, very largely occupied the attention of Congressmen. Lobbyists for all manner of private interests, especially the railroads, crowded the corridors of the capitol and the Washington hotels and not only argued for favorable legislation, but demanded it.

Of this period, Bryce in his "American Commonwealth," says:

"The doors of Congress are besieged by a whole army of commercial and railroad men and their agents to whom, since they have come to form a sort of profession, the name of 'lobbyists' is given. Many Congressmen are personally interested and lobby for themselves among their colleagues from the vantage ground of their official positions. Thus a vast deal of solicitation and bargaining goes on. . . . That the capitol and the hotels at Washington are a nest of intrigues and machinations while Congress is sitting is admitted on all hands; how many of the members are *tainted* no one can tell."

The genesis of the private interest idea in our government is perfectly clear. While the country was developing rapidly, with capital scarce and competition strong, it often seemed that the best way, indeed the only way, to secure the highest public interest was through the encouragement and protection of private interests. To the wisest men of the earlier times in this country it seemed important to encourage private interests, for example, in building railroads; hence vast tracts of land were granted to railroad companies. Our forest and other natural resources seemed unlimited, and it was anything for growth and development. For a long time, only in the case of railroads did the public generally begin to draw the line at which the protection of private interests became the legalized plunder of the public. In the newest and least developed sections of the country, as in Alaska, the line is still somewhat obscured. Private interests, fed thus upon public favors, became enormously strong. Later the combination form of organization appeared, and competition began to be wiped out. Trusts came into existence.

But the private interests, the "infant industries," the "struggling railroads," instead of wanting less government help when they grew strong, demanded more. It was easier to grow rich by gifts from the government than by efficient service and honest effort.

At the time I was in Congress, from 1885 to 1891, the onslaught of these private interests was reaching its height. I did not then fully realize that this was the evidence of a great system of "community of interests," which was rapidly getting control of our political parties, our government, our courts. The issue has since become clear. Whether it shows itself in the tariff, in Alaska, in municipal franchises, in the trusts, in the railroads, or the great banking interests, we know that it is one and the same thing. And there can be no compromise with these interests that seek to control the government. Either they or the people will rule.

I have endeavored in this chapter to show how, in those days, the consideration of private interests of all sorts overwhelmed Congress. I have showed how, in several instances, and in a limited way, I tried to fight against them—singly. But I do not mean to imply that there was no hopeful, no constructive movement then going forward, or that patriotic men, in both branches of Congress, were not doing their best to stem the tide. Such men as Sherman in the Senate and Reagan in the House were real constructive statesmen. While I was in Congress the first efforts were made, through the passage of the Interstate Commerce Law, the Sherman Anti-trust Act and other measures, to reassert the power of popular government and to grapple with these mighty private interests; but of that significant, constructive work I shall speak in the next chapter.

Even then the two diametrically opposite ideas of government had begun a death grapple for mastery in this country. Shall government be for the benefit of private interests, as the Sawyers of those days, and the Quays, Gormans, and the Aldriches believed? Or shall government be for the benefit of the public interest? This is the simple issue involved in the present conflict in the nation.

Chapter III

The Reed Congress and
the New National Issues

I come now with great personal interest to an account of what was, with a single exception, the most tumultuous and exciting session of Congress in all our history, and one of the most important. It was the so-called "Reed Congress" of 1889 to 1891.

For the first time in fourteen years—since 1875—the Republican party had come into full control of all the departments of government; but while Harrison had comfortably defeated Cleveland, and Blaine was in the cabinet, the House of Representatives was Republican by so narrow a majority that there was some talk that we might not be able to organize the House and elect a Speaker.

It developed immediately that McKinley and Reed were to be the two chief candidates of the Republicans for the Speakership, and the lines of the contest were soon sharply drawn. I was for Reed; I was for Reed notwithstanding the fact that I felt for McKinley a peculiar admiration and affection. I thought Reed better equipped in temperament and character for the struggle which we all knew must follow.

McKinley and Reed were not at all alike. McKinley drew men to him by the charm, courtliness, and kindliness of his manner; Reed drove and forced men; he scourged them with his irony—stung them with his wit. McKinley was a magnetic speaker; he had a clear, bell-like quality of voice, with a thrill in it. He spoke with dignity, but with freedom of action. The pupils of his eyes would dilate until they were almost black, and his face, naturally without much color, would become almost like marble—a strong face and a noble head. When interrupted either in a speech or debate, instead of seeking to put his man at a disadvantage, as Reed did, he sought to win him. He never had a harsh word for a harsh word, but rather a kindly appeal: "Come now, let us put the personal element aside and consider the principle involved."

Reed, on the other hand, impressed one with his power. He was rough and sharp and strong. He was one of the ablest men in either house of Congress—next to Sherman, who was a broader statesman, perhaps the ablest. He had a marvelous gift of expression. His sentences were short, crisp, strong, and his diction was perfect, but his voice was harsh and disagreeable, especially in its higher notes. As a debater he has rarely been equaled in our public life; he had a caustic wit, was often sarcastic, ironical, sometimes droll. He would metaphorically lay hold of his opponent, shake him for a few minutes like some great mastiff, and then drop him into his seat all crumpled up. And yet, though witty in his dealings with individual members, he never trifled with the business of the House. Some of his passages with Carlisle, when Carlisle was Speaker, were among the best examples of close forensic reasoning I have ever heard. Both were as fine parliamentary athletes as were ever to be found. I remember vividly a characteristic passage between them. It was near the end of the session, and three o'clock in the morning. An appropriation bill was pending. Some one offered an amendment. If it passed, some advantage would accrue to the Democrats; if it failed, some advantage to the Republicans. A point of order was raised against it and Carlisle overruled the point. Reed was on his feet—Reed, three hundred pounds, six feet tall. He was the leader on the Republican side. I remember he had just two gestures; one an impressive downward movement with his extended index finger, and in the other, during his higher flights, he held one great clenched fist high above his head—like some colossus. He was a striking figure.

"I contend," he said, on the occasion to which I refer, "that the Speaker is wrong."

Carlisle standing there in the Speaker's place answered, "I shall be glad to hear the gentleman from Maine."

Reed retorted: "The Speaker is wrong for this reason"—and put it in a nutshell.

"Ah, but the gentleman from Maine is in error because"—and Carlisle stated his contention without a superfluous word.

"Yes," answered Reed, "but Mr. Speaker"—and for ten or fifteen minutes it was parry and thrust, thrust and parry, Reed pressing Carlisle from position to position until finally the Speaker said:

"The gentleman from Maine is clearly right. The Speaker is wrong and reverses his ruling."

It was during the speakership fight, in which the interest of the country was intense, that I first met Theodore Roosevelt. He was at that time Civil Service Commissioner, and was much interested in the success of Reed. I liked him. I thought him an unusually able and energetic man, but I think no one then realized the power of growth that was in him. We were about the same age; we were both interested in Reed's election, and I saw quite a little of him that winter.

Well, we chose Reed Speaker, and it was not long before the expected clash took place. In previous Congresses and under the old rules it was possible for an obstructive minority, by refusing to vote, to prevent the House from accomplishing anything. A change in the rules seemed absolutely necessary if the Republicans were to enact any legislation, and, indeed, that was one of the issues in Reed's election. The initial test, as I recall, came on some minor matter, and I have never, in any legislative body, seen anything like it for intensity of emotion and excitement.

It was evident beforehand that the Democrats were preparing, by refusing to vote, to make a point of no quorum and prevent the consideration of the motion which was before the House. Reed with McKinley and other members of the Committee on Rules were in conference in the Speaker's room. The time came for action. Reed returned to the floor of the House. I remember how he loomed up behind the Speaker's desk. His face was set and grim. His eyes were dead black, and beyond those of any man I ever knew his were the eyes of power.

The motions necessary to close the debate were made; the yeas and nays were demanded; the clerk was ordered to call the roll.

As we anticipated, the Democrats refused to vote. When the roll was completed a point of no quorum was made. This was the moment of suspense. What would Reed do? What would the Democrats do? A perfect hush fell upon the House; I found myself holding fast to my desk. Reed raised his gavel, and with the mallet end in his hand, deliberately pointed out and called the names of members present and not voting, and directed the clerk to so record them. Then he proclaimed a quorum present, announced the vote, and declared the result.

Instantly members on the Democratic side were on their feet and rushed down the aisles toward the Speaker. An angry roar went

43

up; there were cries of "Czar," "Tyrant." Immediately the Republicans pressed forward to the support of the Speaker. The least thing in the world—if, for example, some one had by accident been thrust against another—might have precipitated a conflict of serious consequences.

As for Reed, he never stirred from his place, but stood unmoved and with a look held them, until one by one they dropped back into their places.

Reed appointed me a member of the Ways and Means Committee, which was then as now the leading committee of the House. Among its members were an unusually talented group of men. On the Republican side were McKinley, the chairman, who afterward became President; McKenna, now a member of the Supreme Court; Burrows of Michigan, who went to the Senate; Dingley of Maine, and Payne of New York, both of whom afterward became leaders of the House; Bayne of Pennsylvania; Gear of Iowa, afterward United States Senator. On the Democratic side were Carlisle of Kentucky, afterward Senator and Secretary of the Treasury; Flower of New York, who served as governor of his state; Roger Q. Mills of Texas, author of the Mills bill, and afterward United States Senator; Breckenridge of Arkansas, afterward Minister to Russia; and McMillan of Tennessee, afterward governor of his state.

I was younger than any of the other members. I think my appointment came largely as the result of a speech I made on the tariff in the preceding session. It was during the discussion of the Mills bill. I had taken no part in the debate, although I had been trying hard to prepare myself on the tariff, studying all the great debates on the subject, going back to Clay and Hamilton.

Ordinarily, Roger Q. Mills, as the father of the measure, should have closed the debate, but for some reason that task fell to Carlisle, the Speaker. Reed closed for the Republicans. Both speeches were very able efforts and made a profound impression; but both had been prepared beforehand and each without reference to the other.

I felt that Carlisle's speech was a dangerous one for the Republicans. It dealt with former tariff legislation, particularly with the effect of the acts of 1846 and 1857. I was sure that Carlisle was not only in error in his statement of historical facts, but misleading in his deductions from statistics.

I believed strongly that Carlisle ought to be answered, though I felt that it would be presumptuous for a member of my youth and inexperience to attempt it. Finally I went to Reed, told him how I felt and urged him to reply to Carlisle. He responded by advising me in a jocular way to answer Carlisle myself. I then went with the same proposition to McKinley. And McKinley also said to me:

"Bob, you answer it."

"Well," I said, a bit nettled, "I will answer it."

I had a cartload of *Congressional Records* and reports sent to my home. I put in two or three weeks of the hardest kind of work and prepared a speech about an hour and a quarter long. I knew that under the rules I could get only five minutes, but I hoped to make enough impression in five minutes to secure an extension of time from some other member. I read the speech in advance to just one member of Congress, William E. Fuller of Iowa, who had been my good friend, and he advised me to deliver it.

I waited my opportunity, and began my answer to Carlisle with the statement, "That the representations and conclusions of the distinguished gentleman from Kentucky in reference to this most interesting decade (1846-1857) remain unchallenged and unanswered, is my only excuse for calling the attention of the House to the subject now." I did my best to crowd everything I could into the first few minutes, keeping my eyes more or less on Reed, the Republican leader. He was working at his desk, writing. After I had been speaking for a time he stopped and turned around to listen to me.

Presently the gavel fell, cutting off my speech. Butterworth and Reed both came to their feet. Butterworth asked that my time be extended so as to enable me to finish my remarks. Reed also interposed—I can recall just how he looked saying:

"Mr. Speaker, I think that courtesy ought to be allowed the gentleman. This speech ought not to be interrupted here."

Unanimous consent was given, and I continued.

The speech, which was afterward widely circulated, evidently so impressed the party leaders as to assure me a place on the Ways and Means Committee.

As soon as the committee was organized we began serious work upon the preparation of the measure afterward known as the McKinley bill. McKinley apportioned the different schedules to sub-committees for special consideration. I was assigned to prepare the agricultural, jute, hemp, flax, and tobacco schedules and was one of three on the metal schedule. Gear, of Iowa, and I made the chief fight to put sugar on the free list.

For many weeks we held open hearings and scores of men of all classes appeared before us and presented their views. Most of the information we then received, as I now realize, consisted of the loose statements of interested men. The facts and figures of the manufacturers were accepted as reliable. I think at that time I did not seriously question this unscientific method of securing information as a basis for such important legislation as that upon the tariff.

We relied upon the historical theory of the protective tariff as advocated by the Republican party. Hamilton, Clay, Blaine, and McKinley believed that it made little difference how high the duties were fixed, because free competition between domestic manufacturers within the tariff wall would inevitably force prices down, insuring the lowest charge to the consumer commensurate with paying American wages to American workmen.

Blaine in his "Twenty Years in Congress" makes domestic competition the cornerstone of protection. He says:

"Protection . . . does not invite competition from abroad, but is based on the contrary principle, that competition at home will always prevent monopoly on the part of capitalists, assure good wages to the laboring man and defend the consumers against the evils of extortion."

But the trouble has been that domestic competition did not prove the strong regulator of commerce that the early protectionists believed it would. Money interests began to form monopolies behind the tariff wall and both consumers and wage-earners began to suffer from extortion.

The difference in view on the tariff between the progressive Republicans and the so-called "stand-pat" Republicans lies exactly here. The Progressives have seen this vast revolution in economic conditions and have recognized the need of radical changes in our tariff system, while the stand-pat Republicans, led by Aldrich, Penrose, Lodge, Smoot, and others, have refused to recognize the changed conditions. They believe in keeping the tariff wall as high as possible notwithstanding the growth of extortionate monopolies. They believe it more important to keep up the profits of the combined manufacturers than to keep down the prices to the people. The passage of the Payne-Aldrich tariff bill of 1909, of which I shall have more to say later in the appropriate place, was the most outrageous assault of private interests upon the people recorded in tariff history.

Progressive Republicans have demanded a Tariff Commission of scientific experts, with power to investigate and discover the actual differences in labor cost between American and foreign products. We do not wish to have the tariff reduced below that difference, but we realize that we cannot accept the statements of interested manufacturers. In my speech in 1890 supporting the McKinley bill, I referred to the wide difference in conditions between farmers and wage-earners in America compared with those in foreign countries. I said:

"Gentlemen may reason upon any line they choose; they may approach the subject from either side; but, sir, there is no escape from the conclusion that labor is the great issue involved. The workers in every field of industry in this broad land are the ones vitally interested."

Where there can be shown to be no difference in labor cost I am for free trade. But the difference must be determined by real experts who understand the use and limits of statistics. This was my criticism at the last session of Congress, of the present so-called tariff board appointed by Mr. Taft. This board reported to Congress the *average* difference on print paper and wood pulp, but I showed that their "average" had no meaning at all. It was made up from many establishments, some of which had old, antiquated machinery which ought long ago to have gone to the scrap heap. In these establishments the labor cost was excessively high, and *we do not believe in protecting inefficient management.* On the other hand, by digging into their report, I showed from their own statistics that the up-to-date efficient plants in this country were making paper just as cheaply as it can be made in Canada, and for that reason I was for free print paper and wood pulp. A tariff board is a poor substitute for the haphazard hearings on the McKinley, Dingley, and Payne-Aldrich bills if the statistical experts do not know how to collect and interpret their statistics. While the present tariff board *may* gather much valuable information, it has no power of commanding the facts from unwilling manufacturers; it does not meet the requirement that every member shall be specially trained for the service, it is insufficiently supplied with funds, and it reports to the executive rather than the legislative branch of the government. Its lack of power was well expressed by its capable chairman, Prof. Henry C. Emery, in a speech to the American Association of Woolen and Worsted Manufacturers on December 8, 1910. He said:

"You must not think I am joking about this thing, but there is a joke about it, and the joke is this: I have no powers whatsoever. The tariff board has no powers. There is really no such thing as a tariff board. The law says that for certain purposes the President may 'employ such persons' as he sees fit. I am one of 'such persons.' That is all."

The Tariff Commission should be at the service of the houses of Congress instead of the semi-confidential advisers of the President. For it is Congress which is charged with the duty of framing the tariff laws, and there are other things besides mere statistics that Congress must pass upon. Congress must determine whether a given industry shall be protected at all. We do not want to protect tropical products not suited to our climate. We do not want to protect raw material, like lumber and phosphates, *where protection merely adds to the exhaustion of our natural resources.* Then, before Congress decides that a given industry shall be protected, we want to know how much of its claim for protection is due to its own inefficiency. We ought to work toward a condition in which American enterprise, good management, clever and powerful machinery, intelligence and skill of the workers will enable us to have *low cost of labor along with high wages to the laborer.*

For this reason we want to know also what are the *actual* wages and *actual* standards of living of American labor in the protected industries. If men are working twelve hours a day seven days a week, as they are in the steel industry, whereas their competitors in England are working eight hours a day six days a week, then the fact that our labor cost is less than the English labor cost does not necessarily require us to adopt free trade in steel products. Our tariff should be based on what American labor *ought* to get in order to reach our ideal of living wages suited to American citizenship. In 1890, when we were working on the McKinley bill, the iron and steel workers had the most powerful trade union in the country. There was no question then that they would be able to get from their employers their fair share of the tariff protection. But their union was broken to pieces afterward by the Homestead strike. The question of how American labor is going to protect itself against the trusts is a serious problem fast looming up ahead of us. Certainly we should not reduce the tariff so low as to shut off their hope of better conditions. If their unions are destroyed *we must supplement our tariff legislation by labor legislation.*

These are some of the facts which a really expert Tariff Commission should furnish to Congress. And I can see, by comparison with our hearings on the McKinley bill, how such a commission would be of incalculable service to the Ways and Means Committee.

But to return to my story: As soon as the hearings were completed the committee divided and the Democratic members, led by Carlisle and Mills, discontinued their attendance. In doing this they were following the precedent set by the Republicans in the former Congress, when the Mills bill was being framed by a Democratic majority. In framing the measure each sub-committee reported and the bill was then drafted by the Republican members. I remember spending night after night with McKinley in his rooms in the Ebbitt House going over, comparing, and arranging the paragraphs of each schedule.

One interesting feature of our deliberations was our various consultations with James G. Blaine. Blaine was a man of extraordinary personality, possessing those peculiarities of temperament and character which made him a great leader of men. I never was an ardent Blaine man. I always shared the Wisconsin admiration for Sherman, and it was a disappointment to me when Blaine was nominated for the Presidency. He was a man who had to be defended; and many Republicans who were not infatuated with him were somewhat afraid of him.

I remember especially one visit that the Republican members of our committee paid to Blaine in his office as Secretary of State. He was not then in good health; the malady to which he finally succumbed had fastened upon him. His face was chalky white and as he talked I remember he leaned upon his desk. It was suggested by McKinley that he sit down. "No, no," he said, "I can't talk when I sit down." The only thing that did not look like death in his face was his brilliant black eyes.

Blaine was one of the most effective talkers we have had—clear, easy, copious, and with a rare grace of expression. He gave us his views on reciprocity, and before the bill finally became law they were substantially incorporated in Section III. At that time Blaine had begun to see clearly the path along which the high protective tariff was driving us, and to realize the necessity of developing our foreign markets. But the sort of reciprocity which he advocated was very different from the reciprocity advocated by President Taft and opposed by many of the Republican Progressives in the last session of Congress.

Nothing surprised me more during that session than the misunderstanding in many minds of the Republican doctrine of reciprocity. It was astonishingly confused with what might be called the Democratic doctrine. The Republican doctrine, as expounded by Blaine, is based upon the protection of all American industries that can economically be conducted in this country. It then places a high tariff on articles, such as tropical and semi-tropical products, that cannot be produced in this country except at excessive cost. But this tariff is not for the purpose of protection. It is for the purpose of "trading capital." Its object is to enable the President to make a trade with foreign countries by offering to them a reduction of duties on articles which we do not care to protect, in exchange for the reduction of their duties on articles which we wish to protect but which we wish also to export. It is a kind of double protection for American industries—protection of the home market against foreigners, and extension of the foreign market for Americans.

But the Democratic doctrine applied to reciprocity is exactly the opposite. It is based upon the free trade theory. It proposes to make "trading capital," not of the industries which we cannot build up economically, but of the industries which we want to protect. In fact, carried to the extreme, as was done by President Taft in his Canadian pact, it sacrificed the farmers, who, with the laborers, are almost the only interests we want to protect, in favor of the trusts, which are the last interests needing protection. It proposed to reduce our tariffs on farm products if the Canadians would reduce their tariffs on our trust products. No wonder the Canadians rejected it! and I believe the Americans would have rejected it if they could have had a similar campaign of education upon it. It would have sacrificed our farmers to Canadian competition, while actually strengthening our trusts by giving them cheaper raw material; and it would have placed the Canadians at the mercy of our trusts, so that they could not have retained the advantages of their cheap raw material after their own manufacturers were driven out. It was also an attractive bait for the American newspapers, which were influenced in its favor by the promises of free print paper and wood pulp. In my speech in the Senate I proclaimed that the suppression by the newspapers of news against reciprocity was a black page in our history.

The McKinley tariff bill was a momentous measure. It aided in defeating the Republican party in 1892, but, when the reaction came, McKinley's connection with it was largely instrumental in making him President of the United States.

McKinley believed profoundly that the interests of the whole country, agricultural as well as manufacturing, were involved in the maintenance of such duties as would insure the protection of all articles which it was economically possible for us to produce in this country. That meant patriotism to him. It was a deep conviction, almost a religion, with him. No one who worked with him could doubt it.

A few months after his inauguration, I received a telegram from President McKinley and also from Senator Spooner, offering me the position of Comptroller of the Treasury. It came out of a clear sky: I was not a candidate for any position under his administration, and I declined by telegraph. Later I called on him at the White House, explaining why I could not accept. We were then in the midst of the Wisconsin fight, and besides I did not desire an appointive office. We sat on a lounge together and talked over our old days in Congress. He told me what his hopes and ambitions were as to extending our trade abroad; that in his selection of appointees in foreign missions and in the consular service he hoped to secure trained business men who were masters in the lines of trade which could be extended in the countries to which they were sent. It was McKinley's greatest ambition, now that the country had reached its highest development under the protective system, with an excess of production demanding outlet, to round out his career by gaining for America a supremacy in the markets of the world; and this he hoped to do without weakening the protective system.

During all the years that I was in Congress the stupendous problems which now confront us, and which will occupy us for a long time to come, had already begun to appear. I mean the problems of the trusts and the railroads: in short, the problems of vast financial power in private hands. In those years the government of the United States for the first time began to consider seriously the condition of the common man—the worker, the farmer. While I was in Congress we passed two measures, which I heartily supported, that were destined to be of incalculable value to the plain people. One of them provided for the organization of a national Bureau of Labor, which has since been joined with bureaus concerned with the interests of commerce to form one of the great departments of the government with a representative in the cabinet. The other was the establishment of the Department of Agriculture—the recognition of the great farming industry of the country. Until that time, while manufacturers had been lavishly protected and while railroads had received vast grants of land, the wage-earner and the farmer had received little attention and no direct benefits. It is fortunate that this cooperation of the government with wage-earners and farmers took the form, not of direct financial advantage, but of investigation, publicity, and education, which in their nature are soundly constructive.

But the great subjects which were dealt with for the first time in those three Congresses were the railroad and trust problems.

Real statesmen like Sherman and Reagan saw that the policy, until then pursued, of serving the public interest by assisting private interests was no longer tenable. Private interests had grown so strong that it was felt that either the government must control them with a strong hand or else they would control the government.

It would not have availed then, nor will it avail now, merely to pursue the negative method of removing the tariff which has encouraged the growth of trusts and combinations. I believe that the reduction of tariffs will furnish a small measure of relief from the extortion of certain combinations, but it will not cure the evil of monopolies in private hands. Many trusts, such as the Standard Oil Company, the Anthracite Coal trust, and the whole group of trusts based upon monopoly of patent rights, do not now depend and never have depended for their existence or their power upon a protective tariff. Foreign competition will not, therefore, cure the trust evil: indeed, it will encourage the movement, already strongly in evidence, toward the organization of international and world-wide monopolies.

No, the constructive statesmen of those times saw clearly that there must be positive action of government either to prevent or to control monopolies. Two very significant laws, both of which I supported heartily, were therefore passed in those years. In one of these—the Sherman Anti-trust Act—the keynote was *prohibition*, the effort to prevent combination and to restore competition by drastic laws. In the other, the act establishing the Interstate Commerce Commission for the control of railroads, the keynote was *regulation*.

Of all the legislation of those years none interested me so deeply as the measure for the creation of the Interstate Commerce Commission, which we passed in 1887. I laid there the foundation of the knowledge which afterward served me well in the fight in Wisconsin, and continued of value after I came back to the Senate nineteen years later when railroad legislation occupied so much of the time of Congress.

I was strongly in favor of the regulation of railroads, and while the bill as proposed did not go as far as I should have liked, I worked for it and voted for it. Of all the speeches I made while a member of Congress, the one on the railroad bill gives me to-day the greatest satisfaction.

It was a bitter fight. To Reagan of Texas, more than any other one man in the House, belongs the credit for the passage of the act. He was a very able man, a Democrat. He was for a time Postmaster-General of the Confederacy. Reagan afterward went to the Senate, but because of his public-spirited interest in transportation questions, his desire to see railroad regulation established upon correct principles, he resigned, went home to Texas, and took the chairmanship of the state railroad commission at a much lower salary. He afterward took a great interest in my fight for railroad regulation in Wisconsin. When I was governor I sent him the original draft of our proposed Wisconsin law, and was much aided by his wise criticisms and suggestions.

Another method of dealing with private interests also appeared during those sessions of Congress in which I personally was particularly interested. I mean the regulation of industry by *internal revenue taxation.* The measure at issue was a bill to check the manufacturers of oleomargarine, mostly the great packers of Chicago, who made a bogus product and sold it as butter. It seriously injured the dairy business all over the country. The bill was debated for months in the House. The constitutional argument in favor of the measure had taken on an apologetic tone. The bill imposed an internal revenue tax on oleomargarine. It could not be defended as a measure to raise revenue, for there was a surplus of revenue in the treasury. When pressed by opponents of the bill to answer whether it was a proper use of the constitutional power to levy a tax when revenue was not needed, advocates of the measure inconsistently and illogically admitted that it was not. In my speech I argued openly that the Constitution authorized the federal government to use the taxing power, that there was no limit to that power for police purposes, and that it could be used not only to raise revenue but frankly and unreservedly to regulate or to destroy an evil. I think now as I thought then, that the power of internal revenue taxation, which has never been extensively used in this country, save for revenue purposes, will in the future be a valuable means of correcting some of the abuses which have grown out of modern business methods.

In my preparation of this oleomargarine debate I got track of a letter written by John Quincy Adams to the Speaker of the House of Representatives, in which I understood there was an extended discussion of the very proposition on which I wished to take my stand. At that period there were no complete records made of the doings of Congress, and I could not find the letter. I took my problem to Mr. Spofford, then at the head of the Congressional Library, who, after several weeks of search, finally discovered a copy of the letter in a newspaper of that day. It was a valuable document in its exposition of the views of the framers of the Constitution regarding the taxing powers of the government. It was eagerly accepted as furnishing high authority for the proposed legislation. In order to make it accessible for future use, I had it printed as an appendix to my speech.

Efforts in those days to bring about constructive reforms, especially if they struck at concrete evils, met with the bitterest opposition, as indeed they do to-day, in the case, for example, of so reasonable and practical a measure as that which provides for a parcels-post.

One single illustration will show the difficulties that beset any man in Congress who tries honestly to press a constructive reform against the power of private interests.

Henry Clay Evans of Tennessee was a friend of mine. He was formerly from Wisconsin, and in the convention in 1896, at St. Louis, I seconded his nomination for the vice-presidency. At that time Vilas of Wisconsin was Postmaster-General in Cleveland's cabinet. One of the first reforms he urged was against the excessive rental charge of railroad companies for postal cars. After a thorough investigation he showed that for the rental which it paid annually the government could actually build outright, equip, and keep in repair all the cars it used—and then save $500,000 a year.

Evans had been appointed to the House Committee on Post Offices and Post Roads, and when he got hold of Vilas' report it amazed him—as it would amaze any one not connected with a railroad company. It seemed to him that he had only to make these facts known in order to have the abuse corrected. He came to me and said very earnestly:

"I am going to get a provision adopted by the committee to stop this abuse and secure an appropriation sufficient to enable the government to build its own mail cars."

It seemed the sensible, honest thing to do. I encouraged him and told him that, if he could get the matter before the House, I would help him.

A few weeks later he gave me the result of his effort in committee:

"I put that thing up to the committee," he said, "with a good plain statement which should have convinced any man, and I couldn't even get a vote in support of the proposition."

If he had tried to get it upon the floor of the House there would not have been a corporal's guard to sustain him. The railroad lobby outside and the railroad members inside would have prevented any action.

Seventeen years afterward, when I came to the Senate, I looked this matter up and there was the same old abuse. During all those years the government had been paying enough rental every year to the railroads to buy the cars outright. I took up the old Vilas report, interested Victor Murdock of Kansas, then on the House Committee on Post Offices, and attempted to get something done. Murdock encountered the same opposition that defeated Evans years before—he could accomplish nothing. But when the Post Office appropriation bill came over to the Senate, I offered an amendment providing for an investigation in order to bring the Vilas data down to date. I believe that legislation should always be preceded by accurate information. I knew that my proposal was subject to a point of order as an amendment to an appropriation bill, but it was so manifestly right and in the public interest that I hoped the point would not be insisted upon. But no! Penrose raised the point of order and the investigation was denied.

The next year, when Penrose got the Post Office appropriation bill up, I was in a stronger position. For some reason he wanted it passed that day. But I stood in its path with my amendment and the power of unlimited debate. He suggested that if the Senator from Wisconsin would not press the matter at that time but would offer his amendment later and independently, that he (Penrose) would promise to have it reported back favorably from the committee and help in passing it. I promptly accepted his proposition, but Penrose went away and did not return until so near the end of the session that when I went to him he said he could not get his committee together—so I lost out again.

At the next session I began earlier, and got a resolution through the Senate which provided for an investigation by the Interstate Commerce Commission. This investigation has been made and reported—and at another session we are going at it again!

During those years in the eighties, while I was in Congress, the lines between the Progressive and stand-pat elements were already beginning to appear. The alignment of forces was not so clear to me then as it is now, but I knew well enough where the leaders stood. Reed always used his great powers in defending the existing system. He sneered at those who desired new legislation. He closed one of his speeches with these words:

"And yet, outside the Patent Office there are no monopolies in this country, and there never can be. Ah, but what is that I see on the far horizon's edge, with tongue of lambent flame and eye of forked fire, serpent-headed and griffin-clawed? Surely it must be the great new chimera 'Trust.' . . . What unreasonable talk this is. A dozen men fix the prices for sixty million freemen! They can never do it! There is no power on earth that can raise the price of any necessity of life above a just price and keep it there. More than that, if the price is raised and maintained even for a short while, it means ruin for the combination and still lower prices for the consumers."

Reed had no sympathy with the Interstate Commerce bill, and voted against it.

I always felt that McKinley represented the newer view. Of course, McKinley was a high protectionist, but on the great new questions as they arose he was generally on the side of the public and against private interests.

And this the people instinctively sensed. In my own State of Wisconsin, during the campaign for the Republican nomination in 1896, I was strongly for McKinley, but the old machine leaders, Payne, Sawyer, Spooner, Pfister, and Keyes, all worked vigorously for Reed. Reed had Big Business with him; but the sentiment in the state was too strong for the bosses. The Wisconsin delegation to the St. Louis convention, of which I had been elected as an anti-machine member, was instructed for and stood solid for McKinley.

I am saying this notwithstanding McKinley's relationships with Mark Hanna. The chief incentive behind Hanna's support of McKinley, I am convinced, was the honest love he felt for his friend. McKinley inspired affection of that sort. And Hanna, having come largely into control of the Republican organization through his genius as a leader and through the enormous expenditure of money, tried to bring all the elements together in harmony. The first and only time I ever met him was at the St. Louis convention. He requested me to come and see him. He was extremely cordial, almost affectionate. I remember he put his arm around me and told me of his relations with McKinley. He told me—and this was the object of the meeting—that he felt sure that McKinley would like to see Payne on the National Committee from Wisconsin. He understood, he said, that I was making a fight on Payne, but hoped that in the interest of harmony I would stand for Payne's selection. I told him very earnestly about our struggle in Wisconsin, that a great movement had started there which could not be arrested or diverted, that Payne and his associates stood for the destruction of representative government, and that we could make no truce with them. Mr. Hanna's manner changed abruptly, and the interview terminated.

I know of my own knowledge that McKinley stood against many of the corrupt influences within his own party—that he even stood firmly against the demands of his best friend, Hanna.

McKinley had no sooner been elected than the Wisconsin machine, backed strongly by Hanna, demanded the appointment of Henry C. Payne as Postmaster-General. And I with others brought forward the name of Governor Hoard of Wisconsin as candidate for Secretary of Agriculture. A few weeks before McKinley's inauguration, upon his invitation, I went to Canton to see him. When I called about ten o'clock he told his secretary that he would not see anybody else before five that afternoon. We drove about town and visited his mother, a beautiful old lady. We had luncheon at his house. We discussed at length the appointment of Payne and Hoard to the cabinet. I explained to him what forces Payne represented in Wisconsin, and indeed he had already known Payne's work as a lobbyist in Washington in connection especially with beef trust matters, and I knew he abominated that sort of thing. But he told me that he believed no other man had ever been so strongly endorsed by prominent influential politicians in every part of the country as was Payne for that appointment. When it was nearly time for me to go McKinley said:

"Bob, I may not be able to appoint Hoard, but I will say to you that Henry Payne shall not be a member of my cabinet."

When I saw McKinley at the White House in the following winter, he told me how the effort to secure Payne's appointment had culminated. He said that Hanna had come to him just before his final decision was made and said: "You may wipe out every obligation that you feel toward me, and I'll ask no further favors of you, if you'll only put Henry Payne in the cabinet."

McKinley's answer was: "Mark, I would do anything in the world I could for you, but I cannot put a man in my cabinet who is known as a lobbyist."

And he kept his word.

McKinley did not fully appreciate the new currents then entering our public life. He was a leader in the old business school of politics which regarded material prosperity as the chief end of all government. But he was a consistently honest man throughout. To illustrate:

It was during his administration that extensive frauds were discovered in the Post Office Department and in the Department of Posts of Cuba. Senator Bristow of Kansas was then the Fourth Assistant Postmaster-General. He is a born investigator, able, original, fearless. McKinley, when he realized the gravity of the frauds, sent for Bristow and told him he had selected him to go to Cuba and make a thorough investigation and clean out any corruption that might be found there.

"I am willing to go, Mr. President," said Bristow, "but before going I want to call your attention to the fact that every appointee in Cuba who has been accused of wrong-doing has been sent there upon the recommendation of members of Congress, Senators, or men influential in the Republican party. When it becomes necessary for me to arrest or remove from office any of these men, they will at once complain to their friends in the states and you will be bombarded with complaints as to my conduct. All I ask is that you withhold judgment until you hear my side of the case."

McKinley said: "Mr. Bristow, I understand just how difficult a task I have assigned to you. But go ahead, do what is right, be cautious, but firm, and shield no man who has been guilty of wrong-doing. As to the complaints, leave them to me; I will take care of them."

Bristow did go ahead and ran his game to cover, and when Hanna and other Senators and Congressmen protested he told them that the Cuban postal service was infested with a gang of thieves and that he was simply doing his duty and proposed to keep it up. Then they went to the White House and McKinley told them that Bristow was acting on his orders. He stood unwaveringly by Bristow against the persistent importunity of many of his most intimate political advisers.

I never felt that McKinley had a fair chance. His first term was broken into by the Spanish War. His second was cut off at the very beginning by assassination. He had no opportunity to develop his carefully wrought-out plans for large trade extension. He had rare tact as a manager of men. Back of his courteous and affable manner was a firmness that never yielded conviction, and while scarcely seeming to force issues he usually achieved exactly what he sought.

In the fall of 1890 I was a candidate for a fourth term in Congress. I was so confident of reelection that I spent much time campaigning in other parts of Wisconsin and in speaking in Iowa and elsewhere. But serious complications had arisen in Wisconsin politics: an act known as the Bennett law had been passed by the preceding legislature which the very large Lutheran and Roman Catholic element in the state believed to be a blow at their parochial school systems, and there was a wholesale cutting of the Republican ticket. Combined with this the machine leaders in

Wisconsin came into my district while I was absent speaking for candidates in other parts of the state, and secretly used all their power against me and in favor of the Democratic candidate. The result was that although I ran seven hundred votes ahead of my ticket, I was defeated. The whole state went heavily Democratic. Every Republican Congressman save one lost his seat.

Thus I was returned to private life and to my law practice; but it was not long before I began the fifteen years' struggle with the machine in Wisconsin which finally resulted in its complete overthrow.

Chapter IV

The Crucial Period
of My Public Life

It would be idle to say that the termination of my career as a Congressman in March, 1891, was not a bitter disappointment to me. It was. I had not made a great many speeches in the six years of my service, but when I did enter the debates it was with careful preparation; and I think I may fairly say that I had attained to such a position as warranted me in looking forward to a career of some distinction had I been permitted to remain in the House. So the defeat came to me as a severe blow. But I had acquired a very valuable experience in my public service and formed delightful and valuable acquaintances. I had been in contact with the strong men of the the country, and as a result had, I think, grown in character and power.

I was but thirty-five years of age, and went back with firm resolutions and good cheer to my law practice at Madison, Wisconsin. I was poor, and the expenses attendant upon readjustment to the new life were matters of consequence. These matters were discussed from time to time by Mrs. La Follette and myself. Our little daughter, Fola, very much impressed with frequently hearing these talks, came one day to her mother, and having in mind my recent failure of reelection, said, "Mama, will papa have to be elected before he can practice law and earn some money?"

I found that my public service, while it had been a serious interruption to my professional life, had extended my reputation materially and tended to draw to me a very substantial clientage. Any thought I had of returning to the public service was vague and remote. That I should continue to be interested in public questions and in matters political was inevitable. I knew that issues of great importance affecting the lives and homes of all the people

60

of the country were coming rapidly forward. I had followed the great debate in the Senate and House on the Sherman Anti-Trust Law, had taken part in the debate in the House on the Interstate Commerce Law, had seen the manifestations of corporate power in the halls of Congress. I recognized, in a way, the evidences of the oncoming struggle. I had come to understand the power of Sawyer, Payne, and a few other prominent Republican politicians, closely associated with railroads and other corporate interests in national and state legislation. I was convinced that Payne had not been seriously disappointed with my defeat; that, in fact, whenever he could exert any influence against my political success, without leaving a trail as broad as a highway, he had for some time lost no opportunity of doing so.

Not so with Sawyer. I had disappointed him again and again in my course upon legislation. But he was a loyal party man and believed in supporting party candidates regardless of personal feeling. Furthermore, as I have said before, I always believed that Sawyer did not violate his standard of political ethics in his course upon legislation. Like many politicians he regarded Congress as a useful agency for the promotion of business enterprises in which he and his friends were identified or interested. If a man did not accept his point of view, he would argue the matter in a blunt, frank, simple way without any display of feeling. The only time I remember to have seen Senator Sawyer manifest the least show of temper was on the floor of the House in connection with the ship subsidy measure, which I have already reviewed. While I understood Senator Sawyer, I think rightly, and know that our standards were not the same and that we would always differ on questions where there was a conflict between corporate and public interests, yet I did not entertain any personal ill will toward him, and I am sure that he then entertained no feeling of personal hostility to me.

I might, therefore, have gone forward with my law practice quite contentedly had it not been for an event which soon took place and changed my whole life. I shall deal with this event considerably at length because it was not only all-powerful in its effect upon me personally, but it will reveal to what lengths corrupt politicians are prepared to go. I had, of course, seen that sooner or later a conflict with the old leaders was inevitable; the people were already restive against the private interest view of government, but if it had not been for the incident to which I refer—which brought the whole system home to me personally in its

61

ugliest and most revolting form—I should not so soon have been forced into the fight.

One of the political grafts of Wisconsin, ancient and time honored, was the farming out of the public funds to favored banks. Excepting the office of governor, the state treasuryship was more sought after than any other place on the ticket. The reason for this lay in the fact that the state treasurer was able to deposit public moneys in such banks as he chose, upon terms satisfactory to the bankers and profitable to himself. Interest upon this money was regarded as a political perquisite.

One of the first acts of the Democratic state administration which came in on January 5, 1891, was to institute suit against all state treasurers of Wisconsin who had occupied that office during the preceding twenty years. The Wisconsin Treasury cases became noted as pioneer cases for the enforcement of the correct principle in the discharge of duty regarding the custody of trust funds. The beginning of these cases produced a profound sensation in the state and attracted much attention throughout the nation. Suits were instituted against former Treasurers Henry B. Harshaw, Edward C. McFettridge, Richard Guenther, Ferdinand Kuehn, Henry Betz and their bondsmen. Senator Sawyer's wishes had largely controlled in the selection of several of these treasurers, and he was one of the principal bondsmen. Certain of the treasurers had little or no property to satisfy judgments of large amounts. Hence, Sawyer, as the wealthiest of all the bondsmen, stood to lose a large sum of money in the event of the state's recovery. The suits finally resulted in judgments in favor of the state aggregating $608,918.23. Of this amount Sawyer was liable for nearly $300,000.00. The estate of Guido Pfister, a leading business man of Milwaukee, was also liable as bondsman for former Treasurer Kuehn to the extent of something more than one hundred thousand dollars. The liability of this estate marks the advent into Wisconsin state politics of Charles F. Pfister of Milwaukee, one of the principal heirs of the Guido Pfister estate, who will figure hereafter in this narrative.

The ex-treasurers and their bondsmen employed a strong array of excellent counsel, among others S. U. Pinney, afterward Supreme Court Justice, and Joseph V. Quarles, afterward United States Senator. The state retained as counsel to assist Attorney-General O'Conner, Col. William F. Vilas, former member of Cleveland's cabinet, afterward United States Senator, and R. M. Bashford, afterward Supreme Court Justice.

Robert G. Siebecker, now one of the justices of the Supreme Court of Wisconsin, was at that time judge of the Circuit Court for Dane County. He had been appointed to that office by Governor Hoard in 1889 to fill a vacancy, and a telegram from Governor Hoard's secretary announcing Siebecker's selection was my first intimation that he had been considered. I was indeed surprised, because Siebecker was a Democrat and was appointed by Governor Hoard to succeed Judge Stuart, who was a Republican. I mention this point in this connection because in so far as the appointment was criticized at all, it was upon the ground that Siebecker was a Democrat. This fact, and the further fact that he was my brother-in-law and my partner in the firm of La Follette, Siebecker & Harper was also the subject of newspaper comment at the time, and his appointment was ascribed to my known friendly relations with Governor Hoard. I have taken pains to state these facts somewhat in detail because of their important connection with the incident which I am about to relate.

Shortly before these cases were to come on for argument in the Circuit Court, I received a letter from Senator Sawyer, whose home was in Oshkosh, Wisconsin, of which the following is an exact copy:

Dictated.
Oshkosh, Wisconsin, September 14, 1891.
Hon. Robert M. La Follette, Madison, Wisconsin.
My dear La Follette:
I will be in Milwaukee, at the state fair, on Thursday. I have some matters of importance that I would like to consult you about, that escaped my mind yesterday. If convenient can you be in Milwaukee on that day and meet me at the Plankinton House at 11 o'clock A.M.? If not on that day, what day would suit your convenience this week? Please answer by telegraph. All you need to say, if you can meet me that day is merely telegraph me "yes." If not simply mention day you can meet me.
Yours truly, PHILETUS SAWYER.

The letter was typewritten on a single sheet of paper, letter size. The top part of the sheet had been torn off, down nearly to the date line, leaving only the printed words, "Dictated. Oshkosh." This fact did not impress me at the time I received the letter but led me to investigate the matter later and to discover that it was written on the office stationery of ex-Treasurer Harshaw, who afterward came to me with a message from Sawyer. The reference to his having seen me the day before it was written, related to our meeting on the 13th of September at Neenah, Wisconsin, on the occasion of the funeral of former Congressman Charles B. Clark.

63

During the services and afterward, until Mr. Sawyer left to take his train, other people had been constantly with us, so that Sawyer had had no opportunity for any private conversation with me.

I conferred with my law partner, Sam Harper, after receiving the letter, and believing that the proposed interview concerned political matters, decided to meet Sawyer. I remember that the brief nature of the response which he requested to the letter impressed me as a precaution taken to forestall newspaper interviewers. And I filed a telegram in response, limited to the word "yes" as directed.

On the 17th of September I went to Milwaukee and met Sawyer at the Plankinton House. The state fair was in progress at that time and the hotel crowded. Sawyer said that he had been unable to secure a room and requested me to go with him to the hotel parlors on the second floor. The parlors were large, and he led me away to a portion of the room remote from the entrance—where we sat down. After some preliminary conversation in which he said, "I wanted to talk with you about Siebecker and the treasury matter," he finally came directly to the point and said:

"These cases are awfully important to us, and we cannot afford to lose them. They cost me a lot of anxiety. I don't want to have to pay——" naming a large sum of money—whether one hundred thousand or more, I am not certain. "Now I came down here to see you alone. No one knows I am to meet you here. I don't want to hire you as an attorney in the cases, La Follette, and don't want you to go into court. But here is fifty dollars, I will give you five hundred more or a thousand—or five hundred more and a thousand [I was never able to recall exactly the sums named] when Siebecker decides the cases right."

I said to him, "Senator Sawyer, you can't know what you are saying to me. If you struck me in the face you could not insult me as you insult me now."

He said, "Wait—hold on!"

I was then standing up. I said: "No, you don't want to employ me as an attorney. You want to hire me to talk to the Judge about your case off the Bench." He said, "I did not think you would take a retainer in the case. I did not think you would want to go into the case as an attorney. How much will you take as a retainer?"

I answered, "You haven't enough money to employ me as an attorney in your case after what you have said to me."

"Well, perhaps I don't understand court rules. Anyway, let me pay you for coming down here."

I said, "Not a dollar, sir," and immediately left the room.

Nothing else ever came into my life that exerted such a powerful influence upon me as that affair. It was the turning point, in a way, of my career. Sooner or later I probably would have done what I did in Wisconsin. But it would have been later. It would have been a matter of much slower evolution. But it shocked me into a complete realization of the extremes to which this power that Sawyer represented would go to secure the results it was after. But in another way its effect upon me as an individual was most profound. I had always had a pride in my family—in my good name. It had been the one thing that my mother had worked into my character. It was the thing that she emphasized when she talked with me about my father, whom I never saw. One who has never been subject to an experience like that cannot realize just what comes over him.

There has always been uncertainty in my mind about the money he offered me—the amounts. He named different amounts. He was going to give me a sum right then, and more, conditioned upon the case being decided "right." He had his pocketbook in one hand, and a roll of money in the other. For an instant I was dazed, and then the thing surged through me. I felt that I could not keep my hands off his throat—I stood over him, said the things to him that I have related and then left him, blindly. I knew he followed me. I went rapidly downstairs, and out of the hotel. The state fair was on, and the hotel lobby crowded with people. I saw nobody. I got out in the street and walked and walked.

Six or eight years afterward, when I was a candidate for governor, I stopped one day in the little town of Sheboygan Falls. Among those who called on me was former Congressman Brickner. He had been on the Democratic side when I was on the Republican side of the House. He came into the hotel to greet me and while he was sitting there he brought up the Sawyer affair. The state, of course, had been aflame after the interview had been published. Sawyer's power over the Republican press of the state was very great, and it was all turned against me. I was denounced as a liar and assassin of character, trying to destroy one of the great and good men of the state. Brickner said, "Mr. La Follette, I knew which one of you two told the truth about what took place in the Plankinton Hotel that day. I saw your face when you came down the stairs, with Sawyer following trying to catch up with you. I knew that there had been serious trouble."

After the interview with Sawyer at the Plankinton Hotel that day I disclosed what had transpired between him and me to a few close personal friends and told them I thought it my plain duty to report the matter to the Court. Several of them took strong ground against this course. They pointed out the great power of Senator Sawyer, his corporation and political connections, his control of newspapers; they argued that he would utterly destroy me. I granted all that, but urged that as a member of the bar, an officer of the Court, I could not be silent; that it was my duty to report to Judge Siebecker exactly what had occurred. Conferences of these friends were held from time to time, they urging their view and I contending that my course, though the harder one, must be followed.

It was finally agreed that the whole matter be submitted to Judge Romanzo Bunn, the federal judge for the Western District of Wisconsin, whose home was in Madison, and who enjoyed the confidence and esteem of all who knew him. I remember the afternoon when I saw him by appointment at his chambers in the federal building in Madison. He listened with patience and understanding, his benign face expressing the utmost pain and sympathy. He did not speak until I had finished. Then he said,

"Robert, have you told Judge Siebecker?"

"No," I answered. "And on the advice of a few friends I came to tell you about it and to ask your counsel."

He said, "Well, you must tell Judge Siebecker. You cannot permit him to sit in the case without telling him all about it. I doubt very much whether he will feel that he can try the cases. That is for him to decide—but you must tell him."

I said to him, "Judge Bunn, I have insisted from the first that it was my duty to tell Judge Siebecker, but my friends have strongly urged against that course, because they realize that Sawyer will follow me relentlessly as long as he lives. I understand that well, for this thing has weighed on me every hour since it occurred."

On the evening of the same day on which I saw Judge Bunn, in the privacy of Judge Siebecker's home I told him exactly what had taken place. He was very much moved. He decided immediately, of course, that, with the knowledge of Sawyer's attempt to corrupt the Court, he could not sit as judge in the cases. He said that if he caused Sawyer to be cited for contempt, the facts would necessarily become public with the result that it would prejudice the cases. So far as either of us knew, many of the defendants probably were ignorant of Sawyer's action. At any rate, it was important that they be given a fair and impartial trial. Before I left him he had determined that he would promptly call together the attorneys on both sides, tell them that he would not hear the cases for reasons which were controlling with him, but that he would call in any other circuit judge in the state upon whom they agreed. Siebecker was then a young man—he had been on the Bench two years and was making an excellent record as judge. These cases were certain to be important, and if he rendered a judgment which should ultimately be sustained by the Supreme Court, it would make a record in which any trial court could take just pride, and might prove an important factor in his judicial career. Indeed, it transpired that Judge A. W. Newman, who was called in to try the cases after Siebecker's withdrawal, was elected to fill the first vacancy upon the Supreme Bench of Wisconsin.

I think it was on Friday that Judge Siebecker informed the attorneys on both sides that he could not try the treasury cases. They were amazed at his announcement, and the news quickly spread. The cases were of such great public interest, involving so many prominent men and such large sums of money, that the keenest speculation and indeed excitement followed Siebecker's withdrawal.

By the following day, newspaper correspondents, representing the principal papers of the state and leading dailies of Chicago, were rushed to Madison, keen on the scent for sensational news. Efforts were made to interview Judge Siebecker. And because of my relationship with the judge and my interest in political matters, every possible effort was made to extract something from me; but I did not regard it as incumbent upon me to make any public statement. Unable to ascertain any facts, a lot of newspaper stories were predicated upon guesses—some wide of the mark and some shrewdly direct in their shot at the facts.

On Sunday morning, October 25, 1891, the Chicago *Times* printed a sensational story with the startling query as to whether there had been an attempt made to "influence" the Court in the Wisconsin Treasury cases, suggesting that if an effort had really been made to influence the Court, causing Siebecker's withdrawal, that the guilty party was known, and stood in the shadow of the penitentiary. Here are the headings from the Chicago *Times:*

BRIBERY THEIR GAME

PERSONS INTERESTED IN THE WISCONSIN STATE TREASURY SUITS ATTEMPT DESPERATE MEANS.

AN EFFORT MADE TO "INFLUENCE" JUDGE SIEBECKER, OF MADISON, WHO WAS TO TRY THE CASES.

THE INDIGNANT OFFICIAL NOTIFIES THE LAWYERS THAT HE WILL NOT SIT DURING THE TRIAL.

HE REFUSES TO AT PRESENT MAKE PUBLIC THE DETAILS OF THE AFFAIR—STARTLING DISCLOSURES EXPECTED.

From what followed I was led to believe that Senator Sawyer had read and been very greatly alarmed by the matter published in the *Times*. His home was in Oshkosh, where also lived former State Treasurer Harshaw. Sunday evening I was surprised to receive a note from Harshaw brought to me by a bellboy from the Park Hotel, Madison. The note, which was written on the hotel stationery, indicating that Harshaw was then in Madison, requested an interview at my law office on the following morning at eight o'clock. I showed it to my law partner, Sam Harper, who happened to be with me at the time. I suggested that Harshaw probably desired to see me regarding the Sawyer matter; that as no witnesses were present when Sawyer made his proposal to me at the Plankinton Hotel in Milwaukee, the time might come when the question of veracity would be raised between us; that Harshaw's proposed interview with me might result in some disclosure which would show conclusively that Sawyer had endeavored to corrupt the Court; and that I would consent to see Harshaw if he (Harper) would be present at the interview.

At eight o'clock the next morning Harshaw came to my office, accompanied by Joseph V. Quarles, afterward United States Senator, one of the attorneys in the treasury cases. They were shown into my private room. After formal greetings, Mr. Quarles made inquiry about Judge Siebecker and said he wanted to see him. I told him where the Judge could be found and he thereupon withdrew. Harshaw remained. As Quarles left Sam accompanied him to the door of the outer office, leaving Harshaw in the private office with me.

The moment we were alone Harshaw leaned across the desk, and said quickly:

"Bob, will you meet Sawyer at the Grand Pacific Hotel in Chicago to-night?"

I was incensed that he had succeeded in communicating to me privately a message from Sawyer, and rising to my feet I said in a tone of voice which immediately brought Sam back into the room.

"No, I will never meet Sawyer or have any communication with him again as long as I live."

I was determined that Harper should know exactly what Harshaw had said to me during his absence, and so leaning across the desk, I repeated:

"You have just asked me if I will meet Sawyer to-night at the Grand Pacific Hotel in Chicago, and I answer you, no, so long as I live, I will never again meet Sawyer or have any communication with him."

Harshaw put up his hand in protest and said, "Don't, Bob, don't be angry with me. I have always respected you and always shall."

I then said to Harshaw that it was wrong for him to come to me with any such proposal; that he knew just what Sawyer had attempted at the Plankinton, and that he ought to have known that I would have nothing more to do with Sawyer. Harshaw said, "I do know what Sawyer did; but had I known beforehand what he intended to do when he met you at Milwaukee, it never would have occurred." This ended the interview, and Harshaw left the office.

From what occurred immediately thereafter it was plain that Sawyer was then in Milwaukee awaiting Harshaw's return, prepared to go on to Chicago provided I consented to meet him at the Grand Pacific; that upon Harshaw's arrival in Milwaukee and his report to Sawyer of the failure of his mission, he (Sawyer) then, apprehensive that the truth might come out, decided that he would forestall any possible statement which I might make. Up to that time no public charge had been made connecting Sawyer with Judge Siebecker's retirement from the treasury cases; but Sawyer knew, and that knowledge impelled him to commit the folly of protesting his innocence in advance of any public charge of guilt. On that same (Monday) evening he personally gave to the *Sentinel,* in Milwaukee, an interview in which he stated that he had "telegraphed" me to meet him at the Plankinton Hotel in Milwaukee; that he had offered me a retainer of five hundred dollars, but no money was paid; that I thought it would not be advisable to take a retainer, as Judge Siebecker was my brother-in-law; that it was the first he knew that Siebecker was my brother-in-law, and that had he known that fact he would not have proposed to retain me; that if I had put any improper interpretation upon his conversation with me, I had misunderstood or misconstrued what he said; and that at the time of the conversation I certainly made no such intimation to him. The interview with Senator Sawyer was published Tuesday morning, October 27th, 1891.

The publication of Sawyer's statement wholly misrepresenting the facts made it necessary that I should make public the truth regarding that interview, and in the Milwaukee *Sentinel* of Wednesday morning, October 28th, in a signed statement, I set forth in detail just what actually did occur between Senator Sawyer and myself. I requested Judge Siebecker's sanction to speak, and received it. I did not point out the weakness and inconsistency of Sawyer's statement; I did not note the fact that he could not be ignorant of the relation existing between Siebecker and myself, which everybody knew, and which had been the subject of public discussion and comment when Siebecker was appointed circuit judge; I made no mention of the fact that I was constantly practising my profession in Siebecker's court, and that there could be no impropriety in my accepting a retainer had it been offered upon honorable terms. In that interview I stated only the naked facts required to make public record of the exact truth.

I believed I fully realized what this would cost me. Sawyer was the power in Wisconsin politics. He was many times a millionaire. His wish was law—his rule unquestioned. His organization extended to every county, town and village. I knew that within twenty-four hours after giving my signed statement to the Milwaukee *Sentinel* his agents would be actively in communication with newspapers, with political committees, with the representatives of prominent business interests throughout the commonwealth.

Party feeling and party loyalty were still strong, and partook in some measure of the zeal and fervor of the days following the war. My veracity had never been questioned by any man. I was confident that the truth of my statement would be accepted. I did anticipate that men who loved the Republican party would resent as an attack upon it a statement which must impeach the honesty and integrity of its leader, and that while members of my party and all men generally would approve of my refusing a bribe, men devoted to the success of the Republican party would say that I might have suppressed the facts, though Sawyer had falsified them; that I might indeed have withheld information from the Court and, for the good of the party, have kept secret all knowledge of the fact that its leader had attempted to corrupt even the courts. This may seem strange in these times of growing independence and keener civic conscience; it was vastly different twenty years ago.

Prepared as I was to meet criticism, no one could have anticipated the violence with which the storm broke upon me. In my own party there was no newspaper that dared to brook Sawyer's disapproval. Besides a little group of personal friends, there was no one to raise his voice in my defense. Prominent politicians denounced me. I was shunned and avoided everywhere by men who feared or sought the favor of Senator Sawyer and his organization. At every turn the way seemed barred to me. No one can ever know what I suffered. As I recall the fearful depression of those months, I wonder where I found strength to endure them. But I went about my work determined that no one should see in my face or daily habit any sign of what I was going through. But the thing gnawed all the while. I went from my office to my house, from my house to my office, and did my work as it came to me day by day. Fortunately I found clients who wanted the services of a man who could not be tempted by money. They came to me with their cases, and I found plenty to do. But I could not shake off or be indifferent to the relentless attacks upon my veracity which came in a steady onset from the Republican press of the state. Anonymous, threatening letters crowded my mail with warnings that if I dared to show my head in politics I would do well to arrange in advance for a lot in the cemetery. I did not know it at the time, nor indeed until after Harper's death, but Mrs. La Follette has since told me that there was a long period following the Sawyer affair when Sam was so apprehensive for my personal safety that he scarcely permitted me to be out of his sight.

But I was resolved that I would not let it break me down. The winter of 1891-92 proved an ordeal. Sam Harper, General Bryant, Charles Van Hise, my classmate, then at the head of the Department of Geology of the University of Wisconsin, and a few friends stayed by me. These friends and the immediate family knew what I suffered during that time, but on the street, in my office and in the courtroom, I carried myself so that no one should know how keenly I felt it all. I slept very little and there was fear that my health would give way. But it did not.

Fourteen years afterward, when I first came to the Senate of the United States, I was placed in a somewhat similar position. I was again alone. When I entered the cloakroom, men turned their backs upon me and conversation ceased. Members left their seats when I began to speak. My amendments to bills were treated with derision and turned down with a lofty wave of the hand. For nearly two years I went through an experience that had seldom failed to bring a fresh, independent member to terms. It was said that I would soon be "eating out of their hands." They did not know the iron that had been driven into me years before.

During that winter of 1891–92 I spent much time alone, in the private room at my law offices, and in the little study at my home in the long hours of the night. I went back over my political experiences. I thought over many things that had occurred during my service in the House. I began to understand their relation. I had seen the evils singly—here and there a manifest wrong, against which I had instinctively revolted. But I had been subjected to a terrible shock that opened my eyes, and I began to see really for the first time. I find now no bitterness and little resentment left in

71

me against individuals. The men of that time filled their places in a system of things, in some measure the outgrowth of the wealth of our resources and the eagerness of the public for their development. Corporations and individuals allied with corporations were invited to come in and take what they would, if only the country might be developed, railroads and factories constructed, towns and cities builded up. Against this organized power it had been my misfortune—perhaps my fortune—to be thrown by circumstances. The experiences of my Congressional life now came back to me with new meaning—the Ship Subsidy bill, the Oleomargarine bill, the Nicaraguan Canal, the Railroad Rate bill, the Sioux Indian land grant and the Menomonie timber steal.

So out of this awful ordeal came understanding; and out of understanding came resolution. I determined that the power of this corrupt influence, which was undermining and destroying every semblance of representative government in Wisconsin, should be broken.

I felt that I had few friends; I knew I had no money—could command the support of no newspaper. And yet I grew strong in the conviction that in the end Wisconsin would be made free.

And in the end it was so. That Sawyer incident had a tremendous effect on the young men of the state. Three years afterward, in the campaign of 1894, they came into the state convention, standing together and taking defeat like veterans. The ten years' fight was on.

I did not underrate the power of the opposition. I had been made to feel its full force. I knew that Sawyer and those with him were allied with the railroads, the big business interests, the press, the leading politicians of every community. I knew the struggle would be a long one; that I would have to encounter defeat again and again. But my resolution never faltered.

I well understood that I must take time to develop my plan; that the first encounter with the organization in Wisconsin must be one which should compel their respect, even though it resulted in temporary defeat for the reform movement. First of all I must make it manifest that I had not been destroyed as an individual. To do this it was necessary to go out and meet men wherever they were gathered together on political occasions.

The national Republican convention was called to meet in Minneapolis, June 7, 1892. There was no serious contest for the presidential nomination. Harrison's administration was generally popular throughout the country. The country was prosperous, and when the country is prosperous a presidential administration is popular.

Harrison himself was a man of superior ability. On a trip across the country in 1891, he accomplished a remarkable feat. It is generally said of these presidential "swings around the circle" that you get substantially all the man has to say in the first three or four days; after that he repeats his thought in varied form. Harrison's speeches, however, made on this trip to the Pacific coast, were a notable series of daily addresses covering a wide range of important subjects, treated broadly and thoughtfully. They aroused a great deal of enthusiasm and were eagerly read by the public. Reserved, undemonstrative, a bit austere in manner, direct, quick to grasp a proposition and decide on its merits, Harrison was a strong executive, commanding the respect and confidence of all with whom he came in contact. He was conservative but not what we would call to-day reactionary. His state papers were noteworthy for the ability and directness with which he discussed public questions. He stood for integrity in every branch of the government; he strengthened, supported and extended the civil service law; he was not in favor with the spoilsman and the jobster. After his retirement from the Presidency he delivered many important addresses throughout the country, one of which in particular was markedly progressive in thought. This address was made to the Union League Club of Chicago, February 22, 1898, on the "Obligations of Wealth." We were then in the midst of our struggle in Wisconsin, and I found his views as expressed therein of great help to me in the speeches I was making in support of reforms in taxation.

I made no attempt to be elected as a delegate to the convention. But I determined, nevertheless, to attend as a spectator. Sam Harper went with me. Of course the delegates elected to the convention by the Wisconsin machine were bitterly hostile to me. My trouble with Sawyer had been given wide publicity and was well known to all prominent politicians in that great gathering. I knew that generally they would not judge the matter upon its real merit, but strictly with reference to its effect upon the political situation in Wisconsin. To the extent that it injured Sawyer, the party leader in the state, it lessened the chances of Republican success; and the delegates to a national convention are looking above all things for immediate political victory. So, to that extent, I anticipated disapproval even among those who had been my personal friends in public life at Washington. It taxed my resolution severely to meet

73

these former political friends. I found all that I had anticipated in the way of coldness and hostility. One encounter which cut me to the quick will illustrate my meaning:

I had served for six years in Congress with David B. Henderson of Iowa, afterward Speaker of the House of Representatives, upon terms of personal intimacy. When the roll was called in the 49th Congress for the allotment of seats, mine chanced to fall almost within touch of Henderson, who was already in the seat which he had chosen—a sturdy figure he was, square face, fine head, covered with thick iron-gray hair. He turned on me a keen, searching, yet withal a kindly look; our eyes met for a moment, and then putting out his hand, he said, "Well, my boy, I think you'll do." That was the beginning, and we were always good friends. We represented adjoining districts, the Mississippi River between. He had called me across the state line to speak for him in the campaign of 1890 when he feared that he was losing, and had often declared that I was a material help in saving him from defeat in that landslide year. When I met him at Minneapolis he came at me quickly with "What are you fighting Sawyer for, and tearing things all to pieces in Wisconsin?" I told him that if he knew the truth he would not ask me such a question. And then the jostling crowd swept between us, and I saw him no more. A few old-time friends, Major McKinley among them, greeted me cordially with a warm hand and an understanding look in the eye, though in the main I was made to feel that they regarded me a political outcast. But it was good training; it was seasoning me for the hard struggle ahead.

With Harrison's nomination, the Wisconsin machine selected its candidates for the state campaign. Former Senator Spooner was its candidate for governor. The rank and file of the party had nothing to say—Sawyer, Payne and a few others made the plans.

I was not yet ready to offer opposition, and decided to wait until two years later. But it was obvious that I must insist on keeping my place as a factor in the Republican campaign of that year.

The defeat of Governor William D. Hoard two years before had seriously divided the party. Hoard's friends felt that he had not been loyally supported by Payne in conducting the state campaign of 1890. In order to mollify Hoard's friends, and they were legion among the farmers of Wisconsin, and to bring about the desired party harmony, Payne withdrew as Chairman of the Republican State Central Committee, and H. C. Thom, a warm personal friend of Hoard was elected in his place.

During my four Congressional campaigns I had been called each time by the Chairman of the State Central Committee to speak outside of my district, and over the state. The facts warrant me in saying, I think, that there was a general demand in campaigns for my work as a speaker. But in the campaign of 1892 I was not invited to speak. This, I understood, was by the orders of the machine.

I had well considered the wisdom of making my fight against the corrupt organization in Wisconsin politics in the Republican party rather than out in the field as an independent. I believed in the integrity of the rank and file of the party. I could see no valid reason why I should stand apart from the great body of men with whom I had been affiliated politically since coming to my majority, so long as I was in substantial agreement with the ideas about which that party was organized. For these reasons, briefly stated, I had settled it in my own mind that I would fight within the ranks. I did not propose that those nominally in control of the party organization should for any reason blacklist and put me outside of the party lines. If I chose at any time to leave the party, it would be because my convictions compelled me to do so. But I would not recognize the authority of any man or any set of men to decide my party status.

After waiting until it became quite apparent that I should not be invited, I wrote to the Chairman of the State Central Committee tendering my services as a speaker in the campaign. He came to see me at my law office in Madison, and suggested that in view of the feeling existing against me on the part of Senator Sawyer and his many friends, it would be inadvisable for me to take part in the campaign. We were personal friends, and discussed the matter frankly. He suggested that Senator Sawyer was an old man, and that if I ever wished to take any part in political matters in Wisconsin, the easier course for me would be to wait until he had passed away. He suggested that the feeling against me was very intense and that my appearance on the platform might be resented with violence. I answered that that would not deter me from entering the campaign; that I proposed to maintain my relations with the party and would not consent to be turned out to pasture to wait for my opponents to die off; that I was opposed to the corrupt machine methods of those in control and intended to stay on the firing line. I furthermore stated that if it was not desired that I should speak under the auspices of the State Central Committee, I would make my own announcements and speak under my own auspices; that I was deeply interested in Harrison's election and wanted to do all in my power for him; and that I was reasonably confident that I would have as good meetings in numbers and results as any managed by the State Central Committee. Chairman Thom thereupon decided that if I was going to speak anyway, he preferred that I should speak under the direction of the State Central Committee.

This I told him would be perfectly agreeable to me, but that I should designate the places where I was to speak. He desired to know what my attitude would be regarding the state ticket. I told him that I should discuss national issues.

I never held better meetings in any political campaign. I found every town placarded with great posters in flaming red, urging that I be called upon in my meetings to discuss the Sawyer affair. These posters contained a list of questions which it was urged should be put up to me for answer. I had little doubt that they emanated from Democratic sources, and it was their purpose to force that issue into my campaign.

Strange as it may seem, in no instance throughout that campaign was there a single unfriendly interruption from the audience, and never was I given a more respectful and attentive hearing. I was greatly encouraged and firmly convinced that whatever the attitude of the politicians, I still had many friends among the people.

In the next campaign, that of 1894, I began my fight on the Wisconsin machine which continued for ten years and resulted in the complete reorganization of the Republican party of the state. Of the details of that fight I shall tell in the following chapters.

Chapter v

Six Years' Struggle
with the Wisconsin Bosses

I had firmly determined to begin my fight on the old political machine in Wisconsin in the campaign of 1894. While I had no money and no newspaper support, and while all the leading politicians of the state were bitterly hostile to me, the success of my meetings in the previous campaign of 1892 convinced me that I could get a hearing.

But it was essential to the success of any such undertaking that some strong man who would appeal to the younger and more independent members of the Republican party should be found to stand as the anti-machine candidate for governor.

Such a man, I felt, was Congressman Nils P. Haugen.

I had known Haugen for many years. He had been a member of the legislature, and railroad commissioner under a weak statute which he administered with marked ability and independence, and having been elected to the 49th Congress, he had served with distinction for nine years. During five years of that time I had been closely associated with him in the House of Representatives. We were agreed in practically all our views upon public questions. I knew him to be fearless, independent, and able. A native of Norway, he was educated in this country, graduating from the Michigan University Law School in 1874. He was a fine representative of the best Scandinavian type—tall, strong, virile, with something of the Viking quality in his character.

I considered the matter carefully. Many of the counties of the western half of the state were well settled by sturdy Scandinavian pioneers—an independent, liberty-loving people. I knew they felt a certain national pride in Congressman Haugen's prominence and success, and I counted on their giving him very strong support.

On my part I still had many friends in my old Congressional district, and among university men all over the state, who could, I knew, be enlisted in any fight upon the machine. Between us, I believed we could carry a good many counties. It seemed to me, therefore, that Haugen was the ideal candidate for the first encounter with the bosses. But would he consider being a candidate?

The chances were all against winning. His hold upon his district was very strong, and there was every reason to believe that he could continue in Congress for many years to come. I knew he enjoyed his work in the House, and he had rendered good service to the state and country. Ought he to be asked to take the chance?

But there was the good State of Wisconsin ruled by a handful of men who had destroyed every vestige of democracy in the commonwealth. They settled in private conference practically all nominations for important offices, controlled conventions, dictated legislation, and had even sought to lay corrupt hands on the courts of justice.

Had I believed that I as a candidate could have led as strong an attack upon this entrenched organization, I should not have asked Haugen or any other man to make that first fight. But I believed then, as I believe now, that however forlorn the hope of immediate achievement, the great final issue at stake demanded that the best and strongest man should meet this call to service as a patriotic duty.

In November, 1893, I requested Haugen to stop at Madison en route to Washington, and I then pressed him to become a candidate for governor. He raised the objections which I had anticipated.

"You know," he said, in his direct, incisive way, "the forces we will have to meet. They have money; we have none. They have a powerful organization extending into every county in the state. Our support will be scattered and isolated. They will have the railroads, the great business interests, and the newspapers back of them. How can we hope to win?"

I proposed to Mr. Haugen that he consent to my writing letters to old university friends over the state, calling upon them to join in supporting him as a candidate for governor.

This was agreed to, and I wrote something like 1200 letters, mainly to young men who were neither allied with the Sawyer-Payne machine nor hitherto active in politics. The replies gave me great encouragement, and I asked Mr. Haugen to meet me in Chicago, where we spent a day going through the correspondence.

Haugen was much gratified; he had no idea that my letters would meet with any such response.

I recall vividly our final conference. It was at my home in Madison. There were present Mrs. La Follette, whose counsel was always valued by our little group, General Bryant, Sam Harper, and Herbert W. Chynoweth, a leading attorney, then a member of the Board of University Regents. After consenting to stand as a candidate, Haugen said: "It is my judgment that we shall lose this fight, and I shall be retired from public life. But there is a chance to win, and in any event, we will make a beginning."

No sooner was Haugen's candidacy announced than the fight was on. I had no misconception of the task which we had undertaken. I knew full well that we were entering upon a long political warfare. We opened headquarters in my law office, and for many weeks the lights never went out. Candidates for governor were brought forward in other sections of the state—W. H. Upham in central Wisconsin, Edward Scofield in the northeast, and "Hod" Taylor, as he was known, from Dane County, in the southern part of the state. These candidates were in perfect accord, and all had the favor of the bosses of Wisconsin. Sooner or later the strength which each could command in the convention would be merged to secure victory for the machine. Sawyer declared that I should never have a seat in a Republican convention in Wisconsin, nor hold political office, as long as he lived. He was friendly to every other candidate, and announced that he had nothing against Haugen, but would oppose him as "La Follette's candidate."

The fight centered on Dane County, which was the heart of my old district. Sawyer's money was everywhere. The opposition controlled the county organization, and Roger C. Spooner, brother of Senator Spooner, was chairman of the county committee. In order to make it as difficult as possible for us, the machine brought forward no fewer than three candidates on the state ticket from Dane County alone, only one of whom (under the usages of conventions in distributing the offices geographically) could hope to be nominated. It was "anything to beat Haugen and kill off La Follette." Considered as a county fight, it was the hottest I ever saw.

The bi-partisan character of machine politics became a prominent feature of the contest. Democratic machine newspapers and politicians joined with Republican machine newspapers and politicians to suppress this first organized revolt. The whole state watched the contest in Dane County. If the machine were successful there, if I were defeated in my own county as a delegate to the state convention, it meant the breaking down of Haugen's campaign. I sat at my desk almost day and night dictating letters to the Republican farmers, among whom I had a very wide personal acquaintance.

The first caucuses, held in the city of Madison and in two other small cities in the county, registered a complete victory for the machine. We were defeated in every ward. It was a gloomy night in our headquarters. Many were disheartened and felt that it was a forerunner of overwhelming defeat. But it only strengthened my resolution to win, and after a brief talk every man went out from the headquarters with zeal to carry the country towns of the county, which might still give us a majority. The struggle from that time on grew fiercer to the end, which came quickly. We fairly swept the country towns, carried the county convention by four to one, and I was elected to head the delegation to the state convention. To give emphasis to the result, the convention adopted strong resolutions declaring for Haugen for governor. The remaining four counties of my former Congressional district were likewise carried in succession, and it was a great satisfaction to lead the old district into the convention to back Haugen's candidacy.

We did not fare so well in Haugen's district. The machine brought forward a leading Scandinavian politician as a candidate for governor, and thus embarrassed the canvass in Haugen's home county, which he lost—together with certain other counties of his district.

The contest for the nomination in the state convention lasted two days. The machine united on W. H. Upham, who was finally nominated. Our forces had passed through such a struggle for election that they were fused together as one man. It was a rigid line-up against the bosses, and while we lost the nomination for governor, their forces so scattered on the remaining nominations that we held the balance of power, and named practically every other man on the ticket. The old machine was tried to the breaking point, and we came out of that campaign tremendously enthused and stimulated for the work ahead. Sawyer, Payne, and the other big ones had been pressed into strenuous and continuous activity throughout the convention to hold their forces in line.

Haugen accepted his defeat with fine spirit. Expressing no regrets, he went back to his home in the little town of River Falls, Pierce County, and resumed his law practice. It was not without a keen pang that I saw him retired from public life, but defeated though we were, the spirit of the campaign of 1894 and the evidence of a growing conviction that held our forces unwaveringly throughout the convention struggle, gave me strong assurance for the future. We had gone down to our defeat in the first battle, but I never doubted we should rise again to fight, and win final victory over the old machine. And when we did win, one of my earliest acts as governor was to bring Haugen's great abilities to the service of the state as a member of the tax commission. He has served continuously in that position since, is now its chairman, and has become a leading authority on taxation in the United States.

I did not at that period put forward a broadly constructive policy. My correspondence of that time shows that appeal was made for support primarily with a view to overthrowing corrupt machine control. It was clear to me that the single issue against boss rule would be more immediately effective in securing support in the first contest than a program for legislation which would necessarily require much more time for educational work.

As I considered the future, it was clear that it would be necessary to devote six weeks to two months out of each biennial period, and possibly each year, in speaking and pamphleteering the state. I therefore withdrew from the firm of La Follette, Harper, Roe & Zimmerman and opened an office by myself. I found it necessary, owing to the steady growth of my law business, to employ two attorneys most of the time to aid me in briefing and preparing cases for trial. But the new arrangement gave me perfect freedom and independence. While I applied myself industriously to my profession, I set aside a brief period in the autumn of each year, which I devoted to speeches and addresses throughout the state.

The campaign of 1894 resulted in a sweeping victory for the Republicans. Upham was elected governor and the old Sawyer-Payne-Spooner machine came back to power with restored confidence. Almost the first thing they did was to tamper with the work of the former Democratic administration in connection with the treasury cases. When the legislature assembled there had already been returned to the state, as a result of the prosecutions of former state treasurers, no less than $427,902.55, and there had been put into judgment the further sum of $181,015.68, making a total of $608,918.23. Other cases were still pending. The bosses at once began developing a plan to relieve the ex-treasurers from the "hardship" of paying their full indebtedness to the state, and, as a feeler, put through legislation releasing one of the treasurers from the payment of a portion of the judgment secured against him, and providing for the discontinuance of all the cases against two of the other ex-treasurers.

Members of the legislature were fearful of public sentiment and reluctant to pass the measures, but a powerful lobby was organized under the immediate charge of Charles F. Pfister of Milwaukee, who had recently appeared as a power in Wisconsin politics. Pfister had inherited several millions from his father, Guido Pfister, who had been a bondsman for one of the state treasurers, against whom a judgment amounting to $106,683.90 had been obtained. Pfister had been associated with Henry C. Payne and Frank G. Bigelow, president of the First National Bank of Milwaukee, in street railway and other municipal enterprises, and had been rapidly promoted to a position of authority in the Wisconsin machine.

The audacity of this attempt to relieve the ex-treasurers by legislation passed under the whip and spur of a powerful lobby is more apparent when it is understood that throughout the campaign of 1894 the Democrats warned voters that if a Republican governor and legislature were elected the ex-treasurers would be "let off."

And they *were* let off: obligations aggregating more than a quarter of a million dollars were cancelled, and the bills were signed by Governor Upham.

At the approach of the next campaign, that of 1896, Sawyer, Spooner, Payne, and Pfister saw plainly that they would have to meet the resentment of the people upon this issue. It would not do to offer Upham again as a candidate. It is true that he had done their bidding: he had served the bosses, but by that very service he had weakened himself as a candidate. Although he was personally entitled to every consideration at their hands, he had gained no independent strength with the people, and it was easy to cast him aside.

Strange as it may seem to the reader unacquainted with machine methods, the question of Upham's renomination in 1896 was disposed of in the Planters' Hotel, at St. Louis, at the time of the national Republican convention. The bosses did not regard the selection of a candidate for governor as a matter in which the voters of Wisconsin were entitled to have any voice. During a recess in the sessions of the convention, Governor Upham was summoned before an executive session of the Wisconsin bosses, informed that he would not be given the endorsement of a renomination, and his successor, Edward Scofield, was chosen. Of course, they expected afterward to go through the formality of calling caucuses and conventions and declare the nomination according to party usage. But it never occurred to these political rulers of the commonwealth that there was anything grotesque in their disposing of the government of the state as a side issue to a national convention.

I came back from the national convention in 1896, to which I had been elected as an anti-machine delegate, and conferred with friends to determine on the strongest and soundest man to stand against Sawyer and his political machine. But with the sacrifice of Haugen fresh in mind, no man was willing to go out in the open as the candidate against that great power.

I was determined that the fight should go on and therefore announced myself as an anti-machine candidate. An address to the independent Republican voters of the state was issued in my behalf by a number of my supporters, headed by ex-Governor W. D. Hoard, in which they said:

"The time is near at hand when the Republican voters must assemble in their respective caucuses and choose delegates to their assembly conventions where in turn delegates will be chosen to the state convention for the purpose of nominating a candidate for governor."

"In our opinion it is of the highest importance that a people's man be chosen as such candidate. There was never a time when such a man was more needed for the important office of chief executive of Wisconsin than now. Will the people take their own work in their own hands, or will they allow, as they have too often done, a ring of shrewd bosses to select their candidates for them? The discontent which has prevailed in our party for nearly two years ought to teach us a lesson. It ought to bring every Republican voter to the primary caucuses with a determination to discharge his own duty as a true Republican citizen."

It was an exciting campaign. My candidacy was at first greeted with jeers, but as it progressed, Sawyer, Spooner, Payne, and Pfister soon realized that their organization was in danger of defeat. Against a practically united press, a veteran army of trained politicians, and the lavish expenditure of money, I came down to the convention at Milwaukee on the fifth day of August, 1896, with delegates enough pledged and instructed to nominate me on the first formal ballot.

There were six candidates for governor, of whom Scofield was the leading machine candidate. All had headquarters at the Hotel Pfister. Shortly after ten o'clock that night, Captain John T. Rice, the leader of a delegation from one of the Assembly districts in

Racine County, informed me that he had been taken aside into a private room and offered seven hundred dollars in money to transfer the seven delegates from his Assembly district to Scofield's support. Between that time and twelve o'clock many other delegates reported like personal experiences. One after another these delegates, in the presence of Sam Harper, General Bryant, and other friends, made detailed statements of what had transpired with them that night. These men had rejected all offers made to them. How many of my delegates had yielded to the temptation I did not know.

Shortly after midnight Charles F. Pfister came to my headquarters and asked to see me alone.

"La Follette," he said, "we've got you skinned. We've got enough of your delegates away from you to defeat you in the convention to-morrow. Now, we don't want any trouble or any scandal. We don't want to hurt the party. And if you will behave yourself, we will take care of you when the time comes."

I told Mr. Pfister that I was able to take care of myself and that I would whip their machine to a standstill in the convention the next day. I was not sure but that they had me beaten, but I didn't propose to run up any white flag. I didn't have one.

When the balloting came on the next day, I was beaten, just as Pfister said. My delegates understood what had defeated them. The work of the bosses had been coarse and rank. When it was over my steadfast supporters came back in a body to the headquarters. Wrought up to a high pitch they indignantly demanded that I stand as an independent candidate, as a rebuke to the methods employed to defeat the will of the people. I shall never forget the excited throng, their flushed faces, their bitter disappointment. One of them, a young fellow—it was his first convention—broke down and sobbed like a child. I stood up and spoke to them: they needed to know that the defeat would not turn me back but drive me on with higher resolve. There came to me those lines of Henley's which had often inspired me, and which I repeated to them:

"Out of the night that covers me,
Black as the pit from pole to pole,
I thank whatever gods there be
For my unconquerable soul.

"In the fell clutch of circumstance
I have not winced nor cried aloud;
Under the bludgeoning of chance,
My head is bloody but unbowed.

"It matters not how strait the gate,
How charged with punishment the scroll,
I am the master of my fate,
I am the captain of my soul."

The outraged spirit of the group quickly changed. The mood to destroy, to get quick redress, gave way, and they faced to the front with courage to fight on. I said to them that the men who win final victories are those who are stimulated to better fighting by defeat; that the people had not betrayed us, but that they themselves had been betrayed by those whom they had sent to serve them in that convention; that the wrong was not here, it was there; that it would be weak and cowardly to abandon the rank and file who believed as we believed; that if any one was forced to leave the Republican party it should be the corrupt leaders; that the bosses were not the party; that the fault lay with the system that permitted corrupt agents to betray their principles; that the evil work of the night before had forced me to do some hard thinking, and that I was going home to find some better way; that we would never compromise, never abandon the fight until we had made government truly representative of the people.

That little army went back to their homes and told the true story of that convention.

At that time, I had never heard of the direct primary. Indeed, there was no direct primary statute in any state, excepting a weak optional law in Kentucky. In order to become familiar with every phase of the caucus and convention system, I briefed all the laws relative to caucuses and conventions. I had resolved to attack and, if possible, overthrow the whole system in Wisconsin.

A little later, I accepted an invitation from President Harper of the Chicago University to make an address before the faculty and students of that institution on the 22d of February, 1897. I took as my theme, "The Menace of the Political Machine." After portraying the evils of caucuses and conventions, and showing how readily they lend themselves to manipulation, defeating the will of the majority, I outlined a complete system of direct nominations for all county, legislative, and state offices, by both parties upon the same day, under the Australian ballot. So far as I am aware, this was the first presentation of a complete direct nominating system. In that speech, I said in conclusion:

"Beginning the work in the state, put aside the caucus and convention. They have been and will continue to be prostituted to the service of corrupt organization. They answer no purpose further than to give respectable form to political robbery. Abolish the caucus and the convention. Go back to the first principles of democracy; go back to the people. Substitute for both the caucus and the convention a primary election—held under the sanctions of law which prevail at the general elections—where the citizen may cast his vote directly to nominate the candidate of the party with which he affiliates and have it canvassed and returned just as he cast it. . . . Then every citizen will share equally in the nomination of the candidates of his party and attend primary elections as a privilege as well as a duty. It will no longer be necessary to create an artificial interest in the general election to induce voters to attend. Intelligent, well-considered judgment will be substituted for unthinking enthusiasm, the lamp of reason for the torchlight. The voter will not require to be persuaded that he has an interest in the election. He will know that he has. The nominations of the party will not be the result of 'compromise' or impulse, or evil design—the 'barrel' and the machine—but the candidates of the majority, honestly and fairly nominated."

Of this address the Chicago *Times Herald* said:

"Mr. La Follette's experience with the machine has resulted in some well considered and well matured plans for the abatement of the evils growing out of our loose primary elections. If the eminently wise and practical suggestions as to how the machine may be stripped of its power in our party politics, which Mr. La Follette elaborated in his address before the students of the University of Chicago, ultimately find embodiment in state laws, the people will have occasion to feel grateful that men of his calibre have been forced into conflict with machine fighters. . . . Laws based on the lines suggested in Mr. La Follette's admirable address will afford the only practical relief from the despotism of machine politics."

Immediately after making this address, I prepared, with the assistance of Sam Harper, a bill incorporating my plan for direct nominations which was introduced in the Legislature of 1897 by William T. Lewis, a member from Racine. It was not expected that it would receive favorable consideration, but it was a beginning. I knew that it would take a long educational campaign to prepare the way for its adoption. I considered, therefore, the best and cheapest means of introducing it into every home in Wisconsin. I had a limited state list which I had used in the campaigns of 1894 and 1896, but pamphleteering through the mails entails considerable expense. I therefore wrote to the owners of country weeklies of both parties, well distributed over the state, and told them of my address at the Chicago University; that the Chicago papers had considered it of sufficient importance to give it two or three columns of space, and that I believed it would be found interesting to their readers. I offered to furnish the address and the draft of the bill in the form of a supplement without charge, to be folded in, and distributed in the next regular issue of their papers. Something over three hundred newspapers agreed to receive it—I do not now recall a single refusal of my offer—and I thus secured the distribution of something like 400,000 copies of my address, press comments on the same, and a copy of the bill. Having some spare space I filled it out with an address by Charles Noble Gregory, now Dean of the Law Department of the George Washington University, on the English Corrupt Practices Act. One of those old supplements lies before me as I write. I think, in all my campaigning, I never got an equal amount of publicity at less cost. There came a time later when the machine was powerful enough to prevent my publishing a line in most of these papers, and forced me to use pamphlets and letters almost entirely. But of this I shall speak later.

I had been defeated in the state convention at Milwaukee through fraud and corruption. But I went into the campaign with zest, and spoke in every important city and town in the state, closing the campaign in Milwaukee before an immense audience. Although the paramount issue in the campaign was sound money, yet with McKinley as the candidate for President, the recent repeal of the McKinley Tariff Act, and the enactment of the Wilson-Gorman Law, made the tariff as a matter of course also a prominent issue. My personal acquaintance with McKinley and my affection for him made my interest in the campaign one of deep feeling and conviction. Having aided in framing and passing the tariff bill, I had a familiarity with the subject which enabled me to discuss it with freedom and confidence.

The bosses would have been pleased had I bolted the convention of 1896. The desperate means to which they were driven to control that convention convinced Sawyer and his associates of the growing strength of the opposition to the machine, and gave them serious apprehension for the future. It was said that in a conference, when it was over, Sawyer, drawing a long breath, mopped his perspiring face and said:

"I never want to go through so hard a fight ag'in."

Years afterward, Stephenson, now Senator, who was then with

the machine and afterward from 1900 to 1908 a supporter of our movement, told me that in a conference with Sawyer and the others after my defeat, he (Stephenson) said to them:

"I can't help feelin' a good deal of sympathy for Bob La Follette. We've got the newspapers, the organization, the railroads, and free passes, and all the money, and he is fightin' us all alone. If he'd a had money enough to buy a few more postage stamps, he'd a beat us sure."

Yes, I think Sawyer, Spooner, Pfister, and Payne would have been glad to see me leave the party and start an independent movement. Many of my close advisers, too, believed that we should break from the Republican organization and try to build up a new reform party in the state. Many Progressives urge this same course to-day. But I do not believe that it lies in the power of any one man or group of men successfully to proclaim the creation of a new political party, and give it life, and being, and achievement, and perpetuity. New parties are brought forth from time to time, and groups of men have come forward as their heralds, and have been called to leadership and command. But the leaders did not create the party. It was the ripe issue of events. It came out of the womb of time, and no man could hinder or hasten the event. No one can foretell the coming of the hour. It may be near at hand. It may be otherwise. But if it should come quickly, we may be sure strong leadership will be there; and some will say that the leaders made the party. But all great movements in society and government, the world over, are the result of growth. Progress may seem to halt; we may even seem to lose ground, but it is my deep conviction that it is our duty to do, day by day, with all our might, as best we can for the good of our country the task which lies nearest at hand. The party does not consist of a few leaders or of a controlling political machine. It consists of the hundreds of thousands of citizens drawn together by a common belief in certain principles. And it seemed to me then that it ought to be in the power of that great body, the overwhelming majority of the party, to smash the machine, to defeat corrupt leaders and to drive the officials of every rank who betray the majority out of public life. Considered as a state problem, I never have questioned the wisdom of our course in remaining within the Republican party.

And so, in the campaign of 1896, I know that I strengthened our movement when I followed my convictions as well as my judgment, and threw myself as strongly as I could into the campaign for the election of McKinley as President.

McKinley carried the state by 103,000; Scofield by nearly 95,000.

In the summer of 1897 I concluded to try the experiment of campaigning for reform in an off year. It had occurred to me that one might obtain a better hearing from people of all parties when they were not in the heat and fever of a political campaign.

On the fourth of July, 1897, I delivered an address at Mineral Point and took as my theme the "Dangers Threatening Representative Government." I delivered substantially the same address at Fern Dell, on August 23d, at the Waukesha fair, and on September 24th at the State Fair in Milwaukee. These speeches were the subject of much controversy throughout the state. The fact that they were strongly assailed by the corporation press served only to excite interest in them, and I received many more invitations to speak than it was possible for me to accept.

/ One might regard a county fair as a very unsuitable place to secure an attentive hearing upon a subject seriously treated, but in all my years of campaigning I think I never made any speeches productive of better results. I found people everywhere open-minded and eager. Almost without exception those in attendance would turn from the amusements and give me their closest and best attention. I found, at every such fair, representatives of almost every township of the county, business men and well-to-do farmers, who took away with them for discussion and consideration the matter which I submitted in the address. /

The opposition criticised the fair committees severely for setting apart a day for the appearance of a "demagogue and disturber" upon their grounds, but so long as the supporters and patrons of the association over the county were satisfied, the protests of the machine availed nothing. I was made, however, to feel their displeasure and resentment on various occasions. On the fair grounds at Oshkosh, which was the home of Senator Sawyer, a determined effort was made to stop my address. I was speaking from a farm wagon which had been drawn on to the race track between the pavilion and the judge's stand. I had scarcely gotten under way with my address when the bell in the judge's stand gave the usual signal for starting the horse races. Dozens of uniformed boys distributed through the audience began shouting, "Score cards for sale; score cards for sale." This was followed by the appearance of half a dozen or more horses coming on to the track a quarter of a mile away, and headed directly down upon the audience, forcing those standing upon the track to stampede to places of safety. I saw that I must act quickly or lose the day, and I directed that the wagon in which I was standing be drawn upon the track. Then, turning to the judge's stand, I announced that I was there on the invitation of the association to deliver an address, and that I should not budge from my place until I had finished and, if again interrupted, my address would occupy the balance of the afternoon to the exclusion of any other performance on that race track. I think not fewer than five thousand people stood up and cheered their approval, and I was not again interrupted.

In the fall of 1897 a few of the friends prominently associated with me in carrying forward our campaign, bought a country weekly then published at Madison, called *Old Dane*. Being busy men, it was necessary for us to select an editor for this paper, and the choice was an easy one.

From the very beginning of our contest we had not only the support of practically all university men throughout the state, but of substantially all of the students of the university old enough to be interested. The spirit of democracy pervaded university life, and a strong body of these fine, clean, brainy fellows—really able men— have been conspicuous in all the Progressive fights of Wisconsin from that day to this. They are the Progressive leaders in their communities throughout the commonwealth, and are filling the first positions in our state—Assemblymen, Senators, the Governor's office. They are to be found upon the commissions, in journalism, in the professions—not even excepting the pulpit—all earnestly striving for civic righteousness. One of the ablest and most active of these students was a boyish-looking, tow-headed Norwegian—now Congressman John M. Nelson—one of the stanchest supporters of the Progressive movement. He came from a farm in the town of Burke, a few miles out of Madison. He had taken rank as a student and a debater in the university society work, and was one of the many students who early came to my office to volunteer his services in the Haugen campaign, and likewise in the campaign of 1896. He accepted the position of editor of *Old Dane,* the name of which we changed to *The State*. As we now had a medium through which to maintain from week to week a campaign of education, the time seemed at hand to propose a constructive program. A new heading for the paper was designed, which set forth the following platform:

Protection for the products of the factory and the farm.
Sound money, a dollar's worth of dollar.
Reciprocity in trade.

Adequate revenues for state and nation.

Equal and just taxation of all the property of each individual and every corporation transacting business within the state.

Abolish caucuses and conventions. Nominate candidates by Australian ballot at a primary election.

Enact and enforce laws to punish bribery in every form by the lobby in the legislature and wherever it assails the integrity of the public service.

Prohibit the acceptance by public officials of railroad passes, sleeping-car passes, express, telegraph, and telephone franks.

Enact and enforce laws making character and competency the requisite for service in our penal and charitable institutions.

Enact and enforce laws that will prohibit corrupt practices in campaigns and elections.

An economical administration of public affairs, reducing expenditures to a business basis.

From the beginning the circulation of the paper rapidly extended, and soon we had readers in every part of the state. It began to exert a strong influence upon public sentiment.

The bosses were alarmed. Here was a publication carrying the truth week by week into every community. Its policy could not be affected in any way—neither money, advertising, nor offices would divert it from its course. Something must be done. So they sought to have the post-office department at Washington deny the paper the second-class mail privilege. I knew that the affair had been instigated by Keyes and the bosses, and I wrote the department, inviting the most searching inspection, but stating what I knew to be the purpose back of the attack. Inspectors from Washington took possession of our books, and made a thorough investigation. I do not know what they reported, but no order came from the post-office department denying us the second-class privilege.

In the meantime we were not only actively at work with our political propaganda and our efforts to overturn the machine, but we were also advancing constructive measures of various sorts as rapidly as we could get them to the attention of the people.

One of these reforms was our effort to secure the passage of a law preventing railroad companies from giving free passes to political leaders and public officials. I will relate the details of the fight to secure an anti-pass law quite fully here because it shows vividly the conditions we had to meet.

The pass abuse had grown to extraordinary proportions in Wisconsin, and the power to give passes, franks on telegraph and telephone lines, free passage on Pullman cars, and free transportation by express companies had become a great asset of the machine politicians. These insidious privileges went far toward corrupting the politics of the state.

I had early to meet the problem of passes in my own case. In 1884, as soon as I was elected to Congress, several railroads sent me passes over their lines. Although there was then little or no agitation of the subject, I talked the whole matter over with Sam Harper and Judge Siebecker, my law partners, and we agreed that I must keep myself absolutely free from any obligations; I never used railroad passes while I was a member of Congress, nor at any other time while I held a public office.

In 1890 I first met A. R. Hall, to whom, more than any other man, belongs the credit for the enactment of the strong statute finally passed, after nine years' struggle, prohibiting state officials from accepting, using, or procuring passes or franks. Hall was one of the pioneers of the Wisconsin movement. I never knew a better man. Plain, modest, without guile, patient, lovable, tender-hearted, his whole life was so simple, so unselfish, so humble that he was sometimes underrated. He feared nothing except to do wrong. He made his way indifferent to abuse and misrepresentation. He did not serve the hour. He was not afraid to break new ground. Fundamental principles appealed to his understanding. He was a man of strong convictions, courageous in defeat, fair in victory.

Hall came to me in the spring of 1891, when I returned from Congress to resume my law practice. The legislature was then in session. We conferred on pending measures, and from that time on we worked together. He was one of our leading supporters in the Haugen campaign, and headed the delegation from his county.

His bill for the abolition of passes and franks was beaten in the session of 1891, and again in 1893. At the Haugen convention, Hall offered a resolution to commit the party against the pass evil, but the machine has a system which takes care of all "crank" resolutions. As soon as a convention is organized, a motion is adopted providing that all resolutions shall be referred, without being read or debated, to the Committee on Resolutions, thereafter to be appointed. Hall's resolution went to the committee, but was never heard from after.

But this did not stop Hall. He was ready with his anti-pass bill when the legislature of 1895 convened. To aid in creating public sentiment against the use of railway passes by members of the legislature and other officials, he and I prepared resolutions which were printed and placed in the hands of reliable men in practically every township of the state. These resolutions were offered on town-meeting day, April, 1895, and generally adopted throughout the state.

During the legislative session of 1895 Hall made a speech for his bill with the usual result. A few members—notably James O. Davidson, afterward governor, and William O'Niel, afterward a senator, supported him. In the meantime, I was aiding as best I could on the platform to organize public sentiment in support of the anti-pass amendment. And public opinion soon began to respond. Members of the legislature found themselves confronted with criticism of their positions on this legislation. But the free pass and the telegraph and telephone frank were valuable assets for the machine, and it was a hard fight.

In the convention of 1896 Hall was again ready with his anti-pass resolution. It was chloroformed as usual by the Committee on Resolutions, but afterward on the floor of the convention, when vigilance was somewhat relaxed, Hall seized the opportunity and again offered his anti-pass resolution, and promptly moved its adoption. It was a dangerous situation for the machine. It is one thing to smother a resolution in committee; it is quite another thing to vote it down in open convention. The vote was taken, and to the consternation of the bosses, it was passed with cheers.

But it was a barren victory so far as actual results were concerned. The legislature of 1897 ignored the action of the convention and again defeated Hall's anti-pass bill. More than this, the bosses and their henchmen denounced it. They said that it had been sprung on the convention; that it had not been considered by the platform committee; that the convention that passed it was nothing more than a mob; that it was not a part of the platform and binding on nobody. This all helped. It provoked discussion and controversy everywhere, and that is all that is required to advance any proposition that is sound and right. The public was now thoroughly aroused, and the defeat of the anti-pass bill in the legislature of 1897 called down upon those responsible for it the sharpest criticism. Then a discovery was made which did more to enable us to destroy the pass bribery system than anything which had theretofore occurred.

H. M. Tusler, the Madison agent of the United States Express Company, who was a strong sympathizer with our reform movement, as are so many employees of corporations, let it be known that Governor Scofield had shipped from his home in Oconto, in the northern part of the state, to Madison, the capital, in the southern part of the state, free on express frank No. 2169, the following:

January 7, 1897; 2 boxes, 2 barrels.
January 8, 1897; 3 barrels, 1 box.
January 9, 1897; 2 boxes, 200 pounds.
January 11, 1897; 2 barrels, 2 boxes, 1,000 pounds.
January 13, 1897; 1 cow (crated).
January 14, 1897; 1 box, 50 pounds; 1 box, 26 pounds.
February 2, 1897; 1 package.
February 26, 1897; a package.
March 26, 1897; 1 sewing machine.
March 26, 1897; 1 buggy pole.
August 26, 1897; 1 barrel potatoes (small).

These facts were published in *The State*. It was no answer to say that this was not in violation of law. It raised a storm of mingled ridicule and resentment. Scofield's cow became famous, her picture appeared in the newspapers, and she came to be known in every home in the state.

Finally, in the session of 1899, Hall's bill was forced through the legislature, and it at once cut off one of the strong props of the boss system in Wisconsin. In the death of Mr. Hall in 1905 the state lost a true patriot.

I come now to the campaign of 1898. We had been beaten twice already—in 1894 and 1896—and there were those who thought it unwise to fight the renomination of Scofield in 1898.

Scofield had been subservient to the bosses in all things throughout his administration. His influence had been exerted in the legislature to aid in defeating compliance with the anti-pass resolution adopted by the convention which nominated him. He had vetoed two bills taxing express companies and sleeping-car companies doing business within the state, upon a technicality. Only three votes were lacking in the Senate to pass these bills over his veto. But the precedent of a second term, usually accorded an executive, gave him a certain advantage. Many of my friends were apprehensive that if I were defeated again it would destroy all possibility of my leadership thereafter, and they urged that a negative campaign be made in the form of a protest against Scofield's renomination, but that we put forward no candidate of our own. I contended that defeat could not destroy any man whose candidacy was based upon important principles; that vital issues were never destroyed by defeat; and that any failure upon our part to oppose the machine would disintegrate our forces, and greatly delay the overthrow of the bosses. I offered my support to any recognized Progressive who would lead the fight as a candidate for governor, but insisted with all the force I could command that the fight must be continued unceasingly. There being no other candidate willing to undertake the campaign, I announced my candidacy.

During this campaign of 1898 I felt deeply the loss of my oldest and best friend and supporter. March 12, 1898, I delivered an address on the Direct Primary at the University of Michigan at Ann Arbor. Upon my return, I was shocked to find my law partner, Samuel A. Harper, desperately ill with pneumonia. I never left him, day or night, till the end came. No man has ever been so completely a part of my own life.

The three weeks' campaign for the choice of candidates in 1898 was one of the fiercest ever conducted in the state. Gilbert E. Roe, my former law partner, now a member of the New York bar, rendered excellent service in that campaign. He was a member of the Committee on Resolutions in the convention and led the fight in committee, securing the adoption of many of the strongest planks of our progressive platform. When the convention met I should have been nominated on the first ballot, except for the use of money with delegates exactly as in the convention of 1896. Senator Stephenson, then a Scofield supporter and a power in the old organization, stated many times to my friends that the total amount of money required to handle delegates the night before the ballotting began was $8,300. I was again defeated.

But we had not fought wholly in vain: we had so stirred the state upon progressive issues that our opponents did not dare risk the rejection of the platform which we presented, and, except in one or two particulars, it was adopted substantially as we drafted it.

It demanded immediate enactment of such laws as would compel all corporations engaged in business to contribute their just and equal share toward the burden of taxation.

It prohibited the giving and receiving of passes and franks, and demanded that it be made a penal offence, both as to the giver and receiver.

It admitted the defects in the caucus and convention system, and favored direct primary legislation to secure to every citizen the freest expression of his choice in the selection of candidates.

It admitted the existence of the lobby to control legislation in the interests of corporations, and promised laws to abolish the same.

In the following legislature, of 1899, none of the pledges of the platform of 1898, aside from the anti-pass law, was redeemed. An effort was made to pass a bill for the more equitable taxation of the railroads, but it was resisted by a strong railroad lobby and finally defeated by substituting a bill for the creation of a commission to investigate the subject. Every forward step was resisted.

A pretense of compliance with the platform promise of direct primaries was made by passing a law which really strengthened and entrenched the caucus and convention system. The bosses thus sought to fortify their position for the future.

We had now lost out in three campaigns—1894, 1896, 1898. But we had tested the machine to the limit of its strength, and we were prepared to go forward with the fight more vigorously than ever before. We had an irresistible platform of principles to appeal to the democratic spirit of the people, and I never doubted that, when once the people understood, they would drive the bosses from control and reclaim their government.

I had then, and have had ever since, absolute confidence in the people. The question was often asked, "How do you expect to make Wisconsin a pioneer progressive state, with its foreign-born, foreign-bred, slow-moving population?" True, a majority of the people of Wisconsin are of foreign birth and foreign parentage. But it is a rare and exceptional people. The spirit of liberty stirring throughout Europe in the late forties and early fifties gave us the best of Germany, Scandinavia, Poland, Ireland. It gave us Carl Schurz and his followers; gave us political refugees who were patriots and hardy peasants, seeking free government as well as homes. An organization known as the German Idealists even flooded Germany with literature urging the founding of a free German state in Wisconsin. In every city and hamlet in the commonwealth are still living the last of these pioneers. And as a heritage to their children they are leaving the story of the oppression which forced them to abandon their native land and intensified their devotion to self-government. Combined with the Puritan Yankee of New England, these sturdy immigrants have produced a courageous, progressive race of men in whom the spirit of democracy dominates.

Our problem was further simplified owing to the predominance of the agricultural population and the absence of great congested centres, which are always the stronghold of machine control through a corrupt combination of big business with municipal graft. During the long winter months the farmer finds time for reading and thinking, but the men in the industries must give their energies more exclusively to their employment and have less leisure for study and reflection, excepting where through organization they are securing shorter hours and better opportunities. To the character of the people of Wisconsin I attribute the progress which we were able to make against machine control.

We entered upon the campaign of 1900, therefore, in which we were destined to be finally victorious, with great enthusiasm.

Chapter VI

My First Term as Governor and
the Problems I Had to Meet

The psychology of a certain type of machine politician is a most interesting study. It is characteristic of him to win if possible, but to *appear* to win in any event. He has a quick, almost prophetic eye for the loaded wagon. He has one rule: beat the opposition man, but if he cannot be beaten, support him. Claim credit for his victory, and at all hazards, keep in with the successful candidate. He believes that if he cannot get what he wants for himself by opposing a candidate, he may possibly succeed in getting what he wants by supporting him.

We had been beaten by the bosses in three successive campaigns in Wisconsin; but when we entered the campaign of 1900, the cumulative effect of our previous work began to be strongly apparent. I announced my candidacy for governor on May 15th. Several candidates were at once brought out by the machine in various parts of the state to carry their own and nearby counties with a view to combining their strength and defeating me in the convention. I had therefore to make a hot fight against each of these candidates in his own stronghold. County after county was carried, and the evidences of victory soon began to be overwhelming.

It was then that a number of politicians who had been opposed to our cause, among them Congressman Babcock, his friend, Emanuel Phillipp, and Isaac Stephenson, now United States Senator, joined our ranks for such time as suited their purposes.

Isaac Stephenson is a man eighty-two years of age. Up to 1900 he had always cooperated with the old Wisconsin machine. Like Sawyer, he was a typical pioneer lumberman, who had acquired great wealth which he was willing to use liberally in political activities. He had never enjoyed any educational advantages, but had read a good deal, and remembered with remarkable accuracy all the details of his active life. He served six years in the House of Representatives, and after he retired at the end of the 50th Congress his political associates gave him frequent assurance that his desire to become United States Senator should be gratified in good time.

When the legislature of 1899 came to elect a United States Senator, Stephenson felt that the hour had come when the oft-repeated promise should be made good. He knew that a word from Sawyer and Spooner would settle the matter, but that word was not spoken. It may be that they had never intended to make Stephenson Senator. It is certain that there were others on the waiting list who wanted the Senatorship and who also expected Sawyer and Spooner to help them. One of these was Congressman Babcock, a machine politician with close political connections with big business.

Now, as a matter of fact, Sawyer and Spooner did not want either Stephenson or Babcock for Senator. The man they really wanted was Henry C. Payne, but his reputation as a lobbyist and boss politician was such that they did not dare propose him openly. They supported Joseph V. Quarles as a "holding candidate." No opportunity offering for Payne they finally elected Quarles Senator. This left Stephenson and Babcock in an unpleasant frame of mind, and both in less than two years came to me with propositions to support the Progressive movement, which by that time began to look like a winning cause.

I remember distinctly the incident which preceded Babcock's alignment with us. Colonel Henry Casson, then Sergeant-at-Arms of the House of Representatives at Washington, and an old friend of Babcock, came to me in January, 1900.

He said: "I come to you with a message from Babcock. He asks nothing from you. But he is angry with the old crowd, because they did not treat him fairly in the senatorial contest. He has such a hold upon his district that he feels he can remain in Congress without asking the favor of any outside support. But he wants to fight in your ranks as a private."

"Well," I replied, "you know what I am fighting for in this state. You know that I am standing for certain issues, and am welcoming all the help that I can get."

Another machine man who also apparently enlisted in the reform movement in that campaign was Emanual L. Phillipp, of Milwaukee, a close friend of Babcock. Phillipp was born of Swiss parentage, with Italian ancestry. Big, heavy, swarthy, adroit, self-possessed, determined, but mild and conciliatory in manner, Phillipp was an out-and-out corporation man. But in the campaign of 1900, he with others of his type professed to have reached the conclusion that there were abuses to reform and that the railroads and other interests recognized this to be so. They were apprehensive that I was hostile to railroad corporations and would, if governor, seek to embarrass them in every conceivable way. Mr. Babcock and Mr. Phillipp assured me that they did not share in this opinion regarding my position; and that they very much wished my true position might be made known. They suggested that Mr. Marvin Hughitt, President of the Chicago and Northwestern Railroad Company, would like to have from me directly a personal statement of my purposes. I replied that I knew of no reason why I should shrink from stating my convictions upon any question of public interest. When I informed A. R. Hall of the proposal he opposed my seeing Mr. Hughitt on the ground that it was the purpose of these gentlemen to draw me into an interview, then cause the matter to be made public for the purpose of arousing popular prejudice. I suggested that if the President of the Wisconsin Dairymen's Association, or the representative of any other business interest, requested a conference for the purpose of ascertaining my position upon legislation which might affect their interests, I would agree to such an interview as a matter of course. To refuse to submit my opinions under such circumstances would tend to justify the belief that I had some ulterior design.

When the subject, therefore, was next brought up I agreed to meet Mr. Hughitt provided ex-Governor Hoard might be present.

At the appointed time, Governor Hoard, Mr. Hughitt, Mr. Babcock and I met in the offices of Mr. Hughitt in Chicago. Mr. Hughitt began by telling us how he started in life as a telegraph messenger boy, and took up most of the time reviewing his career. It appeared that this much desired interview was to begin and end with a recital of Mr. Hughitt's early struggles from poverty to affluence and power. But Babcock knew what the interview was for, and presently suggested that Mr. La Follette was reasonably certain to be elected governor of Wisconsin and that Mr. Hughitt might be interested to know his attitude toward railroad corporations. Mr. Hughitt promptly replied that he had no doubt that Mr. La Follette would be perfectly fair in his treatment of their important interests in Wisconsin. It seemed my time now to speak, and I said:

"Mr. Hughitt, I believe I shall be elected governor and I can state in a very few words my position upon the pressing question of railroad taxation. I shall, if elected, recommend, and, if given the opportunity, shall approve a bill taxing railroad companies upon the value of their property, just as other taxpayers of Wisconsin are assessed and taxed upon their property."

Mr. Hughitt answered, with a wave of the hand, which dismissed the subject, "That is perfectly satisfactory to the Northwestern," and that ended the interview. As I came away I was somewhat at a loss to know just what was the real significance of the meeting, but Mr. Babcock seemed to attach a good deal of importance to it and said, "Well, Hughitt will feel better now that he has seen you. You ought to call on him whenever you are in Chicago. He will always be glad to see you."

I have never met President Hughitt since. I thought then and still think that Mr. Hughitt had been informed that my election as governor could not be headed off; that Babcock and Phillipp were supporting me and proposed to maintain such friendly relations as would give them a footing, if possible, and influence with the administration whenever critical situations arose affecting railroad interests.

Although these old machine leaders thus came to the support of the party ticket in 1900, it is questionable whether on the whole their alliance was not more harmful than helpful to me with the public. Their support not only gave us no additional delegates, but it put us off our guard in campaigning for a really progressive legislature—as we learned later to our cost.

I had another supporter with railroad affiliations in this campaign, but his support was genuine. This was Thomas H. Gill, General Attorney for the Wisconsin Central Railway Company. We were old-time friends, and he had supported my candidacy for governor in 1896 and 1898, asserting his claim to the free exercise of his political rights when questioned about his action by the company.

One evening in May, 1900, just before I made formal announcement of my candidacy, we were in Gill's rooms in Milwaukee, discussing the political situation in the state, when he said, "Bob, the president [meaning the president of the railway company with which he was connected] called me in to-day to inquire definitely as to your views on railroad taxation, and I defined your position as I understand it." "Just how did you state it, Tom?" I asked. He gave me the substance of his conversation with the president and inquired, "Was I not right?" "Well," I said, "you were partially right." I then stated to him as clearly as I could the legislation which I thought ought to be enacted as to the taxation of railroad property in fairness to the people of the state, and the subject was dropped for the evening.

But later that night, thinking it over, I decided it would be better to put my position in writing as a precaution against any possible future misunderstanding. Early next morning I drafted my letter to Tom and delivered it to him personally that same day, saying to him, "There, Tom, you are at liberty to show that to any railroad official, or to publish it if you want to. That is where I stand now, and where I shall stand after I am governor, if I should be nominated and elected." He took the letter, saying laughingly, "That's all right," although he did not think it necessary.

When the railroad taxation bill came up in the legislature, rumors began to be heard about the railroads having an agreement in writing with me on that subject, which would be made public sooner or later to my great embarrassment. Some of my friends came to me, very much disturbed over the story, but my only answer was, "You invite any one who asserts that there is such a statement signed by me to publish it."

The letter had quite a career. It bobbed up at intervals for four years. I could have given it to the press at any time, but I chose to hold it in reserve, preferring to publish it at a time when I could use it most effectively as an example of our opponents' perversion of the truth. In October, 1904, in my last campaign for Governor, when the opposition again revived the story of my "written agreement with the railroads," I gave this famous letter to the public. Here it is:

MADISON, WIS., May 12, 1900.

DEAR TOM:

You have been my personal and political friend for twenty years. Should I become a candidate for the nomination for governor, I want your continued support, if you can consistently accord it to me. But you are the attorney for the Wisconsin Central R.R. Co., and I am not willing that you should be placed in any position where you could be subjected to any criticism or embarrassment with your employers on my account. For this reason I desire to state to you in so far as I am able my position in relation to the question of railway taxation, which has now become one of public interest, and is very likely to so continue until rightly settled. This I can do in a very few words.

Railroad corporations should pay neither more nor less than a justly proportionate share of taxes with the other taxable property of the state. If I were in a position to pass officially upon a bill to change existing law, it would be my first care to know whether the rate therein proposed was just in proportion to the property of other corporations and individuals as then taxed, or as therein proposed to be taxed. The determination of that question would be controlling. If such rate was less than the justly proportionate share which should be borne by the railroads, then I should favor increasing it to make it justly proportionate. If the proposed rate was more than the justly proportionate share, in comparison with the property of other corporations, and of individuals taxed under the law, then I should favor decreasing it to make it justly proportionate.

In other words, I would favor equal and exact justice to each individual and to every interest, yielding neither to clamor on the one hand, nor being swerved from the straight course by any interest on the other. This position, I am sure, is the only one which could commend itself to you, and cannot be criticised by any legitimate business honestly managed.

Sincerely yours,
ROBERT M. LA FOLLETTE.

Success, for a new movement, often presents quite as serious problems as defeat. No only had we to deal with that part of the old machine element which now offered to support us with protestations of confidence, but we had also to hold back and keep together the enthusiasts in our own ranks.

As soon as my nomination in 1900 was a foregone conclusion and I began to think of what our convention platform should be and what we should try to do in our first legislature these problems within our own ranks began to concern me. For example, one of the strongest and ablest men among us was A. R. Hall, who had been so persistent in his efforts to obtain anti-pass legislation. He was now making a dogged fight for a railroad commission to regulate rates. Each session he would introduce a bill, make a speech upon it if possible, and see it go down to defeat. He did not expect to pass a bill, indeed his bill was not such a measure as I should have been willing to make a fight for as a law covering that subject. But it served a good purpose in keeping the matter before the legislature.

Now, I was as keen for railway regulation in Wisconsin as any one could well be. I had been deeply interested in the problem as a boy when it was the leading state issue in the Granger period, and had become a real student of the subject as a member of the House of Representatives in 1886 and 1887. It had an important place in my plans for a comprehensive state program. But as a matter of tactics, I did not consider it wise to bring it forward for immediate and serious consideration. In our campaigns we had emphasized two issues chiefly: direct primaries and railroad taxation. We had found it important to keep the field of discussion narrowed to the subjects which could be adequately treated in a single address. We had tried to make the people masters of these two issues, and, as events proved, we had succeeded. If we now attacked the larger problem of railroad regulation, as Hall urged us to do, we should have too many issues to present clearly and thoroughly to the people in one campaign and would arouse the doubly bitter opposition of the railroads. The railroads had begun to see that some reform in taxation was inevitable, and while they would certainly resist to the end, they believed, secretly, that they could pass on any increase in their taxes to the public by increasing their rates. We might, therefore, get a taxation law, but if we proposed also to push railroad regulation at that time and assert the power of the state to fix rates, the railroads would call to their support all the throng of shippers who were then receiving rebates, and would probably defeat all our railroad measures. If we centred on railroad taxation alone, of course we should have with us, quietly if not openly, all the big shippers and manufacturers who knew perfectly well that railroad taxes should be increased and that such increases would tend to reduce the proportion which they had to pay.

I therefore took time from the campaign and arranged a meeting with Hall at Haugen's home in River Falls. I presented the case strongly to him, urging him not to offer his resolution calling for railroad regulation at the convention. I did not want the convention to go on record against a thing we were all in favor of. We were the best of friends, Hall and I. He was a constant visitor in our home and every member of the family loved him. But he was very insistent about pushing his measure in season and out; he wanted to make a record, and he thought that the fight should be unremitting. Finally, however, he promised to withhold his resolution, and I believe we made better progress in the long run by building our structure of reform step by step. I have always felt that the political reformer, like the engineer or the architect, must know that his foundations are right. To build the superstructure in advance of that is likely to be disastrous to the whole thing. He must not put the roof on before he gets the underpinning in. And the underpinning is education of the people.

In the convention which followed, in August, 1900, I was unanimously nominated for governor, and in November the state gave me the largest majority ever given up to that time to a gubernatorial candidate. On January 7, 1901, I took the oath of office.

Up to the time that the legislature met on January 9th, I felt that we should be able to go forward steadily with the reforms for which the people of the state had declared. I even felt that the machine politicians who came to me offering their support were really convinced that the reforms we demanded were inevitable and that they would no longer oppose them. I was yet to learn the length to which the corporations and the machine politicians who represented them would go in their efforts to defeat our measures. They now carried out openly their plans for stealing the legislature.

When the legislature met there was a general gathering of the machine leaders at the capital. They attended my inauguration and there was no manifestation of hostile purposes. But forty-eight hours afterward the mask was off. The newspapers on the morning of January 9th contained the startling announcement that the "Stalwart" Republicans (as the machine element of the party now for the first time called themselves) were in control of the senate and that they proposed to fight the administration measures. This was the first intimation we had that the old leaders were secretly planning to defeat the legislation pledged in the platform. It was a great shock to us. I found it hard to believe that men elected upon issues so clearly presented would have the hardihood to turn about so quickly.

Our friends were in undisputed control of the lower house of the legislature, the assembly, and after a hasty conference we decided to pay no attention to the sinister reports regarding the senate, hoping that they might not be true.

All the governors before me, so far as I know, had sent in their messages to the legislature to be mumbled over by a reading clerk. I knew that I could make a very much stronger impression with my recommendations if I could present my message in person to the legislature in joint session. I felt that it would invest the whole matter with a new seriousness and dignity that would not only affect the legislators themselves, but react upon the public mind. This I did: and in consequence awakened a wide interest in my recommendations throughout the state.

The predominant notes in the message were direct primaries and railroad taxation—one political and one economic reform.

The railroads at that time paid taxes in the form of a license fee upon their gross earnings. The report of the Tax Commission showed that while real property in Wisconsin paid 1.19 per cent. of its market value in taxes, the railroads paid only .53 per cent. of their market value (based on the average value of stocks and bonds) or less than one half the rate paid by farmers, manufacturers, home owners and others. Upon this showing we contended

105

that the railroads were not bearing their fair share of the burdens of the state. The Tax Commission suggested two measures of reform. One of their bills provided for a simple increase in the license tax, the other provided for a physical valuation of the railroads and a wholly new system of taxation upon an ad valorem basis, measures which I had earnestly advocated in my campaign speeches, and recommended in my message. I regarded this latter as the more scientific method of taxation. The Commission stated that while they had so framed the bills as to err on the side of injustice to the people rather than to the railroads, the passage of either of them would mean an increase of taxes paid by railroads and other public service corporations of more than three quarters of a million dollars annually.

No sooner had the taxation and direct primary bills been introduced than the lobby gathered in Madison in full force. Lobbyists had been there before, but never in such numbers or with such an organization. I never saw anything like it. The railroads, threatened with the taxation bills, and the bosses, threatened by the direct primary, evidently regarded it as the death struggle. Not only were the regular lobbyists in attendance but they made a practice during the entire winter of bringing in delegations of more or less influential men from all parts of the state, some of whom often remained two or three weeks and brought every sort of pressure to bear on the members of the legislature. The whole fight was centred upon me personally. They thought that if they could crush me, that would stop the movement. How little they understood! Even if they had succeeded in eliminating me, the movement, which is fundamental, would still have swept on! They sought to build up in the minds of the people the fear that the executive was controlling the legislative branch of the government. They deliberately organized a campaign of abuse and misrepresentation. Their stories were minutely detailed and spread about among the hotels and on railroad trains. They said that I had completely lost my head. They endeavored to give me a reputation for discourtesy and browbeating; stories were told of my shameless treatment of members, of my backing them up against the wall of the executive office, shaking my fist in their faces and warning them if they did not pass our bills I would use all my power to crush them. In so far as anything was said in disparagement of the administration members of the legislature it was that they were sycophants who took their orders every morning from the executive office. The newspapers, controlled by the machine interests, began to print these abusive statements and sent them broadcast. At first we took no notice of their campaign of misrepresentation, but it grew and grew until it got on the nerves of all of us. It came to be a common thing to have one after another of my friends drop in and say: "Governor, is it true that you have had a row with——? Is it true that you ordered——out of the executive office?"

It seems incredible, as I look back upon it now, that it could be humanly possible to create such an atmosphere of distrust. We felt that we were fighting something in the dark all the while; there was nothing we could get hold of.

In spite of it all, however, we drove straight ahead. After the bills prepared by the Tax Commission were in, the primary election bill was drafted and redrafted and introduced by E. Ray Stevens of Madison, one of the ablest men ever in public life in Wisconsin, and now a judge of the circuit court of the state. The committee having it in charge at once began a series of open meetings, and the lobby brought to Madison people from every part of the state to attend the hearings and to protest. Extended speeches were made against it, and these were promptly printed and sent broadcast. The most preposterous arguments were advanced. They argued that the proposed law was unconstitutional because it interfered with the "right of the people to assemble!" They tried to rouse the country people by arguing that it favored the cities; they said that city people could get out more readily to primaries than country people. It did not seem to occur to them that practically every argument they made against the direct primary applied far more strongly to the old caucus and convention system.

But we fought as vigorously as they, and presently it began to appear that we might get some of our measures through. It evidently made an impression on the lobby. One night, after the legislature had been in session about two months, Emanuel Phillipp came to my office. He moved his chair up close to mine.

"Now, look here," he said, "you want to pass the primary election bill, don't you? I will help you put it through."

"Phillipp," I said, "there is no use in you and me trying to mislead each other. I understand and you understand that the senate is organized against both the direct primary and taxation bills. You know that better than I do."

"Well," he said, "now look here. This railroad taxation matter —wouldn't you be willing to let that go if you could get your primary bill through? What good will it do you, anyhow, to increase railroad taxation? We can meet that all right just by raising rates or by changing a classification here and there. No one will know it and we can take back every cent of increased taxes in rates from the people."

"Phillipp," I said, "you have just driven in and clinched the argument for regulating your rates. And that is the next thing we are going to do. No," I said, "these pledges are straight promises."

"But," he argued, "if you can get this primary election bill through you will have done a great thing. And I will pass it for you, if you will let up on railroad taxation."

"Just how will you pass it?" I asked.

"How will I pass it?" he repeated. "How will I pass it? Why, I'll take those fellows over to a room in the Park Hotel, close the door and stand them up against the wall. And I'll say to them, 'You vote for the primary election bill!' And they'll vote for it, because I own them, they're mine!" And this was Phillipp's last interview with me.

Still other and even more desperate measures were resorted to as the fight advanced. I have already spoken of the manner in which the machine had secured control of most of the newspapers of the state, but there was still one great independent newspaper in Milwaukee—the *Sentinel*. It had been controlled and edited by Horace Rublee, one of that older group of independent journalists which included such men as Joseph Medill, Charles A. Dana, Horace Greeley and Henry J. Raymond. Rublee was temperamentally cold and dispassionate, but endowed with a keen intellect and the highest sense of honor. He treated everything from the heights. He never hesitated to assail corruption wherever it existed, even in the Republican party. After Horace Rublee's death, the *Sentinel* continued to be a thorn in the flesh of the bosses. It attacked Payne and Pfister so sharply for the way in which they were running the politics of Milwaukee, that they finally brought libel suits against it for hundreds of thousands of dollars. The managers of the paper stood their ground and served notice that they would answer and prove their charges. Then suddenly the people of Milwaukee learned that the *Sentinel* had been sold for an immense sum to Pfister.

Thus the bosses gained control of the chief organ of public opinion in our greatest city: the people were left with no large English-speaking Republican daily to fight for their cause. The long series of abuses that arose under a city government controlled by political rings in both parties for the benefit of ringsters—that, in my view, has led to the Socialist uprising in Milwaukee.

Hardly had the news of the transfer of the *Sentinel* been made public than I was afforded strong evidence of its intentions for the future. Mr. Warren, who had been editor of the Chicago *Inter-Ocean* when it was the organ of Charles T. Yerkes of franchise fame, was appointed editor of the *Sentinel*. And one of the first things he did was to come to Madison and call on me at the executive office.

"Governor La Follette," he said, "I suppose you are aware of the fact that Mr. Pfister is now the owner of the Milwaukee *Sentinel*."

I told him I had heard such a report.

"I suppose you know," he said, "the power of the *Sentinel* in state politics. I have come to see you by Mr. Pfister's direction, to say to you that the paper prefers to support your administration and will do so provided you change your attitude on the subject of primary elections and railroad taxation. If the *Sentinel* opposes your administration, you will be defeated and retired to private life. You are a young man. You are popular with the people. With the support of the *Sentinel* you can have a successful career."

He then went on to argue that the people were not fit to make their own nominations, which led to a considerable discussion of the direct primary. "If you will let up," he said finally, "the legislature will be taken care of."

"Mr. Warren," I said, "I have campaigned this state for direct nominations and equal taxation for several years. The convention which nominated me adopted a platform specifically promising that these measures should be enacted into law. These were the two main issues upon which I was elected governor, and I propose to go on fighting for them."

"Well," he said, "if that is your answer, the *Sentinel* will begin skinning you to-morrow."

I replied, "You may be able to prevent the passage of this legislation, and you may defeat me, but I will use all the power that the people have given me to fulfill every pledge in the platform. And you may carry that to Mr. Pfister as my answer."

Mr. Warren bowed himself out of the office, and the war on us began from that moment.

The Milwaukee *Sentinel* had been a sort of political bible in the state. It went into every corner of Wisconsin. The character which Rublee had given to it made it the final authority with thousands of readers.

From that moment it became the organ of the opposition. It supported every form of privilege. The result has been that the party which it championed has lost control of Milwaukee, the boss who owned it and the bosses it so ardently supported have been wholly retired from power in Wisconsin, and the corporations back of those bosses have been firmly reined in by the laws of the state.

But for the time being the change in the *Sentinel* made our fight bitterly hard. It strengthened the opposition. For a long time I paid no attention to its misrepresentations and personal attacks. But finally, about 1904, I began holding a copy of it up to my audiences, telling them just what it stood for and appealing to the people of Wisconsin to drive it out of their homes; saying that the people ought only to support those papers that served the public; that the papers that were organs of corporations should depend upon the corporations for their support. And that is what the people of the country ought to do to-day. They ought to support the newspapers and magazines that are serving their interests. There must always be muckrakers as long as there are muckmakers, and the public owes it to itself to support those publications that stand for the public interest. It does not make any difference what good news service the organs of the corporations offer, turn them out; teach them that they can't prey upon the public and at the same time appeal to the public for support.

Following the change of front in the *Sentinel,* the lobby became more active. Clubs were formed in Madison where members of the legislature could be drawn together in a social way and cleverly led into intimate associations with the corporation men who swarmed the capital. In one of the principal hotels a regular poker game was maintained where members who could not be reached in any other way, could win, very easily, quite large sums of money. In that way bribes were disguised. It was, at that time, against the law to use free transportation in Wisconsin; it was against the law to furnish it; it was against the law to procure it for anybody else. And yet, all through that session of the legislature, members were receiving transportation in the form of mileage books on the state roads for themselves and for their friends. It was notorious that lewd women were an accessory to the lobby organization. Members who could not be reached in any other way were advised that they could receive good positions with railroad corporations after the legislative session was over. Even Congressman Lenroot, then fast rising to the leadership of the assembly, was offered one, which, of course, he did not take.

When we continued to make progress in spite of all this opposition the lobby made another move against us. It brought to bear all the great influence of the federal office-holders who were especially disturbed over the possible effect of a direct primary upon their control of the state. United States District Attorney Wheeler, an appointee of Spooner, and the United States District Attorney of the Eastern District, an appointee of Quarles, were much on the ground; so were United States Marshal Monahan and Collector of Internal Revenue Fink.

Finally, before the vote on the direct primary was taken in the senate, Senator Spooner, who rarely came to Wisconsin while Congress was in session, appeared in Madison. He was there only a few days, but he was visited by members of the senate, and we felt his influence strongly against us.

All the efforts of the lobby, combined with the opposition of the newspapers and the federal office-holders, was not without its effect upon our forces. Every moment from the time the senate convened down to the final vote on the railroad taxation bills they were weakening us, wearing us down, getting some men one way, some another, until finally before the close of the session they had not only the senate but a majority of the Republicans in the assembly. It was a pathetic and tragic thing to see honest men falling before these insidious forces. For many of them it meant plain ruin from which they never afterward recovered.

In order to make very clear the methods employed I shall here relate in detail the stories of several of the cases which came directly under my own observation. I shall withhold the real names of the Senators and Assemblymen concerned, because many of them were the victims of forces and temptations far greater than they could resist. If I could also give the names of the men really responsible for the corruption, bribery and debauchery—the men higher up, the men behind the lobbyists—I would do it without hesitation.

How did the lobby get them? Various ways. There was Senator A. He was a poor fellow from a northern district; a lawyer without much practice—rather a weak fellow. I can't remember just on what bill it was, but they got him. When he returned to his district after the session he built an expensive home, to the amazement of all his friends, and then came down to Washington to a federal position.

We depended on Senator B. He made a statement that he could be relied upon to support the direct primary bill. We figured him

111

on our list until about the time that Spooner visited Madison and *he* got away. Senator C. was another man we had counted upon as one of the old reliables in the movement. He was an Irishman and a good talker and debater. They finally got him, too. I remember he came to me one night and said:

"Well, I don't know but what I'm going to disappoint you in my vote on the direct primary bill."

I could not at first think of a word to say—it was a staggering blow.

"Why, C.," I said finally, "if you were to go over to the other side on these measures, it would seem to me like the end of everything. You couldn't do a thing like that. You have been one of the pillars of the movement."

I don't believe I tried to reason with him. It simply was not a case for argument. There was only one side to it, for he himself had been one of our ablest speakers on the stump in favor of the direct primary.

Well, he voted against us, and it is significant that a few months after the legislature adjourned he was appointed to a federal office and is, I believe, still in the service.

Another instance was that of Assemblyman D., who had been for some time quite an active supporter of the reform movement. He was a small business man and came to the legislature from a county in which I was personally very strong. When the committees were being formed, he was counted so much the friend of our measures that he was placed upon one of the most important committees.

He stood with us in the vote on direct primaries, but some little time after that Assemblyman E., who was one of our leaders in the assembly, came into my office one morning. E. was a fine young fellow, and regarded as thoroughly reliable. He was often in the executive office and I trusted him absolutely. Upon the occasion to which I refer he said:

"Governor, I have changed my boarding place"—he had been boarding with some private family, I think—"I have moved over to the Park Hotel."

The Park Hotel was the principal hotel in Madison, and the headquarters of all the lobbyists. I was somewhat surprised and asked him why he had moved.

"Well," he said, "I propose to be where I can watch the game that these lobbyists are playing. I am satisfied that they are working on some of our weak members, and I am going right into their camp to see what they are doing."

Not long after that he came to me and said:

"How much do you know about D.? I notice him about the Park Hotel a great deal talking with lobbyists. There's something about it that I don't like."

Finally in one of his talks about D. he said: "You want to look out for D., they've got him; you will find him going back on railroad taxation."

I was disturbed about it. We were up pretty close, as I remember it, to final committee action on the bill. I therefore telephoned to one of the leading bankers in the town in which D. lived and asked him to come to Madison. This banker had been a university chum of mine—a man of the highest standing, and a constant and loyal supporter of the Progressive movement. He came to Madison and brought with him a prominent merchant of the town, but before they could reach D. the vote had been taken, and the result was so close that it was found that D. had cast the decisive vote against the bill. The banker and his friends took D. into a room in the capitol, and had a very earnest talk with him. They told him he would never be able to make the people believe that he didn't have the money of the railroads in his pocket for his betrayal of our cause. He never got back to the legislature.

A few days later—when this same bill was before the assembly —we were to have another and a still worse shock. I have said that we trusted E. implicitly. He was one of the most enthusiastic men we had, and being a high-spirited, energetic young fellow, he was of great assistance in our fights. Whenever we gathered a little group of the members in the executive office to talk over any critical situation in the legislature, E. was always with us. He was an active young manufacturer. He often talked with us about his business. I think he had some special machine which enabled him to make his product more cheaply than other manufacturers.

One day E. Ray Stevens came into my office and said, "Governor, I wish you would send up and ask E. to come down here. I don't just like the way he talks."

"Why," I said, "Ray, there can't be anything wrong with E."

Then I began to think that he had not been in to see me for three or four days. "Well," I said, "I will send up."

When he came through the door he did not meet me with his characteristic frankness. But I greeted him exactly as usual and said, "E., I want to have a little talk with you."

I moved my chair right up to his, placed my hands on his knees and looked him in the eye a moment before I spoke. Then I asked, "E., what's the matter?"

The tears started in his eyes and the response came at once.

"Governor, I can't help it. I've got to vote against the railroad taxation bill." After a moment he added, "I haven't slept any for two or three nights. I have walked the floor. I have thought of resigning and going home."

"Tell me all about it, E.," I said.

"Well," he replied, "you know that all I have in the world I have put into that factory of mine. I have told you about how proud I was of the thing. Now," he said, "this railroad lobby tells me that if I vote for that railroad taxation bill they will ruin me in business. They can take everything I've got. They have threatened to give my competitors advantages over me in railroad rates that will offset any advantages I have with my new machinery. Now, I can't beggar my family. I have a wife and babies."

I said, "E., you can't do this wrong. You can't violate your conscience." I talked to him quite a bit. He got up and walked the floor. He said he would always be for our measures, but he could not risk being driven to the wall. And then he left the office.

A few minutes before the roll call on the bill, E., who sat next to Lenroot, turned to him and said, "Lenroot, in five minutes I am going to violate my oath of office." Lenroot was shocked and said, "What do you mean?" He replied: "It is a question between my honor and my bread and butter, and I propose to vote for my bread and butter." And he voted against the bill.

Assemblyman F. was nominated by a convention that was overwhelmingly for the direct primary. It adopted a platform specifically pledging the nominee to support the direct primary bill, and F., the candidate, formally accepted and agreed faithfully to carry out the instructions of the convention.

During the all-night session in the assembly on the primary bill, F. was called from the floor into the clerk's room by a member of the senate who offered him five hundred dollars to vote against the bill. F. told the lobbyist that he would not dare to go back to his constituents if he voted against that bill, as he had solemnly promised them when nominated to vote for it. F. said he would like to do anything the Senator wanted him to and he would like the five hundred, but he did not dare to violate his pledge. After more of this talk they left the clerk's room. The room was not lighted.

At the time there was lying on a lounge in that room Assemblyman G., who was ill and had been brought from a sick room to attend upon this important session. He recognized F.'s voice and also the name of the Senator, which F. repeatedly used during the

114

negotiations. Assemblyman G. reported the whole matter to Lenroot, who informed me. We agreed that here was a case that we could take into the court if G. would swear to the facts as reported to Lenroot. It was hoped that a successful prosecution might check the bribers in their raid on our legislation.

I sent for G. In Lenroot's presence he repeated the conversation between F. and the senator, just as he had given it to Lenroot. I then called F. to the executive chamber. He admitted the conversation as detailed by G., but was slow about confirming G. as to the name of the Senator which he had used again and again in discussing the five-hundred-dollar proposal while in the clerk's room.

Another interview was arranged, at which time he promised to tell everything. Before that interview the lobby did such effective work with both F. and G. that their memories utterly failed them as to every important detail of the whole event, and without these two witnesses there was no case.

Such was the opposition we had to meet on all of our measures, the lobby standing together as one man against both the taxation and the direct primary bills.

It was about the middle of March, after inconceivable delays, before the Direct Primary bill could be finally gotten up in the assembly for consideration, and it was then bitterly opposed.

When the debate was finally exhausted there was an all-night session so managed in a parliamentary way as to prevent a vote being taken. In the meantime lobbyists were calling members of the assembly outside of the chamber, liquor was brought into the capitol, and into the committee rooms. Members were made drunk and brought back in such a condition of intoxication that they had to be supported to their seats. And yet, in spite of all this, we retained the support of enough members to pass the bill.

When it reached the senate, though the members were hostile to it, they dared not kill it outright. The sentiment in the state, they knew, was too strong. Accordingly, they pursued the usual indirect means of accomplishing the same end—by passing a substitute measure called the Hagemeister bill, which defeated the real purpose of the reform.

This substitute was indeed supported by some of our friends who were affected by the argument that it was a good thing to make a start, that "half a loaf is better than no bread"; that it was necessary at any hazard to "get something on the statute books."

But in legislation *no bread* is often better than *half a loaf.* I believe it is usually better to be beaten and come right back at the next session and make a fight for a thoroughgoing law than to have written on the books a weak and indefinite statute. The gentlemen who opposed us were ingenious. Under the Hagemeister substitute they proposed to try out the direct primary principle with respect to county offices alone. Now, they knew well enough that county elections scarcely touch the real problem of party caucuses, conventions and legislation; that they involve little besides personal strife for small local offices. They expected by the application of such a law to discredit the direct primary by bringing out a miserably small vote with a big expense charged up against it. They knew that it would take several years to try out the experiment and that by that time the Progressive group, unable to prove the excellence of their policies, would have merited the distrust of the people.

I had thought all this out years before. All through our earlier contests we could have obtained some mild or harmless compromises and concessions. But I was clear that we should not stand for anything that did not strike at the root of the whole boss system. So I promptly vetoed the Hagemeister bill and took the severe lashing of the same newspapers which had all along been fighting the direct primary.

My attitude in this case, and in several other similar matters, has given me the reputation of being radical and extreme. And if this is radicalism then indeed I am a radical; but I call it common sense. It is simply the clear comprehension of the principle involved, and the clear conception of the utter destruction of that principle if only a part of it is applied. I have always believed that anything that was worth fighting for involved a principle, and I insist on *going far enough to establish that principle* and to give it a fair trial. I believe in going forward a step at a time, but it must be a *full step*. When I went into the primary fight, and afterward into the railroad fight—and it has been my settled policy ever since—I marked off a certain area in which I would not compromise, within which compromise would have done more harm to progress than waiting and fighting would have done.

The Socialists, for example, assert that the regulation of railroads, for which I have always stood firmly, will not work—that it is a compromise, and that we cannot escape governmental ownership. But I say that regulation is in itself a complete step, involving a definite and clear policy or principle. I *think* it will work, and I know it *ought to be thoroughly tested*. If it proves the correct solution of the problem, we have no farther to go; if it does not, we can take the next full step with confidence that we have behind us that great body of the people who can only be convinced by events. Difficulties leading to social explosions are caused not by too lengthy or hasty strides of progress but by holding back and preventing the people from taking the *next full step forward* when they are ready for it.

So I vetoed the Hagemeister bill, and decided to go again before the people with the whole issue. I knew the people of Wisconsin thoroughly. I knew from close contact with them what they were thinking, what they believed. I knew also that I was advocating a sound principle which no amount of abuse or misrepresentation could finally defeat. I felt sure they would support me— as indeed they did when the time came, and most loyally.

After the direct primary matter was disposed of, the railroad taxation bills took foremost place in the legislature. By this time the lobbyists had reached a good many of our men and we began to fear that we could not even control the assembly. They held back the taxation bills and were evidently trying to smother them. I waited patiently and hopefully for the legislature to act. Weeks went by. Hearings were strung out. It was perfectly plain that it was their plan to beat the bills by delay. Every hour, in the meantime, the corroding influence of the lobby was at work. Business connections, social diversions, the poker room, entertainments of every kind, decent and otherwise, were employed, and all I could do, as I sat there day by day watching the precious time go by, was to communicate with the legislature in one of two ways—by message, or by personal appeal to the members to redeem the promises that we had made to the people as a basis for our election. The one way was provided for in the constitution, the other was not. But I could not be stopped from making appeals to those members; I could not. It was very well known that I was the only man in the capitol who could crowd that legislature to do its duty. That is why they attacked me chiefly. As the editor of the *Sentinel* said to me: "If only you will take your hands off, we can take care of the legislature." They argued thus to me: "You have sent in a strong message, you have made good so far as you are concerned, and the people will understand. Now quit, quit, and you can have anything you want."

But I could not see the corruption going on all around me, I could not see honest measures promised to the people beaten by wholesale bribery without doing the utmost I could to prevent it.

About that time the legislature passed and sent up to me a bill taxing the dogs owned in the state. The humorous absurdity of such a measure at once struck me—the attempt to raise a few hundred dollars in taxes upon dogs owned by a class of people already overburdened with taxes, while the corporations of the state were paying hundreds of thousands of dollars less than their just share! I therefore made it the occasion of a message to the legislature in which I vetoed the dog tax bill and in the course of which I endeavored to outline the true principles of taxation. I also held up to view, as I had done in my veto of the Hagemeister bill, the exact conditions in the senate, showing how the lobby had corrupted the representatives of the people. Both of these messages struck home and stung, as I intended they should, and both attracted so much attention throughout the state that the legislature was forced to a consideration of the bills. After a brief fight, however, both of the railroad taxation bills were defeated.

Thus the session of 1901 closed without our having accomplished any of the important things that we had set out to do. More than this, it had enabled the lobby and the bosses, now more strongly organized than ever, to win over some of our leaders. They even secured a manifesto signed by more than half of the Republican members of both branches of the legislature criticising me sharply for what they claimed to be my encroachment upon the constitutional rights of the legislative branch of the state government, and organized themselves into a league to fight the Progressive movement.

I freely admit that as governor I used all the power and prestige of the office to secure the legislation that had been promised to the people. I arraigned the legislature as derelict of duty. No normal condition would warrant any executive, state or federal, in calling the legislative department so sharply to account as I did in the veto of the Hagemeister bill and in the veto of the dog tax bill, but in this case the situation was not normal; after a series of campaigns the Republican party, the party in control of the government of Wisconsin, had pledged in the platform of 1898 a reform of the nominating system, and of the unequal and unjust tax laws, and the legislature elected on that platform had defeated the will of the people and denied them the legislation for which a majority of them had declared.

Again in 1900 the same pledges had been made. The people in the election had by more than one hundred thousand majority voted that such legislation be enacted, and again the legislature had defied the will of the electorate. It was plainly the end of representative government in Wisconsin. It was the rule of a minority through trickery, bribery and corruption. It was a state of revolt. The situation called for extraordinary, aggressive and strong action on the part not only of the executive but of every man who cared to see democracy maintained. The abuse of power was not on the part of the executive. It was on the part of the legislature. The legislators were the ones who were abusing their power. The executive was obeying the mandate of the people.

I understood perfectly well not only that the position which I was taking would raise an issue with the legislature, but that it would be made the basis of a bitter attack upon me. But I was content to go to the people with my messages, and place my record side by side with the record of the legislature, and let it be fully discussed and talked out with plenty of time for the people to consider whether I had taken a course menacing to a republican form of government, or whether this legislature was undermining and destroying every semblance of representative government. So, when this manifesto was promulgated, I accepted the issue. I caused many thousands of copies of the messages which were criticised to be printed and sent broadcast over the state.

If this had been all, therefore, I might have looked upon the situation more hopefully. But the strain under which I had worked for six months, the high pressure, the long hours, the anxiety—I suppose I worked more than eighteen hours a day steadily—had so impaired my health that as soon as the legislature adjourned, I broke down completely, and for practically a year afterward I was ill, part of the time dangerously. This also was made the occasion for unremitting attack. They published stories that I was losing my mind, that I had softening of the brain—anything to discredit me with the people of the state. But there was never a moment that I was not determined that if I lived I would fight it out with them again.

Chapter VII

How We Passed
the Railroad Taxation Laws

At the opening of the legislature of 1903, I felt that the time had arrived to advance vigorously with the railroad regulation issue. There were good reasons for doing this. We had the support of the public. We had discussed the subject pretty thoroughly in the preceding campaign, so that the people were prepared to back us up strongly in our plans. It had been a difficult campaign, but it was indeed illuminating. And that was fortunate, for it was tremendously important at that particular time to have the issue clearly understood and the voters united upon it. As I have already related, the Progressives had suffered defeat in the legislature of 1901. All the important measures they had urged at that session failed of passage. Besides that, I was seriously broken in health for many months. Even a year later, when it became necessary for me to make a campaign for renomination as governor, I was so ill that I could not make a single speech. The old machine seized upon this situation to conduct a campaign of unexampled vigor. Organized in what was called the Eleventh Story League, because they occupied the entire eleventh story of a Milwaukee office building, they spent money without stint. They canvassed the entire state, they purchased the editorial opinions of upward of two hundred Republican newspapers, they issued many pamphlets attacking our movement, their speakers were untiring. But in spite of the furious campaign made against me, I was renominated. This result was brought about chiefly, I think, by the publication of a "Voter's Handbook" of one hundred and forty-four pages in which we set forth the truth about our work, about our plans for railroad taxation and direct primaries, and told specifically by what corrupt methods the Progressives had been defeated in the legislature of 1901. We printed 125,000 copies of this book and placed it in the hands of influential men in every part of the state.

I had not yet regained my strength when I began my speaking campaign in Milwaukee, September 30, 1902, but I improved steadily and spoke every day to the end of the campaign.

Mayor Rose of Milwaukee, the Democrat who ran against me, had the support of the Republican machine; nevertheless I was easily reelected by some 50,000 plurality.

In the course of our campaign we had not only advocated our railroad taxation bills but we had also endeavored to show the people conclusively how futile it was to stop short with laws increasing railroad taxes when the railroads could easily turn around and take back every cent of that increase by raising their rates. But the chief reason for advancing strongly with this issue was a tactical one. I hoped to make such a hot fight for regulation that before the session was over the railroad lobby would be most happy to let our taxation bills go through, if thereby they could prevent the enactment of a law creating a commission to regulate them.

When the legislature of 1903 met we were overjoyed to find that the Progressives were strong enough to organize both houses, though our majority in the senate was very slight. Irvine L. Lenroot, now a member of Congress from Wisconsin, was elected Speaker of the Assembly. Although Lenroot, who is of Swedish parentage, born in Wisconsin, was only thirty years old, and had served but one term previously in the legislature, he made an enviable record. A ready debater, with a special gift as a lawmaker, he forged rapidly ahead to leadership in the legislature, and impressed his strong personality upon the most important statutes of Wisconsin enacted from 1901 to 1905. He is now winning added distinction as a constructive legislator in the House of Representatives.

For years the railroads had been under serious attack in political campaigns. A. R. Hall had long been diligently hammering away on the subject, and had produced a general impression that conditions were wrong, without any concrete proof of his contentions. Hence it had been possible for the railroads by the production of a few made-to-order statistics to confuse and unsettle the public mind.

I aimed, therefore, in my message, not to make a general attack upon the railroads, but rather to set forth the exact conditions regarding railroad rates and services. I presented fifteen different statistical tables, carefully prepared, demonstrating the excessive transportation charges imposed by the railroads upon the people of the state. I compared our railroad-made rates with the state-made rates of the neighboring commonwealths of Illinois and Iowa, applying the comparisons to 151 well-known railroad towns in Wisconsin, Illinois and Iowa, the names of which I gave, together with the specific rates. I showed that these 151 towns were paying on an average 39.9 per cent. more for their transportation charges than towns located at similar distances from markets in Illinois and Iowa. In this way I got down to the vitals of the subject and laid it all before the people so clearly that no one could get away from it. It went straight home to every farmer and shipper in the state. Here was a farmer making shipments, for example, from Baraboo to Milwaukee. I showed that he was paying 59.77 per cent. more freight upon certain products than the farmer of Iowa paid for shipping the same products exactly the same distance to market.

Abusing an individual, calling him a hare-brained theorist, a visionary, a demagogue, an unsafe radical, would not answer these tables and the deductions which I made from them. It was for this reason that the message made such a strong impression throughout the state. However bitterly a newspaper might oppose me, yet my proof of the discrimination in freight rates against the very locality in which it was published simply could not be answered or disregarded.

Immediately the railroads sent their leading lawyers to Madison to meet my charges. One of them published a brief in which he took up table by table the figures I had presented and tried to make some explanation or defense. But he could not budge them; they were unanswerable. Nor could my message be assailed as intemperate; it was as dispassionate as a census report.

One of their statements gave me a further opening. It was charged that in making my comparisons I had unfairly selected stations where exceptional conditions existed, and that I had done this to prove my case, the implication being that elsewhere in the state the rates were not discriminatory.

I decided, therefore, to get out a special message that should once and for all set the whole matter at rest. With the help of Halford Erickson, chief of our bureau of statistics, whom I later appointed a member of the railroad commission, and a corps of clerks, we listed every station on the Northwestern and the St. Paul railroads, the two principal roads of the state, and secured the rates for shipping every sort of merchandise and commodity between those stations and the markets. Then we got corresponding rates and distances in Iowa and Illinois and printed them, with the names of the stations, side by side with those of Wisconsin.

Having in hand this voluminous material, I worked night after night at the executive residence until I wrote a message of 178 printed pages, to which was added many supporting supplementary tables. I sent in this message to the legislature on April 28, 1903, and it furnished a final and unanswerable demonstration that we were paying from 20 per cent. to 69 per cent. higher freight rates in Wisconsin than they were paying for exactly the same service in Iowa or Illinois. I presented it on the day before the hearings on the bill were to open, for I was certain that on that day there would be assembled in Madison, at the behest of the railroads, all the big shippers of Wisconsin. And they actually came by the carload, filled all the hotels, thronged the capitol and surrounded the members of the legislature. They argued, protested, threatened, but they could not controvert my facts.

On the receipt of the message the railroad lobby engineered a plan to break the effect of it by organizing an indignation movement among these big shippers. The meeting, which was held in the state senate, was a cut-and-dried affair at which resolutions were adopted denouncing my message, particularly and especially denying the statements in it that some of the shippers who appeared to oppose the legislation were in receipt of special favors or rebates from the railroads. The greatest excitement prevailed in and about the capitol and all over the state. In fact, I was content to bide my time regarding the action of the shippers. I could not at that moment produce the legal evidence that they were receiving rebates, but I was absolutely sure it existed, and I shall tell later how we secured it.

I knew also that the statement in my message that some of these shippers had been coerced by the railroad companies into appearing before the legislature was perfectly true. I had received calls from some of the smaller manufacturers and merchants who told me confidentially that they were there ostensibly to fight the legislation, but wanted me to know, privately, that they were in favor of it, that they were afraid if they did not come when they were summoned by the railroads they would be punished by increases in their rates, delays in furnishing cars, and in many other ways.

The regulation bill did not pass at that session, nor did we expect it to pass. But the contest accomplished the purposes we had chiefly in mind. It stirred the people of the state as they had never been stirred before, and laid the foundations for an irresistible campaign in 1904. It also gave the lobby so much to do—as we had anticipated—that it could not spend any time in resisting our measures for railroad taxation. It also forced some members of the legislature who were really opposed to us, and who intended to vote against the regulation bill, to vote with us on the taxation bill as a bid for the favor of the people of their districts.

So, at last, after all these years of struggle, we wrote our railroad tax legislation into the statutes of Wisconsin. As an immediate result, railroad taxes were increased more than $600,000 annually. When I came into the governor's office, on January 1, 1901, the state was in debt $330,000 and had only $4,125 in the general fund. But so great were the receipts from our new corporation taxes, and from certain other sources, that in four years' time, on January 1, 1905, we had paid off all our indebtedness and had in the general fund of the treasury $407,506. We had so much on hand, indeed, that we found it unnecessary to raise any taxes for the succeeding two years.

Indeed, we so reorganized and equalized our whole system of taxation that the state to-day is on a sounder, more businesslike foundation than ever before. We brought in so much property hitherto not taxed or unequally taxed that, while the expenses of the state have greatly increased, still the burden of taxation on the people has actually decreased. While corporations in 1900 paid taxes of $2,059,139 a year, in 1910 they paid $4,221,504 a year, or more than double. Wisconsin to-day leads all the states of the union in the proportion of its taxes collected from corporations. It derives 70 per cent. of its total state taxes from that source, while the next nearest state, Ohio, derives 52 per cent.

In 1903 we passed an inheritance tax law which yielded us $26,403 in the following year and has increased steadily since.

In 1905 I recommended a graduated income tax which has since been adopted by the state. It is the most comprehensive income tax system yet adopted in this country. Those who receive incomes of over $500 must make a return to the tax assessor. The tax at 1 per cent. begins on incomes above $800 in the case of unmarried people and above $1,200 in the case of married persons, increasing one half of 1 per cent. or thereabout for each additional $1,000, until $12,000 is reached, when the tax becomes 5.5 per cent. On incomes above $12,000 a year the tax is 6 per cent.

All of these new sources of income have enabled us to increase greatly the service of the state to the people without noticeably increasing the burden upon the people. Especially have we built up our educational system. In 1900 the state was expending $550,000 a year on its university; in 1910 it appropriated over $1,700,000, and there has been a similar increase for our normal and graded schools and charitable institutions. Under the constitution the state debt is limited to $100,000, so that we must practically pay as we go. Recently we have been building a state capitol to cost $6,000,000, at the rate of $700,000 to $1,000,000 a year from current funds.

After the railroad taxation bills were out of the way in the legislature of 1903 a law was passed, upon my recommendation, providing for the appointment of a corps of expert accountants to investigate the books of the railroad companies doing business in Wisconsin with a view to ascertaining whether they were honestly and fully reporting their gross earnings upon Wisconsin business. The railroads had always been left practically free to assess themselves; that is, they transmitted annually to the state treasurer the reports of gross earnings on which they paid a license fee of 4 per cent. in lieu of all taxes, and no one connected with the state knew whether these reports were accurate or not. I was confident, also, and so stated, that such an examination of the companies' books would finally settle the facts as to whether the railroads of Wisconsin were or were not paying rebates to the big shippers. And, as I have said, I wanted the legal evidence. As no one could make an argument against such an investigation, we got the law.

Expert accountants were immediately employed and presented themselves at the main offices of the railroads in Chicago. The railroad officials did not exactly refuse them admittance, but asked them to come again. In this way they succeeded in securing some weeks of delay; for what purpose or for what preparation we were never able to learn. But in course of time the Wisconsin accountants were admitted to their offices, and made a thorough investigation, resulting in the discovery that rebates had been given to the amount of something like $1,100,000 during the preceding period of six years. In short, we found that in reporting gross earnings the railroads had left out all account of these secret rebates and we therefore demanded the payment of taxes upon them. The railroads carried the cases to the supreme court, but the state was finally victorious and we recovered over $400,000 in back taxes from the railroads in this one case.

The investigation also showed clearly that many of the big manufacturers and shippers of Wisconsin had long been receiving very large sums in rebates in violation of the Interstate Commerce act. I recall that one firm received as much as $40,000 in rebates in one year, and this firm had been particularly active among the lobbyists. Another firm received $60,000 a year; others, various sums, large and small. The violence, indeed, of the opposition on the part of the shippers and the fury of their denunciation of the governor for intimating that rebating was practised in Wisconsin could be pretty well gauged by the amounts they were proven to have received.

We had now passed one of the two great measures so long struggled for—the railroad taxation bill. The other, that providing for direct primaries, seemed almost within reach.

I prepared that part of my message which dealt with direct nominations of candidates for office as though on trial for my life. I felt that the legislature simply *must* be made to see its duty and that we *must* pass the direct primary at that session. I feared that if it failed again, after six years of agitation, we might begin to lose ground with the public. There comes a time when public interest cannot be sustained in further discussion of a subject no matter how important. The people will give an administration their support two or three times and then they begin to expect results.

The primary bill as introduced easily passed the assembly, and after a long and hard fight we finally got it through the senate by accepting a provision submitting the act on a referendum to the voters of the state in the election of 1904. The machine senators let it go through with this provision because, first, it left the caucus and convention system in force for nearly two years longer. They felt that they would thus have another chance to secure our defeat and get control of the state. It also gave them a chance to defeat the measure, if they could, at the polls. They believed, I am confident, that the people themselves would fail to adopt it; they still thought that it had back of it only "agitators" and "demagogues." It was necessarily a lengthy measure, with some forty or more sections, and they figured that to present the details of a complex bill was a task too great for us in a campaign involving other important issues. Under the referendum as now adopted in many states publication of such measures is provided for at public expense, months in advance of the election, and there is wide distribution of literature on the subject. But there was no such provision in Wisconsin at that time and they relied on the difficulties and expense we would have in reaching all the voters, and on their own ability to checkmate us.

But, as usual, the bosses were mistaken in their estimate of the intelligence of the people. When the time came the Democratic party as well as the Republican party declared for it, and although a desperate fight was made upon the measure at the polls, nevertheless it carried in the election of 1904 by a majority of over 50,000.

Except for one omission I think it is the most perfect law for the nomination of candidates by direct vote ever enacted. It failed to make provision for the second choice, which permits voters to indicate on the ballot not only their first choice of candidates for each office, but a second choice as well, thereby positively assuring a nomination by the group of the party which is actually in the vast majority.

We struggled for a second choice amendment to our Wisconsin primary law for nearly seven years, and finally obtained it in the session of the legislature of last year (1911). I can trace most of the political misfortunes we have in Wisconsin since the adoption of the primary law to this omission. The machine system of politics requires no second choice, because the boss determines who shall be candidates and prevents rivals from dividing up the machine vote. But it is an essential part of the Progressive belief that there shall be no boss system; no one to give and no one required to take orders; the field is open to everybody, and so there are always men to divide up the Progressive vote, while the machine vote is solid. Thus the machine can win out even when the Progressives are in the vast majority.

This happened in the primary election for United States Senator in Wisconsin in 1908. There were two Progressives in the field against Stephenson, both very strong men—McGovern, now governor, and State Senator Hatton—and they split the Progressive vote between them. Stephenson thus slipped in between and received a plurality of the votes.

It was this omission of the second choice provision, with the opening it gave for a man like Stephenson to spend a large sum of money to secure his nomination (his recorded expenditure was $107,000), that has furnished the chief cause of complaint against the Wisconsin primary system. People do not stop to think that under the old caucus and convention system the amounts spent in an election were often many times as great and no account was made of them. A second choice provision, such as we now have in Wisconsin, ought to be the law of every state which has a direct primary.

We needed one thing more in connection with the primary law, and that was a stringent Corrupt Practices Act to prevent the corrupt use of money in primaries and in elections. We tried hard to get such a law in 1903. We failed at that time, but Wisconsin now has an admirable measure which will make it impossible for any candidate to spend money as Mr. Stephenson did in 1908.

One other measure of great importance also came up strongly in the session of 1903. It grew directly out of our miserable experience with the lobby, and was designed to abolish these corrupt influences which had for decades controlled legislation in Wisconsin. We began fighting for such legislation as early as 1897, and I urged it in messages to three different legislatures, but it was not until 1905 that our anti-lobby law was finally enacted. The Wisconsin statute requires all lobbyists or representatives, employed and paid for their services, to register themselves in the office of the secretary of state, specifying the character of their employment, and by whom employed. The statute prohibits such lobby agents or counsel from having any private communication with members of the legislature upon any subject of legislation. The lobby is given the widest opportunity to present publicly to legislative committees, or to either branch of the legislature, any oral argument; or to present to legislative committees or to individual members of the legislature written or printed arguments in favor of or opposed to any proposed legislation; provided, however, that copies of such written or printed arguments shall be first filed in the office of the secretary of state. This law rests upon the principle that legislation is public business and that the public has a right to know what arguments are presented to members of the legislature to induce them to enact or defeat legislation, so that any citizen or body of citizens shall have opportunity, if they desire, to answer such arguments.

Since I came to the United States Senate I have steadfastly maintained the same position. Again and again I have protested against secret hearings before Congressional committees upon the public business. I have protested against the business of Congress being taken into a secret party caucus and there disposed of by party rule; I have asserted and maintained at all times my right as a public servant to discuss in open Senate, and everywhere publicly, all legislative proceedings, whether originating in the executive sessions of committees or behind closed doors of caucus conferences. When the Tariff bill on wool and woolens was in conference between the two houses last summer, I was determined as a member of that conference that its sessions should be held, if possible, with open doors. I waited upon Senator Bailey, a member of the committee, and told him that I proposed to announce that I should freely discuss on the floor of the Senate any action taken by the committee, and that if support could be had I should move to make the sessions of the committee open and public. Indeed, both Senator Bailey and myself had taken the same position when an attempt had previously been made to hold secret sessions of the Committee on Finance so that Secretary Knox might give in private his testimony on the Reciprocity bill. At that time I moved that a stenographer be present and that all questions and answers be taken down and made of record, and declared that I would not be bound by any action of the committee against making use of the testimony of Secretary Knox if I felt it to be my duty in discussing the Reciprocity bill on the floor of the Senate. I was assured by Senator Bailey that he was heartily in favor of that course. When, later, the committee on conference on the Tariff bill on wool and woolens met in the rooms of the Finance Committee, Senator Bailey moved that the sessions of the conference committee be held with open doors. Objection was made, but finally, on a roll call, Bailey's motion carried, the doors were opened, and the representatives of the newspapers were admitted. For the first time in the history of Congress a conference committee transacted its important business under the eye of the public, with reporters in attendance.

It is to be hoped that this precedent will be followed by all the regular committees and conference committees of Congress in dealing with every subject of legislation. The propriety of considering treaties and matters affecting foreign relations in executive session is conceded, although there are unquestionably cases where public interest would demand open sessions and full publicity even when treaties with foreign nations are under consideration. A case in point is the Honduran Treaty, now pending, in which it is proposed that this government shall become surety for and guarantee loans aggregating millions of dollars made to the Honduran Government by American capitalists.

Evil and corruption thrive best in the dark. Many, if not most, of the acts of legislative dishonesty which have made scandalous the proceedings of Congress and state legislatures could never have reached the first stage had they not been conceived and practically consummated in secret conferences, secret caucuses, secret sessions of committees, and then carried through the legislative body with little or no discussion. I hope to see the rules of the Senate and House of Representatives so changed as to require, in plain terms, every legislative committee to make and keep for public inspection a record of every act of the committee.

In a great body like the Congress of the United States nearly all legislation is controlled by committees. The sanction of a committee goes a long way. The life of a Congressman, a Senator, is a busy one; he is worked early and late, and in some measure he must depend for the details of legislation upon the committees appointed for the purpose of perfecting the legislation. And as the business of the country grows and the subjects of legislation multiply, so committee action upon bills becomes more and more important. We spend a vast sum of money to print a *Congressional Record* in order that the public may be made acquainted with the conduct of their business, and then we transact the important part of the business behind the locked doors of a committee room. The public believes that the *Congressional Record* tells the complete story, when it is in reality only the final chapter.

The whole tendency of democracy, indeed, is toward more openness, more publicity. In the early days of this government not only were the committee meetings secret, but during the first two or three administrations even the sessions of the Senate itself were held behind closed doors. Discussing this subject in the Senate in connection with the Lorimer case, I quoted these stirring words of Charles Sumner, delivered on the floor of the Senate over forty years ago:

"Something has been said about Senatorial caucuses. Now, I shall make no revelation, but I shall repeat what for ten years I have said in this Chamber as often as occasion allowed. A Senatorial caucus is simply a convenience. It is in no respect an obligation on anybody. To hold that it is, is infinitely absurd and unconstitutional. We are all under the obligation of an oath, as Senators, obliged to transact the public business under the Constitution of the United States. We have no right to desert this Chamber and go into a secret conclave, and there dispose of the public business. . . . The Senatorial caucus is secret; it is confidential, if you please; it has no reporters present; it is not in the light of day. Why, sir, to take the public business from this Chamber and carry it into such a caucus is a defiance of reason and of the best principles of government."

I came out of the legislative session of 1903 in good health, and spent that summer and fall chiefly upon the lyceum and chautauqua platforms.

The chautauqua is truly an educational force in the life of the country. It is organized widely among the towns and smaller cities in nearly all of the northern and western states. It is strongly supported by the well-to-do farmers. The people who patronize the chautauquas will not only listen to, but also they demand, the serious discussion of public questions. I called my address "Representative Government," but it was never the same. I spoke extemporaneously, and in connection with my addresses related my experience in Wisconsin. It was the struggle between democracy and privilege which I tried to place on view, and I illustrated it directly from the most recent events in my own state. In that way it always had a live, fresh interest. Whenever I spoke in Wisconsin I never accepted any payment, not even expenses, and elsewhere, if the address was free to the public, I would not accept pay. In this way I have made a thousand or more chautauqua and lyceum addresses, and have pretty well covered all the states of the union except New England and the Old South. I believe these addresses were the most practically effective work I have done, in a national way, for the Progressive movement, though it cannot well be separated from my work as a public official. For it is my work as a public official that has made my work on the platform count. If I had simply discussed principles and their relation to the proceedings of Congress and state legislatures in a theoretical way, I could not have given those addresses the living, vital interest which it was possible to give them where I had been a part of the official proceedings which I presented to my audiences.

Our Progressive cause in Wisconsin has always been supported by what is more technically called the labor vote. Many years ago, in Wisconsin, it was customary, shortly before election, for the bosses to distribute four or five thousand dollars among certain of the old-time labor leaders, who were expected thereafter to deliver the labor vote to the Republican ticket. I have heard it said many times back in those years: "Oh, never mind about the labor vote; Payne will take care of that."

When we began our fight on the bosses they resorted to their usual methods of influencing the labor leaders. The railroads and the big shippers also tried actively to vote their employees against me, but after we had begun to be successful, after the wage-earners had begun to see what our movement meant, we got more and more of their support. This was noticeable in the campaign of 1902. In our great crucial campaign of 1904, of which I shall speak in the next chapter, this effort to influence the labor vote reached its height. It was the final struggle. Congressman Babcock personally called upon large employers of labor and urged them either to prevent their men going to the caucuses to vote for La Follette or else to devise means of controlling the caucuses. In a number of cases railroad men were notified to be at the round-house or shop at a given time when the superintendent would arrive in a special car to address them. The talk was something like this: "It is to our interest and therefore to yours that this man La Follette be defeated for nomination. Your bread and butter depends on your standing by the railroads at the caucuses." And when the caucuses were held, division superintendents and other officials often stood at the entrances to the voting places and handed specially prepared ballots to the railroad employees as they came up to vote.

But in spite of all these efforts I always felt, in fact knew, that I had the sympathy of these employees. Several times in the campaign which followed this desperate attempt to control the caucuses have I had a conductor, as he was taking my ticket, lean down and whisper:

"It's all right, Governor; they had us where we were obliged to take orders in the caucus, but they can't watch us in the election. The Australian ballot will give us a chance."

And in many cases they would say nothing, but grip my hand hard.

I have always had respect for the man who labors with his hands. My own life began that way. Manual labor, industry, the doing of a good day's work, was the thing that gave a man standing and credit in the country neighborhood where I grew up. We all worked hard at home, and the best people I ever knew worked with their hands. I have always had a feeling of kinship for the fellow who carries the load—the man on the under side. I understand the man who works, and I think he has always understood me. In the campaign of 1904 I used, often, the verses of a poem of Whittier's called "The Poor Voter on Election Day:"

> The proudest now is but my peer,
> The highest not more high;
> To-day, of all the weary year,
> A king of men am I.
> To-day, alike are great and small,
> The nameless and the known;
> My palace is the people's hall,
> The ballot-box my throne!

In some cases where the labor vote was very heavy the employers allowed La Follette delegates to be elected and afterward gave them the alternative of losing their jobs or violating their political faith. In Eau Claire County we met with an example of this sort. We had there a very strong supporter who came to us and told us exactly his situation. He said he had been threatened with loss of his job if he voted for me in the convention, and while it would be a great hardship for him to lose his position he could not reconcile himself to obey their orders. We found that we could spare his vote and save his job, so he voted against us with our full understanding of the reason.

As soon as I became governor we began pressing for new labor legislation which should place Wisconsin on a level with the most progressive state or nation; and it can be truthfully said, since the passage last year of a law creating an Industrial Commission, that Wisconsin now easily leads the states of the union in its body of labor legislation. Child labor has been reduced and the children kept in the schools. Excessive hours for women workers have been abolished. The doctrine of comparative negligence has been adopted for railways, and the long hours of trainmen have been done away with. The most carefully drawn of all workmen's compensation laws has been adopted, and the employers of the state have organized, under a new insurance law, an employer's mutual insurance association, similar to those which in Germany have greatly reduced accidents and compensated the workmen. Many other laws have been added and old ones strengthened, and finally our new Industrial Commission, modeled after the Railroad Commission, has been placed in charge of all the labor laws, with *full power to enforce* the laws and protect the life, health, safety and welfare of employees. This commission has employed one of the leading experts of the United States to cooperate with employers in devising ways and means of safety and sanitation.

The commission consists of three members, appointed by Governor McGovern: Charles Crownhart, a very able lawyer and devoted to public service; Dr. John R. Commons, the great constructive economist and a leading authority on labor legislation, and Joseph D. Beck, who had served the state most efficiently as Commissioner of Labor and Industrial Statistics. The Industrial Commission is a new departure of the first importance—the first of its kind in the country. By this measure the state assumes to control and regulate the most difficult questions of sanitation, safety, health and moral well-being which affect the workers of the state. It is one of the most important innovations we have

133

made, one charged with the greatest possibilities for improving the lives of working men and women, and one which should be watched and studied by every one who is interested in forward movements.

In all of my campaigns in Wisconsin I had been much impressed with the fact that women were as keenly interested as men in the questions of railroad taxation, reasonable transportation charges, direct primaries, and indeed in the whole Progressive program. They comprehended its relation to home life and all domestic problems. They understood what it meant for the railroads to escape paying a million dollars of justly due taxes every year. They knew that the educational system of the state must be supported; that every dollar lost to the educational, charitable, and other institutions of the state through tax evasions by railroad and other corporations must be borne by added taxes upon the homes and farms. They understood that freight rates were a part of the purchase price of everything necessary to their daily lives; that when they bought food and fuel and clothing *they* paid the freight. As a result my political meetings were generally as largely attended by women as by men, and these questions were brought directly into the home for study and consideration. It has always been inherent with me to recognize this co-equal interest of women. My widowed mother was a woman of wise judgment; my sisters were my best friends and advisers; and in all the work of my public life my wife has been my constant companion.

Mrs. La Follette and I were classmates at the University of Wisconsin, and naturally we had common interests. The first year of our married life, in order to strengthen myself in the law, I was re-reading Kent and Blackstone at home evenings, and she joined me. This led later to her taking the law course as an intellectual pursuit. She never intended to practise. She was the first woman graduated from the Wisconsin University Law School.

On one occasion when my firm was overwhelmed with work at the circuit, and the time was about to expire within which our brief should be served in a supreme court case, it having been stipulated that the case should be submitted without argument, I proposed to Mrs. La Follette that she prepare the brief. It was a case which broke new ground, and her brief won with the Supreme Court.

About a year afterward Chief Justice Lyon, in the presence of a group of lawyers, complimented me on the brief which my firm had filed in that case, saying, "It is one of the best briefs submitted to the court in years, and in writing the opinion I quoted liberally from it because it was so admirably reasoned and so clearly stated." I said, "Mr. Chief Justice, you make me very proud. That brief was written by an unknown but very able member of our bar— altogether the brainiest member of my family. Mrs. La Follette wrote that brief, from start to finish."

Although Mrs. La Follette never made any further practical use of her law, this training brought her into closer sympathy and companionship with me in my professional work, and in my political career she has been my wisest and best counsellor. That this is no partial judgment, the Progressive leaders of Wisconsin who welcomed her to our conferences would bear witness. Her grasp of the great problems, sociological and economic, is unsurpassed by any of the strong men who have been associated with me in my work.

It has always seemed to me that women should play a larger part than they do in the greater housekeeping of the state. One of the factors in the improvement of conditions in Wisconsin has been the selection of able women for positions in the state service, particularly upon those boards having to do with the welfare of women.

In my first message to the legislature, after I became governor, I recommended the appointment of a woman as factory inspector, and also that women should serve on the Boards of University and Normal School Regents, and on the very important Board of Control, which has charge of all the charitable, penal and reformatory institutions of the state.

At first, even in our own camp, there was some opposition to the appointment of women in the state service—a survival of the old political belief that "the boys ought to have the places"—and especially the places that carried good salaries—but that feeling has disappeared before the evidences of the high character of the services which these women have rendered.

Mrs. La Follette and other interested women exercised a helpful influence in securing the legislation and in making the appointments.

Dr. Almah J. Frisby, a practising physician of Milwaukee, was made a member of the Board of University Regents. She was graduated from the university in 1878, and is a woman of exceptionally strong character and high ability. She remained on the Board until I appointed her to a place on the State Board of Control of Charitable and Penal Institutions, where she has since served with great usefulness.

To succeed Doctor Frisby on the Board of Regents I selected Kate Sabin Stevens, a sister of Ellen Sabin, President of Downer College, Milwaukee, and wife of Judge E. Ray Stevens. She was a graduate of the university, had been Superintendent of Schools of Dane County, and was especially qualified as a representative woman for the place.

As State Inspector of Factories, Miss Ida M. Jackson, now wife of Professor Charles T. Burgess of the University of Wisconsin, was chosen—a bright young woman, who through her newspaper experience had become interested in social questions, and was well prepared for the service.

Mrs. Theodora Youmans, of Waukesha, was placed on the Board of Normal School Regents, a position she has held continuously since. Mrs. Charles M. Morris, of Berlin, was appointed a member of the Wisconsin Free Library Commission. Mrs. Youmans and Mrs. Morris were two out of five members selected on the Board of World's Fair Commissioners. They are women of tact and broad understanding, and unusually fitted for public work, each having served as President of the State Federation of Women's Clubs, in which they have been, since its organization, recognized leaders.

I believe not only in using the peculiar executive abilities of women in the state service, but I cannot remember a time when I did not believe in woman suffrage. The great economic and industrial questions of to-day affect women as directly as they do men. And the interests of men and women are not antagonistic one to the other, but mutual and coordinate. Co-suffrage, like co-education, will react not to the special advantage of either men or women, but will result in a more enlightened, better balanced citizenship, and in a truer democracy. I am glad to say that the legislature of Wisconsin passed, at its last session, a suffrage law which will be submitted on referendum next November to the voters of the state. I shall support it and campaign for it.

Chapter VIII

Progressive Government Produces
Business Prosperity: What Was
Accomplished in Wisconsin

Reformers often stop fighting before the battle is really won: before the new territory is completely occupied. I felt that the campaign of 1904 was the very crux of our whole movement. We had passed our railroad taxation and direct primary measures in 1903; but the railroad taxation law would be a barren victory until it was supplemented by a commission to control railroad rates; and the direct nomination of candidates would fail unless we carried the election and secured the adoption of the primary bill at the referendum that fall. Without the direct primary law it would be an easy matter for the old machine to regain control of the legislature and not only prevent further progressive legislation, but undo part, if not all, of the work already accomplished.

I felt absolutely sure that another term, with another legislature, would securely ground and bulwark self-government in Wisconsin. I knew that the opposition understood this too, and that they would make the most desperate fight in that campaign that they had ever made. I began, therefore, delivering speeches both inside and outside the state as early as December, 1903—nearly a year before the election. As for the old machine, Congressman Joseph W. Babcock early came forward as commander-in-chief. He criticised the methods adopted by Phillipp, Pfister and others in the campaign of 1902 as being too open and noisy. He came right to Madison, rented some rooms and began what he called a "gumshoe campaign." Men were sent quietly about the state, arrangements were made for controlling the employees of the railroads and the big industries, and the federal office-holders were marshaled for duty.

Upon our part the campaign of 1904 was the most comprehensive of the whole series. We went straight to the people with the same facts—the same dry statistics—which we had used so effectively upon the legislature in 1903. We prepared ten different pamphlets and distributed over 1,600,000 separate pieces of mail. Some of these pamphlets contained comparative tables showing transportation rates upon all the principal products shipped to market from *every county seat in the state*. It placed side by side with these items the cost of shipping the same products an equal distance from stations in Illinois and Iowa. In that way it was brought home to every citizen in every county just what he was sacrificing in dollars and cents as the result of the negligence of his representatives in affording him the same protection which his neighbors in Iowa and Illinois had secured many years before. Even in those two states the railroads had controlled the commissions for a long period and the rates had not been lowered in many years, though the volume of traffic had enormously increased and railway profits had more than kept pace with the big tonnage. In this connection I want to credit the Bureau of Labor and Industrial Statistics, Mr. Erickson particularly, as its head, and his assistant, Walter Drew, with the aid rendered in constructing these rate sheets. It was Mr. Erickson's mastery of this subject which suggested to my mind his fitness as a member of the Wisconsin Railway Commission when it was later established and upon which he has served with distinction.

Two or three weeks before the close of the nominating campaign we were surprised by an entirely new tack taken by the old leaders. Word came that in many counties second sets of Republican delegates were being elected under such circumstances that it could have but one meaning—that the opposition was laying the foundation either for stealing the state convention or else bolting it and placing a third ticket in the field. They were desperate; they knew that it was their last chance to win the state under the old system, that the approaching convention would probably be the last ever held in the state for the nomination of candidates, as indeed it proved to be.

When the time arrived for the convention to meet, at Madison, they brought in a veritable army of men. All their leaders were there: Babcock, Pfister, Phillipp, Spooner and Quarles. We realized that we were facing a crisis; that all we had been struggling for in Wisconsin might be lost if we permitted these men by force or by confusion to cast doubt upon the action of the convention.

The convention was called to meet in the university gymnasium, the largest auditorium in Madison. We felt it necessary to protect the doorkeepers from being rushed and swept aside by a crowd of men not entitled to seats as delegates. So during the night before we had constructed at the delegates' entrance a barbed wire passage which would admit of the delegates entering only in single file. Stationed along the line of this fence we had twelve or fifteen of the old university football men—fine, clean, upright fellows who were physically able to meet any emergency. Among them were Arne Lerum, "Norsky" Larson, "Bill" Hazzard, and Fred Kull. The machine crowd formed in a body on the capitol square, a mile from the university, and marched down in large numbers, prepared to take possession of the convention hall. They had printed "fake" badges and delegates' tickets exactly duplicating those issued by the State Central Committee to all regularly elected delegates—theirs as well as ours. It was only by placing initials on the genuine badges and tickets at a late hour that our men stationed at the gymnasium entrance were able to distinguish the genuine from the spurious. When this army appeared at the gymnasium they discovered that provision had been made against a rush and that they had to enter in single file. Whenever a man presented a counterfeit credential he was promptly set outside of the wire fence. All these men, however, came in later with the spectators at the front entrance and found seats in that portion of the hall which had been separated by roping off from the portion occupied by delegates; and along that roping they found another sturdy lot of "Norsky" Larsons. So well was all this preliminary work arranged that the convention organized regularly and in the best of order.

The critical moment came when Mr. Rosenberry, a machine member of the State Central Committee, arose to make his minority report regarding the election contests. The state committee, which was composed partly of our men and partly of their men, had tried out all of these contests before the convention met and they had *unanimously* seated enough of our delegates to give Progressives a comfortable majority of the convention. After the meeting of the committee and before the convention was called to order the machine leaders evidently planned to repudiate the report of the state committee, to ignore the roll of delegates entitled to seats for the preliminary organization of the convention in accord with all precedent, and to seat their "delegates," which the committee had unanimously rejected, and thus get control of the convention —which they knew would probably result in a row.

As I say, Rosenberry came forward to make a speech. It had leaked out that the conclusion of his speech was to be the signal for action; that Rosenberry would then be on the platform, in a good position to seize the gavel, and take possession of the chair, with the fellows down on the floor all primed to have him declared elected chairman. They were simply going to gavel it through, no matter how much protest there might be. The convention was crowded, but we reserved three or four seats close to the front of the platform and near the speaker's chair, where we planted some more "Norsky" Larsons and "Bill" Hazzards. The result of all this precaution was that they dared make no move, and the convention went forward in the most orderly way. Not an unparliamentary thing was done. They voted upon the contests and even upon the nominations, and of course were beaten.

After the convention adjourned that day the machine men were so desperate that they immediately organized a bolt and called a convention at the Madison Opera House, which, we learned afterward, they had rented *weeks before* the caucuses and county conventions were held upon which they based their contests, no doubt with just this contingency in mind. Addresses were made by Spooner, Quarles, Babcock, and others, and they nominated a full state ticket of their own. It was the last stand!

They then proceeded to carry the validity of the regular convention into the supreme court, which supported us at every point, and left so little for the bolters to stand upon that the candidate for governor they had nominated at their convention withdrew his name from their ticket and much of their following deserted them. Indeed, their leaders soon began advising machine men everywhere to vote the Democratic ticket as the only way of beating me. In the election the bolters' candidate received only 12,000 votes.

One other bitter contest was to grow out of these conventions. It being a presidential year, we elected four delegates-at-large to the national convention—Senator Stout, Isaac Stephenson, W. D. Connor, and myself. The bolters' convention also elected four delegates, John C. Spooner, J. V. Quarles, J. W. Babcock, and Emil Baensch. We therefore made ready to meet the contest in the convention. Exhaustive briefs were prepared by Gilbert E. Roe and H. W. Chynoweth; but when we reached Chicago and the case came before the National Committee, they not only would not look at our briefs, but they paid no serious attention to the oral arguments. Of course with Payne of Wisconsin serving as chairman of the National Committee, and Spooner and Babcock strongly influential with the "federal crowd," there was small chance for us, no matter what our claims might be.

The hearing before the committee was a grotesque farce. Payne made a pretense of fairness by withdrawing as presiding officer and called United States Senator Scott of West Virginia to the chair. While the arguments were being made, the members of the committee strolled about the room or chatted with each other in their seats. The few who gave attention interrupted our counsel so constantly with questions manifestly designed to prevent them from submitting a succinct and intelligible statement of the case, that neither had an opportunity to finish his argument in the time allotted. As soon as that time had expired, without even looking at the documents which had been presented, including the printed briefs, the verified statement of the case, the printed case and the affidavits, the committee refused to permit us to be seated as delegates in the convention.

There still remained for us the privilege of submitting our case to the Committee on Credentials, appointed by the convention after it was organized. Such a committee is made up of one representative from each state. Spooner, Babcock, Payne and their associates on the National Committee and in the United States Senate and House of Representatives promptly set at work with the various delegations to secure *right men* from each delegation for the Committee on Credentials. I have been told since by men who were in that national convention that they were approached and urged to see to it that the committeeman on credentials from their delegation was warned that under no circumstances should this Wisconsin movement be allowed to spread; that La Follette was a dangerous man, and that unless he could be stopped right there, he would ultimately break up the Republican party in the nation as he had broken it up in Wisconsin. Under these circumstances we decided not to submit our case to the Committee on Credentials, but instead to file with the committee a statement setting forth the reasons for our decision. I drafted such a statement; the four of us signed it, filed it with the committee—and went back to Wisconsin to take up the campaign for the fall election.

In anticipation of the kind of campaign which I had determined to conduct that year I had secured the incorporation in the state platform of a declaration which read as follows:

"We believe that platform pledges are sacred obligations binding upon every member of the party; that the candidates of the party become its trusted agents to execute in good faith its promises to the voters; that the acceptance of any candidate of any office to the duties of which platform promises may relate imposes upon the candidate the obligation to the party and to the voter to aid in redeeming every pledge in letter and spirit; that to receive the vote of the citizen as the candidate of the party which has promised the legislation and then to oppose such legislation, or to connive at its defeat, is a fraud upon the voter and deprives him of his right of suffrage as effectually as though he were disfranchised by law.

"That the platform pledges of both parties have been openly and flagrantly violated in Wisconsin must be regarded as the political history of the last six years. Legislation promised by the accredited delegates of the Republican party has been defeated session after session by the members of the party chosen from its ranks to represent it in the legislature. Sometimes these men have secured the votes of constituents by silent acquiescence in the promises of the platform; sometimes by open declarations to support the legislation pledged by the party; in either case, as trustees of the honor of the party and the rights of the voter and taxpayer, they are guilty of having betrayed their trust. No party can retain and no party deserves to retain the confidence and support of the citizen if it knowingly entraps him to vote for candidates who repudiate its pledged obligation. The regular party organization can therefore regard as the candidates of the Republican party for state and legislative offices only such men as are pledged to its support, and whose record and good faith are above question. . . ."

I took that as authoritative support for the plea that only such men should be regarded as Republicans as pledged themselves to support the principles and declarations of the platform and whose record assured fulfilment of the pledge. And in my speech of acceptance I emphasized that.

In all my campaigning, covering a period of twenty years, it had been a rigid rule with me never to engage in personal controversy. I assailed abuses, attacked bad practices with all the power I could command, and though the newspaper files of that day will record the fact that I was subjected to every form of abuse and misrepresentation, I had not been diverted from my course. I saw clearly that if I gave heed to personal attack and retaliated in kind that the principles would be lost sight of and the contest degenerate into one of mere abuse and recrimination. But after my legislative experiences of 1901 I had seen many men returned to the legislature of 1903 who had made conspicuously bad records and yet were able so to confuse the issues that they could and did secure their reelection. It was plain to me that the people needed to be educated on men as well as measures. I therefore formulated my plan so to conduct the discussion with respect to men that it would be impersonal in its character and would go directly to the record of the representative and deal with concrete facts. It seemed to me logical and unanswerable that the people were entitled to know exactly how they were represented, and that no man had a right to complain if his constituents were fully informed as to his record on every bill of public interest.

I am free to confess that it had been my great ambition to be governor of Wisconsin, not just to be governor (for that seemed to me in itself but an empty honor), but to be in reality the chief executive of the state; to be a strong factor in securing legislation that should build into the life of the people a new order of things —laws that should be a recognition of human rights, that should make safe the vital principles of representative government. To aid in achieving such results was the realization of my highest ambition. I had gone through two sessions of the legislature, through three hard campaigns prior to that time; I had given to the work some of the best years of my life, and here I was at the end of my second term as governor with almost nothing of a lasting nature accomplished. I was determined, therefore, to make this a campaign that should result in the election of a legislature that would finally execute the will of the people. It was an unheard of thing for the governor of the state to "interfere" in the nomination of candidates for the legislature; but I knew perfectly well that those members of the legislature who had served the political machine instead of their constituents would, many of them, seek renomination and reelection to the legislature, when they would again repudiate their party pledges. And so, with the calling of the caucuses, I went out into senate and assembly districts, announced public meetings and executed the new policy upon which I had resolved. I did not engage in personalities; I did not attack individuals as such, but I took the journals of the two houses of the legislature on to the public platform, and presented fairly and clearly the character of the different measures of public importance, and then read from the journal the record vote of the candidate seeking reelection upon those measures. I selected districts in which those men who had wronged the public were seeking renomination, and almost without exception in those districts where I held meetings I secured the defeat of the candidates who sought renomination.

It was not possible for one man to cover, during the caucus period, all of the seventy-two counties of the state, but I did as well as I could; and in those senatorial and assembly districts which I was unable to reach and in which Republican candidates secured renomination whose records would have defeated them if they had been properly placed before their constituents, I now resolved to make the contest against them at the election, although they were nominally members of my own party. Wherever I found a Democratic nominee for the assembly or senate whose standing was such as to warrant confidence in his pledges, and who was willing to come into my meetings and give assurance of his support of the measures for the public good embodied in the Republican platform, I besought the voters of such legislative districts to support him and defeat the Republican nominee who had betrayed them in the preceding legislatures. I utterly ignored the campaign for my own election. In nearly one half of the counties of the state I never held a single meeting in that campaign. But I picked out those legislative districts that were the battleground for the accomplishment of legislation and I campaigned those as they had never been campaigned before. I spoke forty-eight days in succession, never missing one single day, excepting Sundays. I averaged eight and one quarter hours a day on the platform. We had two automobiles, so that if one broke down or got out of order in any way I could transfer to the other. I began speaking about nine o'clock in the morning. I would go into a county and speak at every little hamlet or crossroads, talking to small groups of men during the day, often from the automobile, and sometimes in a store. Then we would have a meeting in the evening, probably at the county seat, where I always had a large audience, finishing my work about eleven o'clock at night. Some of those night meetings were enormous; when I closed the campaign at Milwaukee I spoke to about 10,000 people for four hours.

I took only one meal a day at the table during those forty-eight days. My noon luncheon consisted of a bottle of good rich milk and two slices of the crust of bread buttered, and sometimes a little well-cured cheese shaved off and put in between. For my supper I duplicated my luncheon. I got the bread and milk at the farmhouses along the road, and ate it on the way. It was a real whirlwind campaign, and I came out of it weighing only two pounds less than when I went in. The opposition tried for a time to follow me and catch my crowds, but they were soon worn out, and their reception, just after I had furnished my audiences with the ammunition for asking concrete questions, was discouraging, so that they soon desisted.

I discussed chiefly freight rates. I would tell them how much it cost them to ship a carload of hogs from that town to Chicago, and how much it would cost an Iowa farmer to ship a carload of hogs from his town the same distance to market. And then I would tell them that we were trying to create in Wisconsin a railroad commission to which appeal could be made, instead of to a railroad official, for fair freight rates and adequate service. Then I would take the record of the last legislature on that question. I would say: "Now, I think you are entitled to know how your representative voted on this question. I am going to make no personal attack upon any individual, but he is your servant, and the servant of all the people of this state. His vote counts not only against your interests, but against the interests of the district in which I live as well, and I am here to-day to lay before you his record, and let you then decide whether that is the sort of service you want. There is no politics in this thing; it does not matter whether you get this legislation upon the vote of a Republican or a Democrat." Then I would tell them that I had interviewed the candidate on the Democratic side, and found him to be a man of integrity, that I had received from him assurance that he would support the important legislation pledged in the Republican platform, and submitted to them whether the promise of this man was not better than the performance of the man who had betrayed them in the preceding session.

And I cleaned up the legislature. That was the origin of the "roll call" which I have since used with such effectiveness. It is simply a form of publicity, of letting the light in on dark records. I have developed a department called "The Roll Call" in *La Follette's Magazine* which has presented accurately the records of many Senators and Congressmen, and has been instrumental, I am positive, in putting more than one bad Congressman and Senator out of business. In my chautauqua work also I have found the roll call a most potent instrument for political regeneration.

I was elected by about 50,000, and the direct primary law, for which we had campaigned vigorously, carried by about the same majority. We also elected a safe majority of both houses of the legislature.

Now, it is never safe to be satisfied with victory at an election. The real test comes later, when the bills incorporating new principles are written. It is one thing to talk of general propositions on the stump: it is quite another thing to perform the careful, cautious, thoughtful task of reducing those propositions into closely worded legal provisions which will afterward serve the public interest and stand the scrutiny of the courts. The trouble comes when the powerful opposition appears to cease, when the skilful corporation lawyer comes to you and says:

"You shall have no further opposition. All we ask is that the measure be fair and reasonable. We have had large practical experience, and we can make a few suggestions really for the good of the legislation."

He then presents changes which seem very plausible, but in which may lurk the weaknesses and uncertainties that will afterward lead the court to break down the statute by construction. It is then that sincere friends of reform may be misled, because they have not the expert knowledge to meet the situation. At the outset of the legislature of 1905, therefore, we took the greatest pains in drawing our railroad bill. We got together leading members of the legislature and discussed the first draft exhaustively: Senators Hatton, Sanborn, Martin, Frear, Morris, and Assemblymen Lenroot, Braddock, Ekern, Dahl and others. Senator Hatton was especially helpful not only in framing the bill but in managing it in committee. Then I had copies of the bill retyped, with wide margins, and sent them to disinterested experts throughout the country—men like Commissioner Prouty, ex-Governor Larrabee of Iowa, Judge Reagan and Judge Cowan of Texas, A. B. Stickney, President of the Great Western Railroad, and many others. We took all the notes and criticisms of these men and went over our bill again before it was finally introduced.

It was a very strong regulatory bill. It provided for a commission with power not only to fix rates but to control service and to make a complete physical valuation of all the railroad property in the state. It was more sweeping than any legislation enacted by any state up to that time; and there is still, I believe, no law which compares with it—and none, certainly, more successfully enforced both to the advantage of the railroads and to that of the people—as I shall show later.

Of course, the railroad representatives opposed the bill at every step. The hearings continued for many weeks, and the strain was at times serious.

While we were in the stress of the fight I was called one evening from the dinner table to answer the telephone. Some one said:

"Hello, Governor! how are you getting on with your legislation?"

I answered instantly, for I recognized his voice: "Colonel Bryan, where are you?"

He told me that he was to speak in Milwaukee that night, and the next day at Oshkosh. I said:

"Colonel, come this way. Some of the best provisions of our railroad bill are in danger. Come this way and help us."

He was in doubt about being able to do so without interfering with his engagement at Oshkosh, but the next morning a telegram from him was delivered to me at the breakfast table. It said, "I am just taking the train for Madison; will arrive at 10:45."

I went down to the capitol early and called into the executive office several leading members of the legislature, both Republicans and Democrats. I informed them Colonel Bryan would be in Madison that day a couple of hours between trains, and suggested that the legislature adopt a resolution inviting him to address them in joint session at about eleven o'clock. This suggestion met with the favor of the men whom I had called in, and they secured the passage of the resolution.

I met Colonel Bryan at the train. He was in fine spirits, keenly alive to the situation and deeply interested in a non-partisan way in our achieving the very best results we could in that important session. The galleries of the assembly chamber were crowded with citizens, and all the members of the legislature were present on the floor. I presented Colonel Bryan, and he made one of the finest speeches I ever listened to. He was witty and eloquent; he appealed to the patriotism of the legislature without regard to party, especially urging the Democratic members to support our measure. He said he was not afraid of Republicans stealing Democratic thunder; that he would be willing to leave all the good Democratic propositions that had ever been advanced out on the porch over night if only the Republicans would steal them and enact them into law.

I had Bryan's speech taken down by a stenographer and circulated it widely in Democratic districts, thus starting a back fire on the Democratic legislators who were doubtful. The result justified the effort. It aided us materially, and when the bill came up for the final vote it was passed unanimously.

I have always felt grateful to Colonel Bryan for this broadminded and patriotic action. It showed that his interest in principles was truly uppermost. I first met Bryan near the close of the last session of the 49th Congress. I had been defeated and was going out; he had just been elected and was coming in. He was then a tall, slender, handsome fellow who looked like a young divine. Since then I have met him very often, and have come to feel a strong personal attachment for him. He helped us often during our long fight in Wisconsin when the Democratic machine as well as the Republican machine was opposing the things we stood for. He helped us in *The Commoner* with his support of our campaign for direct primaries. I have brought audiences to their feet by quoting Bryan or by reading from *The Commoner* his words approving our measures.

In the campaign of 1902 efforts were made to get him to come into Wisconsin to speak in behalf of the Democratic ticket. I knew that he did not come. I did not know why until the next summer, when I went to Lincoln, Nebraska, to speak at the Epworth League State Assembly. I was resting in my room in the afternoon when there came a knock at my door and Bryan entered. I had not seen him for years. During our conversation he told me that he could not hear me speak that evening as he wanted to, because he had a convention on his hands. "But," he said, "I am tremendously interested in what you are doing in Wisconsin and I want to see you succeed. It is more important in its example to the country than any triumph of the Democratic party in that state. I want to see you get a state primary. I want to see you carry out your taxation propositions. I want to see you win out in your contest with the corporations." And he went on, "I have been supporting your cause in *The Commoner,* and as long as you are advocating the things you are now advocating, I shall continue to support you. In the last campaign the Democrats tried very hard to get me to come into the state to speak, but I would not do it because I did not want to aid in solidifying the Democratic party against your work there. I wanted you to have all the Democratic support you could get to take the place of the corporation Republicans who were attacking you."

There was a strong minority in the Democratic party, all through our contests, which favored direct primaries, railroad and other corporate taxation, the regulation of railway rates and services, and practically every reform measure incorporated in the Republican state platform. And though this element of the party was not strong enough under the caucus and convention system to control their state conventions and frame the platforms, they were independent and patriotic enough to use their influence and their votes in favor of the principles in which they believed. Many thousands of Democrats in Wisconsin voted for Republican members of the legislature known to stand for the enactment of these principles into law, and gave me active support in my campaigns and election.

I have met Bryan often in recent years. We have talked from the same platforms and been in the same lyceum and chautauqua courses season after season. I consider him a great moral teacher and believe that he has exerted a powerful influence for good upon the political thought and standards of his time.

As soon as the legislature passed our regulation law I appointed the three commissioners. I had contended all along for an appointive rather than an elective commission. I felt that the state should have the best experts in the country in these positions, whether residents of Wisconsin or not, for much would depend upon the way in which our new law was administered. They would have to match wits with the highly skilled, highly paid agents of the railroads, and they would have to make their work pass the critical consideration of the courts. Now, the men best equipped by study and experience for such work might, if the commission were elective, prove very poor campaigners. If pitted against brilliant talkers or good "mixers" they might stand no show at all. The submission also of a large number of candidates to the voter to be selected at a time when his mind is occupied with the consideration of questions under discussion, as well as candidates, tends still further to lessen the chances of the selection of the best man for particular service. For these reasons I have always strongly advocated the appointive method for filling all places requiring the services of trained experts.

I tried to persuade Commissioner Prouty of the Interstate Commerce Commission to come to Wisconsin, organize our commission, and take the chairmanship, but failing in that, I turned at once to the head of the transportation department of the University of Wisconsin, B. H. Meyer. A native of Wisconsin and a graduate of the university, Professor Meyer had made himself an authority upon railroad affairs in the country. He served upon our commission with great distinction, resigning in January of last year (1911) to accept a position upon the Interstate Commerce Commission at Washington. As another commissioner I appointed John Barnes, a Democrat, one of the foremost lawyers of the state, who sacrificed much in taking the place at the salary we paid. He has since been elected to the Supreme Court of the State. The third member was Halford Erickson, who had rendered invaluable service as Commissioner of Industrial and Labor Statistics. He had practical knowledge of railroading and has steadily grown in power until to-day he has no superior as a railroad authority on any state commission in the country.

The commission proceeded with wisdom. Though under great pressure at first, it refused to consider complaints until it had laid a broad foundation of scientific knowledge. Expert engineers and contractors were employed and many months were spent in making a physical valuation of all railroad property in the state. This is the logical first step if you are going to fix rates. It then became necessary to determine the actual cost of maintenance and operation—a very difficult matter in our case—because the railroads of Wisconsin are parts of great systems.

When all this immense work was done, the commission had the wisdom and foresight to submit its findings to the railroad officials, who went over them and approved them. This prevented disputes in the future upon fundamental facts.

Having all this data, the commissioners began to entertain complaints, and to fix rates upon a basis which they knew positively was fair to the public and fair to the railroads. They so reduced transportation charges as to effect a saving of over $2,000,000 per year to the people of the state, and they have only made a beginning. Generally the rates of public utility corporations have been reduced, but in some cases the investigation showed that the rates were too low already and the commission raised them. The result is that individuals may be found in communities where rates have been increased or have not been promptly or radically reduced who declare that the Railroad Commission has not met expectations by "going after" the corporations.

All through our fight for railroad control the lobbyists and the railroad newspapers made the most mournful prophecies of disaster: they predicted that capital would fly from the state, that new construction would stop, that equipment would deteriorate, and so on and so on. What are the facts?

The object of our legislation was not to "smash" corporations, but to drive them out of politics, and then to treat them exactly the same as other people are treated. Equality under the law was our guiding star. It is the special discriminations and unjust rates that are being corrected; the privileges, unfair advantages, and political corruption that have been abolished. Where these do not exist the object has been to foster and encourage business activity. Consequently, no state in the union to-day offers better security for the savings of its people than Wisconsin. The honest investor, or business man, or farmer, or laborer, who simply wants equal opportunity with others and security for what he honestly earns, is protected and encouraged by the laws. The mere speculator, or monopolist, or promoter, who wants to take advantage of others under protection of law, is held down or driven out. The result is that instead of falling behind, the state has actually gone forward more rapidly than the rest of the country. This may be shown by incontrovertible facts and figures in practically every direction where there has been progressive legislation affecting business.

The Railroad Commission keeps accurate account of all the business of every railroad and public utility in the state. It has jurisdiction over property whose total value amounts to $450,000,000. The books are kept exactly as the commission orders them to be kept. These accounts show that while during the first five years of its existence the commission reduced rates by more than $2,000,000 a year, the *net earnings* of the railroads of Wisconsin increased relatively just a little more than the net earnings for all railways in the United States. The increase in Wisconsin was 18.45 per cent., and in the United States it was 18.41 per cent.

How did this come about? Simply from the fact that the decrease in rates for freight and passengers was followed by an enormous increase in the amount of freight and number of passengers carried. So it happened that, notwithstanding the *reduction in rates,* there was an actual increase of nearly 20 per cent. in the revenue, while the increase of revenue of all the railroads in the United States was only 16 per cent.

This remarkable increase took place notwithstanding the fact that, mainly on account of the greatly improved service which the commission required the railroads to perform, the expense of railroad operation in Wisconsin increased 33 per cent. more than the average rate of increase in the entire United States.

Much of what the railroads lost in the reduction of open rates that everybody shares they recovered by being compelled to abolish free passes and secret cut rates that went only to insiders and grafters. The special examiners whom I appointed in 1903 uncovered $5,992,731.58 as Wisconsin's share of rebates paid by twelve roads during the six years 1898 to 1903. By stopping rebates alone the railroads have gained at least $1,000,000 a year toward offsetting $2,000,000 they lost by reduction of rates. They must also have gained largely by the stoppage of political contributions and expenses. The railroads to-day are gaining far more by treating everybody on an equality than they could have gained if their old methods of politics and secret favoritism had continued.

It is not claimed that railroads are both *making* and *keeping* more money in Wisconsin than they did before the progressive legislation began. Indeed, they are *making more but keeping a smaller proportion of it.* They are now paying taxes the same as other people on exactly what their property is worth. This they began to do in 1904. Under the old system of unequal taxation, in 1903, when the railroads practically assessed themselves, they paid taxes in the state amounting to $1,711,900. Under the new system, in 1910, when the State Tax Commission assessed them exactly like farms and other property, they paid $3,142,886. This was an increase of 83 per cent. in the amount of their taxes. But during the years 1903 to 1909 the taxes of all railroads in the United States increased only 41 per cent. That is, railroad taxation in Wisconsin has been increased by the progressive legislation in six years nearly twice as much as the increase for all of the United States. If this increase in taxation* is a hardship on the railroads, it is simply because equal taxation is always a hardship on those who had not been formerly paying their equal share of taxes.

Nor did progressive legislation stop new construction: During the years 1903 to 1909 the railroads invested in new construction in Wisconsin an amount estimated by the Railroad Commission at $39,000,000, an increase of 15 per cent. over 1903. This is not a fictitious increase in capitalization. It is *actual cash paid out* for new road and equipment. A cash investment by railroads of $6,500,000 a year for six years of progressive legislation refutes their prophecies of disaster.

Other public utilities besides railroads were not brought under the control of the Railroad Commission until 1907, and it was not until 1909 that the commission was able to get their accounts into such shape as to be reliable. But, for the year 1910, compared with 1909, notwithstanding reductions in rates and improvements in service, the water utilities increased their net earnings 7.1 per cent., the telephone utilities 7.1 per cent., gas utilities 7.4 per cent., and electric utilities 25 per cent. These utilities have even exceeded the railroads in the rate at which they have made cash investments for new construction. While the increase in railroad construction has averaged 2.5 per cent. a year for six years, the water utilities in 1910 increased their new construction of property 2.5 per cent. over what it had been in 1909; the telephone utilities 5.4 per cent., gas utilities 1.6 per cent., and electric utilities 35.5 per cent. For the year 1911 compared with 1910 the water utilities increased their net earnings 4.3 per cent., the telephone utilities 15.9 per cent., gas utilities 5.7 per cent., and electric utilities 24.2 per cent. The water utilities in 1911 increased their property by new construction 4 per cent. over that of 1910; the telephone utilities 5.7 per cent., gas utilities 6.1 per cent., and electric utilities, 22.1 per cent.

Wisconsin is certainly not driving capital out of the state when the electrical business in the single year 1910, after two years of regulation by the state, made *bona fide* new investments 35 per cent. greater than it had done in 1909. All of this has been accomplished notwithstanding the fact that the Railroad Commission has reduced the rates charged by public utilities $250,000 a year, and has required improvements in the quality of service amounting to $125,000 a year—a total saving to the consumers of gas, water, and electricity of $375,000 a year.

A single example will show how these different results have been brought about. In April, 1910, after two years of careful investigation, the Railroad Commission, after improving the quality of service, reduced the maximum price of electricity in the city of Madison from 16 cents to 14 cents per kilowatt-hour, and adjusted the other rates on a lower basis. The result was that the sales of electricity increased 16 per cent., the net earnings increased 24 per cent., the company increased its investment 12 per cent., and the savings to consumers, comparing old rates with new rates, was $18,308 a year. At the end of another fifteen months, in July, 1911, after such an increase in profits following the reduction in rates, the company accepted without protest another reduction to 12 cents. No additional investigation was necessary, because the books of the company had been kept in the way prescribed by the commission so as to show every item of expense, income, and investment. Supervision by the state commission has thus proven of great benefit to the private corporation itself.

How has it been possible that both the people of Wisconsin and the investors in public utilities have been so greatly benefited by this regulation? *Simply because the regulation is scientific.* The Railroad Commission has found out through its engineers, accountants, and statisticians what it actually costs to build and operate the road and utilities. Watered stock and balloon bonds get no consideration. On the other hand, since the commission knows the costs, it knows exactly the point below which rates cannot be reduced. It even raises rates when they are below the cost, including reasonable profit.

The people are benefited because they are not now paying profits on inflated capital. The investors are benefited because the commission has all the facts needed to prevent a reduction of rates below a fair profit on their true value. So honestly, capably, and scientifically has the work of our commission been done that the railroads and other utility corporations have accepted their reductions without any contest at all. Our law makes it perfectly easy for the railroads to seek redress in the courts if they feel wronged in any way. Yet it is significant that there has never been an appeal taken in any railroad rate case decided by the Railroad Commission. The corporations know that the Railroad Commission has all the data for making rates that they (the railroads) have, and that it can go into court and show that it is making rates not by guess, not by estimate, but by the most careful calculation based upon definite information. Thus while the railroad companies do not enjoy having their rates cut down, they are not over-eager to advertise the Wisconsin system of rate making. When the other states of the country and the federal government make rates as we do in Wisconsin, the shippers of the country will be saved millions of dollars every year in excessive transportation charges.

In Wisconsin we regulate services as well as rates. When the services of a railroad are not satisfactory to the public, complaint can be made to the Railroad Commission. Under our law that complaint does not need to be a formal legal document, but a simple statement of grievance by letter or postal card. In 1906 I rode over the branch of the Chicago, Milwaukee and St. Paul road which runs from Madison to Prairie du Chien. The train was not so very crowded when I got on two or three stations east of Prairie du Chien, but it kept filling up and pretty soon I found myself standing in the aisle. I kept being crowded back and back until when I got to Madison I was sitting on the tail end of the train, and I was thoroughly angry. I had a canvass made of the regular patrons of the train who were aboard, to find out how the service that morning compared with the average service. I found it was the usual thing, and I wrote at once on the back of an envelope which I took from my pocket something like this:

"Mr. Commissioner: I call your attention to the bad service on the Prairie du Chien division of the Chicago, Milwaukee and St. Paul road. It is not adequately equipped either with cars or trains. Passenger train so-and-so crowded to the platforms. I think the matter should be investigated by your commission."

I think inside of ten days there was a new train running on that road. The travelling men called it the "Bob" train in honor of me, but I am sure that no more attention was paid to my complaint than would have been paid to one from any other source.

154

The complaint is taken up by the commission in an informal way. A representative of the railroad and the party making complaint are then brought together, quite informally. I should say hundreds of cases of that sort are disposed of and adjusted to the satisfaction of both parties to one case requiring a formal presentation and the employment of counsel. This system makes it cheaper for the railroads, cheaper for the people, and it is a speedy way to get justice in a lot of little things. Most people deal with railroads in a large way only a few times in their lives. But they are brought into intimate contact with the railroad on little freight shipments, or with relation to crossings and depots—small annoyances which often cause more bitterness than large matters. As the result of the easy and just settlement of such difficulties I think to-day there is a better feeling in the state toward the railroads and railroad men than ever before in our history.

In other ways our progressive legislation has materially benefited all the people of the state. For example, beginning in 1903, I secured in every water-power franchise the insertion of a provision that the rates charged should be regulated by arbitration. Since that time the water powers of the state serving as public utilities have been placed under the control of the Railroad Commission, and a great corporation, supervised by the Railroad Commission, with its profits limited to 6 per cent. on actual cost, has been created and has improved the headwaters of the Wisconsin River in order to secure a steady flow through the year. Several enormous power dams have been constructed, and through these means the state has gone far toward utilizing its 1,000,000 available horsepower, while protecting the state against water-power monopoly.

Wisconsin began in 1905 to build up a state forest reserve on the headwaters of its principal rivers. It now ranks next to New York and Pennsylvania in its areas of forests belonging to the state, and has adopted a permanent policy of adding annually to the reserve.

Wisconsin has also taken hold of the insurance problem with vigor. The special session of the legislature which I called in 1905 provided for a committee to investigate insurance corporations. This was about the time of the Hughes investigation in New York, and the committee appointed pursuant to that legislation rendered a very signal service to our state. As a member of that committee H. L. Ekern, who was then Speaker of the Assembly—a legislator of real creative power—developed a very remarkable aptitude for the insurance problem. It was most extraordinary. Ekern is a

Norwegian, a university graduate, a lawyer. In the legislature of 1907 he appeared before the committee having charge of the insurance legislation, and there demonstrated his ability to more than hold his own against the ablest actuaries and lawyers representing the largest insurance companies in the United States.

In 1910 he was elected Insurance Commissioner of the state and in the legislature of 1911 he brought about a complete recodification of our insurance laws. He has indeed practically laid the basis for a system of state insurance—the first, I think, in the United States.

The public service of the state has been democratized by a civil service law opening it to men and women on an equal footing independent of everything excepting qualification and fitness for office. I think the passing of this law was the only case of the kind where the employees then holding office were not blanketed into the service, but were required to take the regular competitive examinations in order to retain their jobs. The law has worked to the great advantage of the service and to the general improvement of political standards. There is no longer any political pull in Wisconsin.

I give here, also, some further facts to show that Wisconsin, instead of being retarded by progressive legislation, is advancing more rapidly than the country taken as a whole.

Since 1904, when we recodified our whole system for the examination of state banks, there has not been a single failure among the 573 state banks in Wisconsin, with $27,000,000 of capital, surplus and undivided profits. The only bank failures in the state have been those of three national banks through embezzlement.

During the years 1903 to 1911 the capital, surplus and undivided profits of all state and national banks in Wisconsin increased 72 per cent., whereas for the United States they increased only 48 per cent. Individual deposits for the same years in Wisconsin banks increased 82 per cent., while in the United States as a whole they increased but 74 per cent.

The clearing-house exchanges for Milwaukee increased 117.5 per cent. from 1900 to 1910, whereas for the United States the increase was 106 per cent. Milwaukee's increase was greater than Chicago's.

Judged by commercial failures, Wisconsin has prospered better in proportion than the country. The total liabilities in commercial failures for the entire United States in the four years 1906 to 1909 increased 33 per cent. over the total amount for the preceding four years 1902 to 1905. But the liabilities in Wisconsin for the same years *fell off* 5.3 per cent. In other words, comparing the four years that followed the progressive victory of 1905 with the four years that preceded it, the business failures in Wisconsin *fell off* one twentieth, but for the whole United States they *increased one third.*

These are a few of the conclusive proofs that progressive legislation in Wisconsin has not been destructive, as its enemies predicted. Instead of driving capital out of the state it has attracted capital more than other states. It has made investments safe for all, instead of speculative for a few. It has been conservative and constructive as well as progressive. Only one of the progressive laws—a law passed in 1911, declaring flowing water public property—has been overturned by the supreme court of the state, and not one has been carried into the federal courts.

No account of the long and successful struggle in Wisconsin would be fair and complete that did not record the splendid services of the men who led the fight for progressive principles. I regret that I cannot here give to each the individual recognition that is merited. That must wait for a more detailed history of the Wisconsin movement. It was a day-and-night service with them; they left their offices and business interests and devoted years to the great constructive work which has made Wisconsin the safest guide in dealing with the political, economic and social problems of our time.

This closes the account of my services in Wisconsin—a time full of struggle, and yet a time that I like to look back upon. It has been a fight supremely worth making, and I want it to be judged, as it will be ultimately, by results actually attained. If it can be shown that Wisconsin is a happier and better state to live in, that its institutions are more democratic, that the opportunities of all its people are more equal, that social justice more nearly prevails, that human life is safer and sweeter—then I shall rest content in the feeling that the Progressive movement has been successful. And I believe all these things can really be shown, and that there is no reason now why the movement should not expand until it covers the entire nation. While much has been accomplished, there is still a world of problems yet to be solved; we have just begun; there is hard fighting, and a chance for the highest patriotism, still ahead of us. The fundamental problem as to which shall rule, men or property, is still unsettled; it will require the highest qualities of heroism, the profoundest devotion to duty in this and in the coming generation, to reconstruct our institutions to meet the requirements of a new age. May such brave and true leaders develop that the people will not be led astray.

Chapter IX

Alone in the Senate: Experiences
with Roosevelt: Railroad
Rate Legislation

I was elected to the United States Senate on January 25, 1905, four weeks after the legislature met. At first I was very doubtful whether I ought to resign the governorship and go to Washington. Much work still remained to be done in Wisconsin, and I felt that I could not accept until all the pledges which we had made to the people were redeemed in letter and spirit.

For this reason I determined not to resign as governor until the legislation we had under way was not only passed but actually in operation. While I recognized that the work of democracy is never finished, I resolved for myself that I would not leave Wisconsin until our legislation had been enacted and its efficiency proven. In the following spring we tested our new direct primary law at the polls, and we tried out the railroad taxation law before the circuit court.

Having thus discovered the weaknesses in our program of legislation, I called a special session of the legislature to meet in December, 1905, in order to correct the defects and fully to complete our work. When the session adjourned, eleven months after my election to the Senate, I resigned as governor of Wisconsin and prepared to go on to Washington.

In making this final decision I was not a little influenced by the urgent letters and interviews with people of prominence outside of Wisconsin. During that summer I lectured in some twenty-five different states and I never went anywhere that leading Progressives did not urge me to go to Washington and carry forward the fight on the wider national platform. I remember meeting Colonel Bryan once or twice during the summer.

"La Follette," he said, "I hear you are not going to the Senate. I do hope that is not true. You must go and make the fight there in the public interest."

I found not a little amusement in the treatment by the press of the country of my decision to accept the senatorship. Most of the important papers prophesied an early suppression of all my reform notions. It was suggested that a few months in the Senate refrigerator, to which I would be promptly consigned, would considerably cool my ardor and give me time for reflection and the adoption of saner, more rational views of business and government. I remember one of the cartoons of the time pictured my approach to the Senate end of the Capitol apparently all unconscious of the fact that every window was open and that the Senate leaders were leaning halfway out, each holding aloft a mallet with which to extend a senatorial welcome.

On the evening of January 3, 1906, Mrs. La Follette and I arrived in Washington. Senator Chandler of New Hampshire, who had been most friendly, came to the Raleigh Hotel to call upon us, and I learned from him the proper methods of procedure in presenting my credentials. I had anticipated some departure from precedents owing to the fact that the senior Senator from Wisconsin, John C. Spooner, and I had long been upon opposite sides in the Wisconsin fight, and while it had not been personal in its character, the struggle had resulted in a very wide division. I did not know how he might feel about conforming to the usual custom of the Senate in presenting my credentials.

The next day at twelve o'clock I went to call on the Vice-President, Mr. Fairbanks, in his official capacity as President of the Senate; and upon returning to the floor of the Senate, Senator Spooner met me and introduced me to a number of the Senators who were coming in to take their places. There were some dozen or fifteen men in the Senate whom I knew as members of the House—Burrows, Hopkins, Rayner, and others. Spooner invited me to sit next to him. Mrs. La Follette and other friends were in the gallery. After the divine blessing had been invoked Senator Spooner arose and presented my credentials. The Senator offered his arm, I took it, and we marched down to the Vice-President's desk, where the oath of office was administered. I was then escorted to my desk in what was called the Cherokee Strip—a group of seats on the Democratic side of the house which was then occupied by Republicans, there being at that time 61 Republicans in the Senate and only 31 Democrats. Thus it came about that at

12:30 o'clock on the 4th day of January, 1906, I found myself occupying a seat on the outskirts of the Democratic side of the Senate as a member of the 59th Congress.

After my election to the Senate I had received the usual form letter from Senator Hale, chairman of the Committee on Committees, asking me to state my preference as to committee assignments. In my reply I expressed but one preference—the Committee on Interstate Commerce. I suggested that my interest in the subject of transportation, to which I had given some years of study and investigation, led me to believe that I could render better service upon that committee than upon any other. I had never received any response to that letter, and I was naturally interested to know what my assignments were. I need scarcely say that I was not appointed to the Committee on Interstate Commerce. Of all my assignments the Committee on Indian Affairs was altogether the best; though I should not overlook the bestowal upon me of a chairmanship which carried with it a committee room, a clerk, and a messenger. The title of this committee impressed me considerably. It was the "Committee to Investigate the Condition of the Potomac River Front. (Select.)" I had immediate visions of cleaning up the whole Potomac River front until I found that in all its history the committee had never had a bill referred to it for consideration, and had never held a meeting. My committee room was reached by going down into the sub-cellar of the capitol, along a dark winding passage lighted by dim skylights which leaked badly, to a room carved out of the terrace on the west side of the Capitol.

It is scarcely necessary to emphasize the very great importance of committee appointments in the Senate. They are the gateways of legislation. A powerful committee in secret session has almost autocratic power in deciding what laws shall or shall not be passed: and it is in the committees that the great financial interests of the country have found their securest entrenchment. Of first importance is the great Finance Committee, which has charge of all bills affecting the tariff, currency and banking. Other very powerful committees are Interstate Commerce, with its control of bills, relating to railroads, trusts and combinations, and the Committees on Rules, on Appropriations, on Foreign Relations, and on the Judiciary.

I decided to make the best of my committee appointments. I knew, of course, what they thought when they placed me on at least three of them: Claims, Indian Affairs and Pensions—"We will give the gentleman so much routine work to do that he will not trouble us at all"—for these committees, more than almost any others, are occupied by a multiplicity of unimportant legislation. But while I resolved to do my duty, I determined not to permit my attention to be diverted from the really great and important questions of the day. Upon one of the committees, indeed, that of Indian Affairs, I found immediately most congenial service. My interest in the Indians, awakened during my service in the House of Representatives fifteen years before, had always been active.

The most important bill under consideration by that committee was the bill for the settlement of the affairs of the Five Civilized Tribes in the Indian Territory, one of the most important provisions of which related to the segregated coal lands of the Choctaw and Chickasaw Indians. The bill, as passed by the House, provided for a continuation and extension of the policy of leasing the coal lands to private mining companies. The Senate committee proposed to amend this provision of the House bill and provide for the sale of the lands. It was a new question for me, but I went to see the Secretary of the Interior and got his views upon the subject. I then called upon the Director of the Geological Survey, and learned that bituminous coal of a very superior quality had been located upon 413,000 acres of this land. I also discovered that leases covering about 112,000 acres in area, while taken in the name of private coal-mining companies, were really controlled by the railroads of the territory. I found that there was little or no competition in prices, and that the transportation rates for shipments from the mines to the consumers were enormously high.

I therefore opposed in committee the sale of these coal lands. Being voted down on that proposition, I proposed such amendments as seemed to me to better the measure, such, for instance, as limiting the amount of coal land which could be acquired by any one company; providing for a condition in the deeds making the lands revert to the United States in trust for the Indians when the land went to any railroad corporation or the officers or directors of any railroad corporation.

I was, of course, voted down overwhelmingly in the committee on all of these propositions; indeed, as I now remember it, my own was the only vote which I was able to get for any of them. I reserved the right to oppose the committee as to these provisions in any and all respects when the bill should be brought up on the floor of the Senate. The committee smiled a broad smile. I was regarded at that time, I am sure, by every man upon that committee as a crank, a disturber of peace and prosperity. I knew what was back of that smile. The members of the committee were thinking what the Senate would do to me when I attempted to oppose the action of the committee in selling these coal lands.

Well, when the bill came before the Senate, I offered amendments which led to a two days' discussion. Though they were voted down, the whole subject was so effectively aired in the newspapers as a scheme of the railroads and other special interests connected with them to get hold of the Indian coal lands, that the plan to sell the coal had to be abandoned.

But from that day to this the railroads and other important interests have never ceased their efforts to get control of these valuable deposits.

At every session of Congress, from that session of 1906 down to the last day of the extra session of 1911, the protection of the interests of the Indians and of the public generally in that coal field has required constant vigilance. Many lobbies have been organized; measures have been introduced in one form and another at every session—independent bills, riders on appropriation bills, jokers in conference reports have concealed in some form an attempt to exploit these coal lands and the people dependent upon them for fuel supply.

This first fight in the Senate proved to be an important one. It was the beginning of the battle for conservation of coal lands belonging to the people. I am not aware that President Roosevelt had ever, prior to this time, given expression to any views in regard to a policy upon this subject, but as an evidence of the quickness with which his mind grasps an important subject, I mention my first call upon him after the debate in the Senate. I do not now remember the purpose of my visit; I do remember his greeting:

"Senator La Follette, by Jove! you struck a mighty good lead on that coal matter in Indian Territory. I think that is a very important subject."

And I said to him: "Yes, Mr. President, its importance will develop. I am going to work out a bill providing that the government shall take over that coal and save it from being exploited by monopoly control."

"Bully! It is a bully good thing!"

"Mr. President," I said, "I think it would also be a good thing applied to all the coal fields of the government, and I want to come and talk to you about that when you haven't so many in waiting to see you."

He said, "I would be very much interested. I wish you would come."

I did go to have a talk with him and I found him not only open-minded upon the subject, but ready to assent to the importance of some action in that direction. I then suggested to him the withdrawal from sale and entry of all coal, asphalt, and oil lands by executive order, but he at once raised the question of the power of the President to act without Congressional authority. I argued that the President had such authority, but he said that he would get Attorney-General Moody's opinion on it. When I saw him afterward he said that Moody's opinion left the matter still in doubt. I then told him that I would introduce a joint resolution in the Senate clothing him with power to withdraw the public lands from entry.

Accordingly, on the 20th of June, I offered such a joint resolution authorizing the President "to withdraw from entry and sale all public lands known to be underlaid with coal, lignite, or oil and all such lands which, in the judgment of the Director of the Geological Survey, contain deposits of coal, lignite, or oil, and that all such lands be withheld from entry or sale until such time as Congress shall determine otherwise."

I was not able, however, to secure action on the resolution in the Senate.

I next saw President Roosevelt on the 30th of June a few hours prior to the adjournment of Congress. He was then in the President's room at the capitol. I told him it had been impossible to get action upon the joint resolution authorizing him to withdraw the coal lands from sale and entry, at the same time saying that I did not think that such action was necessary on the part of Congress.

"Well," he said in his characteristic and energetic way, "Moody thinks there is some doubt about it, but I'll resolve that doubt in favor of the public, and after Congress adjourns I'll withdraw all government lands known to contain coal deposits."

I told him I believed that such action on his part would have the backing of all the people of the country, and that I proposed to give such time as I could during the summer to a study of the subject with a view to introducing a comprehensive bill not only dealing with the coal lands belonging to the Indians but with all the coal lands belonging to the general government.

He said, "Good. You go ahead, get your bill ready, and I will make it the leading subject in my message to Congress in December. Come and see me as soon as you return."

Not long after Congress adjourned, while on the road in the

middle west filling lecture engagements, I saw a Washington dispatch announcing the withdrawal by the President of many millions of acres of government coal lands, and that afternoon, in an address on the dangers threatening representative government, I told the story of the coal lands and of the President's keen interest in the whole subject.

On my return to Washington in December, 1906, I called promptly upon the President. Almost his first words were:

"Senator La Follette, I have got it in the message!"

I told him I had made a first draft of my bill, but that I needed some further assistance in perfecting it. Upon my request he gave me a card to Attorney-General Moody, and one of the best men in the Department of Justice was assigned to help me. Many weeks were spent in mastering all the literature and legislation upon this question in Great Britain, Germany and New Zealand, and we then prepared a broad conservation measure. In view of the fact that the bill was in a large degree the work of the able assistant assigned by the Attorney-General I may be pardoned for saying that it is the one bill that has been put before Congress that deals with the whole subject in a comprehensive way.

Its essential provisions are that all coal lands shall be reserved by the general government and shall not be sold, but shall be operated under license. By the passage of such a measure the government would forever control its coal reserves.

Before I introduced the bill, however, I called at the executive office and went over it section by section with the President. At every important point Mr. Roosevelt would smite the table and declare his approval with an emphatic:

"Admirable, admirable! that does the business!"

When we had finished with the bill, he said:

"How soon will you introduce it?"

"To-morrow," I answered.

He said, "You may announce, if you desire, that it is an administration measure."

I was delighted, and expressed my appreciation that this important measure could have the active support of the administration. I introduced the bill, and gave to the press a brief statement of its provisions. Within three days I was surprised to receive a note from the President advising me that he had conferred with friends about the coal bill which I had introduced, and found that it would be impossible to get support for any such measure; that its provisions were regarded as too drastic, and that in order to get "something through" it would be necessary to agree upon a less comprehensive plan. He said it had been suggested to him that Senator Nelson had introduced a bill shortly before which would be acceptable to everybody. The joint resolution which I had introduced on the 20th of June, 1906, with its preamble reciting the conditions that existed, followed by the President's withdrawal of the coal lands, had served as a warning that action in some form, thoroughgoing or otherwise, was likely to be undertaken, and Senator Nelson of Minnesota had on the 3rd day of January, 1907, introduced a bill upon the subject. I replied to President Roosevelt's note by letter, as I wished to place before him a careful analysis of the Nelson bill to the end that he might see that legislation of that character would be not only worth while, but would, if enacted, serve only to bring government control and leasing into actual disrepute, and end, as do all compromises with principle, in defeating the very object in view. In my letter to the President I assured him that no pride of authorship would impel me to insist upon my bill; that in order to secure legislation upon this important subject I stood ready to support any bill, provided it embodied the principles essential to make this new legislation really effective. In reply, the President did not attempt to answer the objections which I presented to the Nelson bill, but said substantially that if those who were supporting the new policy were not willing to agree upon "something which could be passed," he would wash his hands of the whole matter and would cancel his withdrawal of the lands and open them again to sale and entry.

I state the facts here just as they transpired, because they illustrate the difference in methods which sometimes rendered it impossible for President Roosevelt and myself to cooperate on important legislation. He acted upon the maxim that half a loaf is better than no bread. I believe that half a loaf is fatal whenever it is accepted at the sacrifice of the basic principle sought to be attained. Half a loaf, as a rule, dulls the appetite, and destroys the keenness of interest in attaining the full loaf. A halfway measure never fairly tests the principle and may utterly discredit it. It is certain to weaken, disappoint, and dissipate public interest. Concession and compromise are almost always necessary in legislation, but they call for the most thorough and complete mastery of the principles involved, in order to fix the limit beyond which not one hair's breadth can be yielded.

Roosevelt is the keenest and ablest living interpreter of what I would call the superficial public sentiment of a given time and he is spontaneous in his response to it; but he does not distinguish between that which is a mere surface indication of a sentiment and the building up by a long process of education of a public opinion which is as deep-rooted as life. Had Roosevelt, for example, when he came to consider railroad rate regulation, estimated correctly the value of the public opinion that had been created upon that subject through a space of nine years, he would have known to a certainty that it lay in his power to secure legislation which should effectually control the great transportation companies of the country. But either through a desire to get immediate results, or through a misunderstanding of the really profound depth of that public sentiment, he chose to get what little he could then, rather than to take a temporary defeat and go on fighting at the succeeding session of Congress for legislation that would be fundamentally sound.

To get back to the coal matter: I knew instinctively what had taken place immediately after the introduction of my bill. Representatives of the railroads and of the corporations both inside and outside of Congress had probably swarmed to the White House, denounced the bill, denounced me, and told the President that the plan I had offered was socialistic and that the committee would not tolerate it.

Well, after the President decided he could not support the bill which I had introduced it had no chance of passing the Committee on Public Lands. And no other measure proposed received the support of the people of the country who were in favor of genuine conservation. That ended, for the time being, any chance of legislation on that subject. But I have presented the same bill at every session of Congress since 1907 and it is now before the Committee on Public Lands. I am very hopeful that public sentiment and the changes that are gradually taking place in the personnel of the committee will soon make it possible to secure favorable action. I am glad to see, indeed, that the Secretary of the Interior has used this bill as well as that which I introduced to provide for the control of the Indian coal land of Oklahoma as a basis for his plan for the control of coal and other mineral resources in Alaska.

The simple scheme of dominating the committees in the Senate and the House, as exemplified in the case of these coal land bills, is the familiar procedure of those private interests both inside and outside of Congress which seek to direct national legislation. Any attempt to bring about progressive reforms is met by this en-

167

trenched opposition. For example, the Committee on Naval Affairs will be found composed almost entirely of members representing states or districts within which have been built up, often wrongfully, great land naval establishments, harbors, docks and the like. I venture to say that an expert, unbiased naval board so chosen as to represent the highest authority of our country on all matters pertaining to our navy would close many if not most of the principal naval yards and docks and never permit the expenditure of another dollar upon them. Every experienced naval officer will tell you that owing to channel and currents every large battleship docks at Portsmouth at the risk of serious injury or total loss, and yet Hale of Maine and Gallinger of New Hampshire were for years important members of the Committee on Naval Affairs, and Portsmouth was maintained. The same is in a measure true of the Mare Island yard at San Francisco, but Senator Perkins of California is now chairman of the Committee on Naval Affairs. Every principle of naval warfare requires that this government should have one of its most important stations at Guantanamo, Cuba. But we have no Senator from Guantanamo, and so we have no harbor there.

Now, I had grown tired of sitting in the Senate and seeing appropriation bills carrying hundreds of millions of dollars brought in, not reasonably early in the session, but held back, held back, until near its close. Such delay served two purposes: The appropriation bill having the right of way under the rules could be used to kill off any measure that the interests did not want passed. Furthermore, it could be urged that there was no time for full debate. One afternoon, therefore, when Mr. Hale arose and presented the Naval Appropriation bill, stating that he hoped the first reading of the bill would be dispensed with, I said that I had had no opportunity to see what was in the bill; that I thought the time had come when the Senate should stop such proceedings; that my remarks were not intended as an affront to the committee, but that each of us had his personal responsibility to his state and to the country, and that the organization of the Senate contemplated that legislation should not be enacted by the fifteen or seventeen men who constituted the committee, about whose selection the Senate itself had had very little to say. At once Mr. Hale started in to rebuke me. I told him that I was not accountable to him for the course that I was taking; that I stood ready to assume all the responsibility for any loss of time to the country on this important legislation; that appropriation bills, it seemed to me, should be reported early enough so that members of the Senate could have a few days at least in which to investigate them, and I asked that he defer pressing the bill for a day or two. But Hale made no response and the clerk started in to read the bill.

I had not studied the Naval Appropriation bill at all, but I began to send for documents, which were piled up on my desk, and I determined to speak on the bill until adjournment for the day and thus gain time to study it. Hale saw that I was quite determined to prevent the passage of the bill that afternoon and so he rose and said that he wanted to be reasonable about these things, and the bill went over finally until the following Monday.

I went home that night and immediately began getting telephone calls from naval officers here in Washington, who said they were gratified to see that there was to be some discussion of the bill; that there were many things about it that were bad; that we were making expenditures wastefully; that they had pride in the navy and that they wanted to see a navy built up for the ocean, and not for the land. I answered that I would be glad to have them meet me and certain of my associates who would be selected with the greatest care, and who would protect them absolutely. Then I called in Cummins, Borah and Dixon. I called Dixon because he had come to me after my tilt with Hale and expressed sympathy with the course I had taken. This was the first gathering of the group of so-called Progressives in the Senate for concerted action on legislation. We spent the entire Sunday on it, assisted by a number of naval officers, and threshed out the whole bill. When we had determined on the items in the bill that should be opposed, we shared them among us and each one went to work.

In the course of the debate on the Naval Appropriation bill which followed, the Senate bosses for the first time were vigorously attacked for the way they made up the committees. I contended that members from states where appropriations were to be expended ought not to be on committees which controlled those expenditures. I said that no one would think of permitting a jury to sit in any case where that jury was directly or indirectly interested in the result of the verdict. And that it was against human nature that the men on the committee would not give preference to the yards and docks in their own states; that they were unfit to weigh the claims of a harbor in another state. Of course, it was taken by my associates as theoretical preaching and sneered at, but it had its effect just the same. We did not, indeed, get any change in that particular bill, for they had a big majority and passed it in spite of us, but at the close of the debate I offered a resolution as fundamentally important in principle as the resolution that I offered for the reservation of the coal lands, with reference to naval appropriations in the future. That resolution provided that the President should appoint a board of naval experts to investigate all of the naval harbors, yards and drydocks in the United States, and report to the next Congress whether appropriations were being made in the best interests of the service, and whether appropriations for the future ought to be continued for these various purposes. They voted me down, but a few weeks after this, Roosevelt, just before he went out of office, appointed just such a board, which has since made a valuable report.

I made a fight for time to investigate all important appropriation bills during that session, and since then immediate consideration is rarely asked upon the report of an appropriation bill.

There is indeed a great field for reform, not only in the method of selecting the members of the various committees of the Senate, but in the principle that should control. I do not believe that any committee charged with the responsibility of the expenditure of hundreds of millions of dollars of the public moneys should be composed of Senators or members of the House representing states within which such expenditures are made. Frye, I remember, picked me up in that debate, and asked me if I would apply that same rule to the Committee on Commerce, of which he was chairman. I answered, "By all means." I contended that the final expenditure should be made with a single purpose in mind, and that was the public interest, their general good, and that could only be made by men who had no political interest to serve. It is a common thing for members and Senators to urge, as one of the arguments in making their personal and semi-confidential appeal to their friends upon the various committees, that the expenditure of so many hundreds of thousands of dollars in their districts or their states would materially help them in their coming election. Every man who has ever served in either branch of Congress has heard it over and over again. It is not an exceptional thing for a man to support his claims for reelection on the size of the appropriations he has secured. Senator Warren of Wyoming, within a year, in a speech made to his constituents, compared the amount he and his colleague had obtained in the way of appropriations for Wyoming with what other Senators had been able to get for some of the most important states in our union—and boasted of it as meritorious achievement.

The most important thing of all is to send honest men to Washington—men in this time of stress who want to serve the public, and nobody else. The abler these men are, the better, but above all the people should see to it that their representatives are honest —not merely money honest, but intellectually honest.

If they have the highest standards of integrity and the highest ideals of service, all our problems, however complex, will be easily solved.

Jethro was a wise counsellor when he said to Moses, "Thou shalt provide out of all the people, able men such as fear God, men of truth, hating covetousness."

I have said before in the course of this narrative that the legislation in which I took the greatest interest as a member of the House of Representatives was the enactment of the Interstate Commerce Act. And when I came to the Senate, nineteen years later, I found the same subject as the most important legislation pending. The Hepburn bill, amending the Interstate Commerce Act, had passed the House and was before the Senate.

There followed months of debate—one of the most important debates of recent years—through which I sat waiting for some one to raise what seemed to me to be the real issues—the real questions as we had met them in our years of struggle with the railroad problem in Wisconsin.

Now, there are just three principal purposes in the governmental regulation of railroad rates: The first, to prevent unjust and extortionate rates from being imposed upon the country; the second, to prevent discriminations between shippers, or localities, or commodities; the third, to enforce and regulate an adequate service.

The primary purpose in the enactment of the Interstate Commerce Act in 1887—I recall clearly the arguments and hearings— was to prevent the imposition of unreasonable and unjust rates. It was passed in response to a demand of the public which had been growing in volume ever since the days of Granger legislation.

In saying this I do not wish to belittle the abuses arising from discriminations of which rebates furnish one example. They have been most serious in their consequences: but the early advocates of railroad regulation saw clearly that the subject of deepest importance was not discriminations but unreasonable rates.

One school of advocates of railway regulation has adopted as its platform the prevention of discrimination, because it is the least difficult of the two branches of the subject to deal with. It provokes the least opposition from the railroads, and it is always backed by powerful organizations of shippers. Again and again President Roosevelt laid it down in his messages and public addresses that there was very little complaint that rates were unreasonable, but that there was much complaint against discriminations. And that statement was true. It was true for this reason. The shippers can easily organize and can make themselves heard and felt. The thing in which the shipper is vitally interested is that his competitor shall not have a better rate or better facilities than he has. But he is not concerned as to whether that rate is high or low, because he does not pay the rate, excepting in the first instance. He always charges the rate in as a part of the cost to the consumer, who is the real freight payer the country over.

Now, the consumer who is primarily interested in unreasonable rates has little or no opportunity to be heard. Nor has he the means of knowing, when he buys his coal, his supplies, his food, his lumber, his hardware, how much of the price he has to pay is due to excessive freight charges. He realizes that year by year it costs more for everything he must buy, but he is not able to put his finger upon the particular amount of that excessive cost which is due to freight charges made in the shipment of raw material to the factory, in the shipment of the partially finished product to some other factory, and in the further shipment of the finished product to the wholesaler or jobber, and in the final shipment to the retailer, from whom he buys it. He cannot organize and come before a legislative committee and make himself heard. Furthermore, Congress has taken care that no body of men, no commission created anywhere, should have either the authority or the instrumentalities through which it could ascertain what was really a reasonable freight rate.

It is true that the Interstate Commerce Commission has assumed from time to time to say that rates were reasonable or unreasonable, but it has based its decisions, in that regard, merely upon comparisons of one rate with another, both of which may be wholly unreasonable. It has never had, and has not now, any real standard of judgment.

For ten years after its organization in 1887 the Commission did assume the right to fix rates; then in 1897 came a crushing decision of the Supreme Court which robbed it of this power and, indeed, left it worse than helpless. During the next nine years, down to 1906, when the Hepburn bill to which I have referred was introduced, the committees were so organized in both Senate and House and so dominated by railroad and other corporation interests that it was impossible to get any real reform measure reported out.

During all the years from 1897 to 1906 the commission, which was a very able one, kept calling the attention of Congress and the country to its utter helplessness and urging legislation. Year after year it repeated its pleas, it appeared before committees, it showed how the railroads were rapidly combining in enormous monopolies. It showed in 1905 that unwarranted increases in transportation rates amounting to more than $100,000,000 a year had been levied upon the people since the commission lost its power in 1897—but Congress would not move.

All this time, however, the clamor of both the shippers and the public had been increasing in volume and intensity. In 1903 Congress passed the Elkins law which dealt with rebates and discriminations—for the railroads by that time had grown weary of paying rebates, and were not unfavorable to having the practice forbidden. But nothing was done for the people—the consumers who were still suffering from unreasonable rates.

By 1906 the situation had become so unbearable and centres of production throughout the country had suffered to such an extent that there arose a great outcry of protest. Organized bodies of men were sent to Washington to appear before the committees and attempt to arouse them to a sense of their responsibility to the public, and finally the railroads, realizing that something must be done to quiet the public clamor, loosened their hold sufficiently to permit a bill to be reported out from the Committee on Interstate Commerce of the House of Representatives, known as the Hepburn bill. It passed the House and came to the Senate, and there it fell into the hands of the Senate Committee on Interstate Commerce, a majority of which was absolutely opposed to any legislation restoring any power to the Interstate Commerce Commission.

Finally, however, through an alliance of Doliver and Clapp with the Democrats, the bill was reported out, and the debate began. But incredible as it may seem, it is nevertheless true that the bill did not include in its terms the recommendations which the Interstate Commerce Commission had urged as necessary to make it a workable statute—the amendments which, through these years, it had been pleading with Congress to enact into law. It never touched the heart of the matter, namely, whether the commission should be given the power to determine what was a reasonable rate, and to enforce its decisions.

For months I sat through these debates, as I say, waiting for some one to raise the real question. I had studied the bill with great care. There was just one portion of it which was important and did really improve the law, and that was the amendment empowering the Interstate Commerce Commission to require all railroads engaged in interstate commerce to adopt a uniform system of bookkeeping, and authorizing the commission through its examiners and accountants to examine the books and accounts of railroad companies at all times. The value of that provision could not be overestimated. But that was about all there was of a vital character to the act of 1906.

I was very loath to see the bill pass in its imperfect form, but I was a new man in the Senate, without influence with the members of that body. I felt strongly that if President Roosevelt rightly estimated the strength of the public sentiment in favor of effective legislation, and would exert his influence upon the Senate, that legislation which would really count could be secured. I believed I knew exactly what was required to meet the necessities of the situation, but I did not feel that I could thrust my views upon the President. I had known him for fifteen years, but I was conscious that he had been warned that I was dangerous and extreme in my views, and I was in no position to offer him any suggestions unsolicited.

Lincoln Steffens was in Washington during that winter. On one occasion he asked me why I did not go to see the President and warn him of the defects in the bill.

"I have been seeing the President," he said, "and I am going to suggest to him that you have gone all over this question in Wisconsin, that you have been at it for years up there, and it will do no harm for him to have a talk with you about it."

This he did, with the result that I received an invitation to go to the White House and see the President one Sunday evening at ten o'clock. It was at a time when newspaper reporters were not about, and there was no one to take note of the fact or publish to the country that the President was conferring with so dangerous a person. He was alone, and after chatting with me a few moments, he said: "Senator La Follette, I sent for you to come and talk with me about the rate bill."

Then he proceeded to say that the most needful thing to be done in the way of changes in the law was to strengthen it, so that the injustice done to a great many shippers by discriminations would be made impossible.

"Discrimination is important," I said, "and should not be tolerated. Every man who deals with a common carrier has a right to treatment on an equal footing with every other shipper of the same product. But the question, Mr. President, is very much bigger than that. To begin with, the first and the vital thing in which the great body of the people of this country are interested is in having transportation charges *reasonable*."

Then I took up and discussed with him the changes that ought to be made in the bill. I sat with him until twelve o'clock that night, and I did not outstay my welcome either. I found him a very good listener and I had the feeling that I had made some impression upon him. In the course of my talk he stopped me to say, "But you can't get any such bill as that through this Congress."

My answer was, "That is not the first consideration, Mr. President."

"But," he said, "I want to get something through."

And I remember very clearly saying to him, "Mr. President, you pass such a bill as is pending in the Senate, and a successor in your place will have to tear it to pieces and build it all over again. The record that your administration leaves on this legislation will count for a world more in your history, and in the history of the country, if you will try to get what is right even though you fail, than if you take what you can get, knowing that it does not reach the vitals of this question." I said: "If you will send a special message to Congress right now, while this bill is pending, pointing out the things needful to be done, you may not get it through this session, but you have got an organized sentiment that has been building up for nine years; and if you lay down clearly, so the public can understand just what ought to be done, and this Congress fails to act, in the next Congress you will have the people back of you more strongly than ever. If you went to the end of your service as President, reiterating in your messages every time you dealt with the subject the true lines upon which this legislation should be written and the public interest protected, you will have left in your messages a monument compared with which such a statute as this would be trivial."

But however the President may have been impressed by what I said, and I am quite sure he was impressed, no message came from him on the subject of strengthening the bill fundamentally. So I marked out my own course and made up my mind that I would put before the Senate and the country the defects in the bill and would offer the necessary amendments to make it an effective statute. I had no expectation of being able to secure the adoption of any amendments unless I could get the support of the administration for them, but I knew that a beginning must be made to build up public opinion for another try at the law a few years later. I spent several weeks preparing my argument and beginning on April 19, 1906, I spoke for about two hours and a half, the same length of time on the 20th, and the same on the 21st. I reviewed the history of the whole subject. The printed speeches (published together) numbered 148 pages.

I had not been speaking more than ten minutes before I found myself without any Republican colleagues to listen to me, aside from the presiding officer, and the Senator from New Jersey, Mr. Kean, who seemed to have been left on guard. I understood perfectly well that I was being rebuked. It was not altogether because I was a new man in the Senate, but I had no sympathy, no fellowship, no welcome from Republican members of the Senate when I entered. I knew that I was familiar with my subject. I had studied it for several years. In Wisconsin it had been the one subject, above all others, which had been discussed, investigated, and legislated upon. I knew that things had been done there in a fundamental way, and that I had been a part of the doing, and I felt that my experience should be of some value to the country. So I could not help saying:

"Mr. President, I pause in my remarks to say this. I cannot be wholly indifferent to the fact that Senators by their absence at this time indicate their want of interest in what I may have to say upon this subject. The public is interested. Unless this important subject is rightly settled, seats now temporarily vacant may be permanently vacated by those who have the right to occupy them at this time."

It was said very quietly, but it elicited general applause in the galleries, which immediately brought Senator Kean to his feet to demand that the rule of the Senate be enforced and the galleries cleared. The presiding officer thereupon admonished the occupants of the galleries that upon a recurrence of what had transpired the galleries would be cleared.

What occurred in the Senate gallery found its way into the cloak rooms and committee rooms, whence the Senators had retired, and before long they began drifting back into the Senate, and it is fair to say that throughout the remainder of my speech I had exceptional attention.

Senator Dolliver was a member of the committee that had framed this bill, and when I began to attack what was called the

Hepburn-Dolliver bill, naturally he felt compelled to defend it. He had been for six or seven years a member of the Committee on Interstate Commerce and he did not seem to understand what I was talking about when I suggested the radical defect in the bill —that it was not possible for the commission to make and enforce reasonable rates, even if this bill passed. He thought my statement preposterous. Then he proceeded to point out that section so and so of the bill declared every unreasonable rate to be unlawful; and then almost in the next sentence it stated that the commission should have authority to enforce reasonable rates. He seemed to think that this was all that was necessary, and I do not believe that Dolliver or any other man in the Senate at that time had ever seriously considered the idea of determining the value of the property, the cost of maintenance and the cost of operation as a necessary basis for fixing the reasonableness of rates. The thing seemed to break upon the Senate as a startling idea, and yet most of them as business men would never have thought of fixing a price on a commodity or for a service without knowing definitely what that service cost. True, the commission had recommended and urged a valuation of the railroads in its reports, but it had never been aired on the floor of the Senate.

I pointed out to Senator Dolliver in the course of the debate that there were no means by which the commission could ascertain what was a reasonable rate; that under the law of 1887, as proposed to be amended by the pending bill, it would be possible for the commission to determine whether rates were *relatively reasonable,* but not that they were *reasonable per se;* that one rate could be compared with another, but that the commission had no means of determining whether either rate so compared was itself a reasonable rate. And then I proceeded to lay down the basis for determining reasonable rates, and we had a running debate for about an hour, when Dolliver, who had come down until he stood squarely in front of my desk, said:

"Mr. President, I am disposed to sympathize with the views of the Senator from Wisconsin: I believe that the bill ought to be amended."

And he was one of five other Senators besides myself on the Republican side who voted for the amendment to authorize the Interstate Commerce Commission to ascertain the value of the railroad property of the country. And from that time on Senator Dolliver, as long as he lived, stood with me whenever the question of valuation was raised.

Dolliver was honest-minded, and when his intellect pointed the way, that way Dolliver went always. I shall have more to say of him later in this narrative.

I do not think the "stand-patters" of the Senate understood what I was talking about when I discussed the Hepburn-Dolliver bill. They did not follow me closely enough to understand. But on the Democratic side of the Senate chamber I had excellent attention, and before I finished I had a goodly number on the other side.

When the time came to offer amendments I carefully canvassed the Democratic side of the house, and secured the pledges of enough Senators to enable me to get a roll call on the amendments as I offered them. I made no personal appeal to any Senator to vote for any amendment. All that I asked was that they give me an opportunity to put the Senate on record. And I found the Democrats very ready to do that.

In offering each amendment I made perhaps a five or ten minute statement, and then demanded the yeas and nays. On the amendment for the valuation of railways engaged in interstate commerce I demonstrated conclusively the overcapitalization of the railroads of the country. I argued that if the same system were applied which we were then applying in Wisconsin—that is, the true value of the property ascertained together with the cost of maintaining the property and the cost of operating the property, and the rates so adjusted as to make a fair return to the railroads upon the actual investment made by the roads and not upon capitalization—that it would be working a saving in transportation charges of something more than $400,000,000 to the people of this country every twelve months. In support of that amendment I used the reports of the Interstate Commerce Commission, the decisions of the Supreme Court of the United States, and the demonstration made in Wisconsin. And yet, when the roll was called, my amendment was beaten 40 to 27, the only Republicans voting for it being Burkett, Dolliver, Elkins, Gamble, La Follette, Warner.

There were nine amendments in all. Eight of them had the endorsement of the Interstate Commerce Commission, an unprejudiced body. Each had reason and justice back of it. No argument could be made against any one of them, and no argument ever was made on the floor against their merits either at that time or since. There was nothing to be said on the other side.

Coming home on the street car one day, I wondered how far they would go. And I took a tab out of my pocket and outlined an amendment to the effect that any federal judge should be disqualified from hearing, trying or determining any case for the regulation of railway rates against any road in which he was a stockholder, or whose bonds he owned, or upon which he used free passes. And that amendment was lost 40 to 27. There were only three Republicans who thought that a federal judge ought not to own stock in a road and then hear, try and determine a case involving its interests!

Formerly, record votes on delicate questions were always avoided in the Senate, if possible; but I had a purpose in thus committing the Senators on these phases of railroad control. I wanted to show exactly where they stood and why.

During the summer which followed I made a speaking tour that covered nearly all the states from New York to California, and everywhere I went I used these roll-call records of the Senate. I made twenty-one speeches in which I showed the record of Dryden of New Jersey, and I have no doubt that the proof which these roll calls furnished of the true attitude of Senators served to retire not a few of them. There were twenty-four "stand-pat" members of the Senate at that time (1906) who are not there to-day.

At the beginning of the next session (1907) I determined to press forward with constructive railroad legislation and I introduced a bill providing for a comprehensive valuation of the railroads as a basis for establishing just and reasonable rates. I submitted the bill before its introduction to the Interstate Commerce Commissioners and had the benefit of their advice and suggestions.

After introducing it in the Senate I tried for weeks to get a hearing upon it before the committee, but was wholly unable to do so.

I introduced the bill again at the beginning of the next session of Congress in March, 1909, and I have kept it before the Senate committee ever since. I believe absolutely that it is the only basis of a just settlement of the problem. I know how well the plan is being worked out in Wisconsin, and I am certain sooner or later that the national government must adopt it.

To illustrate the futility of the Hepburn law as passed, it is worth noting that the railroads began almost immediately to raise their rates, and they accompanied these raises by a systematic and costly campaign of publicity to make the public believe that the advances were necessary. But in spite of this, during the years 1907, 1908 and 1909 a number of large meetings were held at which shippers, manufacturers and producers protested against the raises.

And in 1910, the next railroad legislation which really got before Congress was the so-called Commerce Court bill, though the establishment of a Commerce Court was only one of its provisions. That bill as it came from Attorney-General Wickersham with the approval of President Taft was, in all the history of railroad legislation, the rankest, boldest betrayal of public interest ever proposed in any legislative body. If it had been passed as introduced it would have lost to the people all the ground that had been gained in the long struggle with the railroad corporations. The bill as it was originally presented practically took all the power away from the Interstate Commerce Commission, deprived it of the right of employing counsel to defend its own orders and transferred all that authority to the Attorney-General's office. It bestowed upon the railroads much larger rights in contesting before the courts the orders of the commission than they had ever had before, and cut out, root and branch, the right formerly enjoyed by outside interested parties and communities of appearing and paying their own attorneys to aid in sustaining the orders of the commission.

In short, it threw the determination of railroad questions back into the hands of the Attorney-General and the courts.

Before the Progressives in the Senate began an attack upon this bill I made a speech reviewing the acts of the present Attorney-General, Mr. Wickersham, in the very important matter of the New Haven Railroad cases. The dismissal of these suits, which had been brought before Mr. Roosevelt left the White House, was almost the first act of surrender to the interests on the part of the Taft administration.

In my speech I showed the strength of the government's case against the New Haven merger, yet the first act of the Taft administration, through the Attorney-General, was to hand over all that great section of New England to the New Haven Railroad, which had acquired control not only of all means of transportation by rail, but had bankrupted or bought in practically all of the steamship and trolley lines, so that to-day you cannot ship a pound of anything from Massachusetts excepting on the terms imposed by a single corporation. That whole speech was specifically aimed against that provision of the law which gave the Attorney-General exclusive power in connection with the prosecution of cases. It was aimed to sound a warning in the ears of the Senate when we came to consider the question of clothing the Department of Justice with the sole power of saying the final word with reference to litigation between the people and the railroads.

And I think my speech had much to do in preventing the adoption of this provision of the law.

The first speech that I made on the Commerce Court bill was on April 12, 1910, on the New Haven merger. I made the other speeches on the bill April 29, May 25 and 26, May 31, and June 3. On May 31 I offered my amendment for the valuation of railroads as a part of this bill, and made an argument upon it. My amendment was defeated by a vote of 33 to 29; 11 of the 29 were Republican; the 33 who opposed it were all Republicans.

The reception of my speeches by the Senate in 1910 on the railroad question was markedly in contrast with the reception given in 1906.

In the fight made on the President's railroad bill Senators Clapp and Cummins, who were members of the committee, took very active part. Senator Cummins, particularly during the earlier weeks of the contest, was almost constantly in the debate. The entire Progressive group carried the great burden of the contest against the administration bill, and so strong and so effective was their attack, and so reasonable their arguments, that the administration Senators on the floor were compelled to abandon entire sections of the bill to avoid the humiliation of being overwhelmingly voted down in the Senate.

Several sections of the bill were put forward in the beginning under the guise of reforming abuses in watering and overcapitalizing railroad properties. These sections, under the mask of preventing overcapitalization, were in fact designed to legalize every dollar of the railroad capitalization of the country, and under cover of ingeniously worded phraseology would have made possible unlimited railroad stock-jobbing for all future time.

Mr. Taft, in an interview published in the *Outlook* December 2, 1911, takes to himself credit for the railroad legislation as it finally passed. As a matter of fact, the fangs in this bill as originally introduced were, with the exception of the Commerce Court provisions, all drawn by the fight of the Progressives. We could not, however, prevent the establishment of a Commerce Court, which is in a position to destroy, and is now actually destroying, the work of the most progressive Interstate Commerce Commission the country has ever had. It is scarcely possible to speak of the course of the administration upon this legislation in temperate language.

I wish in this place to refer briefly—and I must do it more briefly than the matter deserves—to another fight I made in which I had to meet the railroad interests as they had entrenched themselves in the Interstate Commerce Committee. The Railroad Brotherhoods of Engineers, Firemen and Trainmen, a remarkably intelligent body of men, had long maintained a very efficient and faithful legislative representative, Mr. Hugh Fuller, here at the national capital, but they had found it impossible even to get a record vote on important measures in which they were interested. No bill in their interests relating to hours of service or liability of the employer for negligence was permitted to get out of the committee. I took up the matter of an Employers' Liability law and attempted in 1906 to have it adopted as an amendment to the Interstate Commerce Act. Failing in this, by an unexpected move I got a bill before the Senate where I could force a record vote. Now, no Senator wanted to put himself wrong with the railway employees, and so after fencing for delay I finally got it passed without a roll call. This law, having been held unconstitutional by the supreme court (by a vote of five to four), I introduced another Employers' Liability bill in the next session, and had it referred to the Committee on Education and Labor (of which Dolliver was chairman) instead of to the Committee on Interstate Commerce. The bill was reported out by Dolliver, was passed and is now the law.

I also secured the passage in 1907, after much opposition and filibustering, of a law to limit the hours of continuous service of railroad employees. This law has been of great use in preventing those accidents which formerly arose from the continuous employment of men for twenty-four or even thirty-six hours without sleep or rest.

Chapter x

Reinforcements: A National
Progressive Movement

What is undoubtedly the most significant development of recent years in the Congress of the United States, especially in the Senate, has been the growth of the so-called Progressive group—reflecting a similar change in political view upon the part of the people of the country.

When I entered the Senate I was alone. Dolliver, Clapp, and Beveridge, all of whom were afterward active Progressives, had been members of the Senate for some time and were still recognized as regular, though Dolliver had shown some symptoms of revolt. I have already described the first occasion upon which the few Republican Senators who were willing to oppose the reactionary bosses were brought together—upon the Naval Appropriation bill in January, 1909. Later, after we got into the tariff fight in 1909, we began to know who could be depended upon, and our meetings were frequent. Dolliver, Beveridge, and Clapp were here when I came; Dixon and Bourne entered March 4, 1907; Borah, March, 1908; Cummins, November, 1908; and Bristow, March, 1909. This was the group which generally worked together.

I cannot let this occasion pass without some special reference to Dolliver, who, in the last year of his service in the Senate, became a great power for good.

Dolliver was a wonderfully gifted man. His command of language and facility of expression equaled that of any man I ever knew. He had imagination, humor, alertness. He could command all of his powers instantly. This was something of a misfortune to Dolliver, because it tempted him often to depend upon this wonderful readiness of power instead of engaging in the drudgery which is necessary to enable any man to master first the principles and then the details of a complex problem. He entered public life very young and everything came to him easily. He did not have to encounter opposition in his own district. He did not have to fight for anything in his own state. He was taken up by the leaders here in the House and afterward in the Senate. He was always in demand as a speaker at banquets, always flattered and applauded, and he drifted along with the old crowd. So, when I came to the Senate Dolliver was one of the men put forward to answer any criticism that I might offer against things as they existed. Even after the debate on the railroad bill, to which I referred in the last chapter, Dolliver was lecturing in the same field that I was covering. I had been out through Iowa before I came to the Senate, and I had reviewed the struggle that was then on in Congress to amend the Interstate Commerce Act. I spoke in Dolliver's town and I spoke in Hepburn's town, and they came in for my criticism against the committees for holding up legislation. Senator Dolliver was piqued and prepared a speech for the chautauqua platform designed to answer my criticism, though he never mentioned my name. So, when I came to the Senate, although we had been good friends in the House, and though he greeted me cordially, I felt that he was more than a little against me.

In 1908 I was the one Republican in the Senate who made a fight on the Emergency Currency bill. Dolliver came back a day or two before the vote was to be taken. And he was staged for an eloquent fifteen or twenty minute talk aimed directly at me. He did not mention my name, of course, but it was intended as a rebuke to me.

I used to say to Mrs. La Follette, "Dolliver sometime or other will come to himself," and so I never would be drawn into any controversy with him which would lead to a breach in our friendly personal relations.

As we were coming into the new session, in 1909, and the tariff bill was coming up, I thought a great deal about Dolliver. One day I went over to his seat and said, "Senator, I want you to come down to my committee room. I want to talk with you."

He said, "Sit down and talk here."

"No," I said, "I want a serious talk with you. We will both get angry before we get through, but we will stay until we get it over with."

"What is it all about, Bob?" he asked.

"I want to make you see that you ought to break away from Aldrich," and I pointed to the other fellows sitting all about him. "These fellows are not serving the public; they are betraying the public and you are following them. Your place is at the head of a movement here in the Senate and in the country for the public interest."

He said, "Bob, your liver is all out of order; you're jaundiced. You see things awry: cheer up."

So he laughed and turned me off with a joke, and I did not get any serious talk with him until March, after the committees were selected. Allison was dead and Cummins had succeeded him. Dolliver surrendered his place on the Committee on Interstate Commerce so that Cummins could have a good committee assignment. According to Senate usage two Senators representing the same state and belonging to the same political party cannot serve on the same committee. Dolliver had gone to the boss of the Senate, Mr. Aldrich, and said, "Will you put Cummins on that committee if I resign?"

"Why, if you want it, I will," said Aldrich.

Having resigned from that committee to make way for Cummins, he applied for appointment to the vacancy created by Allison's death on the Committee on Finance. Dolliver had a right to expect that his friends, Aldrich and the rest, would put him on. But after getting his resignation from the Committee on Interstate Commerce, Dolliver was not only denied a place on the Committee on Finance, upon which he had set his heart, but Cummins himself came within a hair's breadth of losing the appointment to the Committee on Interstate Commerce.

Meeting Dolliver in the corridor one day after the appointments were announced, I said to him, "Jonathan, are you pretty nearly ready to have that conference with me?"

He answered, "Yes, I am coming over to see you."

"Well," I said, "come now."

And he went with me to my committee room. We spent several hours together. Dolliver reviewed all of his associations with these masters of legislation in the House and in the Senate. He went back to the treatment which he had received on the Committee on Interstate Commerce when Aldrich took his railroad bill away from him by a combination of votes in the committee and placed him in the humiliating situation of having to see his bill reported by a Democratic member of the committee. He told me then of the difficulty with which he held himself in restraint from making an outbreak against Aldrich and the system, but that he had yielded to the counsel of his old colleague, Senator Allison. But he said that he had told Allison that he could not stand it much longer; that he was going to break away and declare his independence of the system in the Senate which was manipulating legislation for the benefit of great interests. And Allison, whom he loved like a father, had said to him:

"Jonathan, don't do it; don't do it now: wait until I am gone. I know it is wrong. It has grown up here gradually in the last quarter of a century. I have gone along with it. These men are my associates. I have only a little while left, and I haven't the strength to break away. It has got to come. It is a cancer; it's got to be cut out. But wait until I am gone, and then go into this new movement where you belong."

Dolliver said to me, "From this time on I am going to be independent. I am going to serve my conscience. I have been lecturing, I have saved my dollars and put them into a farm up there in Iowa. I am going to judgment in the next twenty years, and I am going so I can look my Maker in the face. I do not have to stay in public life. I can take my books, my wife, and my children, and if I am dismissed from the service for following my conviction I will go out to my farm, and stay there until the call comes."

After that I don't know how many times Dolliver, when our little group would be conferring, would turn toward me and say, "Bob has been taking the gaff all these years, and isn't going to take it alone any longer."

Dolliver never came to the fulness of his strength until this great political revolution took place within him. And then it awaked the sleeping giant and he became a student of the details of the tariff; he dug it out by the roots.

Dolliver had a very remarkable memory. He often told me about how he had trained it. His father had insisted upon his committing all of his Latin themes and whole books of the Bible to memory. He could write out a speech and deliver it almost literally as it was written.

He was attacked by the stand-patters of Iowa when he became a Progressive, and he was not credited even by Progressives with that sincerity of conviction which he was in every way entitled to. Many of those in the Progressive ranks who had suffered under his keen witticisms could not believe that Dolliver had changed from conviction. But I know that he did. A close study of his record will show how, even while Allison still lived, he was constantly straining at the bonds which kept him in the ranks on that side. He and Clapp came together. They were very dear friends—often together in a social way. They understood and appreciated each other. They were not at all alike, but they had a very strong affection for each other.

It was the fight on the Payne-Aldrich tariff bill which brought us all together. The administration of Roosevelt had come to an end on March 4, 1909, with nothing to its credit in the way of tariff revision. That thorny problem fell to the unfortunate Mr. Taft.

Now, Mr. Taft, fully appreciating the public clamor for tariff changes, and knowing that he could not be elected unless he took a strong stand, interpreted the platform pledge with respect to tariff revision in a speech at Milwaukee on September 24, 1908, as follows:

"I can say that our party is pledged to a genuine revision, and as temporary head of that party and President of the United States, if it be successful in November, I expect to use all the influence I have by calling immediately a special session and by recommendations to Congress to secure a *genuine and honest revision.*"

He also promised a *"substantial revision downward."*

As soon as he was inaugurated President Taft called an extraordinary session of Congress to meet on March 15, 1909—and the work of the tariff revision began.

Immediately, as will be remembered, the struggle began for control of the organization of both houses. In the House an attempt made to defeat Cannon, whom Taft had in the campaign called "An old man of the Sea," was frustrated through the influence of no other person than Mr. Taft himself—and to the dismay of every one. And in the Senate, in spite of opposition, the old control, with Aldrich as its leader, organized all the committees.

We had expected that Taft's first state paper to the extra session which he had called would be a vigorous demand for downward revision of the tariff. The Senate and House were crowded. The attention was keen everywhere. The clerk began to read. At the end of two minutes he stopped. There was a hush, an expectation that he would resume. But he laid aside the paper. A look of amazement was on every face. The one thing emphasized in the President's message was the importance of disposing of the tariff as early as possible in order that business might not be long disturbed by uncertainties regarding customs tariffs. Not a word about honest revision or revision downward!

But the Progressives did not then lose hope in the President. We believed that he would still carry out his promises. We had all supported him heartily in his campaign. I had been the candidate of the state of Wisconsin for the Presidency at the convention which nominated Taft, and while I had no expectation of being nominated, I did hope that we should have some influence in molding the platform. When Taft was nominated, I immediately sent him the following telegram:

"Hon. William H. Taft,
    "Washington, D. C.
"While the platform is disappointing in some fundamental provisions and omissions, and I shall claim the right to say so, I congratulate you most sincerely, and in the faith that you are more nearly in accord with the great body of Republican voters than the platform, I shall do all in my power to insure your election."

When the tariff bill passed the House, therefore, after being bitterly opposed by the House insurgents as the thoroughly bad measure that it was, I felt at liberty to call upon the President and talk with him about it. I still had hope that he would keep faith with the people. He agreed with me, on that occasion, that the bill as it passed the House was not a compliance with platform pledges, and he said distinctly that unless it were thoroughly overhauled he would veto it. I suggested to the President that it was plainly his duty now to transmit a message to Congress making it clear that the House bill was in violation of the pledges of the party and against the public interests.

"Well," he said, "I don't much believe in a President's interfering with the legislative department while it is doing its work. They have their responsibility and I have mine. And if they send that bill to me, and it isn't a better bill than it is now, I will veto it."

I suggested that if he remained silent he would never find himself able, after the record was made up, to turn about and fall upon Congress with a veto. His answer came quick and strong.

"You and your associates in the Senate go ahead, criticise the bill, amend it, cut down the duties—go after it hard. I will keep track of your amendments. I will read every word of the speeches you make, and when they lay that bill down before me, unless it complies with the platform, I will veto it."

And he brought his fist down on the desk with a thump to emphasize the firmness of his purpose.

"Very well," I said, "Mr. President, but I predict that when it passes the Senate it will be a far worse measure than it is now."

"Well," he retorted, "I will show you."

Aldrich kept the bill in possession of his committee for forty-eight hours. The corridors about his committee rooms were crowded with the representatives of the big protected interests. Some were admitted from time to time for brief conferences. When Aldrich reported the bill he made a brief oral statement devoted solely to an estimate of the revenues which would be produced under the proposed duties. No written report accompanied the bill, and no explanation, written or oral, was placed before the Senate, offering any reason for the six hundred increases over the rates fixed in the House bill. Thereupon, Aldrich demanded immediate consideration of the bill, which contained three hundred pages, and of which most of the Senators had no knowledge whatever. He was preparing, as usual, to drive roughshod over all opposition.

I was not altogether unprepared for this action on the Senator's part, and, taking the floor, I protested against the present consideration of the bill. I made it plain that never before in our history had the Senate Committee on Finance failed to submit with a tariff bill an extended printed report setting forth the arguments for every change of duty. Furthermore, I proved from the record that it had been the invariable custom of the Senate committee to place the tariff bill and the accompanying report upon the desks of Senators, with a notice that the bill would be taken up some two to six weeks later, giving Senators full opportunity to familiarize themselves with the proposed changes.

No answer was made to my speech. It was manifestly the purpose of Senator Aldrich to allow Senators no chance to prepare in advance to resist the sort of tariff legislation which the Payne-Aldrich bill provided. And in furtherance of this plan, as the consideration of the bill advanced, he secured the adoption of an order that the Senate should meet, until further order, at 10 o'clock in the morning, and that the sessions should continue without recess or adjournment until 11 o'clock at night. The reason which he advanced for this was that the business interests were suffering because of the uncertainties regarding the tariff; but the effect of this order was to force those Senators who were conscientiously investigating schedules either to abandon all of their efforts or to take the course pursued by our little group. I personally know that it was the practice of a number of Progressives, as it was my practice, to leave the Senate at the close of the session at 11 o'clock and, reaching home at midnight, to work well into the small hours of the morning over the provisions certain to be reached on the succeeding day, then snatch a brief rest and be ready for the session at ten o'clock in the morning. This work continued week after week all through the hot months of a sultry Washington summer.

It was taxing to the last degree, and reduced the vitality of the hardiest members of the group. I shall always believe that the exactions of that session were the primary cause of Dolliver's death a year later.

Two of the members of the group, Senator Dolliver and myself, had been members of the Ways and Means Committee of the House of Representatives and had taken part in framing the tariff bills in other sessions. Senator Dolliver performed a prodigious amount of labor, particularly upon the cotton schedule, followed by one of the most brilliant speeches of his entire public career. Senator Bristow devoted much time to the lead and sugar schedules; Senator Cummins made special preparation upon the metal schedule, glass, and other important products of general consumption. He was in the debate day by day, rendering most excellent public service. I endeavored to acquire as complete a knowledge as possible of the cotton schedule, the woolen schedule and important items in several other schedules of the bill, which I presented as thoroughly as I could.

The feature of the work done by the insurgents upon the bill is characteristic of the Progressive attitude toward all matters of public interest—and that is *service to the public* as against special interests. It is incumbent upon the reformer who seeks to establish a new order to come equipped with complete mastery of all the information upon which the established order is based. And it is for this reason that the thoroughgoing, uncompromising, Progressive movement is essentially a safe one for the public and for all legitimate business.

It soon became apparent as we got into the thickest of the fight that the lines were set and the combinations effected to advance instead of reduce tariff duties. Reductions here and there in no way beneficial to the consuming public were made with a view to offsetting in the general average advances upon many of the necessaries of life, which already enjoyed an excessive protection under the Dingley law.

The bi-partisan character of the tariff issue also soon developed. In any case where the Progressive attack menaced the duty on any product, Aldrich as a rule summoned to his support a sufficient number of reactionary Democrats to prevent breaking his lines.

Mr. Aldrich soon discovered that with all his experience in piloting tariff bills through Congress he was in no wise equipped to meet the opposition of the Progressives. And after a few encounters, when either of the three or four men in the Progressive group took the floor to attack some schedule, Aldrich would beat a hasty retreat from the floor of the Senate to escape the mortification certain to follow such encounters. In all of his long leadership in the Senate on all questions, tariff or otherwise, it had been sufficient for Mr. Aldrich to say, "It is so," or "It is not so," or "It is necessary"—but a new day had dawned. The insurgents stood in the pathway of Mr. Aldrich's program of legislation with searching interrogatories demanding reasons for all things. The Senate boss was thrown into confusion. He had been accustomed to issue orders —not furnish reasons.

The consideration of the tariff bill had proceeded but a little way when it became certain that no important changes could be effected. But that did not deter the Progressives. Defeated again and again, they returned to the attack. It was a splendid exhibition of the true spirit of moral reform. *Defeat was a matter of no consequence to them.*

The great service rendered by the Progressives in the extra tariff session was a clean-cut, straightaway, undeviating fight for principle. The extra tariff session did more to give the Progressive movement a clear definition in the public mind than any one thing that has transpired in Congress.

There were ten Republicans, not all of whom could be classed as Progressives, who voted against the bill on its first passage through the Senate: Beveridge, Bristow, Brown, Burkett, Clapp, Crawford, Cummins, Dolliver, Nelson and myself. The bill then went to conference.

While most of the Progressives were disappointed in the President's attitude, they still hoped that he might do something. During the debate, in appealing to the Republican side of the Senate to make good the pledges of the Republican platform, I had quoted President Taft in Milwaukee, in Des Moines, in Kansas City, interpreting the pledge of that platform to mean downward revision. Other Progressives made reference to these speeches for the same reason. We felt that there could be no gainsaying his position.

While the bill was in conference I took the occasion to go to my home in Wisconsin, and called at the White House to pay my respects before leaving. The President said:

"Come and sit down. I want to talk with you about the tariff. What am I to do with this bill?"

I said, "Mr. President, you ought to veto it. You remember you said you would unless it was a better bill than when it passed the

House. Instead of being a better bill, it is much worse. Hundreds of increases have been made in the Senate."

"Well," he said, "suppose I find that I can't do that. What changes ought I to insist upon in conference?"

I could not help remembering what the President had said previously about his being opposed to executive interference with the legislative department of government. But the country was all wrought up and the President had thrown his scruples to the winds. Picking up a pencil and pad of paper, he said,

"Tell me what things ought to be reduced in duty."

He wrote as I talked until he had filled the page of the tablet. Then, laying it down, he said,

"Will you write me a letter stating succinctly the things that you think ought to be done?"

I had made my preparations to go home, but I waited over, and the following day I sent to the White House a somewhat lengthy typewritten document giving my views. I started out by saying that I thought he ought to veto the bill, but that if he decided not to veto it, it ought to be changed in certain particulars which I outlined. I got a note from him a day or two after I reached home thanking me for that letter.

At the end of ten days the conferees reached an agreement and reported to the two houses. The final test came on the adoption of the conference report, the effect of which would be to send the bill to the President. The bill was not so changed in conference as to materially alter its character. Mr. Taft had failed to get his stand-pat friends who conducted the conference to make changes that really amounted to anything. It was still a violation of the platform pledges; it still broke faith with the people. There were indeed slight modifications in duties on lumber, and three or four other articles, and upon these slight changes the administration based its hope of securing the support of some of the Senators and Representatives who had voted against the bill before it went to conference. There was a basis for this hope. After making a record in the House or the Senate against the bill to present to his constituents a member was in a position to say that he had done his best to improve the bill and that he now chose to vote with his party for a protective measure, though it were too radically protective, rather than vote with the Democrats against the bill reported by the conference committee.

Again it became a question in our little group as to how many would stand against the conference report and complete a record

of consistent opposition to a bill that represented the consummation of privilege more reprehensible than had ever before found a
place upon the statutes of the country.

I recall distinctly the efforts put forth to break our lines. Insurgents were invited to the White House to meet the President, and
others saw him from time to time. Among these were Dolliver,
Cummins and Beveridge. I recall Dolliver's comment:

"Bob," he said, "I was invited up to the White House to a tariff
breakfast." And then he paused and looked at me with a twinkle
in his eye and added, "The muskmelon he served was not very
good."

I knew that Dolliver had not changed. Neither Bristow, Clapp,
nor I was invited to sample the President's breakfast melons. We
were regarded as hopelessly lost to the administration.

The conference report was agreed upon during the night, and
the stand-pat papers announced that the changes made a great
"moral victory" for President Taft. This was to open the door for
the "near" insurgents to come back to the party and vote for the
conference report. One not experienced in the life of the national
capital can hardly conceive the tensity of the situation. Party
loyalty is still a fetish in Congress. The air of the Senate chamber
and cloak-rooms was charged with partisan feeling. It fairly
crackled.

But in spite of all this pressure, our little group held together
wonderfully, and at the final vote the following Republicans cast
their ballots against the bill: Beveridge, Bristow, Clapp, Cummins, Dolliver and myself. Senator Nelson, who cannot be classed
as a Progressive, also voted against the bill.

All during the struggle over the Payne-Aldrich bill partisan
power and partisan methods were used in all their forms to force
the Progressives into line upon a measure which they knew to be
bad. The insurgent members of the House, for example, were
made apprehensive about their patronage. A great many of their
post-office appointments were delayed—and a little later the appointments growing out of the taking of the new census became a
critical matter.

One night nearly all of the Wisconsin delegation came up to my
residence. They were very much wrought up. They had discovered
that the administration was discriminating against the Progressive
members in Wisconsin and in favor of Senator Stephenson, who
was voting regularly with Aldrich. Senator Stephenson had said
to them that the President was going to allow Mr. E. A. Edmonds

to name the supervisors of census in all the districts of Wisconsin. Edmonds was chairman of the State Central Committee of Wisconsin and the man who had managed Stephenson's campaign when he spent $107,000 in the primary election. They said they came to me because I was chairman of the Committee on Census of the Senate, and they thought that I might ascertain if Mr. Taft was going to turn over all the patronage of the state to the "standpatters." I told them that such an action as this was directly contrary to what he had said to me when discussing the civil service features of the census bill; that I had seen him about strengthening those sections of the bill and he had then assured me that the census bureau was not to be made a political machine. I told the delegation that if it would be any satisfaction to them I would bring the matter to the President's attention. So I saw the President and told him just what had been reported. He looked out of the window and said, "It's a lie; not a word of truth in it."

"Well," I said, "may I say to them, Mr. President, that they can file their recommendations with the expectation that they will be treated as other Republican Congressmen are treated?"

"Well," he said, "I can't take this matter up *until after the tariff bill is passed.*"

Then I knew that this patronage matter was being held as a club over the Progressives.

When the tariff bill was passed, Mr. Lenroot, Mr. Nelson and Mr. Cary, Wisconsin Republican members, all voted against it. When they filed their recommendations before leaving Washington for supervisors in their respective districts they were promptly turned down and stand-patters recommended by Stephenson and Edmonds appointed in their places. There was one Democratic district in Wisconsin where no recommendation had been made. Doctor Durand said he would be glad to have me make a recommendation for that district. The man I suggested was promptly turned down, and the man appointed by the President was recommended by Mr. Edmonds and Senator Stephenson.

Now these appointments were made during the recess, and their nominations all had to come through the Senate Committee on Census, of which I was chairman. When the committee met I stated exactly what the President had done with respect to supervisors of census in Wisconsin. Hale, Carter, and a number of members of the committee said:

"You report against the confirmation of those Wisconsin supervisors, and every member of this committee and the whole Senate will stand with you. Not one of them will be confirmed."

But I saw plainly enough that I was going to have some differences with the administration upon important legislative matters and so I resolved to report these nominations for confirmation, determined that my differences with the administration, if any, should be upon matters of principle and not be obscured by squabbles over patronage.

I wish to refer here in passing to another experience I had, as chairman of the Census Committee, with the President. On one of my visits to the White House while the census bill was pending I called the President's attention to a section of the bill that provided for taking the valuation of the manufacturing plants of the country. I said, "Mr. President, I have been a member of the Senate for three or four years. I have been trying to secure consideration of an amendment to the Interstate Commerce Act authorizing the commission to make a valuation of the railroads of the country. But as the committees are organized in the Senate and in the House we can't get a bill out of the committee. Now there is an opportunity here to put a provision into the census bill employing engineers of the army and other experts under the direction of the Department of Commerce and Labor to make a physical valuation of the railroads, and I am very strongly tempted to use all the power and influence I have as chairman of that committee to get some action upon this important subject."

"Senator La Follette," he said, "I am afraid that will delay consideration of the bill. If you will not do that, I will recommend valuation strongly in my message next fall; I will put the whole influence of the administration behind your proposition."

I said, "Very well, Mr. President. I will act on your suggestion, and with the support of the administration next fall we will have a good show of getting some action."

He did not recommend the legislation in his message. Instead, he put in a statement that no legislation of the sort was necessary; that the Interstate Commerce Commission should proceed under the law just as it was. And that was the end of the valuation of railroad property under the Taft administration.

It was acts such as these, together with his attitude upon the tariff question, his failure to support the plain pledges of the party, his interference in behalf of Cannon, his use of patronage to discipline members, his alignment with Aldrich and the stand-patters of the party, and his whole course in the Ballinger affair, which absolutely alienated the Progressive group.

One of the most important measures which has come before the Senate since I became a member is the Aldrich Emergency Currency bill, afterward known as the Aldrich-Vreeland Currency bill. In some ways no bill ever introduced in Congress was more significant of the control of legislation by great financial interests. This bill proposed an issue of $500,000,000 of additional notes to national banking associations, such issue to be based upon state bonds, municipal bonds, and as reported by the committee and advocated by Senator Aldrich, *railroad bonds* as well. The country had just gone through the panic of 1907 and banks and business had been made to feel the pinch. There was a plausible reason to urge, and, indeed, considering the character of our currency system and the imperfection of our banking laws, a sound reason, for making provision against a sudden withdrawal of the money necessary for the daily exchanges of business, whether such contraction was due to the fear resulting from a panic inaugurated for speculative purposes or otherwise. For even a managed panic may become unmanageable, and in any event legitimate commercial enterprises are certain to suffer.

But there were reasons back of the emergency features of this bill more important vastly to the interests than those prominently urged. It was inevitable that the years of stock-watering and promotion, the inflation of railway securities, industrial securities, mining, traction, gas and electricity, should bring its harvest of financial distress and reaction. It was inevitable that the crime of overcapitalization should meet its punishment. There was urgent demand that these securities should be restored to public confidence. The emergency currency measure offered the opportunity, and for the first time in history it was proposed that railroad bonds should be wrought into our monetary system as a basis for currency issue.

To secure the acceptance of railroad bonds as a basis for even an emergency currency would accomplish two vitally important things for the special interests: First, it would restore confidence in such railroad securities, stocks as well as bonds; second, it would avert an impending danger to such securities, which had been seriously menaced by a proposal to ascertain the true value of the properties of the railroads, against which stocks and bonds had been issued without limit.

When I entered the Senate in 1906, as before stated, I had proposed as an amendment to the Hepburn rate bill a provision authorizing and directing the Interstate Commerce Commission to make such valuation as a basis for establishing reasonable rates. The Senate had voted down my proposed amendment.

For two years I had awaited an opportunity to offer my amendment providing for valuation to any measure pending before the Senate to which it would be germane. Apparently it had never occurred to the committee reporting the currency bill that my valuation measure, which had been bottled up in the Committee on Interstate Commerce, would be germane as an amendment to the railroad bond provision in the currency bill.

This opportunity now presented itself in connection with the Emergency Currency bill. I promptly offered an amendment providing that the Secretary of the Treasury should be authorized to accept railroad bonds as security for the emergency currency issue *only after the Interstate Commerce Commission had ascertained the value of the physical properties of the railroads,* upon which the bonds in question constituted a first mortgage; and provided further that no such railroad bonds should be accepted unless the value of the property of the railroad company were found to be ample security for such bonds.

The offering of the amendment produced a flutter of excitement. Disgust and consternation were plainly manifest. For two years they had been able to deny me a vote in the Senate on the valuation of railway property and the reactionary Senators had learned to fear being placed on record with roll calls. And here I was rudely thrusting this troublesome proposition upon them in violation of all the regulations governing "senatorial courtesy."

I had announced that on March 17th I would address the Senate on the pending bill, and in that connection would oppose the railroad bonds provision. Thirty minutes before I was to begin my argument on that day Senator Aldrich arose and informed the Senate that he was directed by the Committee on Finance to withdraw from the bill all that portion of it relating to railway bonds!

But if it was Mr. Aldrich's purpose to avoid a discussion of his plan to make railroad bonds a security for currency issue he failed. For in opening my argument I referred to the announcement of Senator Aldrich, and predicted that at some later stage in the course of the legislation that same provision would again make its appearance in the bill. Therefore I covered in my argument the railroad bonds provision and discussed it thoroughly. I presented facts to show that 75 per cent. of the railroad bonds which would be affected by the provision were held by banks in New England and eastern states, and only 25 per cent. distributed throughout the west, middle west, and south. With its highly organized banking system the entire holdings would be at the command of the big group banks. In the course of my argument I was also able to demonstrate that the legislation would operate to place the money trust in a position to control for their own advantage any issue of emergency currency.

When government bonds were made the basis for national bank issues, it was avowedly for the purpose of enhancing their market value. It had that effect. It would have a like effect upon railroad, municipal and other bonds. It would be difficult to conceive of a better way to boom the market for railroad bonds than to put behind them the mandate of the law compelling national banks to go into the market and bid for them. Could anything be conceived by the ingenuity of man that would more quickly enhance the price of railroad bonds held by a limited number of speculative banks and by a few capitalists, or better promote certain great related interests?

In the course of my speech on the Emergency Currency bill I showed clearly how the industrial and banking interests are closely controlled by a small group of financiers. I asserted that fewer than one hundred men control the great business interests of the country.

The following day the great newspapers of the country, with very rare exceptions, denied my statements and denounced me as a demagogue. The *Review of Reviews* editorially characterized my utterances as sensational and much to be regretted.

A few days later I replied to my critics and out of the Directories of Directors and other record data proved my assertions, and demonstrated that in fact less than a dozen men control the business of the country—indeed, that Standard Oil and Morgan are the real business kings of America.

In a way the public had understood that the railroads had consolidated and even that the great manufacturing corporations of the country had combined to control production and prices. But I think I may say that never before March, 1908, had the facts been brought together in any discussion in Congress. I then demonstrated through an analysis of the directorates of Big Business that the railroads, telegraph, shipping, street car and interurban lines, cable, telephone, express, mining, iron, coal, oil, gas, electric light, manufacturing, steel, agricultural implements, machinery of all kinds, cotton, woolens, tobacco, sugar, and the food products are completely controlled and mainly owned by a small group of men.

I was very much interested and not a little gratified a few weeks ago to have the statements I made in 1908, as applied to the control of capital and credit, corroborated by the president of one of the largest banks in the United States—George M. Reynolds of the Continental and Commercial Bank of Chicago. On the 13th day of December, 1911, he was one of the speakers at the somewhat exclusive banquet held under the auspices of the National Business League of America. I might add parenthetically that this National Business League of America is an organization that is behind the Aldrich currency scheme and this meeting was held in Chicago primarily to advance the Aldrich scheme, which is now being pressed upon the attention of Senators and members of the House.

It was a company of bankers, a financial family gathering, as it were. Mr. Reynolds said:

"I believe the money power now lies in the hands of a dozen men. I plead guilty to being one, in the last analysis, of those men."

I quote this from page 296 of the official report of the "Proceedings of the National Business Congress." A limited number of the volumes giving these proceedings were issued, but, since Mr. Reynolds' overfrank statement has been quoted publicly, I am informed that the reports have been called in and consigned to deposit vaults. There are a few, however, in the hands of individuals who will endeavor to keep alive the confessions of Mr. Reynolds, speaking as one of the twelve.

The withdrawal of the railroad bond provision by Mr. Aldrich before I began my speech on the currency bill prevented, as he intended it should, any plan on my part to force the consideration of railroad valuation, and on March 27, 1908, by a vote of 42 to 16 the bill passed the Senate. The only Republicans who voted against it were Borah, Bourne, Brown, and La Follette.

In the House the Vreeland bill was substituted for the Aldrich bill and the whole matter was finally thrown into conference. At an early meeting the conference committee announced that an agreement between the two houses was utterly impossible and that therefore no bill could be passed.

I did not place as great reliance as others upon the statement issued. I could not believe that the interests would permit the session to close without another effort to carry out their plans, but Congress and the country generally accepted the statement with expressions of general satisfaction that the whole matter should go over to a later period, when something of substantial merit might be secured.

For many weeks not a word was heard from this committee on

conference, and then suddenly on May 27th, three days before adjournment, this measure of vital importance was thrust upon the consideration of Congress in the form of a conference report, which might be debated but could not be amended in any respect. Upon examining the measure it was clearly apparent that the bill was in no respect better than the bill which had passed the Senate, and in many particulars it was infinitely worse.

As I had predicted, the railroad bonds provision had been restored to the bill, but buried under an obscure phrase. The bill also contained an infamous provision which permitted the use of bonds as security for currency at *less than par value.*

I determined to resist its passage with all my strength. I felt assured that with the assistance of three or four other Senators I could protract the discussion until the rankly objectionable features of the measure would elicit such a protest from independent bankers and business men of the country as would compel Congress radically to amend or to defeat it. I sought for help among the few recently elected Republican Senators, but found them timid about joining me in the undertaking. I then resolved to make the best opposition I could to the measure and extend the debate in the hope that some Democratic Senator or Senators might later come to my assistance.

Before the conference report was called up for action in the Senate I was assured by Senators Gore and Stone that one or the other of them would take the floor when I concluded, Stone saying that he would speak for five or six hours against the bill and Gore agreeing to follow Stone for at least two hours. The conference report having been called up shortly before 12 o'clock on the 29th of May, I very soon thereafter obtained the floor and began my discussion of its most objectionable provisions, which I continued for the balance of the afternoon, throughout the night and until 7 o'clock on the morning of the 30th of May, having spoken nineteen hours without surrendering the floor.

It was not expected that I would be able to hold the floor for more than a few hours at most, but as the afternoon wore away, and I continued speaking past the usual adjourning time, there were manifestations of some uneasiness on the part of the chairman of the Finance Committee and his more immediate supporters.

The newspaper dispatches carried the information to the country that a fight was on against the Emergency Currency conference report, and by midnight telegrams began to come to Senators from independent bankers and businessmen asking them to support me in my opposition to the measure.

But bills had been held back by the Senate managers of legislation to serve as guards to this conference report. One of these measures was the great public buildings "pork barrel" bill carrying appropriations in which many Senators felt deeply interested. Senators who would naturally be in sympathy with my fight were warned that if they aided me the public buildings bill would be permitted to fail at that session.

Another measure used as a club to beat off the aid of a number of Southern Senators who were strongly opposed to the Emergency Currency bill was a measure, then pending, to cut down the number of representatives in the House from the southern states.

But I got on fairly well with my single-handed opposition. The interest was very great. Scores of representatives came over from the House, and the galleries were crowded.

When I first took the floor Aldrich, Hale, and the other managers of Senate business were inclined to chaff me, but, after I had been speaking for some time, they grew impatient. I noticed that they had their heads together and before long it was whispered to me by a friendly Senator that I would have to be on my guard if I kept the floor, as they proposed to get me to yield to some interruption, and then have the presiding officer recognize the interrupting Senator as having the floor in his own right, thus compelling me if I desired to go on again to secure a fresh recognition from the Chair, which would be held to be my second recognition upon the same question upon the same legislative day. As Mr. Aldrich intended to keep the Senate in continuous session until the conference report was adopted, the legislative day might continue indefinitely. I would then be placed in a position where, when I yielded the floor to procure rest and refreshment, I could not be recognized, as this would be in violation of one of the standing rules of the Senate. The rule in question provides that no Senator shall speak more than twice upon any one question in debate upon the same day. This rule is never enforced, but it was proposed to enforce it against me.

Senator Hale addressed the Chair as follows:

"Mr. President—

"The Vice-President. Does the Senator from Wisconsin yield to the Senator from Maine?

"Mr. La Follette. I yield to the Senator from Maine.

"Mr. Hale. I do not ask the Senator to yield. The Senator

yielded the floor, and I secured the recognition of the Vice-President."

This was not in accordance with the fact. Senator Hale had not secured recognition of the Vice-President which entitled him to the floor in his own right.

I was surprised on the following morning to find that the *Congressional Record* as printed changed the form of the Vice-President's recognition. As it appeared in the *Record* the next morning it was as follows:

"Mr. Hale. Mr. President—

"The Vice-President. The Senator from Maine."

Thus it was made to appear from the *Record* that the Senator from Maine was recognized as having the right to the floor, and not as having the floor yielded to him by me. On procuring the official shorthand report of the proceedings, I found it had been "doctored," and I caused a photograph to be made for future use. Thus the foundation was laid by altering the *Record* to have me barred from the floor when I yielded it again.

Having held the floor for nineteen hours, I surrendered to Senator Stone of Missouri, who had come to my assistance. He was relieved after occupying the floor for six or seven hours by Senator Gore, who spoke for two hours. It was the understanding that Senator Stone would follow Senator Gore for an hour, at which time I would again take the floor. We intended to continue the "filibuster" until the leaders should give in.

I was in my committee room arranging material for use when I was hurriedly summoned to the Senate floor with the information that the debate had been closed. The roll call was in progress when I reached the floor, and it was therefore impossible for me to attempt to secure recognition and continue the fight. It seems that Senator Stone was not in the chamber when the blind Senator Gore, supposing that Stone was present according to previous arrangement, yielded. There being no one at hand to ask recognition in opposition to the conference report, the call of the roll began at once, and the fight was over. The conference report was adopted by a vote of 43 to 22. The debate had at least exposed the character of the conference report and the methods employed by the masters of legislation for enforcing it upon the country. It added another chapter to the record of the subserviency of Congress to special interests.

It is my settled belief that this great power over government legislation can only be overthrown by resisting at every step, seizing upon every important occasion which offers opportunity to uncover the methods of the system. It matters little whether the particular question at issue is the tariff, the railroads, or the currency. The fight is the same. It is not a question of party politics. The great issue strikes down to the very foundation of our free institutions. It is against the system built up by privilege, which has taken possession of government and legislation, that we must make unceasing warfare.

It was in this Emergency Currency bill that Aldrich laid the foundation for the upbuilding of his scheme, which is now backed by powerful financial and business interests to secure stronger control upon the capital and credit of our country. This has now crystallized in the so-called Aldrich currency plan, a measure which the interests will take the first available opportunity to force upon Congress.

Chapter XI

Why I Became a Candidate for the Presidency—Taft's Unavailability—A Complete History of Roosevelt's Course after His Return from Africa—Formation of the Organized Progressive Movement—Pressure for a Real Progressive Candidate

B_y the close of the extra session convened on the fifteenth of March, 1909, President Taft's course upon the tariff legislation had raised, in the mind of every real Progressive, doubts as to his availability as a candidate to succeed himself. In his campaign for election he had interpreted the platform as a pledge for tariff revision downward. Five months after he was inaugurated he signed a bill that revised the tariff upward. And the tariff protected trust beneficiaries, availing themselves of their increased rates, promptly advanced prices to the consumer.

The President started on a tour across the country in September, 1909. At the outset in an address at Boston he lauded Aldrich as the greatest statesman of his time. Then followed his Winona speech in which he declared the Payne-Aldrich Bill to be the best tariff bill ever enacted, and in effect challenged the Progressives in Congress who had voted against the measure, and the progressive judgment of the country, which had already condemned it.

During the succeeding sessions of Congress President Taft's sponsorship for the administration railroad bill, with its commerce court, its repeal of the anti-trust act in its application to railroads, and its legalizing of all watered railroad capitalization; his course regarding Ballinger and the Cunningham claims, and the subterfuges resorted to by his administration in defence of Ballinger; his attempt to foist upon the country a sham reciprocity measure; his complete surrender to the legislative reactionary program of Aldrich and Cannon and the discredited representatives of special interests who had so long managed congressional legislation, rendered it utterly impossible for the Progressive Republicans of the country to support him for reelection.

Former President Roosevelt, after the expiration of his term of office, absented himself from the country for a period of about fifteen months. It was during this interval that the Progressive movement made its greatest progress nationally. The reason for this is obvious. Taft's openly reactionary course on legislation during the first two sessions of Congress following his inauguration welded together the Progressive strength of the country, and sharpened and clearly defined the issues. While Roosevelt was President, his public utterances through state papers, addresses, and the press were highly colored with rhetorical radicalism. His administrative policies as set forth in his recommendations to Congress were vigorously and picturesquely presented, but characterized by an absence of definite economic conception. One trait was always pronounced. His most savage assault upon special interests was invariably offset with an equally drastic attack upon those who were seeking to reform abuses. These were indiscriminately classed as demagogues and dangerous persons. In this way he sought to win approval, both from the radicals and the conservatives. This cannonading, first in one direction and then in another, filled the air with noise and smoke, which confused and obscured the line of action, but, when the battle cloud drifted by and quiet was restored, it was always a matter of surprise that so little had really been accomplished. Roosevelt is deserving of credit for his appeals made from time to time for higher ethical standards, social decency, and civic honesty. He discussed these matters strikingly and with vigor, investing every utterance with his unique personality. He would seize upon some ancient and accepted precept—as, "Honesty is the best policy"—and treat it with a spirit and energy and in a manner that made him seem almost the original discoverer of the truth. He often confessed, however, a distaste for and lack of interest in economic problems, and his want of definite conception always invited to compromise, retarding or defeating real progress.

It was not strange, therefore, that he approved the Hepburn Rate Bill, and claimed it as an achievement for his administration. For nine years the public had demanded relief from Congress that would restore to the Interstate Commerce Commission some measure of the power of which it had been deprived by a Supreme Court decision in 1897. And, finally, the Hepburn Bill was enacted as a pretended compliance with that public demand. Except for section twenty, which authorized the Commission to enforce upon the railroads a uniform system of bookkeeping, the bill omitted every provision which the Commission had for nine years urged upon Congress as necessary to make the Interstate Commerce Law a workable statute for the protection of the public interest.

Nor was it strange that he approved the Emergency Currency Law—which was but another ragged patch upon our makeshift monetary system, placed there through the powerful influence of the speculative banking interests—and commended it as a "wholesome progressive law."

It was for these reasons that, after a service of seven and one half years as President of the United States, he left no great constructive statute as an enduring record of his service. To the credit of his administration may justly be placed, however, in large measure the more recent progress of the conservation movement. But conservation did not originate with the Roosevelt administration. The Forestry Bureau in the Department of Agriculture was established as a result of a memorial presented by the American Association for the Advancement of Science in 1873, reinforced by another memorial of the Association in 1890. The first national forest reservation was established in 1891. This was the beginning of conservation, which was further promoted by a more elaborate treatment of the subject by the National Academy of Sciences in 1897. Through the publication of a volume entitled "Lands of the Arid West," by Major J. W. Powell, Director of the Geological Survey, and as a result of the foresight and influence of Director Powell, an irrigation division of the United States Geological Survey was established in 1888, and authority conferred upon the Secretary of the Interior to withdraw from private entry reservoir sites and areas of land necessary for irrigation purposes. From this time on the growth of conservation as a governmental policy was commensurate to its great importance to the public. In response to the steadily growing demands, numerous withdrawals of public lands from private sale or entry, for the protection of forests, fuel supply, irrigation, and waterpowers, were made during the Roosevelt administration. In this department of the public service Roosevelt made a distinctly progressive record, due in large degree to the zeal and activity of Chief Forester Pinchot. The enthusiasm of the Chief Forester which led him to include within forest reserves extended areas of purely agricultural lands, thus retarding agricultural development in some of the western states, naturally caused bitterness and hostility to the whole movement on the part of many people in those states whose prosperity depended chiefly upon the development of their agricultural lands. This resulted in building up the only well-grounded opposition to conservation progress. While injustice was done in many cases, the administration of the forestry service has been one of incalculable benefit to the public as a whole.

But the fact remains that the Roosevelt administration came to a close on the fourth of March, 1909, without leaving to its credit a definite Progressive national movement with a clearly defined body of issues. There was the comprehensive and well recognized Progressive movement in Wisconsin. A good beginning had been made in a number of other states, and for three years I had labored in the Senate, making some gain against a solid opposition, but wholly unable to rely on the administration of President Roosevelt for support or cooperation.

On the twenty-fourth of March, 1909, Roosevelt sailed for Africa. He was absent from the country until June, 1910. In that period, under the administration of President Taft, the Progressive Republican movement made greater headway than during the entire Roosevelt administration. This was largely due to the fact that Taft's course was more direct, Roosevelt's devious. Openly denouncing trusts and combinations, Roosevelt made concessions and compromises which tremendously strengthened these special interests. Thus he smeared the issue, but caught the imagination of the younger men of the country by his dash and mock heroics. Taft cooperated with Cannon and Aldrich on legislation. Roosevelt cooperated with Aldrich and Cannon on legislation. Neither President took issue with the reactionary bosses of the Senate upon any legislation of national importance. Taft's talk was generally in line with his legislative policy. Roosevelt's talk was generally at right-angles to his legislative policy. Taft's messages were the more directly reactionary; Roosevelt's the more "progressive." But adhering to his conception of a "square deal," his strongest declarations in the public interest were invariably offset with something comforting for Privilege; every phrase denouncing "bad" trusts was deftly balanced with praise for "good" trusts.

So uncertain were the Progressive leaders in the Senate and House as to the position which Roosevelt would take upon progressive issues after his return from Africa that it was almost daily a matter of discussion among them. Would he ally himself with Taft or would he stand with the Progressive movement, which had by that time become a concrete and well understood political entity? Indeed, so uncertain were even his close personal friends, some of whom had fallen out with the administration, that they were anxious to get his ear first as he turned his face homeward, in order to forestall, if possible, any announcement from him favorable to the Taft administration. To that end Gifford Pinchot, who had been removed by Taft from his position of Chief Forester—and had become an active Progressive—as early as December 31, 1909, had written an extended letter to Roosevelt which would meet him at the African border, and give his mind the right slant on the political situation. Pinchot followed his letter abroad, to supplement it with verbal explanation and personal persuasion. A throng of American newspaper correspondents crossed the ocean to get some word from Roosevelt which could be cabled back to enlighten the people on the momentous question as to whether Roosevelt, when he finally landed in America, would ally himself with the Progressives or with the Taft administration. Their diligence and ingenuity were rewarded with no syllable to indicate his course. He landed in New York, June 18th, and for weeks the daily press teemed with questioning and speculation. But still the American public was left in ignorance as to the future action of the former President. At the capital of the nation and throughout the country the line of battle had been drawn, and there was no faltering on either side. Every citizen possessed of any conviction, had taken his stand long before, and the contest was on in every state.

The extra session of 1909 on the tariff had been followed by the regular session of 1909–10, in which the Progressives had torn to pieces the administration railroad bill, and written the measure almost entirely anew, on the floor of the Senate. The tariff session had rent asunder the Republican party. Quarter was neither sought nor given between the progressive and stand-pat forces. The session of 1910, preceding the congressional elections, had intensified the differences, widened the breach; and still the former

President had nothing to say. He had been received with great acclaim in the old world, and likewise upon his arrival in New York. It was a time in the life of the Progressive movement when his support would have been a tremendous gain.

Upon the twenty-seventh of June, 1910, on invitation which came to me through Gilson Gardner, close personal friend of Roosevelt, and Washington correspondent of the Scripps papers, I visited him at Oyster Bay. A colored attendant showed me into the library, and informed me that the Colonel would see me presently. He soon made his appearance, wearing linen knickerbockers, and after a cordial greeting said that he had just come in from pitching hay, confirming his statement by removing a rather liberal quantity of timothy from his person. He asked me about the work of Congress and the new administration, and I told him definitely of the tariff and railroad legislation, and of the great advance which the Progressive movement had really made. I asked some direct questions, both regarding issues and President Taft, but excepting as to one matter he was very guarded in his statements.

Speaking of the initiative and referendum, he said he had arrived at no settled conviction; but upon the recall his mind was definitely made up, at least in so far as it related to the recall of judges. He said: "I am not sure whether the recall should be applied to public officials generally, but I have been so disappointed in many of the judges commissioned during my administration, that it is perfectly clear to me that the recall should be established and enforced as to judges, and particularly, federal judges appointed for life." I received the statement with some expression of surprise, suggesting as my viewpoint that if the recall were applied to the judiciary, the percentage of petitioners demanding recall should be fixed at a much higher rate than was commonly accepted as proper basis for recall of legislative and other public officials. He replied that he had given no particular thought to the details, but that he had a settled and fixed opinion as to the importance of applying the principle to the federal judiciary. At the close of the interview I left with him some speeches bearing upon the tariff and railroad bills which he said he would read with care. I told him very explicitly of Taft's course upon the tariff, of his Winona speech, in which he declared the Payne-Aldrich Bill the best bill ever enacted by a Republican Congress. His only comment upon Taft was that "sometimes a man makes a very good lieutenant but a poor captain."

I was not a little surprised to find, less than three months later, a Roosevelt editorial in the *Outlook,* under date of September 17, 1910, in which he commented upon the Payne-Aldrich Tariff Law as follows:

"I think that the present tariff is better than the last, and considerably better than the one before the last."

Neither the foregoing statement, nor anything akin to it, however, was made in Roosevelt's speeches upon his tour in the months of August and early September in the west, where public sentiment was very pronouncedly against the Payne-Aldrich Tariff Law. The *Outlook* editorial above quoted was a portion of a more extended reference to the tariff in the speech which he had prepared for his trip through the west. Obviously he left a copy of his tariff views with the *Outlook* before leaving for his western tour. The reason why the portion quoted above and published as a Roosevelt editorial was not delivered as a part of any of his addresses on the tariff in the west was due to the fact that one of the Progressive Senators who rode with him on his special train during part of the trip, and to whom he submitted the speech which he proposed to deliver, directed his attention to the fact that the utterance was almost identical with that made a year before by Taft at Winona, which had called down upon the President the fiercest sort of denunciation. But this did not at all embarrass ex-President Roosevelt. He promptly adjusted himself to western ideas upon the tariff, by cutting out of his speeches in Iowa, Kansas, and other western states the approval of the Aldrich bill which had been written in when the speeches were prepared for delivery. Thus he made the right impression upon the west for the time being. But it was a distinct shock to his admirers beyond the Mississippi a little later when Roosevelt joined with the New York stand-patters in the Republican State Convention in praising the Payne-Aldrich Tariff Bill and President Taft's administration. In this convention, which met at Saratoga, Roosevelt had such absolute control that he was able to elect himself chairman, make the keynote speech, and nominate his personal friend Stimson for Governor. He *agreed to, voted for,* and throughout the campaign *supported* the New York State platform, containing the following:

"The Payne-Aldrich Tariff Law reduced the average rate of all duties 11 per cent. By increasing the duties on some luxuries and articles not of ordinary use, making, however, no increases on any common food product, it turned a national deficit into a surplus."

The New York platform also contained this further declaration:

"We enthusiastically endorse the progressive and statesmanlike leadership of William Howard Taft, and declare our pride in the achievements of his first eighteen months as President of the United States. Each succeeding month since his inauguration has confirmed the nation in its high estimate of his greatness of character, intellectual ability, sturdy common sense, extraordinary patience and perseverance, broad and statesmanlike comprehension of public questions, and unfaltering and unswerving adherence to duty."

Roosevelt's course in the Saratoga convention was a staggering blow to Progressive Republicans throughout the middle and western states, where press and people alike condemned him. He led the campaign for Stimson and the New York platform in the election of 1910—making it his own fight—and was overwhelmingly defeated.

For many months little was heard from him. It was plain that the Progressive movement could not be tied up with the Taft administration by anybody. The Progressives in the Senate and House of Representatives held steadily to their course. They could not be coerced by the administration, through the use of patronage, into supporting measures not in the public interest. Every day strengthened their cause before the people. Every question with which they dealt placed Progressive issues more clearly and definitely before the public, as the most fundamentally important political movement in a generation of time.

As we drew on toward the close of 1910 word was frequently brought to the Progressive leaders in Washington by some of Roosevelt's close personal friends that he had been chastened by his recent experience and enlightened by a better understanding of public opinion; that he was becoming more progressive and would eventually be found in the ranks of those who were, day by day, giving that movement its distinct place in political history.

For nearly a year the formation of a national league to promote progressive legislation in the different states had been under discussion among a few of the Progressive Senators and Members of the House of Representatives. And during the holiday recess in the last days of December, 1910, I drafted a Declaration of Principles and form of constitution for the organization of such a league, and submitted the same to Senators Bourne and Bristow. With some modifications suggested by the Senators in our conference, the declaration and constitution were prepared for signatures and copies mailed to Senators and Members who had returned to their homes for the recess, and to leading Progressives in different states. The organization was effected at a meeting held at my residence, 1864 Wyoming Avenue, Washington, D. C., on the twenty-first day of January, 1911. Jonathan Bourne was elected President; Frederic C. Howe, Secretary; Charles R. Crane, Treasurer. Following is the Declaration of Principles adopted:

We, the undersigned, associate ourselves together as The National Progressive Republican League.

The object of the League is the promotion of popular government and progressive legislation.

Popular government in America has been thwarted and progressive legislation strangled by the special interests, which control caucuses, delegates, conventions, and party organizations; and, through this control of the machinery of government, dictate nominations and platforms, elect administrations, legislatures, representatives in Congress, United States Senators, and control cabinet officers.

Under existing conditions legislation in the public interest has been baffled and defeated. This is evidenced by the long struggle to secure laws but partially effective for the control of railway rates and services, the revision of the tariff in the interest of the producer and consumer, statutes dealing wih trusts and combinations, based on sound economic principles, as applied to modern industrial and commercial conditions; wise, comprehensive and impartial reconstruction of banking and monetary laws, the conservation of coal, oil, gas, timber, water powers, and other natural resources belonging to the people, and for the enactment of all legislation solely for the common good.

Just in proportion as popular government has, in certain states superseded the delegate convention system, and the people have assumed control of the machinery of government, has government become responsive to the popular will, and progressive legislation been secured.

The Progressive Republican League believes that popular government is fundamental to all other questions. To this end it advocates:

(1) The election of United States Senators by direct vote of the people.

(2) Direct primaries for the nomination of elective officials.

(3) The direct election of delegates to national conventions with opportunity for the voter to express his choice for President and Vice-President.

(4) Amendment to state constitutions providing for the Initiative, Referendum and Recall.

(5) A thoroughgoing corrupt practices act.

Roosevelt was invited to become a member of the National Progressive Republican League, founded upon this simple declaration of elementary principles, but he had not become enough of a Progressive at that time to be willing to identify himself with the organization, and therefore declined. He was urged to join the League for several reasons. The name of a former President would give strength to the organization. It would help, sooner or later, to place him in open opposition to the Taft administration. It would commit him to a clear-cut and definite position upon the five propositions embodied in the Declaration of Principles. This would be very important, as it is his political habit so to state and qualify his positions that you are never quite sure of him.

I think it is fair to say that the activities of this League resulted in the enactment of the presidential preference laws in the several states during the legislative sessions of 1912. Oregon had already adopted its statute. Wisconsin, five years before, had enacted a law under which the delegates to the National Republican Convention of 1908 were elected by direct vote of the people. This law was supplemented by the legislature of 1912 providing for a direct vote on presidential and vice-presidential candidates. North Dakota, Nebraska, California, New Jersey, Illinois, and Massachusetts enacted similar statutes, and in South Dakota steps were taken to elect delegates by direct vote under an existing primary law, though the provision authorizing such election of delegates had not previously been invoked. The League, under the direction of its president, Senator Bourne, did, and is continuing to do, effective work in advancing the principles to promote which it was organized.

That the Progressive Republicans should present a candidate for nomination for the presidency in opposition to Mr. Taft had long been considered by the leaders of that element of the party, and with the beginning of the new year (1911) many conferences were held on that subject. These gatherings were attended not only by Progressive members of the Senate and House, but also by representative Progressives who visited Washington from time to time. The interest of the Progressive cause was the controlling thought in all of those deliberations. None of the men whose availability as candidates was discussed manifested any eagerness to undertake the contest, though all were agreed that Progressive Republicans were in duty bound to oppose the renomination of President Taft. Not only because of the division which had arisen in the Republican party upon principle was it conceded that his nomination must be opposed, but because whatever the outcome, the integrity and perpetuity of the Progressive movement demanded that it should present for the support of Progressive Republicans throughout the country a candidate who represented its principles.

It was well understood that owing to the peculiar conditions existing in the south, which made it certain that the administration through patronage could control the selection of practically all delegates from that section of the country, Mr. Taft had a very great advantage at the outset. Even in the northern states the federal machine is a powerful factor in the election of delegates, though the candidate may be personally weak, or even obnoxious, and the power of the President's steam roller had been demonstrated so thoroughly in the previous convention that every one familiar with that campaign accepted it as a tremendous force to be reckoned with. Taft had almost no individual strength or following in 1908. But President Roosevelt put his personality behind an army of federal officials and nominated him against all opposition. I was in a position at that time to know definitely the public sentiment of the west and middle western states. For many years I had addressed great audiences throughout those states, beginning while I was governor of Wisconsin and continuing the work after I came to the Senate in the recesses between sessions of Congress. I had received much encouragement, particularly from that portion of the country, in support of my own candidacy for the Republican nomination months prior to the meeting of the convention in 1908. But political sentiment, however strong, unsupported by organization and the finances with which to meet the necessary expenses of a campaign, cannot withstand the assault of a compact, well-disciplined, well-managed federal machine, directed by one trained in the arts of modern political campaigning.

Incredible as it may seem, it is nevertheless a fact in political history, that Roosevelt planned and consummated Taft's succession to the presidency. The campaign of 1912 witnessed the publication by Roosevelt of a letter written to him by President Taft shortly after his inauguration which contained this startling acknowledgment:

"I can never forget that the power I now exercise was voluntarily transferred from you to me, and that I am under obligation to you to see that your judgment in selecting me as your successor and bringing about the succession shall be vindicated according to the standards which you and I in conversation have always formulated."

When this was given to the public by the former President, in a speech at Worcester, Mass., April 26, 1912, it was with the naive comment: "It is a bad trait to bite the hand that feeds you."

The admission of the beneficiary of this crime against democracy, with the comment of the man who planned and executed it, should have taken both Taft and Roosevelt out of the 1912 campaign. The presidency is the people's office. That it was passed as one might transfer the title to a house and lot makes a mockery of every principle upon which constitutional government is founded.

But, to resume my narrative: With a single exception those who professed any interest in the Progressive cause regarded it as an imperative duty to oppose the renomination of Taft with a pronounced and thoroughgoing Progressive candidate. Roosevelt was the exception. He was opposed to bringing out a Progressive candidate. Before the close of the session in March, 1911, he had caused it to be made known to the Progressives in Washington, through a number of his close personal friends who sustained intimate relations with them, that while he was *at last* hostile to Taft, he was not in favor of opposing his renomination. Among those who saw him often in New York, and constituted the medium of communication with Progressives in Washington, were Gifford Pinchot, E. A. Van Valkenberg, manager of the Philadelphia *North American,* and Gilson Gardner. They especially were the bearers of frequent messages, and the accepted spokesmen of Roosevelt in published interviews regarding Taft's administration. Through these men we were informed that while Roosevelt was at *this time,* in the winter of 1911, against Taft, that he (Roosevelt) did not want to see any Progressive candidate put in the field against him; that he was confident of two things: first, that Taft could not be beaten for nomination; and second, 1912 would be a Democratic year and no Republican, either Progressive or reactionary, could be elected President; that, therefore, he would prefer to see Taft renominated without opposition, and beaten at the polls. None of these men who reported Roosevelt's position at that time agreed fully with him. Pinchot from the first was insistent that a fight should be made against Taft's nomination; that it could not be made without a Progressive candidate, and that the future of the Progressive movement demanded that such a contest be waged. In the event of failure Pinchot then, and afterward, urged that he would like to see such candidate lead a third party fight upon Taft, should the latter secure the nomination.

Many conferences were held. Indeed, scarcely a day passed when the subject was not informally discussed between the Progressive Senators and Members of the House, as they met from time to time. The third session of the 61st Congress closed on the fourth of March, 1911, without any definite conclusion being reached, although it was pretty generally understood that we must take some formal action soon.

The President convened Congress in extra session on the fifteenth of April, 1911, for the consideration of the so-called "Reciprocity" agreement with Canada, which had been defeated in the closing days of the previous session. The Progressives in both houses of Congress quite generally opposed the pact with Canada, upon the ground that it was not a fairly reciprocal agreement—that it discriminated against the agricultural interests of this country and in favor of the already over-protected trusts and combinations. Gifford Pinchot and also his brother Amos Pinchot, who had joined in some of the conferences before referred to, and, likewise, Van Valkenberg, were very much exercised over what they termed the political mistake of the Progressives in opposing the Canadian Pact. While I do not now recall that either of those men quoted Roosevelt as being in accord with them on this legislation, he was nevertheless strongly in favor of the Canadian Pact, as will appear later in this narrative.

As the session advanced, the strength of the Progressive position on reciprocity developed markedly. Though the press of the country, which derived a special advantage from the proposed agreement, denounced all opposition to the President's program, the agricultural interests were so solidly arrayed against it that Roosevelt and his friends ceased to advocate the President's policy for this legislation. Later, as I shall show, when it became politically expedient, Roosevelt took a positive stand against reciprocity.

Early in the spring of 1911 Roosevelt prepared for another tour of the country. This trip was arranged pursuant to invitations which he had received during the preceding months to deliver addresses in several states. It offered an excellent opportunity to try out public sentiment to determine whether time had in some measure restored him to the popular favor, which he had sacrificed as a result of his course in the Saratoga Convention and the crushing defeat of his candidate in the New York election.

Up to this time there had been no change in his opinion regarding opposition to Taft's renomination, as the Progressives in Washington were advised from time to time through those friends of his who kept us informed. He was deadly hostile to Taft, but still felt that he could not be beaten in the convention, and that he should be allowed to take the nomination without contest and then be given a beating at the polls. But so far as reported to our group in Washington, the idea of a Progressive candidate for the presidency, even if defeated in the convention, as a means of holding together an advance Progressive movement, seemed to have no place in his political thinking. His mind was dwelling upon immediate political victory or defeat. In all that we heard from Roosevelt, through these near friends of his, the continued upbuilding of the Progressive movement for the restoration of representative government was not a subject which he was considering at all.

While this was the attitude of Roosevelt toward a Progressive candidacy, I cannot too strongly emphasize the fact that the Progressives in Washington, indeed all over the country, were of one mind—that there should be a Progressive candidate. My own mail, and that, I think, of other Progressive Senators and Representatives, was filled with urgent appeals from Progressives, east as well as west, that some action be taken at once to place a candidate in the field. While able men in nearly every state in the north were active in promoting Progressive principles they seemed to look to the group in Washington to take the initiative. Scarcely a day passed when I did not receive calls from strong men identified with the Progressive movement, who came to Washington on other missions, but made it a part of their business to press this matter for early action. Editors and publishers of progressive magazines and papers were heard from directly and indirectly, insisting that there should be no further delay in taking formal action to the end that Progressive Republicans should be given an opportunity to support some one who could be recognized and supported as representing the Progressive movement. Among those urging action none were more aggressive and persistent than the Pinchots, James R. Garfield, formerly a member of Roosevelt's cabinet, Van Valkenberg, and Gardner. The peculiarly close relation of these men to Roosevelt and their active cooperation was a source of special encouragement of the Progressive group in Washington. The question of Roosevelt's attitude toward such a candidacy was, of course, a matter of much concern, and the possibility of his coming into the field himself as a candidate was often raised in our interviews with these men, both in casual meetings and in our more or less formal conferences. At this time the invariable answer to any question touching this subject was that he did not believe there should be a candidate at all; and *as to himself, it was not to be thought of.* On one occasion, I remember, it was stated by Gardner that the Colonel, referring to the 1910 election in New York as a Roosevelt defeat, said that he would be literally eaten up if he were to become a candidate, and that he could not consider such a thing.

Roosevelt's speaking tour of the country beginning in March, 1911, lasted more than six weeks. He came back quite another man. There was no mistaking the fact that the New York gubernatorial campaign of 1910 had left him in a sorry plight politically. This was the construction which he himself put upon the situation. But this 1911 trip restored his self-confidence in a marked degree.

In the light of subsequent events, there can be little doubt that when Roosevelt left the White House he had 1916 firmly in his mind. He was more than half piqued at that time because his suggestions as to appointments had been ignored by his successor. He returned from Africa to find that many changes had taken place; the Progressive movement he found far in advance of him; he neither understood it, nor was he in sympathy with its manifest purposes, in so far as he comprehended them. He deliberated for a time as to whether he would stand with the administration, supporting Taft for renomination, or seek to identify himself with the Progressives—or straddle. He straddled. It left him awkwardly stranded in the election of 1910. He halted to take account of stock. Events were rapidly transpiring. It was evident that the Taft administration was losing ground day by day. While Taft made some effort at reconciliation, he was not willing wholly to subordinate himself to his former chief. Nothing less would have satisfied Roosevelt. Besides, every month made it clear that the Taft administration was becoming more and more impossible. The congressional elections of 1910 forecast disaster for the Republican party in 1912. Roosevelt was *still looking to 1916,* and as the political situation developed in the following year, in his political philosophy, which is always personal, Taft's renomination and defeat in 1912 fitted admirably into his plan.

Then came this tour in the Spring of 1911. It fired his blood. There were the old-time crowds, the music, the cheers. *He began to think of 1912 for himself.* It was four years better than 1916; and four years counts in the life of a man turned fifty-three; a world of things may happen in four years. But every one saw the uncertainties of 1912. Roosevelt clearly saw them. He could take no chance. He could not afford to become a candidate against Taft and fail. Why not put forth another man, and feel out the Taft strength? If it became apparent that Taft could not be beaten for the nomination, a contest would nevertheless weaken him and make his defeat in the election the more certain. If it became clear that Taft could be beaten in the convention and furthermore that he (Roosevelt) could win in the election against a Democrat, his restored confidence, resulting from the tour of 1911, made him reasonably certain that he could displace the candidate put out against Taft, stampede the convention, and secure the nomination for himself. Now, let us see how this Roosevelt psychosis fits the facts as they have transpired.

Shortly after Roosevelt's return from his tour of 1911 Gilson Gardner paid him another visit. I do not know whether this was at Roosevelt's solicitation, or whether he went over on his own motion, as he often did. But be that as it may, he came back the bearer of a most important message. Roosevelt, he said, had entirely changed his mind regarding a Progressive candidate against Taft; he *now* believed that the Progressives should put forward a candidate, that *I should be that candidate,* and that I should get into the fight *at once;* that I stood before the country in a different relation to the Progressive movement than any other man; that I had done the pioneer work; that upon his return from the west he had visited Madison, while the Wisconsin legislature was still in session; that he had been very much surprised at the thoroughly scientific character of the work under way in that state, and the fundamentally sound body of laws which had been enacted under my administration as governor; that the Progressive movement in Wisconsin had reached a stage of practical demonstration of its wisdom and thorough soundness. He said that he was still inclined to believe that Taft could not be beaten; that he (Roosevelt) could not openly oppose him as a candidate because he had made him President; that he could not, for the same reason, openly advocate my candidacy against Taft; but that he would, if I became a candidate, commend my work from time to time in the *Outlook* and help along in that way; that while visiting the legislature in Madison he had spoken there and strongly endorsed my work; that he did it, having in mind the possible announcement of my candidacy, with the idea that it would be useful and helpful as an expression of approval. He said further that if Taft could not be beaten for the nomination, as he was still inclined to believe, I could nevertheless stand as a candidate, and if defeated in the convention, I would not be weakened before the country.

This same statement was made by Gardner many times to me and to my friends in Washington and elsewhere.

Secretary of War Stimson visited Roosevelt in January, 1912, and upon his return to Washington reported to his college friends, Gifford Pinchot and Congressman William Kent, that Roosevelt was not really opposed to Taft's renomination, and that he (Roosevelt) had said he regarded Taft as the most available man for the Republican nomination. Gardner, when he heard Stimson's statement reported at our headquarters, became quite resentful against

Roosevelt, and said to me in the presence of Houser, my campaign manager, and others that he would make a signed statement setting forth the fact that he had brought Roosevelt's message to me urging me to be the candidate and to declare my candidacy at once. Subsequently, when it became certain that Roosevelt would be a candidate, I requested Houser to ask Gardner for this statement. He then refused to make it, unless Houser promised it would not be used against Roosevelt. And as Houser could not make such a promise, Gardner declined to furnish the statement.

During the North Dakota campaign, in reply to a letter published by Gifford Pinchot and sent broadcast throughout the state, Houser gave to the press a statement reviewing the history of my candidacy, including Roosevelt's connection with it, and his message delivered to me through Gardner. To meet this, Gardner came out with a denial of the truth of Houser's statement. Gardner's denial promptly called forth an interview from George S. Loftus, President of the Minnesota Progressive League, which is contained in the following dispatch printed in the New York *Tribune:*

URGED LA FOLLETTE TO RUN

"Minneapolis, March 17.—An answer to the letter of Gilson Gardner, in which it was said that any statement that Colonel Roosevelt had urged Senator La Follette to become a candidate was untrue, was issued here last night by George Loftus, President of the Minnesota Progressive League. It is as follows:

"The statement made by Walter L. Houser relating to the message that Gilson Gardner carried from Colonel Roosevelt to Senator La Follette is correct, according to a statement made by Mr. Gardner himself to a number of Progressives at a luncheon which they tendered Mr. Gardner at the Odin Club on October 9, 1911.

Mr. Gardner stated further that the Colonel advised him that he would not be a candidate, and under no circumstances would he accept the nomination if tendered to him. That statement somewhat surprised a number present, and they questioned him again concerning it. He repeated his statement and said that when the time came 'we would find the Colonel lined up with La Follette against Taft.'"

On the thirtieth of April a conference of Progressives was held in Senator Bourne's committee room in the capitol, attended by several Senators and Representatives—Senators Cummins, Clapp, Bourne, Gronna, Poindexter; Representatives Lenroot, Hubbard, Norris; Professor Merriam, Senator Clyde Jones, and Walter S. Rogers, of Chicago, the latter representing Charles R. Crane; Gilson Gardner; Angus McSween, representing Mr. Van Valkenberg of the Philadelphia *North American,* and a number of others whom I do not now recall. Professor Merriam, Senator Jones, and Mr. Rogers, leading Progressives of Illinois, had come on to Washington to urge that action be taken to bring out a Progressive candidate for the presidency; that such action would greatly aid the Progressive movement in Illinois. Merriam had been the Progressive candidate for Mayor of Chicago, had made a brilliant campaign, and a splendid run. Senator Jones, the Progressive leader in the Illinois State Senate, was then a candidate for the nomination for governor. Practically all who were present took part in the discussion. There was unanimity of sentiment that the Progressives must unite upon one of the Progressive leaders as a candidate. Though some one suggested the favorite son plan, putting forth several Progressive candidates, no one seriously regarded such plan as feasible.

Senator Cummins, whose name had been widely mentioned in the press as a possible candidate, took prominent part in the discussion. He said:

"There is but one man who should be considered as the Progressive candidate, and that is Senator La Follette."

When asked as to his own candidacy, he emphatically replied, "I shall not be a candidate; it is out of the question."

He added that he felt he ought to say regarding Iowa that there would be a sharp contest between the stand-patters and the Progressives, and that no Progressive candidate, himself or any other, could carry the state solidly; he had no doubt he said that a number of districts could be carried for Senator La Follette, and added, "If he consents to make the fight, I will do everything in my power in Iowa to elect as many delegates as possible to support him in the convention."

I said at that time, what I said in all of our conferences, and to leading Progressives who wrote me from various parts of the country, or called on me in Washington—that the Progressives of the country could not support President Taft for renomination, nor could they, without stultification, remain silent and permit him to be nominated; that we must put forward a candidate, whether that candidate win or lose; that Taft, with the power of southern patronage, would certainly secure the southern delegates to start with, which would give him a long lead; that I was confident, however, he would be found to have little strength west of the Alleghenies; that to stand as the candidate meant the sacrifice of much time and strength, with the chance in favor of a defeat in the convention; that I was willing to support any thoroughgoing

Progressive; that I was willing to make the fight as the candidate if the Progressives agreed that I ought to do so, provided men could be found to contribute the money required to meet the necessary expenses—a sufficient sum to make it certain that the campaign could be carried forward, headquarters maintained, literature printed and distributed, a force of clerks and stenographers employed to take care of correspondence; without this assurance, I said it were better not to undertake it at all. I think every man present stated it as his opinion that I should become the candidate. Gardner told of his interview with Roosevelt. McSween presented the views of Van Valkenberg, giving his (Van Valkenberg's) reasons why I should become the Progressive candidate: Wisconsin, he said, had carried the Progressive movement to the point of demonstration; my work there and in the Senate, in itself, should settle the question as to my candidacy.

In the minds of those who were present at this conference the whole matter was regarded as settled, subject to our being able to secure such contributions as would make the campaign possible.

I have given what took place in this conference somewhat in detail, because it is typical of many others that were held before and after, attended by some of those who were present on this occasion, and by other Senators and Representatives who likewise urged me to stand as the candidate. Among other Senators and Representatives who tendered support to my candidacy were: Bristow of Kansas, Works of California, Crawford of South Dakota, Murdock of Kansas, Lindbergh of Minnesota, Helgeson of North Dakota, Haugen of Iowa, Kent of California, Nelson, Morse, and Cary of Wisconsin. Senator Borah of Idaho stated that there were complications in his state which he thought he could best take care of by making no open declaration at the time, but gave assurance that the delegation from his state could be depended upon for support in the convention.

The foregoing recital can give but an imperfect idea of the activity and zeal of many of the gentlemen above named in pressing for the opening of the campaign. Hardly a day passed that I was not urged to give the final word. But I was resolved that I would not consent to be a candidate until we had assurance of such financial support as would enable us to conduct a campaign worthy of the movement. Also I withheld consent for another reason—a personal one. For twenty years I had given the very heart out of my life to the restoration of representative government in Wisconsin, and thereafter to carrying the work over into the national field. It had been single-handed work in the beginning of the Wisconsin struggle, and I likewise found myself alone in the national contest when I came to the United States Senate. I would not over-estimate or magnify my own importance in that work, nor was I willing to under-estimate it. It had become my life work, and I felt that I had achieved results of a character too important and substantial to lend myself to any campaign plans which might permit me to be made a mere pawn in the national game. I may be thought to have taken myself too seriously, but, I must set down here the truth, subject to whatever judgment may be passed upon it. In other words, I estimated my own worth to the Progressive cause too highly to consent to being used as a candidate for a time, and then, to serve some ulterior purpose, conveniently broken and cast upon the political scrap heap, my ability to serve the Progressive cause seriously damaged, and possibly the movement itself diverted and subordinated to mere personal ambition. I would have been unwilling to see the movement, after it was committed to the support of any thoroughgoing Progressive, shifted for political expediency to another candidate, either in the convention or in the campaign leading up to it.

In every contest situations may arise, or be created, inviting to a compromise on candidate or principle. The temptation to yield is strong. Yet in my whole course I have always insisted on driving straight ahead. To do otherwise not only weakens the cause for which you are contending but destroys confidence in your constancy of purpose.

For these reasons before beginning a national campaign for the Progressive cause I was impelled to exercise every reasonable precaution against miscarriage and disaster. I could foresee the possibility, as the campaign progressed, and Taft's real weakness developed, as I personally believed it would, that either Cummins or Roosevelt, or perhaps both, might then be tempted to thrust in, thus dividing the Progressive strength and defeating the real progress which a clean-cut, uncompromising campaign, even though a losing one, would insure for Progressive principles. But Senator Cummins's word had already been passed, and his position affirmed by his repeated assurances made to others, as well as to myself. Indeed, in the last interview I had with him, at the close of the reciprocity session, he said to me:

"I want to say to you, Bob, before going home, that I think it impossible to carry the state of Iowa for you solidly; but we can carry a number of districts and give you ten or a dozen delegates.

And I have come to say that you can depend upon my doing everything in my power to secure you the largest possible number of votes in Iowa."

I answered: "That is all that any one can ask, Albert. I am certain if you will give me your best support, that I shall have a good representation out of the Iowa delegation to the National Convention."

As to Roosevelt, Gifford Pinchot said again and again: "Roosevelt will not be a candidate. He has said repeatedly that he could not be a candidate against Taft. And from many talks with him I am as certain as I live that he will be found actively and openly supporting your candidacy before the campaign ends. It will be impossible for him to take any other course."

Mr. Van Valkenberg, in one of his last conferences with me in Washington, told of an extended interview with Roosevelt which represented his position as one of strong encouragement to my candidacy. Roosevelt had read to him an article which he had prepared on Wisconsin for publication in the *Outlook*. It was subsequently published on the twenty-seventh of May, 1911. Van Valkenberg stated that Roosevelt was growing more and more hostile to Taft and that he would never under any circumstances support his nomination; that while he did not feel that he could go farther in the *Outlook* than to speak in commendatory terms of my work and its sound and rational character, that nevertheless he would certainly, in a personal way, with political friends who called upon him from all parts of the country, say the right word, which would prove immensely helpful. It is just to Van Valkenberg to say that he was always careful to give it as his own opinion that Taft could not be beaten, but no one was more insistent than he that the Progressive fight should be made against Taft, and that I was the one man in the country to make it.

With these assurances I decided to become a candidate. It was some time before contributions were assured which warranted the formal opening of a campaign. Finally such assurances of financial support were given by Charles R. Crane, William Kent, Gifford and Amos Pinchot, and Alfred L. Baker as warranted the opening of headquarters and the inauguration of the campaign for my nomination as the Progressive candidate.

Before taking this final step I took the precaution, however, to say to those who became contributors to my campaign, and particularly to Gifford Pinchot, because of his close friendship for Roosevelt, that it must be understood, if I became a candidate, I should remain a candidate until I was nominated or defeated in the convention. Indeed, I had been careful to have this well understood by all of my supporters in the Senate and House of Representatives, and all others who had offered me their support. I said to them again and again that I would make the best fight I could, understanding, as everybody did, that the chances were in favor of Taft's renomination, as at that time they appeared to be; but that it would be unfair to me, and more than that, seriously harmful to the Progressive movement, to put me or any other candidate into the field, to feel out the strength of the opposition, become a target for the enemy's fire, and then be cast aside for some one who had been watching from behind the breastworks for favorable opportunity.

There were many conferences and much discussion as to whether there should be a formal announcement of my candidacy. At one time a call was drafted, and signed, by a number of my supporters as a basis for presenting the matter to the public. To my surprise Senator Cummins declined to sign such a call. This raised again the question in my mind as to whether it did not indicate some mental reservation regarding the pledge which he had given to support me, and renewed my concern that later he might enter the field as a candidate himself, in the event that my campaign should demonstrate that Taft was very much weaker in the northern states than was commonly believed at that time. But Bourne and others, who had many personal interviews with Cummins on this subject, gave me every assurance that such was not the case, and that Cummins would, under no circumstances, become a candidate; that his reluctance to sign a call for me was solely because he did not regard that as the best form of introducing my candidacy to the public. The publication of any call not signed by Senator Cummins would, however, at once have led the opposition press to charge that I did not have the united support of prominent Progressives. And for that reason the call was not published.

I could not wholly dismiss from my mind an apprehension regarding both Roosevelt and Cummins. From time to time it would intrude itself into my reflections. I was confident that both were eager for the presidency. I knew that either of them would be more acceptable to the reactionaries than I, because both, judged by their public records, would compromise and make terms with the opposition. And I conceived it possible, notwithstanding Taft's great advantage through patronage and the federal machine, that a strong campaign would show him hopelessly weak as a candidate throughout all of the northern states, excepting New England, and that a break might be made even in New England. And to a few of my most intimate friends I said from the beginning that I would not be leading a wholly forlorn hope.

Chapter XII

The True History of the Campaign
of 1912 for the Republican
Nomination to the Presidency

Setting aside all doubts, and accepting the promises of support
from the Progressives at face value, I entered upon the campaign
for the nomination with vigor and determination. I secured the
services of Walter L. Houser, former Secretary of State of Wisconsin, as campaign manager. Headquarters were established in
Washington, and he took charge, with a clerical force. The campaign was diligently prosecuted, beginning in July, 1911. We sent
out thousands of letters into the northern states, especially the
states west of the Ohio River. My candidacy was treated with derision by supporters of the Taft administration, and the great
body of the metropolitan press. But in less than three months it
had taken on proportions which compelled recognition. The correspondence became so heavy, and the demand for literature and
campaign speakers so urgent, that it was soon necessary to double
the working force at headquarters, and extend plans for organization by states throughout the country, excepting in the south, in
New York, and in a part of New England. Even in the extreme
east it would have been possible to have made much headway had
our means permitted. Indeed, we found the whole country ready
to break away from the reactionary control of politics and government. Many times I had said to my associates that the people were
much in advance of the Progressives in Washington, and overwhelming proof of this came to us from every side. Strong Progressive organizations were soon perfected in numerous states, and we
were greatly strengthened and encouraged.

By October the campaign had attained such proportions that it
seemed desirable and necessary to bring together the leading Progressives of the country for a better understanding as to local con-

ditions in carrying forward the work in a national way. Pursuant to a call issued by Chairman Houser, three hundred leading Progressives representing thirty states assembled in Chicago on the sixteenth of October, 1911. It was a remarkably impressive gathering and continued in session for three days perfecting an organization. Many addresses were made, and throughout all of its deliberations there prevailed a spirit of the deepest fervor and patriotism. Resolutions were adopted declaratory of Progressive principles and endorsing my candidacy in the strongest terms, from which I quote the following:

"The record of Senator La Follette in state and nation makes him the logical candidate for President of the United States. His experience, his character, his courage, his record in constructive legislation and administrative ability meet the requirements for leadership such as present conditions demand. This conference endorses him as a candidate for the Republican nomination for President and urges that in all states organizations be formed to promote his nomination."

In that great conference, from first to last, there was but one discordant note. It was sounded by James R. Garfield. He came to the meeting direct from New York, where he had been closeted with Roosevelt. He was careful to say that he spoke only for himself, but he was singularly persistent in opposing any endorsement of my candidacy. He did his work chiefly with the Committee on Resolutions, but finding himself quite alone and his efforts futile, he withdrew further opposition. A few days later I received a letter from him in which he urged that the action of the conference be not interpreted as an endorsement of my candidacy. Garfield's course was rendered the more significant by the appearance of an editorial in the *Outlook* (October 28, 1911), in which the unqualified endorsement of the Chicago conference is referred to as follows:

"This endorsement is to be regarded as a recommendation rather than a committal of the movement to any one man."

Garfield's action in connection with the Chicago conference revived my distrust regarding Roosevelt, as it did that of Mr. Houser and other of my intimate friends who attended the Chicago meeting, and knew of Garfield's efforts with the Committee on Resolutions to block the endorsement of my candidacy.

Just prior to the Chicago conference, Gardner had visited a number of the middle western states, through which President Taft was then filling a series of speaking engagements. This trip was made by Gardner, representing the syndicate of papers for which he was the Washington correspondent, and was primarily for the purpose of forming a judgment with respect to Taft's strength as a candidate and the strength of my opposing candidacy. He returned to Washington and advised me that in his opinion Taft had little or no real following west of the Mississippi River, and he said: "I have come definitely to the conclusion that you now have a fair chance to win the nomination in the convention." He gave it as his opinion that the Progressives from the Pacific coast and middle western states were certain to send three hundred to three hundred and fifty delegates to the National Convention. He announced that he was going over to New York to acquaint Roosevelt with the situation as he saw it, and urge him to a more active and more open support of my candidacy.

Upon his return Gardner came to see me. I saw at once that his interview had given him some new impressions of Roosevelt's attitude toward my candidacy. Apparently it had suddenly dawned upon Roosevelt that Taft could be beaten. Indeed, Gardner reported that when he told Roosevelt that there would be three hundred and fifty Progressive delegates opposed to Taft's renomination, elected west of the Mississippi, Roosevelt at once declared that Taft could not be nominated in the face of that opposition; that even if with the southern delegates there were votes enough to force his renomination, no federal machine would dare to name him in the face of so much opposition. Moreover, the Chicago conference had very greatly impressed Roosevelt with the Progressive support that was coming to me. In reporting his interview to me, Gardner said:

"Roosevelt is not only surprised at the development of your candidacy, but he is disappointed as well." And then explaining, he said further: "Roosevelt wants to be President again, but you know it has heretofore been his judgment that Taft could not be beaten. However, he now believes that he will be beaten. This change of opinion is not due alone to my report of the conditions in the west, but others have seen him; and then this Chicago conference has been very informing to him. He begins to see that this Progressive movement is a whole lot bigger than he has ever believed it to be. Now you are developing such strength that being nominated in 1912 becomes a possibility. And even if you should fail of the nomination, your leadership of the Progressive movement would become so established that you would be in the way in 1916."

Gardner was plainly impressed by the change in Roosevelt.

While more the Colonel's friend than mine, he often said that in his opinion Roosevelt could not be elected if nominated; that he had repeatedly urged this view upon Roosevelt, and, furthermore, that notwithstanding his great personal attachment for Roosevelt, he knew his weakness, his tendency to compromise, and he believed that "more progress would be made in four years under a La Follette administration than in ten years under a Roosevelt administration."

Gardner had found Roosevelt up on the bit. Others had been ahead of him in reporting the decline of the Taft strength and the astonishing progress of my candidacy. Dan Hanna of Ohio, son of the late Mark Hanna, and Nat Wright, his editor of the Cleveland *Leader,* had visited Roosevelt just ahead of Gardner, and had urged that it was time for him to "cut the string" and turn his candidacy loose. Roosevelt had received also a report in writing from O'Laughlin, correspondent for the Chicago *Tribune,* who had been with Taft on his "swing around the circle," and he reported Taft a "dead one," and urged upon Roosevelt that it was time for him to get in. "Still," Gardner said, "he will not do it. He cannot come out as a candidate against Taft. He knows it. He has said so himself again and again."

While there was this flaming up of Roosevelt's inner desire, he did not "cut the string." But manifestly he loosened it, giving his friends an opportunity to start here and there an "insistent demand" that he should be the candidate of the Progressives. Thus, following the visit of Hanna and Wright to Roosevelt, the Cleveland *Leader,* and the Toledo *Blade,* another Hanna paper, became more pronounced in advocacy of Roosevelt as a candidate.

This stirring of Roosevelt sentiment was cleverly directed. There was not enough of it to require any outward change of attitude on the part of Roosevelt himself, but just sufficient in Ohio and elsewhere to indicate an apparent outcropping of a powerful underground Roosevelt sentiment in certain localities. This would serve to check or confuse the Progressive support for me resulting from the action of the Chicago conference, and still leave Roosevelt in the choice position where he could let the contest go on, deciding later what course it would be advantageous for him to take. It had exactly the desired effect upon my campaign and we began to receive complaints from Progressive leaders in Ohio and various other states that division was being created in the Progressive ranks by Roosevelt's friends who were giving out that my candidacy was really in Roosevelt's interest and that at the right time he would be brought out as the real candidate. This situation was seized upon by papers favorable to the Taft administration, and extensively circulated. In some cases it was represented as a disagreement in the Progressive ranks. In some cases it was announced that the Progressives supporting my candidacy were being hoodwinked, and that delegates elected for me would be delivered to Roosevelt in the convention. Altogether it became a very serious hindrance to the progress of our canvass.

Houser complained daily that his work was being delayed and at many important points brought to a standstill. Our most earnest workers, men who were supporting my campaign upon the record of achievement in Wisconsin, the work done in the Senate, and in short my whole course as a Progressive; men who would not have enlisted in a campaign for Roosevelt, and who, further than this, were unwilling to play a double part, urged that some definite statement be issued clearing the whole matter up. Of course, the confusion and trouble could have been easily disposed of by a few plain words from Roosevelt. Gardner and Pinchot, with whom we talked the matter over, insisted again and again that Roosevelt did not intend to be a candidate, but that he was unwilling to make any statement to that effect. They said he had, while President, announced that he would not again be a candidate, and that advantage had been taken of this by his opponents to embarrass him in so many ways and to such an extent that he had declared that he would never again make such a statement. This obviously was no answer, and seemed to be an evasion of the point in issue. There was no way in which Roosevelt as a private citizen could be embarrassed by a statement that he would not under any circumstances be a candidate for the Republican nomination for the Presidency in 1912—*unless he intended to be a candidate*.

It was at this time and in this connection that I found myself beginning to be uncertain as to Pinchot and Gardner. Among all of my supporters none had been more insistent upon my becoming a candidate, nor stronger in their assurances that Roosevelt was acting in perfect good faith. But we were confronted with a serious situation in the campaign. Whatever Roosevelt's real position, he was certainly taking exactly the course to embarrass and weaken my candidacy, and injure the whole Progressive movement. It was no satisfaction to our correspondents, whose inquiries multiplied every day, to say that we had repeated assurances from Roosevelt through his closest friends that he would not be a candidate against Taft. The reply invariably came back, "Roosevelt

231

should be willing to say this plainly to the public over his own signature. We can make no progress with La Follette's candidacy so long as we are constantly confronted with the statement, 'Are you certain that he will continue as a candidate, or, if we support delegates for La Follette, will they be turned over to Roosevelt later?' This we must know."

While we were in this baffling and distracting situation, Houser proposed that a letter be written Roosevelt which would compel him in his answer to say definitely whether he would under any circumstances be a candidate. Houser contended that there still was sufficient uncertainty as to Progressive success to deter Roosevelt from coming out as an open candidate, even if he were tendered the united Progressive support, and that a letter could be so framed as to force him to a public declaration, which would take him out of the way, and leave me a clear field. I answered that I could not write a letter to Mr. Roosevelt or consent that one be written which might in any way bind me to support him if he decided to become a candidate; that I felt that I could not bring myself to support Roosevelt as the Progressive candidate, but that it could do no harm to call a conference to be attended by the Pinchots, Gardner, and other supporters to discuss the matter; and, indeed, that some good might result in securing an expression from certain of these men upon the subject.

Such a conference was held at the Pinchot residence, in Washington, which resulted in two or three tentative drafts of letters being made. But after it finally became apparent that any letter requesting him, in the interests of the Progressive movement, to publicly announce that he would not be a candidate, must carry with it a give and take proposal which might contingently pledge me to his support if he should become a candidate, I put an end to the whole matter, repeating in substance what I had said whenever there had been any serious discussion of Roosevelt as a Progressive candidate for the presidency: that I had always credited him with having rendered an important public service in what he had said and written on social and political evils, but when it came to doing the thing necessary to be done, he had failed utterly; that the time for preaching generalities had gone by and the time to do the big constructive work had come; that Roosevelt had never shown any constructive ability; that he had no settled convictions upon the economics of the Progressive movement, and therefore would certainly compromise it whenever he thought it expedient; that this would defeat real progress; that because of this quality of mind and this element in his character the Progressive movement had made more progress when he was out of the country than in all the seven years he was President; that I was certain he was wrong on the question of the valuation of railway property; that he attached no importance or very little importance to valuation as the correct basis for regulating railway rates and had declared that he did not believe there was any water in the stocks and bonds of the great railways systems; that if he were President again I feared he would confirm or bring about the confirmation of the thousands of millions of fictitious capitalization of the public service corporations and the industrial combinations of the country, fastening forever upon the American people the burden of the present high prices; and that if I were brought face to face with the question for final decision, I was not prepared to say that I would accept him as a Progressive candidate, or could even support him if he were nominated.

This conference was not in vain. It served to strengthen my doubts as to certain of my supporters. On the evening of the same day I received a visit from Gifford Pinchot, who called to inform me that, following the conference, he, Gardner, and Medill McCormick had conferred together, and that he desired to notify me that there must be no break with Roosevelt; that should one come, he and the other two had decided that they would go with Roosevelt. I said to Pinchot:

"You know that Roosevelt favored my being a candidate; you know that he sent Gilson Gardner to me to urge me to be a candidate. Now all appearances indicate that he is encouraging the use of his name. As soon as my candidacy began to take on proportions that looked like success there was what seemed to me to be unmistakable evidence of his doing everything in his power to block it, excepting to come out openly against me. Such a course cannot fail to divide the Progressive strength and seriously injure, if not destroy for the time being, the whole Progressive movement."

Pinchot reiterated the statements which he had made before that Roosevelt was not and would not be a candidate; that he (Pinchot) was still absolutely certain that if nothing were done to oppose Roosevelt he would ultimately support me openly; that I had no right to question his motives or his good faith. I asked him if, knowing as he did, the relations between Roosevelt and Garfield, he thought Garfield would be found taking a decided position regarding this campaign or any candidate that was not in accord with Roosevelt's wishes. He frankly admitted that he would not

233

expect Garfield to take any important action in this campaign against Roosevelt's judgment. I then reminded him that Garfield had gone from a conference with Roosevelt directly to the Progressive meeting in Chicago, and there, standing practically alone, had opposed as vigorously as he could in the executive session of the Committee on Resolutions any endorsement of my candidacy. And I asked him if he did not regard that as a plain indication of Roosevelt's position. He was forced to admit that it had that appearance, and with some spirit added:

"But suppose you are right about it, and Roosevelt comes out as a candidate, what can you do? You must know that he has this thing in his own hands and can do whatever he likes."

I said: "I grant you that he can come into this campaign as a candidate if he chooses to do so. There is no way to prevent that. The fact that he has encouraged my candidacy will not, I am sure, deter him if he thinks at any time the opportunity is favorable. But let me serve notice on you now, that if he does so, you and he may understand that he will be confronted with his record, which is not that of a Progressive. I said, "I know Roosevelt's strength, and I know his weakness. He has never been subjected to criticism by men of position in his own party. His whole course on the tariff during the seven years he was President proves him to have been as much a stand-patter as Aldrich or Cannon. Now, I am not seeking any break with Roosevelt. I have no doubt he could take a large Progressive following with him because he is accepted by many people unacquainted with the details of his record, as a Progressive. He is probably in a position to divide the Progressives and destroy all chance of success in this campaign. But I say now, that if he undertakes such a course, he will surely fail. I know your strong friendship for Roosevelt, and I appreciate the support you have given me. I sincerely hope you are not mistaken when you say that Roosevelt has no intention of becoming a candidate and that he will, as you say, ultimately openly and actively support me for the nomination. Surely you must see, and he must see, that the public is warranted in inferring from his present course that he is contemplating an announcement of his candidacy, and that introduces confusion and uncertainty into our campaign which is very harmful. But there is no other way for me than to go on making the best fight I can for the nomination." With my last statement Pinchot apparently agreed and we talked for some time further on the details of our campaign.

234

A short time prior to this, on the seventh of December, Pinchot had made a speech before the Chicago Press Club, from which I quote the following:

"If Colonel Roosevelt had not made his recent statement, and I am in a position to know that he means what he says, he might have been the candidate. I do not assert that La Follette is yet sure of the nomination, but now that circumstances have made Mr. Taft's renomination either impossible or extremely improbable, the attention of the country is turning swiftly and eagerly to Bob La Follette of Wisconsin."

Just what occurred between Pinchot and Roosevelt after this speech was delivered in Chicago on the seventh, and before it was repeated in Boston on the sixteenth of December in Tremont Temple, upon the occasion of the forming of a Progressive organization for Massachusetts, I, of course, have no means of knowing. That Pinchot saw Roosevelt during this interval is certain. It was significant that in delivering the Chicago Press Club speech at the Boston meeting Pinchot omitted from the paragraph above quoted the statement regarding Roosevelt's not being a candidate.

Except for this omission he gave the speech as delivered in Chicago. This circumstance is open to the inference that Roosevelt no longer wanted Pinchot emphasizing this statement by repetition.

It is also certain that Pinchot saw Roosevelt after calling on me that evening following the conference at Pinchot's house, when we had the very plain talk just detailed concerning Roosevelt's candidacy and my purpose, which I believe was communicated to Roosevelt. Within forty-eight hours thereafter there came a pressing invitation over the long distance telephone for Houser and Lenroot to meet Roosevelt with Gardner and Gifford Pinchot at the residence of Amos Pinchot in New York, on Sunday, December 17th. It is clear that Roosevelt was still desirous of keeping the soft pedal on his candidacy, the time not yet having arrived when it would serve his purpose to break in. I declined to permit Houser to go (suggesting that Kent go instead) for the same reason that I had declined to permit either Pinchot or Gardner to arrange any meetings between Roosevelt and myself, which they often sought to bring about. I was unwilling that there should be established any beaten pathway between my headquarters and Mr. Roosevelt's offices in New York, upon which at any time might be predicated a relationship committing me to Roosevelt's brand of Progressivism.

The substance of Roosevelt's statement to these men, as reported to me by Lenroot, Kent, and Gardner immediately upon their return to Washington, was as follows: Roosevelt said he was not a candidate, but he should never again declare that he would not be a candidate; that he did not think he ought to make such an announcement anyway, because if it were found in the convention that I could not beat Taft, it might be necessary for him to permit his name to be presented to the convention; that even then he could not do so, if upon the whole situation it appeared that he might be beaten in the election; that he could not afford to be beaten in the election, as it would spoil his place in history, but that a defeat would not injure me; that I should go ahead with the campaign, and if I could be nominated, all right; that if it were found in the convention that I could not make it, then he might come in; but that "under no circumstances ought we to permit the wires to be crossed" or any division or contention come between our friends in the campaign. The North Dakota primary, which was to occur on the nineteenth of March, was then brought to his attention by Lenroot, who pointed out the danger of his (Roosevelt's) name being placed on the ballot there, either by friends, without his consent, or by Taft's supporters, for the purpose of dividing the Progressive vote, thus enabling the reactionaries to carry the state, unless he would (as he could under the law) *forbid the use of his name.* To this suggestion of Lenroot's he replied that he had not thought of that; but that if such unwarranted action were taken by his friends, or enemies, division could be averted by an understanding that delegates elected for me might be for him for second choice, in the event that his name had to be brought forward in the convention to prevent Taft's nomination, and it appeared he could win in the election.

Gardner expressed great satisfaction at the result of the interview, contending that Roosevelt was acting in perfect good faith; that he was not a candidate and did not intend to be a candidate. Kent agreed that they would be justified in reaching that conclusion if Roosevelt's word could be relied on; but thought that notwithstanding his repeated assurances he might be expected to break in at any time and attempt to carry off the nomination; that he certainly would do so if he thought he could get away with it and win in the election against a Democrat. After Kent and Gardner had gone, Lenroot gave it as his opinion that, notwithstanding all Roosevelt had said, he was at that very moment a candidate, but that he would never come out in the open until he had secured such pledges of support as would insure his nomination and also felt sure that he could win in the election.

Arrangements had been made for me to begin a speaking campaign extending through the states of Ohio, Michigan, and Illinois, the latter part of December and the first of January. My campaign had now been under way for many months. Hundreds of thousands of letters had been written and great quantities of documents and speeches distributed. We had set aside from our campaign fund a sufficient sum to print several thousand copies of a document reviewing my public record as a member of the House of Representatives for six years, and governor of Wisconsin for three terms, giving a brief analysis of the progressive laws enacted and the effect of the administration of those laws upon the public service and other corporations of the state, and also covering my six years of service in the Senate. The manuscript for this document had been prepared with care, since it was to be the one given the largest general distribution, and turned over to the publicity department in our headquarters to be printed. I had been closely occupied with my official duties and the writing of my autobiography, and could only occasionally look in on the headquarters. Shortly before leaving for Ohio to begin my campaign, I asked for some printed copies of this record, and was surprised to find that it had not yet been printed. As Houser was also leaving for Ohio, at my request Congressman John M. Nelson of Wisconsin consented to spend such time at the headquarters as could be spared from his work in the House, and his attention was called to the importance of printing and distributing this pamphlet containing my record.

Some months before this Medill McCormick, with whom I had had no previous acquaintance, calling at my residence to see me, had tendered his services to aid in the campaign. He referred to his former connection with the Chicago *Tribune,* and his wide acquaintance with newspaper publishers throughout the country, all of which he mentioned as fitting him to aid in promoting the campaign. He said if his services were acceptable he wanted me to give him a letter to Mr. Houser with directions that he be provided with office space at the headquarters for the work which he proposed to do. He stated that he had no active business engagements, as he had been recuperating his health for a considerable period of time, and was therefore absolutely free to lend a hand. He saw Mr. Houser and soon came to have general charge of matters connected with printing and publicity at the headquarters.

After I had left to fill my Ohio engagements, Congressman Nelson found that the printing of the manuscript covering my public record was not under way. In the course of a conference relating to other matters, McCormick incidentally placed in Nelson's hands a copy of what Nelson supposed was the approved manuscript. It developed, however, that a manuscript written by McCormick himself had been substituted for the original. Upon reading the document which he proposed to have printed, the significance of the exchange was at once apparent to Nelson, who went directly to McCormick, and with some warmth inquired why a eulogy of Roosevelt was to be sent out ostensibly in the interest of La Follette's candidacy from our headquarters, and stated very positively that it would never be done with his consent in my absence. McCormick took possession of the manuscript and subsequently directed the clerk to have it put in type, telling him to offer the printer a bonus of two hundred dollars for rushing the printing of the document. After taking this extraordinary course to secure the immediate printing of his manuscript, McCormick left for Chicago, in order to be on the ground in Illinois some time in advance of my entering that state to fill the speaking engagements for which I had been scheduled. From Chicago he wired Nelson, again urging that the printing of his manuscript be rushed. Obviously the deep cut which the expenditure for printing this document would make in our limited campaign fund was taken into account, and it was assumed that when once printed, although objectionable, the chances were that it would be sent out instead of the document originally prepared, as we could not afford to print both.

McCormick's manuscript was cleverly written. It highly commended my work and my candidacy, but contained flattering references to Roosevelt so framed that, if it had been sent out from my headquarters, it would have *committed me to him* as a thorough-going Progressive in the event that he later came out as a candidate. The loyalty of the clerk, however, saved the situation. He carried the manuscript to Nelson, and informed him of the offer which he (the clerk) was authorized to make to the printer in McCormick's behalf. It is to be remembered that at this time Houser and I were both absent and, except for Nelson, McCormick was the one man in authority at my headquarters. Nelson submitted the McCormick manuscript to Mrs. La Follette and Professor Commons, who chanced to be a guest of ours in Washington at the time. They promptly decided that it should not, under any circumstances, be issued, and proceeded at once to have printed the manuscript which had been originally prepared.

Something like a month before I began my speaking campaign in Ohio a Progressive organization had been formed in that state of which Judge Wanamaker of Akron was elected chairman, and John D. Fackler of Cleveland secretary. At the time of the formation of this Progressive organization it had been proposed to adopt resolutions declaring for my candidacy. But it was suggested to Houser, who was present, that it would be more effective to offer such a resolution at a state-wide conference which it was proposed should be held in Columbus on the first of January following the tour through the state which I was expected to make during the last days of December. Houser reported this to me on his return to Washington. I asked him if it were not possible that work was being done for Roosevelt by Wanamaker and others who had devised this course, and whether the postponement was not for the purpose of enabling them to develop enough Roosevelt sentiment at the Ohio state conference to defeat a resolution endorsing my candidacy. He assured me that there was not the slightest ground for any such suspicion; that Wanamaker was very friendly to my candidacy, though it was true that he had been at one time a strong Roosevelt man.

My first meeting in Ohio was at Youngstown in the afternoon of December 27th. Shortly before going to the opera house, where I was to speak, Judge Wanamaker, accompanied by Mr. Fackler, called on me at my rooms in the hotel. I had previously been warned to be somewhat on my guard as to Wanamaker. He had called to suggest, he said, that in the course of my speech it would be a fine thing if I would mention the names of former Presidents Garfield, McKinley, and Roosevelt, as it always had a good effect upon an audience and tended to promote enthusiasm to refer to the old-time Republican leaders of the party. I told him that I was not much given to talking about individuals; that I purposed to discuss the present-day evils oppressing the people and the Progressive remedies which we proposed to meet existing conditions. After some further talk I was escorted to the opera house. Newspaper correspondents representing the press associations and many of the leading papers of the country were present. Indeed, I was accompanied throughout this campaign tour by a large corps of newspaper men, who reported very fully all of my meetings. I never had a more enthusiastic reception nor a more responsive audience, but I afterward learned that cards had been distributed to those entering on which was printed in black-faced type, "We are for Roosevelt." I do not know whether there was any connection between this circumstance and Judge Wanamaker's suggestion that I mention the name of Roosevelt in the course of my speech, but I strongly suspect that had I done so an attempt would have followed to turn the meeting into a Roosevelt demonstration which would have been reported over the country, giving out the impression that the first meeting of my campaign had developed an overwhelming sentiment for Roosevelt as the Progressive candidate.

The meetings in Ohio, Michigan, and Illinois were really remarkable. I think I may say that never in the heat of a campaign was greater enthusiasm witnessed, and still the primaries were months off. Roosevelt and his friends were surprised and alarmed. When they could neither ignore nor disparage, they were at some pains to restrain the public from committing the error of becoming too enthusiastic about the candidate.

The *Outlook* of January 13, 1912, after commenting upon the size of my audiences, added, with exquisite refinement of analysis:

"Whether the crowds that have gathered to hear him have been impelled by enthusiasm for the man, belief in the principles he advocates, or a desire to protest against present political conditions, it would be hard to say; probably all three in varying proportions."

In judging of Roosevelt's conduct, it is quite important to know whether he entered the field because my candidacy was failing, or because it was succeeding. That is the test of the man's sincerity and reliability of character as involved in this affair, and of the ultimate effect, for good or ill, of his manifest determination to take control of the Progressive movement. It therefore becomes an essential part of the history of this whole matter to study step by step the progress or failure of my campaign and candidacy.

The first practical test came with the Chicago conference of October 16th. The second and more important test came with my first speaking campaign through these three states. I have said that I never witnessed a deeper and more intense public interest, with all the outward manifestations of enthusiasm and devotion, than on this tour through Ohio, Michigan and Illinois. But I do not rest that statement alone on my own impressions. The brief excerpts herewith added, taken from extended press comments by papers, with one or two exceptions, unfriendly to my candidacy and the Progressive movement, are typical of what the newspapers reported, and are submitted solely that the reader may judge of the matter for himself.

Of the Youngstown meeting, the Philadelphia *North American* said:

"It was an impressive opening, and one which has filled his admirers in Ohio with enthusiasm."

The Cincinnati *Enquirer* made this comment on the Cleveland meeting:

"At Gray's Armory, which was packed to the doors half an hour before the Senator's arrival, a band burst forth with the national anthem when La Follette appeared. For several minutes Senator La Follette was deterred from speaking by the cheers of the crowd."

Of the Cleveland meeting the Philadelphia *North American* said:

"Senator La Follette got a reception here tonight so genuinely enthusiastic, so demonstrative of tremendous public interest in the man and the Progressive movement, as to astonish his friends and arouse alarm among the reactionary Republicans. The Cleveland newspapers declared to-day that nothing like this was ever known in Cleveland before."

The same paper said of the Toledo meeting:

"The hall in which Senator La Follette spoke here to-night was so crowded before the Senator arrived that the police took charge and locked the doors. Two thousand and more persons were turned away. It was the most enthusiastic audience the Senator had addressed, and cheered him frequently."

The Cincinnati *Enquirer* gave this as a part of its report of the Toledo speech:

"If any one had gained the impression that Republican State Chairman Walter F. Brown's Progressive organization had robbed the visit of Senator Robert M. La Follette of any of its enthusiasm, it was dispelled to-night when the doughty Wisconsin fighter stepped upon the platform in Memorial Hall.

"The cheering of more than three thousand men and women greeted him, and this demonstration lasted for five minutes. There were more than two thousand outside the hall who failed to get admittance. They stood around for half an hour in the cold in efforts to make their way indoors."

Referring to the Dayton meeting, the Philadelphia *North American* said:

"Senator La Follette closed the most remarkable day he has spent in Ohio with a meeting here to-night attended by five thousand persons. At North Baltimore to-day the Senator got a reception which astonished him. The actual number of men present exceeded many times the voting population of North Baltimore and must have pretty well exhausted the rural strength of both sections for miles around. Nothing like this North Baltimore meeting was ever known in that section of Ohio in any political campaign."

Of this same meeting the Cincinnati *Enquirer* said:

"Senator Robert M. La Follette of Wisconsin talked to an audience here to-night that comfortably filled the Memorial Hall, the largest auditorium in the city. His sentiments were loudly cheered and his climaxes evoked tremendous applause.

"Upon his entrance upon the stage he was given such an ovation as clearly showed his immense audience heartily in sympathy with the principles he is representing."

My last meeting in Ohio, at Cincinnati on Saturday night, December 30th, was referred to by the Philadelphia *North American* as follows:

"Senator La Follette was given to-night, in Cincinnati, President Taft's home town, the most enthusiastic reception accorded him since he entered the state of Ohio. As he proceeded with his speech the enthusiasm increased, and his telling points were greeted with cheers."

In Michigan I addressed meetings January 1st, 2nd and 3rd at Flint, Bay City, Saginaw, Grand Rapids, and Kalamazoo.

The following from the Detroit *Free Press* are typical of the notices given my meetings in Michigan:

"Flint, Mich., January 1.—Senator Robert M. La Follette opened the New Year and his campaign in Michigan simultaneously to-day with a meeting in the auditorium of the Masonic Temple. He was greeted by an audience of about 1,200 persons, which included a considerable number of farmers from the surrounding country. The Senator was accorded a hearty reception."

"Bay City, Mich., January 1.—Senator Robert M. La Follette addressed three thousand people in the armory here this afternoon. The audience was enthusiastic and appreciative."

Beginning with a meeting on the evening of January 3rd, in Orchestra Hall, Chicago, from which more than three thousand people were turned away, I continued on through the state, concluding a series of seventeen speeches in Illinois at East St. Louis on the evening of January 5th.

Respecting the Chicago meeting, I quote from the Philadelphia *North American:*

"The public interest in Senator La Follette and the hold he obtained upon his audience here are causing the same amazement to the newspapers and politicians that marked his entry into Ohio. Both the newspapers and the politicians have been sneering at the La Follette movement and at Senator La Follette in particular. There was plenty of progressive sentiment in the state, they have admitted, but they have been emphatically declaring that it was not La Follette sentiment, and if it were to assume the form of hostility to Taft and the Republican administration it would be found to be Roosevelt sentiment. La Follette's trip to-day and his meeting in Chicago last night have demonstrated that the voters are intensely interested in the Wisconsin Senator and that they believe in him and in his doctrines. The comment in Chicago was that the audience which greeted and cheered Senator La Follette was more like the great mass meeting held against the Allan bill than any political gathering which the city has known since that time."

And this from the Chicago *Inter-Ocean:*

"The meeting last night was the largest and surely the most enthusiastic political gathering ever held in Orchestra Hall. Every seat in the hall was occupied before eight o'clock.

"Senator La Follette had a friendly audience to talk to. They frequently interrupted him with applause. When he rose to speak he was cheered for five minutes. He talked two hours and a half and the audience seemed willing to remain indefinitely."

The principal meetings in Illinois were held in the following cities: Chicago, Joliet, Morris, Ottawa, Streator, La Salle, Spring Valley, Peoria, Bloomington, Decatur, Springfield, East St. Louis, and Danville.

The Chicago *Tribune* said this of the Peoria meeting:

"Illinois political 'jackpotters' were castigated without mercy to-day by Senator Robert M. La Follette in a speech at Ottawa, Ill., the home of Lee O'Neil Brown, as well as in speeches at other cities.

"The Senator completed the first leg of the stiff course mapped out for him in Illinois with an address here to-night before five thousand persons."

And this of the Joliet meeting:

. . . "The demonstration to-night, as viewed by expert politicians in the second city in the state, was a record breaker for enthusiasm and cordiality."

The following from the Philadelphia *North American* is characteristic of the general press comment:

"At Bloomington, Springfield, Decatur, and finally here at East St. Louis he was greeted by crowds that packed every available space in the buildings in which he spoke. It was a typical La Follette welcome in every town where he stopped. The men who came to hear him were earnest Progressives, and his utterances pleading for a return to popular rule were enthusiastically applauded."

And this from the Chicago *Tribune:*

"Senator La Follette was tremendously pleased with his reception in Illinois to-day. He let it be known that he feels he has been received most kindly, and far in excess of the most optimistic predictions of his friends when the Illinois invasion was first planned."

. . . .

"There were big crowds at every point he touched—Bloomington, Clinton, Decatur, Springfield, Carlinville, Staunton, Edwardsville, and to-night (at East St. Louis) an audience which tested the popularity of Senator La Follette in the face of allegations from local Progressive managers that the regular organization, which is particularly strong here, had made efforts to throw cold water on the meeting."

I spoke once in Indiana, at Terre Haute, on my way back to Washington.

It was the most remarkable series of midwinter meetings ever held. The weather was bitterly cold; yet there were immense audiences everywhere for both the day and night speeches, and I never found people more responsive or more deeply and earnestly interested.

My tour of these states was really a triumph. And it destroyed the effect of the jack-in-the-box statements emanating from New York regarding Roosevelt's purposes, which had produced so much confusion in the field work that was being carried on from the headquarters.

Realizing the importance of taking advantage of the strong current which had set in for my candidacy following the meetings in Ohio, Michigan, and Illinois, I should have extended my tour into Minnesota, the Dakotas, Iowa, Nebraska, and Kansas before returning to Washington, excepting for the fact that it was necessary to return to Washington on account of some matters pending in the Senate, and to fill engagements in New York, Pennsylvania, and New Jersey which had been made some time before.

I had been back in Washington but a few days when it became apparent that there was a marked change of policy on the part of Roosevelt and his friends. Systematic and organized efforts of a more clearly definite character were being vigorously put forth to check and set back the rising tide of sentiment in my favor. The Progressives of the country were taking my candidacy too seriously!

At the very time when my meetings were overtaxing the largest auditoriums that could be secured, Roosevelt wrote a letter to Governor Hiram Johnson, of California, who had been strongly committed to my candidacy, in which he stated in substance that it was necessary I should be set aside, and suggested that he (Johnson) would make an admirable candidate for Vice-President. The Vice-Presidential bait was dangled before the eyes of the governor on a separate and detached sheet of paper in the form of an unsigned postscript. Johnson afterward visited Roosevelt in New York, and became one of the group who finally succeeded in cornering the coy and diffident candidate and wringing from him a "reluctant consent."

Dispatches began to appear in the papers here and there quite systematically, and from significant sources, asserting that Roosevelt would be a candidate. I quote from one dated at Poughkeepsie, N. Y., published in the Philadelphia *North American,* January 1, 1912,

"That Theodore Roosevelt will be a candidate for President again if the call comes strong enough for him to respond is the statement made to-day by John Burroughs, the author-naturalist in an interview published in the Poughkeepsie *Courier.* Much significance is attached to this prediction on account of Mr. Burroughs' intimacy with Mr. Roosevelt."

On January 1, 1912, I opened my campaign in Michigan. On the same day the much talked of Ohio state conference was held at Columbus. It had been announced several weeks before. Ninety-two of the leading Progressives of the state were present. In this meeting, for the first time and in an open and formal way, the friends of Roosevelt disclosed their real purpose. Walter F. Brown, reactionary boss and chairman of the Republican State Central Committee, was present, working actively in support of Roosevelt, and to prevent any endorsement of my candidacy by the Ohio conference. Brown is to Ohio politics exactly what Platt, Quay, Henry C. Payne, and men of that type were to the political affairs of their time. The morning of the conference he spent much time with Pinchot and Fackler.

It had been accepted that a formal endorsement of my candidacy would be adopted in this meeting. But a small minority, led by Pinchot, Garfield, Wanamaker, and Brown, appealed to those in attendance not to adopt a resolution making formal declaration for any candidate for President, urging that the friends of Roosevelt should not be antagonized. Pinchot especially gave assurance that they would later all be found supporting my candidacy. He stated further that he knew from his repeated conferences with Roosevelt that he was not a candidate, and expressed the strongest belief that Roosevelt himself would be found before long openly supporting me. My friends attending upon that conference, who were eager to endorse me, outnumbered the friends of Roosevelt eight to one. But yielding to Pinchot, and the appeal for harmony, the following resolution was finally agreed to:

"We are opposed to the renomination of President Taft. We hereby declare it to be the determined purpose of the Ohio Progressive Republican League to work in harmony and unison to nominate a Progressive Republican for President, recognizing as fellow Progressives all who hold the principles for which we stand, whether they be for the presidential nomination of Robert M. La Follette or Theodore Roosevelt, or any other Progressive Republican.

"We assert the essential unity of the Progressive movement throughout the entire state and nation.

"We favor the election of delegates who will favor the nomination of a candidate who will fully represent the Progressive principles."

Speaking for these resolutions, Pinchot said:

"I believe most intensely that it would be foolish not to crystallize the Roosevelt sentiment and the Progressive sentiment of all other men, whatever candidates they may prefer, so that we can elect delegates to the Chicago convention who will vote for the Progressive candidate, which we know will be Mr. La Follette."

The convention then voted 81 to 11 in favor of a resolution as a "personal expression" of the delegates, naming me as "the living embodiment of the principles of the Progressive movement and the logical candidate to carry them to successful fruition."

January 5th, Garfield made a hurried trip to New York, and had an interview with Roosevelt at a private club. He was in a position to report on the great stirring that Ohio had just been given, and the clever work done by himself, Pinchot, Wanamaker, and Walter Brown, the machine boss, in averting an affirmative endorsement of my candidacy by the Ohio conference at Columbus three days before.

Pinchot, immediately after the Ohio conference, went to Battle Creek, Mich., for a brief rest, and on January 3rd the newspapers generally published the following:

"Gifford Pinchot, in an interview given out here to-day, denied that he had made any statements in speeches or interviews, that Theodore Roosevelt had told him that he would not accept the presidential nomination if it were tendered. 'I know nothing of Mr. Roosevelt's affairs, either as to whether he would accept the nomination, or whether he believes he could be elected.' "

Just one month before, he had said in his speech to the Chicago Press club:

"If Colonel Roosevelt had not made his recent statement, and I am in a position to know that he means what he says, he might have been the candidate."

And only two days before he had said in his speech before the Ohio conference that he was advocating the plan which he contended would secure the election of "delegates to the Chicago convention who will vote for the Progressive candidate which we *know* will be Mr. La Follette."

But Progressive sentiment was crystallizing about my candidacy so rapidly that the near friends of Roosevelt who had been professing loyalty to me, while at heart for him, were being forced by developments more and more to disclose their real design. And we were fast approaching a time when Roosevelt himself would have to show his hand.

On the nineteenth of January Mr. Homer Mann, chairman of the Fifth District Congressional Committee, called a meeting of party workers together in Kansas City, to whom he said:

"Some time ago I wrote to Mr. Roosevelt telling him that it was impossible to carry the state unless he again assumed the leadership of the party. I got a reply. I am not at liberty to give the answer now, but it suffices to say that this meeting was called."

I had spoken many times in Kansas. Some three years before Bristow became a candidate for the United States Senate I had urged my audiences to elect him to succeed Senator Long, and in my meetings throughout the state had reviewed Long's senatorial record. Finally, when Bristow did become a candidate, I had gone to Kansas on the urgent call of William Allen White to speak for Bristow. I had every reason to believe that White, who is very strong in Kansas, was supporting my candidacy.

On the ninth of January a letter was received at our headquarters in Washington from Rodney A. Elward of Castleton, Kan., an old Wisconsin University friend and supporter of mine, and at present one of the regents of the Kansas State University. In this letter, Elward said:

"I received a letter from William Allen White this morning saying he is for La Follette."

This letter of White's must have been written a day or two before and about the time I had concluded my tour of Ohio, Michigan, and Illinois.

I was amazed to see it followed on the tenth of January by an editorial in White's paper, the *Emporia Gazette,* concluding an appeal to Progressives to organize for Roosevelt, with the words, "Roosevelt or bust!"

What came to White in that brief interval to change his attitude, I do not know.

The day after the publication of Mr. White's "Roosevelt or bust" editorial, Frank A. Munsey, owner of several newspapers and periodicals, very much interested in the United States Steel Corporation, and one of Roosevelt's financial backers and intimates, published in large type a double column signed editorial on the front page of his papers, of which the following is the concluding paragraph:

"Situated as he is, my guess is that Mr. Roosevelt is quite content to let political matters shape themselves up as they will. If no call comes to him to lead the fight, he will keep right on having a good time with his work, as he is now doing. But if the call does come, he will buckle on his armor and 'go to it' with all his old-time impetuosity and energy."

In view of Mr. Munsey's relations with Mr. Roosevelt, and the financial backing which he furnished to promote Roosevelt's campaign, it will hardly be questioned that the publication of this editorial was inspired.

Two days later the story that a campaign for Roosevelt was being quietly financed by George W. Perkins of the Steel Trust, and that Ormsby McHarg had been sent into the southern states to "see" the right parties, was printed as coming from Indianapolis, and widely copied in New York, Washington, and other papers. It produced a great sensation. When the newspaper reporters saw Roosevelt at the *Outlook* office to interrogate him on the subject, they experienced considerable difficulty. The session was very brief, and was reported by one of them as follows:

"Mr. Roosevelt's jaws snapped shut as he listened, and when they opened it was to say, 'I will not discuss pipe dreams from Indianapolis or anywhere else. There are depths of tomfoolery that I can't notice.'"

But the financing of Roosevelt's campaign by Morgan's friend Perkins was a subject of too great public interest to be disposed of as "tomfoolery." And the watchful newspaper correspondents were soon able to report that private meetings and conferences were being held between Perkins and Roosevelt. The support of Morgan's man, Perkins, recalled to the public mind Roosevelt's great service to the Steel Trust in permitting it to swallow up its principal rival, the Tennessee Coal and Iron Company, and, consequently, the demand for something definite as to Perkins' financial backing of Roosevelt's candidacy became so insistent that it could not be silenced by brushing it aside as a "pipe dream." Some one had to speak, and the speaking part was assigned to Perkins, who issued a "frank statement" announcing that he was supporting Roosevelt because "they looked at public questions in the same way." When taken red handed the very boldness of an open admission is the best and only recourse. Before many weeks all reserve as to Perkins, Munsey, and the Steel Trust was thrown aside, and later men most prominently connected with the Harvester Trust were likewise openly supporting the Roosevelt candidacy. That Wall Street interests generally were in accord was soon well understood among those who noted the kindly references to Roosevelt and the difference in expression whenever his name was mentioned around the Stock Exchange.

While the whole plan in the light of subsequent events became perfectly plain, so cleverly was it all managed, so rapidly were the scenes shifted, so swiftly did the unauthorized announcements and the qualified denials follow one upon the other, that doubt and confusion prevailed everywhere, outside of the little circle of which Roosevelt was the centre. One day it would seem certain that my candidacy had already been betrayed by the friends of Roosevelt who were in my own organization; the next day I would be assured that he would announce his refusal to be a candidate; that there would be no division in the Progressive ranks and that his supporters would be my supporters. But events were driving ahead rapidly. With each day the double play became more difficult.

Finally, on the 14th of January, we were surprised at our headquarters to receive a visit from John D. Fackler, our campaign manager for Ohio, who said he came with a proposition from Walter Brown and Dan Hanna for a working combination of La Follette and Roosevelt forces. They proposed that the campaign be carried on in Ohio with La Follette as the candidate, but that in each congressional district one Roosevelt delegate should be placed upon the ballot with one La Follette delegate. Roosevelt was not to be known as an open and avowed candidate. The inducement was held out that they would furnish all the money for the campaign in Ohio, but they stipulated that the La Follette Progressive literature which had been supplied from Washington, and was then on hand at our Ohio headquarters in considerable quantity, should be destroyed, and no more sent out into the state.

Fackler was told that I would enter into no deal or combination with the men who stood for the very things in politics to which I was opposed, and that I would consent to no arrangement which involved either coupling Roosevelt's candidacy with mine, or conducting a campaign in which Roosevelt delegates should be put on a ticket under cover of my candidacy. Fackler professed to agree with the position which I took, but he said in the course of the conversation that it had been very strongly intimated to him if the Brown-Hanna-Roosevelt scheme could be carried out he (Fackler) could have the nomination to Congress from that district. He protested that he had no desire to go to Congress and that such an offer, if squarely made, would have no influence with him. He said several times that when he reached his office on Monday morning he would find these men there with their check or the money ready. Fackler returned to Ohio with directions to say to Brown and Hanna that their offer was rejected; that we should continue to make a straight-out fight for Progressive principles and for my candidacy, and that we would enter into no combination of any character whatsoever.

A few days later Fackler, accompanied by Walter Brown, visited Roosevelt at the *Outlook* office in New York. He returned to Ohio by way of Washington, calling upon Houser at the headquarters, where he gave positive assurance of his continued loyalty, explaining his visit by saying that he had gone to see Roosevelt at the suggestion of Brown, but that the conference was confidential, and that he was not at liberty to state what Roosevelt had said to him. Fackler subsequently went over to the support of Roosevelt, taking with him as much of my organization as he could influence. He was given the support of the Roosevelt organization as a candidate for the congressional nomination in the Cleveland district, but was defeated in the primary.

We now began to have serious differences with Gifford Pinchot. He insisted that the Brown-Hanna combination should be made, and that the La Follette organization in Ohio should put a Roosevelt delegate on the ticket in each congressional district. My answer was that my candidacy should not be made a shield and cover for Roosevelt; that if he was to be a candidate, he should come out in the open; that I would never consent to be a stalking horse for Roosevelt or any other man; that for many years I had fought a clean, straight fight for definite Progressive principles; that I had been urged by Progressives to stand as the presidential candidate for that reason; that I would not compromise these principles or permit my name to be used in any way to secure delegates for any other candidate; that he (Pinchot) understood all this before he contributed in support of my campaign, and that as I repeatedly asserted, this would be my position through to the end.

I was now to be reminded that "nothing weighs lighter than a promise." On the twentieth of January Cummins announced his candidacy for the presidential nomination. It was little more than eight months since the conference of Progressives in Senator Bourne's committee room, on the thirtieth of April, when Cummins had said, "I shall not be a candidate. It is out of the question." To Houser, in explaining his action in coming out as a candidate, Cummins stated that it was his purpose to hold Iowa from going to Taft. Houser protested and urged him to keep his promise. But he issued his announcement. In the end he was only able to get ten of the twenty-six delegates from the state of Iowa to the national convention. Judged by his estimates of what I would be able to do in that state and from the correspondence at our headquarters, I could scarcely have done worse.

I had been announced to speak in Carnegie Hall on the twenty-second of January. A few days before this meeting Pinchot proposed that on the occasion of my visit to New York a luncheon should be arranged at Amos Pinchot's house, where Roosevelt and I should meet. As I had now become convinced that Roosevelt was an active, though not an open, candidate, and was only waiting to create a situation which would seem to compel his candidacy, I would not consent to be drawn into any situation which would lead the public to believe that there was a combination between us, or which could thereafter be interpreted to mean that I accepted Roosevelt as representing real Progressive principles. For some days New York dispatches had appeared in Roosevelt's interest, reiterating the statement that (to quote from one of them) "there will be absolutely no rivalry between Senator La Follette and Theodore Roosevelt in case the latter should become a candidate. . . . On the other hand, it is becoming apparent that should Roosevelt decide that he will not accept the nomination under any circumstances, then the real Roosevelt strength will undoubtedly go to Senator La Follette."

The time had not quite arrived openly to desert me. My campaign work and that of our headquarters was effective in arousing and organizing Progressive sentiment, and it was still a part of the Roosevelt plan to wear down my strength and entice away my active supporters, one after another, so that when the right time came for a final stroke my situation would be such that I would either go in and help promote the Roosevelt campaign or strike my colors and retire from the field. When Fackler was given his specific instructions, directing that the Ohio campaign must have no connection whatever with those who were supporting any other candidate, the same instructions in effect were sent to my headquarters in Chicago. Medill McCormick was now spending most of his time in and about the Chicago headquarters.

I had already seen enough to make me wholly distrustful of McCormick's loyalty, and was apprehensive that he was doing everything in his power to undermine and weaken my organization. I was therefore determined to take such steps as would force the Roosevelt men in my camp to show their hands. I was resolved to seek no quarrel, but I would have no more double work going on in my headquarters. This had the effect of forcing the Roosevelt men in our organization to make their stand, and about January 18th Pinchot, acting upon his own motion, called a conference of those who had contributed to support my campaign, and such others as he saw fit to invite, to meet at the Washington headquarters. There were present at that meeting Gifford and Amos Pinchot, Congressman Kent, Walter S. Rogers (secretary to Charles R. Crane), who were the principal contributors; Houser, Congressman Lenroot, my private secretary, John J. Hannan, and as I now remember it, Gilson Gardner. Medill McCormick was there. McCormick came on from Chicago, I presume, on Gifford Pinchot's invitation. I declined to participate in the conference so long as McCormick was present and he later withdrew. Francis J. Heney happened to be in Washington at this time. He was then one of my warmest supporters and strongly opposed to Roosevelt's becoming a candidate. After I learned that Pinchot had called the conference I requested Heney to attend and he did so.

Gifford Pinchot was insistent that the campaign should be conducted according to the scheme suggested by Walter Brown and Dan Hanna, continuing the campaign for me as the Progressive candidate, but putting Roosevelt delegates on the ticket with the La Follette delegates in Ohio and elsewhere.

In this conference Heney vigorously opposed Gifford Pinchot's plan. He pointed out the rank injustice of the course Roosevelt was pursuing, and emphasized, as did others, the uncertainty of Roosevelt's position on Progressive principles. He argued that it was altogether too late for Roosevelt to come into the campaign; that months before he had personally interviewed Roosevelt on the subject of his candidacy; that Roosevelt had said that he was not a candidate; that Heney had replied to Roosevelt that it was not enough for him to say that he was not a candidate; that the Progressives of California and other states had a right to know whether he would under *any circumstances become a candidate,* and that thereupon Roosevelt had said most emphatically and positively that he would not under any circumstances become a candidate. Gifford Pinchot reiterated his oft-repeated statement that Roosevelt was not and would not be a candidate, but contended that we could elect some delegates by putting Roosevelt men on the tickets, and thus get some votes which otherwise might not be cast for us. Lenroot expressed the opinion that as a matter of political expediency such a course would be advantageous. Houser said that while he had been favorably inclined toward the plan as a matter

252

of political tactics, still he did not think we could stand for any combination with the representatives of the Steel Trust, who were evidently behind Roosevelt.

As I was firmly against this course Pinchot was voted down. Amos Pinchot strongly supported my position throughout the conference, and at its conclusion pointedly remarked to his brother:

"Gifford, I think you will sleep better tonight now that it is settled that we are not to be tied up with representatives of machine politics and the Steel Trust."

Amos Pinchot said to me just before going into the conference in excusing his brother's insistence that I should consent to the combination:

"I agree with you perfectly that there must be no combination with Roosevelt. I have no doubt whatever about his having been an active candidate all along, but I am sure Gifford is honest in the position he is taking. Roosevelt has always been able to pull the wool over his eyes."

Gifford Pinchot apparently acquiesced in the decision of the conference, and I was gratified to believe that the whole matter was definitely and finally settled.

A few days later, on the twenty-second of January, I went to New York to fill an engagement at Carnegie Hall. Gifford Pinchot presided at the meeting, which was an exceptional success. A representative audience filled the great hall, and when I arrived I found the streets packed for blocks by people unable to gain admission. I was obliged to address a large overflow meeting before entering the hall. Of this meeting the New York *Times* said:

"It was the Wisconsin candidate's first appearance in New York and the reception accorded him he himself said was as great as any he ever received in his home state. Carnegie Hall never held a bigger nor a more enthusiastic audience."

The *Sun* said:

"Carnegie Hall was packed at eight o'clock, and the reserves of two police stations were called out to take care of the crowds that were jammed into Seventh Avenue north and south of the hall."

Roosevelt did not attend my meeting. He was, as I was informed, at a dinner given in his honor on that evening by one of the Progressive clubs of the city. Several members of this club called on me later to express regret that this dinner could not have been given at some other time, and to say that it would have been so arranged but that no other date was acceptable to Roosevelt.

Though my New York friends were jubilant over my campaign

opening there and the progress made in other states, I found them very fearful that Roosevelt was determined to "break in," as they expressed it.

There was still no open declaration from him, but it was understood that leading Progressives were being summoned to confer with him and give out newspaper interviews of the "pressing demands" in their respective states that he should become a candidate.

Upon my return to Washington I was surprised to find that Gifford Pinchot had called still another conference of the same men to meet at our headquarters. The date which he fixed for this conference was January 29th, and he had been urgent that Mr. Crane should be present. I learned that he had seen Roosevelt just before my New York meeting. I felt that this conference would be the last which Pinchot would attend if he failed in his plan, and I understood why he was so determined that Crane should be present. The two Pinchots and Kent had each furnished a contribution of $10,000, all of which had been contributed months before, and which had been substantially expended by this time. Crane was contributing $5,000 a month, and had agreed to continue his payments monthly until the time of the meeting of the National Convention in Chicago. If Crane could be drawn to the support of Pinchot's position, it was Pinchot's reasoning, as I believe, that I would be compelled to masquerade as the candidate behind whom Roosevelt's campaign could be prosecuted, without his being forced to announce his candidacy until the convention should meet, when it would be sprung, the convention stampeded, and the nomination "forced" upon him.

This final conference met pursuant to Pinchot's call at my Washington headquarters on Monday afternoon, January 29th. There were present Gifford and Amos Pinchot, Charles R. Crane, and his secretary, Walter S. Rogers, the manager of our Chicago headquarters; Professor Charles E. Merriam, Louis D. Brandeis, William Kent, Congressman Lenroot, Gilson Gardner, Angus McSween, the Washington correspondent of the Philadelphia *North American,* Houser and Hannan. Medill McCormick was again brought into this conference from Chicago, uninvited, unless by Pinchot. Their discussion consumed the afternoon, and was marked by plainness of speech all around. It was evident from the beginning that the Roosevelt element represented in the group had come prepared to force the issue. It was manifest to them that my candidacy could no longer serve the Roosevelt interest, and they submitted an alternative in writing which I quote:

(1) That La Follette shall withdraw in favor of Roosevelt, with reservations as to differences of opinion, and continue to stump.

(2) That La Follette shall withdraw, but not in favor of anybody, and continue to stump, leaving the individuals of the group to take what course they choose.

In order to insure the fullest and freest discussion, I did not myself enter the room where the conference was being held until they had about exhausted the subject under consideration. Moreover, I had been resolved upon my course from the beginning, and even if I stood alone I knew I must go straight ahead. When they had threshed the whole matter out among themselves I was invited to come in. It was then about five o'clock. I had just been called to the telephone by a representative of the Associated Press, who informed me that a Chicago paper was running a story that afternoon stating in effect that Medill McCormick, Crane, Pinchot, and others were holding a conference that day at the Washington headquarters, and that a statement would be issued as a result of the conference announcing my withdrawal. It would appear that information must have been furnished to the Chicago paper regarding the conference before McCormick left Chicago. I immediately called Houser out of the conference, and caused to be issued by him the following statement:

"Washington, D. C., January 29, 1912.—Once for all I want to settle the rumors in circulation that Senator La Follette contemplates withdrawing as a presidential candidate. Senator La Follette never has been and is not now a quitter. When he entered the contest for the nomination he assured those who induced him to become a candidate that he would go through to the end, and that is his determination. He will be there until the gavel falls in the convention announcing the nominee. Senator La Follette is making this campaign to promote the principles in a national way for which he has stood and fought in his own state and in the United States Senate. He will make a campaign in every state to elect delegates pledged to those principles, and to his candidacy as the Republican nominee for President, first, last, and all the time.

"(Signed) WALTER L. HOUSER."

Before giving out this statement, I called Mr. Crane, Professor Merriam, and Mr. Rogers out of the conference, and informed them of the Chicago story which I believed had been given out by McCormick before leaving Chicago; that the Associated Press had called for confirmation or denial, and that I had prepared the only statement which I could consent to have issued on the subject. I knew from what Houser had reported as to the proceedings in the conference that the Pinchots, Gardner, and possibly some others, had already decided to desert, and I submitted this statement to Mr. Crane. I had never for one moment believed that he would abandon me. He is a man of few words, but with great constancy of purpose. He had been in the conference with the Pinchots for hours, and subject to as strong an appeal as it was possible for them to make, and I watched his face with keen interest as he read the statement. There was no change of expression. He returned it to Houser, saying very quietly:

"I think that statement is all right."

So I knew that I would at least have one strong supporter to the end. With Crane, Merriam, and Rogers I then joined the conference. Pinchot at once entered upon a review of what he had said to the conference regarding my candidacy and that of Roosevelt. In order to bring the discussion directly to the point, I called up the alternative statement which Houser informed me had been under discussion, regarding my withdrawal in favor of Roosevelt. I told them that I had but one answer to make; that I had never played that kind of politics and never would; that I did not recognize Roosevelt as standing for Progressive principles; that I had resisted from the time of its proposal every effort on the part of Pinchot and others to make me serve as a stalking horse for Roosevelt's candidacy; that I had not sought the support of Pinchot or any one else, and had not made myself the Progressive candidate; that they had joined in urging me to stand; that I had made a clean fight for principle which had tremendously strengthened the Progressive movement all over the country, but now, when there seemed to be some prospect of success, it was proposed to turn everything over to Roosevelt; that if this were done the campaign would be converted into a contest to nominate Roosevelt rather than advance a cause; principles would be compromised or wholly ignored, and the Progressive movement suffer untold injury; that Pinchot had pledged his support to me as long as I continued a candidate; that I could not prevent his withdrawal of that support, but that I would say nothing which he could construe to be a consent or release from his obligation to continue his support. The Pinchots, Gardner, and McCormick then withdrew, but Crane, Merriam, Rogers, Kent, Lenroot, and all of the others assured me that they would go through with me to the end. It was a great relief to have it settled and over with. For weeks the strain had been severe. The Pinchots, however, still hesitated to make any statement respecting the course which they proposed to take.

A few days later (February 2nd) I attended the annual banquet of the Periodical Publishers' Association at Philadelphia, an engagement which had been made some weeks before. In my speech I dealt with the centralized control over the nation's affairs, and concluded with the statement that this control by great special interests extended even to the newspapers and was rapidly reaching out for the magazines. This occasion offered the opportunity to say things which seemed to me supremely important. I understood perfectly that it must subject me to criticism but felt that that ought not to deter me. I spoke as the publisher of a magazine to publishers. I was speaking to men who knew, many of them from bitter experience, the powerful influence which the modern business system exerts directly and indirectly over the publisher through the centralized control of great national advertising agencies. The representatives of the largest publishing companies present understood the subtle working out of plans by which these immense advertising agencies have become the publicity agents of great business interests, the placing of whose national advertising they control; and that the placing or withholding of advertising by these agencies with a given publication, determines whether that publication shall fail or succeed. It lies in the power of these agencies to serve their clients by giving their advertisements to publications which are well behaved toward the great interests and to starve out those publications which freely criticise privileged business; or, in other words, to make the stand-pat publication prosper and the Progressive publication fail.

I print here exactly what I said upon this subject:

"I have sketched the growth and power of the great interests that to-day control our property and our governments. I have shown how subtle and elusive, yet relentless, they are. Rising up against them is the confused voice of the people. Their heart is true but their eyes do not yet see all the intricate sources of power. Who shall show them? There are only two agencies that in any way can reach the whole people. These are the press and the platform. But the platform in no way compares with the press in its power of continuous repeated instruction.

"One would think that in a democracy like ours, seeking for instruction, able to read and understand, the press would be their eager and willing instructors—such was the press of Horace Greeley, Henry Raymond, Charles A. Dana, Joseph Medill, and Horace Rublee.

"But what do we find has occurred in the past few years since the money power has gained control of our industry and government? It controls the newspaper press. The people know this. Their confidence is weakened and destroyed. No longer are the editorial columns of newspapers a potent force in educating public opinion. The newspapers, of course, are still patronized for news. But even as to news, the public is fast coming to understand that wherever news items bear in any way upon the control of government by

257

business, the news is colored; so confidence in the newspaper as a newspaper is being undermined.

"Cultured and able men are still to be found upon the editorial staffs of all great dailies, but the public understands them to be hired men who no longer express honest judgments and sincere conviction, who write what they are told to write, and whose judgments are salaried.

"To the subserviency of the press to special interests in no small degree is due the power and influence and prosperity of the weekly and monthly magazines. A decade ago young men trained in journalism came to see this control of the newspapers of the country. They saw also an unoccupied field. And they went out and built up great periodicals and magazines. They were free.

"Their pages were open to publicists and scholars; and liberty and justice and equal rights found a free press beyond the reach of the corrupt influence of consolidated business and machine politics. We entered upon a new era.

"The periodical, reduced in price, attractive and artistic in dress, strode like a young giant into the arena of public service. Filled with this spirit, quickened with human interest, it assailed social and political evils in high places and low. It found the power of the public service corporation and the evil influences of money in the municipal government of every large city. It found franchises worth millions of dollars secured by bribery; police in partnership with thieves and crooks and prostitutes. It found juries 'fixed' and an established business plying its trade between litigants and the back door of blinking justice.

"It found Philadelphia giving away franchises, franchises not supposedly or estimated to be worth $2,500,000, but for which she had been openly offered and had refused $2,500,000. Milwaukee they found giving away street car franchises worth $8,000,000 against the protests of her indignant citizens. It found Chicago robbed in tax-payments of immense value by corporate owners of property through fraud and forgery on a gigantic scale; it found the aldermen of St. Louis organized to boodle the city with a criminal compact, on file in the dark corner of a safety deposit vault.

"The free and independent periodical turned its searchlight on state legislatures, and made plain as the sun at noonday the absolute control of the corrupt lobby. It opened the closed doors of the secret caucus, the secret committee, the secret conference, behind which United States Senators and Members of Congress betrayed the public interest into the hands of the railroads, the trusts, the tariff mongers, and the centralized banking power of the country. It revealed the same influences back of judicial and other appointments. It took the public through the great steel plants and into the homes of the men who toil twelve hours a day and seven days in the week. And the public heard their cry of despair. It turned its camera on to the mills and shops where little children are robbed of every chance of life that nourishes vigorous bodies and sound minds, and the pinched faces and dwarfed figures told their pathetic story on its clean white pages.

"The control of the newspaper press is not the simple and expensive one of ownership and investment. There is here and there a 'kept sheet' owned by a man of great wealth to further his own interests. But the papers of this class are few. The control comes through that community of interests, that interdependence of investments and credits which ties the publisher up to the banks, the advertisers and the special interests.

"We may expect this same kind of control, sooner or later, to reach out for the magazines. But more than this. I warn you of a subtle new peril, the centralization of advertising that will in time seek to gag you. What has occurred on a small scale in almost every city in the country will extend to the national scale, and will ere long close in on the magazines. No men ever faced graver responsibilities. No men have ever been called to a more unselfish, patriotic service. I believe that when the final test comes you will not be found wanting; you will not desert and leave the people to depend upon the public platform alone, but you will hold aloft the lamp of Truth, lighting the way for the preservation of representative government and the liberty of the American people."

But I entirely underestimated the character and extent of the criticism which I called down upon myself. I was a candidate and the interests did not overlook their opportunity. Sensational accounts of this speech and its reception were published throughout the country, and at the same time equally sensational and false reports were spread concerning my physical condition.

It is true that I was not feeling as fit as usual. As on one or two previous occasions I had overtaxed my strength. But each time a very brief rest sufficed to restore me to full vigor; as it did in this instance. I attended this gathering with some reluctance, knowing that to speak there would make demands upon me which, at that time, I could ill afford. I had just returned from a speaking trip, part of which was made under most trying circumstances, and all of which taxed my reserve. Besides, I was seriously troubled at the evidences I had discovered at headquarters of the studied undermining of my candidacy by some of my supporters. Added to this, the doctors had decided that our little daughter must undergo an operation, the seriousness of which could not be foretold, on the morning following the Publishers' banquet. For every reason I felt that I ought not to go, but was reluctant to break my engagement. I went, arriving after the dinner. It was very late when I began to speak. I was not at my best and did not at once get hold of my audience. It was, I do not doubt, entirely my own fault—but I determined to make them hear me to the end. In my effort to do so I talked too long without realizing it. I went home, really ill from exhaustion, but was at the hospital early next morning when my daughter went under the surgeon's knife. After that, with a short rest, I was able to go on with my work as usual, and into the campaign in North Dakota, disproving the stories circulated, not only at that time but since, as to my having broken down. I went through a campaign carrying me from coast to coast, making

259

nearly two hundred speeches, and have not lost a moment's time since. I mention this incident, not because it is important of itself, but for the reason that it was given a bearing upon the campaign by those who were quick to use it as a cover under which they felt they could plausibly make their switch to Roosevelt. The men who had already abandoned my candidacy, because I could not stand as a shield for another, or agree to any deals or combinations that would confuse the issue or mislead the people, seized upon what they were pleased to call my "shattered health" as an excuse for their action.

Following the session of the Wisconsin legislature of 1901, I was made the object of a somewhat similar attack for the purpose of demoralizing my support. Combined with the incessant work accompanying the legislative session came the abandonment of the fight by men in whose zeal and devotion I had found courage and inspiration, and finally the defeat of the legislation I had hoped to see enacted. In 1901, however, as a result of the strain, my health was actually impaired; but the nature of my illness was at that time likewise maliciously misrepresented, because my unfitness was the thing most desired by those who were opposed to the Progressive movement, and particularly to my part in it.

Again and again the friends who were supporting my candidacy had heard my interpretation of the fight; and they appreciated the spirit in which I had consented to make it. I had not gone into it for the purpose of beating Taft as an individual. I had not gone into it as a political game to be played according to the rule of expediency. I had campaigned only for supporters willing to make the fight for principle, ready to win, or to lose, if need be, in the interest of a cause. My whole public life had been given to a struggle in which countless battles were necessarily lost in the course of the warfare, so a temporary defeat meant less to me, perhaps than to men unseasoned in strife.

As before stated, the Pinchots and Gilson Gardner definitely withdrew from my support at the conference held at my headquarters in Washington, January 29th, but apparently found some embarrassment in announcing the fact. The critical attitude of the press following the Publishers' banquet of February 2nd opened the way. It furnished a pretext for the desertion which it was now plain to be seen had been under consideration for a long time. They waited for two weeks after the final conference in which they definitely withdrew their support, before making any public announcement. Then there was published in the Philadelphia *North American* the following, giving the condition of my health as the reason for the action taken:

LA FOLLETTE DROPPED BY PINCHOT FOR PRESIDENCY

Senator's Condition Makes His Candidacy Impossible Declares Pinchot—Roosevelt Boom in Minnesota

JERSEY CITY, New Jersey,
February 10, 1912.

Hugh T. Halbert, St. Paul, Minnesota:

In my judgment La Follette's condition makes further serious candidacy impossible.   GIFFORD PINCHOT.

The above is the wording of a telegram read last night at a meeting of the Board of Directors of the Minnesota Republican League called to consider the probable withdrawal of Senator La Follette as a candidate for the Republican nomination for President. Mr. Halbert, a member of the Board, made a speech insisting that La Follette was out of the running, and that the league should turn its support to Roosevelt. The committee, however, refused to take this course, and adopted resolutions pledging unanimous support to La Follette. Mr. Halbert then resigned from the Board. He has for seven years been President of the Saint Paul Roosevelt Club.

On the eighteenth of February Pinchot published a formal statement announcing that he had withdrawn his support from me and would thereafter advocate Roosevelt's nomination, *this time* setting up the claim that my candidacy had only been a sort of temporary convenience. I quote from this statement the following:

"Senator La Follette's candidacy was undertaken for two clear and specific purposes: first to hold the Progressives together as an effective fighting force, and second, to prevent the renomination of a reactionary Republican for the presidency."

If this statement were true, then the campaign which we had been making for months to induce support of my candidacy was plainly a fraud upon those who were led to believe that I was a candidate in good faith.

In this connection it is interesting to refer to the Call for me to become a candidate, which was signed by a number of Progressive Republican Senators and Congressmen, but which was not published because, as before stated, Cummins did not sign it, giving as his reason for withholding his signature that he did not think it the best way to inaugurate my candidacy. Pinchot wrote in part and approved in its entirety that document, from which, passing over a review of my public services, I quote the following:

"This seems to us a very splendid record, a record of patient, fearless and effective public service, achieved in the face of almost insurmountable difficulty and opposition.

261

"To guide the Progressive movement, a chief executive is required whose life has been devoted to the task of freeing our political institutions from the control of organized wealth, who understands the problem which is before the country, who has proved by what he has done that he is able to deal with it, and who will use the power of his great office in the interests of the people. The people are progressive and it is necessary, just, and right that their chief magistrate should be progressive also. If the republican voters of the country could make their wishes effective at this time, we believe that your record as citizen, governor, representative and senator, your unswerving fidelity to principle and your long, fearless, and successful leadership would cause them to choose you as their next presidential nominee. We therefore earnestly urge you to permit your name to be presented as a candidate for the Republican nomination for President of the United States."

It would seem that at this time, when I was being urged to become a candidate, and by none more strongly than Pinchot, it was with a view of nominating and electing me President, rather than drafting me into a temporary service as a sort of political "minute man" to hold the field until a favorable opportunity should present itself for bringing out the real candidate.

Pinchot's announcement of his support of Roosevelt, in view of their intimate relations, was everywhere accepted as the immediate forerunner of a declaration of candidacy by Roosevelt himself.

The time had come for them to act openly. Roosevelt organizations made their appearance here and there with all of the evidences of pre-arrangement. Then came the speech by Roosevelt before the Constitutional Convention at Columbus, Ohio. This speech was accepted as a statement of his "principles." It dealt in his characteristic way with many issues which had been raised by Progressives. It sounded progressive enough to satisfy men of that belief, who did not weigh carefully qualifying phraseology, and at the same time was not definitely progressive enough to alarm big business. He favored the Initiative and Referendum with "proper restrictions." He favored the Recall "with such restrictions as will make it available only when there is a widespread and genuine public feeling among a majority of the voters." The Recall, as applied to judges, he declared to be a question of "expediency merely" which each community has a right to try for itself in "whatever shape it pleases." As to labor legislation he suggested that "no restrictions be placed on legislative powers that will prevent the enactment of laws under which your people can promote the general welfare, the common good." His discussion of trust regulation was equally indefinite, declaring that the mere size of business is no offence, and that any corporation, big or little, which has

262

gained its position by unfair methods, and by interference with the rights of others which has "raised prices or limited output in *improper fashion*" should be broken up. As to other national issues, including the tariff, he said, "I stand to-day exactly where I stood in 1910."

As to where he stood in 1910, it will be remembered that, in a signed editorial in the *Outlook* under date of September 17th, of that year, speaking of the Payne-Aldrich Tariff Law, Roosevelt said: "I believe that the present tariff is better than the last, and considerably better than the one before the last." This was equivalent to saying what Taft said at Winona and shows Roosevelt, on the tariff, to be just the same sort of a Progressive—and just the same sort of a Standpatter—as Taft, as indeed does President Roosevelt's entire record of seven years.

While this speech was undergoing preparation, some of my former supporters who were now openly for Roosevelt evidenced anxiety lest the address would not be definitely Progressive, and informed friends in Washington that they were keeping in close touch with the Colonel for the purpose of stiffening him up on his Progressive declarations. It was reported that when the completed address was read to one of them and he was asked for his opinion, he answered with the single word "punk."

Few men of our time have Roosevelt's appreciation of the importance of keeping the public guessing in order to stimulate political interest. Although the Columbus speech could not, of course, carry any statement as to his candidacy, Roosevelt gave to the occasion just the right turn by tossing off to the newspaper reporters afterward the observation, "My hat is in the ring." This meant that he was a candidate. But it was followed at once with the serious statement that he was still considering what answer he should make to the half dozen governors whom he had informally invited to formally invite him to become a candidate for the Republican nomination for the presidency. This answer, it was given out, he would make later. But all things must have an end.

Finally, upon the twenty-sixth of February, Roosevelt made a formal statement in which he said he would accept the nomination for President if tendered him by the Republican presidential convention. At last the public had definite word. Men no longer guessed or made wagers that he would or would not. It was settled. And now, to the surprise and disappointment of Roosevelt enthusiasts, the interest of the general public began to abate. The speculative element which prompts men to stake fortunes on the turn of the market was eliminated, and the public settled down to a serious consideration of the real meaning and significance of Roosevelt's candidacy. His friends had predicted that his statement "would fire the country"; that "it would only be necessary for him to consent to be a candidate." He had thought so too. "I will accept the nomination for President if it is tendered to me," he wrote to the governors.

But after the press had made its formal comment on his announcement, interest began to drag perceptibly. His friends in Washington became very anxious about it. Roosevelt himself soon realized that he had misjudged the situation; that the call for him again to serve the public was not so urgent as he had supposed; that he must drop the receptive role which he had assumed and go out and create a demand for his candidacy. He decided to try a trip to Boston and did so. But it proved disappointing. In short, his Boston speech and reception were admitted by his friends to be a frost. He came back very much discouraged. After this failure he understood that when he went out again he must "make a killing." His next public appearance must be an unqualified success, or it might set the tide running the wrong way.

The primary election in North Dakota was near at hand. It was the first presidential preference test. He must carry that state by a good majority for its effect upon the country. North Dakota, by the rules that govern in all contests, should be his. It was the state in which he had spent his cowboy days, and the whole section west of the Missouri River was still called the cow country. Every effort was put forth by the brother of Governor Bass of New Hampshire, who was in charge of Roosevelt's campaign, to stir the state pride for the Colonel as a North Dakota pioneer. A day or two before the election Roosevelt sent a long telegram into North Dakota pleading with the voters for their support. His managers spared no efforts to win the state for Roosevelt. A large force of clerks and stenographers was employed at their headquarters, and a campaign attended with a very lavish expenditure of money was prosecuted for weeks. It would scarcely be an exaggeration to say that through their headquarters they spent more money in one day than the entire campaign in North Dakota cost my supporters.

An interesting feature of Roosevelt's campaign in North Dakota, and one illustrating his peculiar political methods, was his change of front on the reciprocity issue. North Dakota, as a grain-growing state, was strongly opposed to Taft's Canadian agreement, and the feeling of resentment against him was so intense that he scarcely figured in the campaign at all. Roosevelt was as strongly in favor of the Canadian Pact as Taft, and through editorials in the *Outlook* and public addresses he had given vigorous support to Taft's Canadian policy and specifically endorsed the agreement. After Roosevelt became an announced candidate, our headquarters at Washington made an investigation of his record upon this subject. Taft had transmitted the Canadian agreement to Congress by special message January 26, 1911. In a signed editorial on January 28th, in which he commended reciprocity with Canada, Roosevelt said:

"Our tariff policy with Canada can well afford to stand by itself, not only because of our close relationship to the great Dominion to the north of us, but because of the substantial identity of conditions on each side of the line dividing us, so that as regards Canada I should be glad to see the most complete measure of reciprocity to which Canada will consent."

And again, on February 25, 1911, the *Outlook* said, editorially:

"Canadian reciprocity was commended last week in notable speeches both from President Taft and ex-President Roosevelt."

In a speech made at Grand Rapids, Mich., February 11th, Roosevelt said:

"I welcome the proposed reciprocity treaty (with Canada) as making a signal advance in bringing about the closest and most friendly relations between the two countries."

Two days later, in a speech before the Republican Club at the hotel Waldorf, New York City, Roosevelt declared:

"I want to say how glad I am to hear of the way in which the club, the members of the club here to-night, responded to the two appeals made to them to uphold the hands of President Taft [terrific applause] both in his effort to secure reciprocity with Canada, and in his effort to secure the fortification of the Panama Canal [applause]. . . . I hail the reciprocity agreement, because it represents an effort to bring about a closer, a more intimate and friendly relationship of mutual advantage on equal terms between Canada and the United States."

As soon as Roosevelt's endorsement of reciprocity, as shown by his speeches and editorials, was printed in the North Dakota papers, he reversed his position through a letter furnished to the publisher of a Minneapolis agricultural journal having a North Dakota circulation, and came out flatly against the Canadian agreement.

Nothing could more clearly expose Roosevelt's shiftiness in politics than his course on Canadian reciprocity. When proposed by Taft and exploited by the newspapers, who were the special beneficiaries under the plan, it appeared to be a very popular issue.

And Roosevelt, as the above quotations show, originally advocated it. It was defeated at the close of the 61st Congress, and again in the extra session called by Taft at the beginning of the 62d Congress. The extended debate upon it exposed it as a sham, and by the time the North Dakota primary was at hand, it was no longer a popular issue. Hence, Roosevelt faced the other way and repudiated his former endorsement.

In his campaign, as the candidate of the Roosevelt party, he spoke on the fifth of September, 1912, to the farmers of Minnesota, on the state fair grounds at Saint Paul. His audience was 90 per cent. hostile to Canadian reciprocity. So Roosevelt, never missing the popular side, had this to say of Canadian reciprocity to the Minnesota farmers:

"At first many of us, myself among the number, thought reciprocity might be a good thing. But we took it for granted that the bill would be drawn right. Later we found it was a jug-handle proposition, with the farmers paying the freight."

That is to say, Roosevelt had advocated Canadian reciprocity at the outset because he took it for granted the bill would be drawn right, from which he would have it inferred that he advocated Canadian reciprocity before he understood the nature of the Canadian agreement, and the bill drawn in compliance with the agreement. Now, what are the facts?

In the recent contest between Taft and Roosevelt for the Republican nomination, the fact that Roosevelt changed his position on Canadian reciprocity, when he found it unpopular, led Taft to make a very remarkable disclosure. In a speech delivered at Boston, on April 25, 1912, President Taft said:

"Mr. Roosevelt now seeks to take advantage of the supposed feeling among the farmers of the country against the reciprocity agreement with Canada, which I made and induced Congress to adopt, but which Canada finally rejected. I would not object to this as a legitimate argument in a political controversy against me and in his favor, if the fact were not that I consulted him ten days before I made the agreement, and explained to him, in full, its probable terms, stated the arguments pro and con, especially the effect of it on agricultural products, and asked him to confer with his colleagues of the *Outlook* as to its wisdom and public benefit, and let me know his and their judgment. He replied approving the agreement in the most enthusiastic terms and complimenting me for having brought it forward. I submit below our correspondence on the subject of reciprocity:

" '(Confidential)
" 'The White House, Washington, D. C.
" 'January 10, 1911.

. . . .

" 'The probability is that we shall reach an agreement with our Canadian friends by which all natural products—cereals, lumber, dairy products, fruits, meats, and cattle—shall enter both countries free, and that we shall get a revision—not as heavy a one as I would like, but a substantial one, and equivalent certainly to the French reciprocity treaty and probably more— on manufactures.' "

Here follows about half a column of further quotation from Taft's letter, giving the arguments pro and con on the subject. The letter concludes as follows:

" 'I shall be glad to hear from you as soon as you conveniently can write on this subject, because the matter is just at hand and it is quite likely that within ten days we shall reach an agreement.

" 'Sincerely yours,

" 'WILLIAM H. TAFT.' "

To this letter Roosevelt replied as follows:

" 'NEW YORK, January 12, 1911.

" 'Dear Mr. President:

" 'I at once took your letter and went over it with the *Outlook* editors. . . . It seems to me that what you propose to do with Canada is admirable from every standpoint. I firmly believe in free trade with Canada for both economic and political reasons. As you say, labor cost is substantially the same in the two countries, so that you are amply justified by the platform. Whether Canada will accept such reciprocity I do not know, but it is greatly to your credit to make the effort. It may damage the Republican party for a while, but it will surely benefit the party in the end, especially if you tackle wool, cotton, etc., as you propose.

" 'Ever yours,

" 'THEODORE ROOSEVELT.' "

Taft's letter to Roosevelt explicitly stated the essentials of the agreement as made, and incorporated in the bill which became a law. His letter informed Roosevelt that cereals, lumber, dairy products, fruits, meats, and cattle were to be made free, and in exchange for that, Canada reduced the duties on manufactured products. So Roosevelt had specific information that all these agricultural products were to be admitted from Canada free of duty, and declared it to be "admirable from every standpoint." Now, he says, he thought reciprocity might be a good thing but "took it for granted the bill would be drawn right." Roosevelt ought to have told the Minnesota farmers how he would draw a bill which would be "right," as to their interests so long as it admitted free of duty agricultural products, as he knew from Taft's letter this agreement proposed to do. Now, we know that Roosevelt was fully advised, before the agreement was made, of everything to which the farmer objects in the agreement as made, and the bill drawn in conformity with it. Possessing this information, he approved it in the strongest terms in his letter to Taft, January 12th. After this identical agreement had been entered into, and after the President had transmitted it to Congress, and after the bill based on the agreement had been introduced in Congress, he wrote editorials and made speeches for it. He understood then quite as well as he does now that it was a "jug-handle proposition with the farmer paying the freight."

The above quotations from the *Outlook* and from Roosevelt's speeches were incorporated in a typewritten statement prepared at our headquarters for publication in the North Dakota papers. The following morning an incident occurred which furnishes a side light on the difficulties under which my campaign was conducted. We were surprised to learn that this typewritten statement had been clandestinely sent from our headquarters to the office of Gilson Gardner, who had more than a month before severed all relations with my campaign, and become an open supporter of Roosevelt. It was at once suspected that an employe in our headquarters, who had access to the material that we were sending out, had transmitted this statement of Roosevelt's position on the Canadian pact to Gardner's office. When questioned he vigorously denied having done so. Anticipating that he might try to warn his confederate in Gardner's office, a watch was set over the telephone connections. A few minutes later, indeed, as soon as he could reach a telephone in the office, where he supposed he could talk without being overheard, he called up Kirby, Gardner's confidential stenographer, and directed Kirby to destroy the envelope in which the typewritten record had been enclosed.

This affair would be scarcely worth mentioning except as it tends to show the difficulties under which I was compelled to prosecute my campaign. It was a most critical time when everything counted. The North Dakota contest was engaging the attention of the whole country. Everything bearing upon the Roosevelt candidacy there was of the keenest interest.

The employe whose name I withhold, because it would appear that he was simply the tool of others, was appointed to a position of some responsibility months before, upon the endorsement of Kirby, who stood in such relation to Gardner that his endorsement was accepted by the headquarters. Of this fact I had not known personally. F. M. Kirby is the same Kirby who was private stenographer to Secretary of the Interior Ballinger, and who created a great sensation in the Ballinger-Pinchot investigation, by appearing before the committee and giving testimony against Ballinger and in the interest of Pinchot, concerning matters of which he claimed personal knowledge on account of his confidential relations with Secretary Ballinger. Kirby was therefore employed by Gardner, who offered me his services from time to time as a stenographer while Gardner was, as I believed, supporting my candidacy. I did not accept his tender of the services of Kirby and it is needless to say that the employé in our headquarters appointed upon Kirby's recommendation was dismissed as soon as it became known that he had sent the Roosevelt reciprocity document to Gardner's office.

Roosevelt was urged by his supporters to take the stump in North Dakota, and it was given out to the press in New York that he might do so. But the reports which he was receiving from North Dakota were not encouraging. He appeared to vacillate between the desire to take a hand and the fear that if he did so and lost the state the hurtful effect upon his campaign would be very much accentuated. He therefore took the more prudent course of sending some of his closest adherents and most effective campaigners instead. Pinchot, Garfield, and others appeared upon the platform in North Dakota in the interest of his candidacy. Pinchot found himself at once confronted with a demand for an explanation of his shift to Roosevelt. In his speeches he assigned as the sole reason for his action that I had become disabled, and that in consequence it became necessary for the Progressive Republicans to have a candidate who could carry on the campaign actively and personally. The hollowness of this pretext was promptly exposed when I appeared in the campaign in North Dakota in such excellent trim as to be able to make from ten to fifteen speeches a day. At the end of four days of this sort of campaigning, I left North Dakota the night before the election, confident of the result.

The vote on the nineteenth of March in the North Dakota presidential primary election—the first presidential preference election ever held—astounded the country. Roosevelt was overwhelmingly beaten. I had carried the state by more than ten thousand, while Taft's total vote was but little more than eighteen hundred. Taft's small vote in North Dakota, due, in part at least, to the resentment felt by the farmers on account of his stand upon the Canadian pact, nevertheless disclosed his great personal weakness as a vote getter.

The North Dakota result thoroughly alarmed the special interests, who were backing Roosevelt in order to capture or to divide and checkmate the Progressive movement. It is a cardinal principle with the interests to so manipulate national politics, if possible, as to bring about the nomination of satisfactory presidential candidates by both political parties. Either Taft or Roosevelt would be quite to their liking, but North Dakota disclosed to them an amazing situation. If the middle western states were to vote as North Dakota, then there was the gravest danger that a real Progressive might be nominated by the Republicans at Chicago. If Roosevelt could not break down my strength, and Taft were to prove so weak as not to be counted in the contest throughout that section of the country, then it was obvious that I would enter the convention with enough votes either to be nominated or to force the nomination of some pronounced Progressive candidate.

The North Dakota result called for heroic treatment. So confident had been the supporters of Roosevelt that he would sweep the country, that they regarded a fund of three hundred thousand dollars as quite sufficient to carry his campaign through from start to finish, and shortly after his announcement boasted that this amount had already been provided. But the recession of interest and enthusiasm coming shortly after he became a candidate and followed by the North Dakota landslide against him swept aside all previous hopes and calculations. Something had to be done, and done quickly. Something was done. Just what and by whom the public may eventually know. But this much may be said now. If Perkins (United States Steel) contributed to Roosevelt's campaign, it must have been because Roosevelt's treatment of trusts in the past was, and his promised treatment of trusts in the future is, so very satisfactory to Perkins that he willingly put money into the campaign as an investment. Roosevelt's position upon trusts must have likewise appealed very strongly to others whose interests were akin to those of Perkins. For shortly after the North Dakota primary Munsey, one of the prominent owners of United States Steel stocks, and Dan Hanna, also heavily interested, and others with kindred interests, became directly and indirectly the largest contributors to Roosevelt's campaign. Contributions from men with these connections would account, in part, for the character of campaign which Roosevelt carried on for months, the lavish

270

expenditures of which were proof overwhelming of unlimited sources of supply. Headquarters were established east and west, north and south, and an army of men employed and put in the field. Special trains, private cars, literary bureaus, newspapers, documents, special dailies—the whole conduct of the campaign itself was proof overwhelming that big finance was behind Roosevelt.

My resources were very limited, and it was decided best to confine my speaking campaign to those states having statutes providing for a popular preferential vote for presidential candidates. As Nebraska, Oregon, and California were the first states, under these statutes, to hold elections, I planned to campaign them next after the North Dakota election.

After I had been announced to speak in Nebraska, an extra session of the legislature was unexpectedly called by Governor Deneen of Illinois. Pursuant to this call the legislature of Illinois passed a presidential preference primary law. While my supporters were inclined to advise against placing my name upon the Illinois ballot so long as I could not personally campaign the state (my engagements in Nebraska rendered it impossible for me to make a speaking campaign in Illinois), yet, feeling that real Progressives, who believed in the principles which my candidacy represented, should have an opportunity wherever there was a presidential preference law, to record their convictions, I requested my friends to take the necessary steps to place my name on the ballot. This they did. I should have had no expectation of carrying Illinois even had my engagements or my finances admitted of making a campaign in that state, because I did not consider Illinois Progressive. In support of this opinion there stands the undisputed fact that her congressional delegation in the United States Senate and House of Representatives is ultrareactionary, and the record of her state legislature likewise. The adoption of a presidential preference primary was no more proof that Illinois is a Progressive state than a like legislative enactment by the state of Massachusetts about the same time would be accepted as proof that Massachusetts is a Progressive state.

My name was placed upon the ballot in Illinois in accordance with my wishes, but there was little else that could be done, as I have before stated. I received some forty-five thousand votes. Roosevelt, with a very large outlay of money, carried the state overwhelmingly. He made a special train canvass. Three Roosevelt headquarters were maintained in Chicago, and bureaus throughout the state. On primary day the polling places swarmed

271

with workers, and carriages and automobiles scoured the cities and towns and rural districts for votes. His support was not Progressive. This fact is attested by the action of the Illinois state convention, which voted down the Initiative, the Referendum, the Recall, votes for women, and substantially every distinctly Progressive issue which was presented.

The following week, with the prestige of Illinois, the same sort of a campaign was made in Pennsylvania, with practically the same results. Roosevelt's success in these two stand-pat states stamped his candidacy with its true character. No real Progressive could have secured anything like such a vote as did Roosevelt in those states. It had, however, the outward seeming of success— the sort of success that intoxicates the crowd.

There is a time in every campaign when the tide sets in a given direction. It then seems quite impossible to arrest attention long enough to distinguish between the real and the counterfeit. In the 80's, when Indiana and Ohio held state elections in October, the national committees of both parties, counting on the effect of a winning in those two states upon the November elections to follow, put forth every effort, summoned their ablest campaigners and spent money without limit to carry the state elections.

Illinois and Pennsylvania were both ultrareactionary, one the centre of Steel Trust power, and the bulwark of high protection; the other the home of the Harvester Trust, the Beef Trust, and many of the greatest business combinations of the country. In both states Taft's campaign was conducted by a discredited political state machine, rankly offensive to the people. The Steel Trust and other special interests supported Roosevelt because through him they could divide the Progressives and defeat the nomination of any real Progressive candidate. And, if it resulted in Roosevelt's nomination and election, they remembered that whatever he had *said* about them, in all the time he was President, he never *did* anything to hurt them. He was just enough of a reactionary to retain the favor of a large body of the reactionary element, and just enough of a Progressive to attract unseasoned Progressives who wanted to beat Taft, regardless of the means employed to carry their states against him. Progressives of this type wanted to "win"; not a real Progressive victory—just a victory. And they did win precisely that kind of a victory in those two states. And thus, having won in Illinois and Pennsylvania, Roosevelt carried several really Progressive states in the elections that followed.

The result in Illinois and Pennsylvania made no difference with my plans. I had known defeat before, and had been trained to meet it with strengthened resolution to press on, building up a real Progressive support, so fixed in convictions as to be utterly indifferent to reverses. The momentum of a victorious army is hard to resist, but an army disciplined by defeat, that will still fight on, is invincible.

No campaign for principle is ever in vain. And I felt an abiding faith that the work which I was doing in the presidential primary states would be lasting in its effects. A splendid body of men and women were deeply interested. In each of the states the foundation for a permanent Progressive organization was laid, with leaders of real power in charge.

My campaign in California was exceptional in many respects. Governor Hiram Johnson had gone over to Roosevelt, taking with him his strong state machine and the La Follette League of several thousand members organized some months before. When I reached the state, a little more than two weeks before the primary, it seemed that it would be impossible to make a campaign at all. But Rudolph Spreckels, who had carried through the San Francisco graft prosecution, came forward with splendid spirit, and not only paid all the expenses of the California campaign, but although suffering from recent illness, he personally gave his time and strength and ability to its management.

And likewise in varying degree did a number of loyal friends attest their devotion to the cause—state campaign managers Harry N. Tucker, North Dakota; R. O. Richards, South Dakota; Frank A. Harrison, Nebraska; Thomas McCusker, Oregon; Walter W. Pollock, Ohio; James E. Pope, New Jersey; Elizabeth G. Evans, Massachusetts, besides many others in those states—all of whom gave freely of their time and means in the contest.

So, in the face of desertion and defeat, I fought on, contesting in every direct primary state until election day in the last state to hold a primary election. I lost Nebraska, Oregon, California, three districts which I campaigned in Ohio, New Jersey, and South Dakota. I had carried Wisconsin with twenty-six delegates and North Dakota with ten, which gave me thirty-six delegates to the National Convention—a very effective fighting force as it finally proved.

Roosevelt's willingness to "accept" merged into a desire to receive, and then into a determination to pursue the Republican presidential nomination, which he did in person to the very doors of the convention. Progressive principles were lost sight of in his campaign. For definite issues and purpose there was substituted a standard of personal loyalty to him. Until he came into the open as a candidate, five months before the convention, there had been a strong and rapidly growing Progressive movement within the Republican party. It was based upon clearly defined principles. It stood forth as the representative of modern political thought on fundamental democracy. It had assumed national proportions. It was united. Into this movement, when it gave promise of national success, Roosevelt projected his ambition to be President a third time.

When the campaign was finished both Taft and Roosevelt claimed a majority of the delegates elected to the convention. I felt confident that neither had a majority, and believed that if the contests were settled with anything like fairness, it would leave them with their strength so nearly even that the twenty-six delegates from Wisconsin and the ten from North Dakota instructed for me would constitute the balance of power in the convention. I knew that I could depend upon the steadfastness of these thirty-six and felt confident that they would be in a position to force the adoption of a strong Progressive platform and the nomination of a thoroughgoing Progressive candidate. Roosevelt and Taft had conducted a campaign so bitterly personal that the nomination of either could not, I believed, commend itself to the wisdom of a majority of the convention. Furthermore, the conditions which had aroused public resentment and indignation—the control of government by the railroads, the trusts, the money power—had come upon the country mainly in the last dozen years under the administrations of Roosevelt and Taft. In view of the whole situation, I urged those representing me in that convention to stand to the last against the nomination of either Taft or Roosevelt.

The Republican National Convention of 1912 met in Chicago June 18th and lasted until the 22nd. For about a week before the convention the Republican National Committee had been in session, hearing and deciding contests, in order to prepare the preliminary roll of delegates of those entitled to participate in the temporary organization of the convention. According to custom, the credentials committee, consisting of one member from each state, chosen by the several state delegations—the choice being ratified by the convention—went into session shortly after the convention met, and passed upon the results arrived at by the National Committee.

Knowing that he did not have a majority of the delegates honestly elected to the convention, Roosevelt made a loud outcry against the fraud which he professed to believe the National Committee intended to perpetrate in passing upon contests to be brought before it. This served the double purpose of diverting attention from his own fraudulent contests and discredited the decisions of the National Committee in advance of its action. While the National Committee was engaged in hearing and deciding the contests, Roosevelt and his followers vigorously denounced at every stage the seating of Taft delegates as "robbery" and "theft." Their protest was quite as violent when the committee decided justly against Roosevelt as when it decided unjustly against him. Before the National Committee had completed its hearing of contests, preliminary to perfecting the temporary roll of delegates, it was apparent that the Taft people would control the convention for temporary organization.

Prior to the time when Roosevelt became an avowed candidate, the men who were to constitute my delegation from Wisconsin had been selected, and at his request Governor F. E. McGovern had been named as one of the delegates at large and placed at the head of the ticket. The men so selected were all supposed to be my friends and strongly in favor of my nomination. They were elected in the presidential primary by nearly one hundred thousand majority. Some days before the Chicago convention I learned that McGovern and Henry Cochems, another delegate and a close friend of McGovern, had had an interview with Roosevelt in his private car on the twenty-seventh of March (1912) in the city of Milwaukee, as he was passing through the state on his return from campaigning in Minnesota. I did not know just what this interview signified until a few days before the meeting of the convention, when the word reached me from friends in Wisconsin that McGovern would be Roosevelt's candidate for temporary chairman of the convention. As soon as I learned of this I sent my private secretary, John J. Hannan, to McGovern, directing him to say that I should regard his standing as Roosevelt's candidate for temporary chairman as most inimical to my candidacy; that the placing of McGovern's name before the convention as Roosevelt's candidate for temporary chairman and his election by Roosevelt delegates would at once be accepted by the convention and the country as evidence of an alliance with Roosevelt; that I desired that my candidacy be kept entirely free from any deal or bargain or combination with any other candidate; that the effect of such a proceeding would at once array every delegate in the convention opposed to Roosevelt (and many real Progressives were opposed to him) against me; that if Wisconsin and North Dakota held the balance of power between the Taft and Roosevelt delegates, this would be equivalent to surrendering that position of vantage, and in the end would operate to carry my delegates to the support of Roosevelt and secure his nomination; that as my delegates were for the nomination of neither Taft nor Roosevelt, they should take no action which would strengthen either Taft or Roosevelt.

Hannan found McGovern determined to be the Roosevelt candidate for temporary chairman. He declared that he had his speech all prepared; that it was the greatest opportunity of his life, and although strongly urged by Hannan to hold off from any such combination with Roosevelt, he refused absolutely to yield.

It now became plain that it was a part of the Roosevelt plan to form a secret alliance with McGovern, tempt him with the Chairmanship of the Convention, secure the support of the Wisconsin and North Dakota delegations, and with Cummins' Iowa strength added to the Roosevelt strength, elect him chairman; that McGovern, as chairman, should rule out as fraudulent, and not entitled to participate in the temporary organization a sufficient number of the Taft delegates seated by the National Committee, to give Roosevelt a majority of the convention, and then once in control they would be able to steam-roll Roosevelt's nomination.

A pretence was made that McGovern's candidacy was in my interest, and would, in some mysterious way, have aided in my nomination. But this valuable service in my behalf was conceived and carried along toward consummation without consultation with or indeed without an intimation to me, and kept carefully under cover until the Chicago convention was right at hand— and then attempted to be forced through over my earnest protest. It must always stand upon the record as a betrayal, not merely of my candidacy, but of the Progressive principles which the Wisconsin voters instructed these men to represent with fidelity.

McGovern stated in an interview in explanation of his persistency in being a candidate for temporary chairman, given out to Wisconsin papers after his return to the state from the convention, that if he had been elected temporary chairman he would have ruled that the seventy-two delegates contested by Roosevelt should have been stricken from the roll and denied the right to participate in the temporary organization. He put together some figures attempting to show that, if the deal had not been repudiated from the platform in my behalf by Houser, he (McGovern) would have been elected temporary chairman. The absurdity of this claim is obvious to any one who, even remotely, followed the proceedings of the convention. The fact that all the anti-Taft votes combined were not sufficient to control became apparent on the first test of strength in the convention. This was the "seating" of contested delegates for the temporary organization. And in this proceeding *all* the Roosevelt forces participated and were outvoted. These delegates safely seated, the Taft forces were strong enough to dominate every subsequent roll call, including that upon the temporary chairmanship. There is no way of juggling figures to prove that *after* the seating of these delegates McGovern could have been elected temporary chairman, even were he given the votes of all my delegates. But that is relatively unimportant. Even had it been possible for such a combination to elect McGovern, I could not have consented to it. Such a course would have been a repudiation of my whole career and of my pledges to the people to enter into no deals or combinations. What is significant is McGovern's admission that *if* he had been elected temporary chairman he would have "gaveled" the seventy-two delegates contested by Roosevelt out of their seats. In other words, he confesses that he would have done even more unjustifiable "steam-rolling" as chairman in Roosevelt's interest than he says was done by the convention in Taft's interest. Such a decision as this, had it been rendered, would have violated the precedents of every national convention ever held, and arbitrarily and wrongfully have nominated Roosevelt as the Republican candidate.

Upon the arrival of the Wisconsin delegates at Chicago prior to the meeting of the convention, a caucus of the delegates was held to consider McGovern's candidacy for temporary chairman. The caucus decided by a vote of 15 to 11 not to present McGovern's name to the convention as a candidate. In violation of this action by the delegation and to their great amazement, Henry Cochems nevertheless did nominate McGovern for temporary chairman. Immediately Roosevelt followers in the convention, without regard to the alphabetical order of the states, were on their feet seconding the nomination of McGovern. That there was a perfect understanding with the Roosevelt forces now became evident.

The placing of McGovern in nomination caused a stir throughout the convention hall. Many interpreted it as evidence of a combination between the Roosevelt and La Follette forces. No answer was forthcoming until after the seconding speeches had been made. And then Walter L. Houser, my campaign manager, who was a delegate at large, in a forceful, earnest speech, informed the convention that the action of Cochems and the others who seconded McGovern's nomination, whose speeches had adroitly carried the impression that I sanctioned the nomination of McGovern, totally misrepresented my attitude; that my candidacy was uncompromising and unwavering, and would remain to the end free from combinations of any sort.

In an editorial printed generally in the Scripps papers, Herbert Quick says of this incident of the convention:

"The one sharp shock of unexpectedness, the dramatic thrill which lifts the spectators to erect grip on the arms of their seats, was furnished the first day of the convention by the La Follette clash in the Wisconsin delegation. . . .

"The Roosevelt people wanted to get the temporary chairman. The fight was so close that nobody could tell how it would end. Borah of Idaho was the Roosevelt candidate. But the politics of the situation pointed unerringly to McGovern of Wisconsin. For the La Follette votes in Wisconsin and North Dakota, numbering 36, were bitterly needed. It was plain that with ordinary men and ordinary convention standards, these 36 votes could be secured by the honor to this little group of giving one of their number the temporary chairmanship.

"They offered the glittering prize to McGovern. The delegation, under the general instructions to avoid deals, dickers, and affiliations refused it. It decided that it would not present the name of Governor McGovern. But Henry Cochems, a personal chum of the governor, with the governor's consent, and acting as an individual, presented his name in a ringing speech.

"The Roosevelt leaders—Hadley, Glasscock, Heney, Johnson, and others —seconded the nomination. To the convention it looked as though the Roosevelt people had annexed the La Follette strength on this vote, and probably on everything save the formal votes for President.

"And then the lightning flashed! Walter L. Houser, La Follette's manager, took the platform, and in a speech thrilling with passion, laid the La Follette cards face up on the convention table.

" 'This nomination is not with Senator La Follette's consent,' he shouted. 'We make no deals with Roosevelt. We make no trades with Taft. Not even this great honor to our governor and an honored member of our delegation can bribe Wisconsin's representatives. Let no man think that La Follette has traded with any one. We make no trades.' . . . 'I'm going to wire La Follette to-night,' said an Indiana Roosevelt leader, 'that he reaps more glory out of this than any other man gets in the day's doings. It tells in a single dramatic moment what he has been trying to tell the country for a year—that he is playing the game without deals, without bargains, and with sole reference to accomplishing results which he believes to be necessary to the welfare of the country. If this episode had been staged by a skilful dramatist for the express purpose of doing this very thing, it could not have been more splendidly done. It put Wisconsin in the spotlight. But the real significance of the incident is its value in giving the world a flashlight picture of the La Follette way of doing things.'

"The incident made a lot of Roosevelt men fiercely angry. They asserted that La Follette was trying to wreak his wrath on Roosevelt and to aid Taft. But the country will know better. And the Roosevelt men themselves, most of them, know better. The picture thrown on the screen of the fateful first day of the fateful Republican convention of 1912 will stay in the nation's mind.

"It shows an indomitable figure—erect, unbending, swayed by no wind of expediency, moved by no temporary advantage, playing the long game, building influence and opinion rather than winning victories, making no deals or trades, taking defeat gamely, and when met by a facer coming back for more punishment, until his foe finally goes down beaten by an adversary who does not know how to quit."

After the final vote for President on Saturday, June 22d, Roosevelt and his followers held a meeting in Orchestra Hall, where, in a speech to the delegates, he bade them return to their constituencies, to test the sentiment of the people, and meet again at a later time to determine as to the advisability of creating a new party—a Roosevelt party—a party, the sole excuse for the formation of which was based upon the contention that delegates in the Republican Convention were stolen from one candidate and given to another. "Thou shalt not steal," was made the keynote of the Roosevelt bolting convention. "Thou shalt not steal—from *me*," would have been more in keeping as a Roosevelt slogan. The importance of principles, of issues, was wholly lost sight of. The methods resorted to by the National Committee, it may be said in passing, however wrongful, were not unique. In 1908, when they were necessary to steam-roll the nomination of Mr. Roosevelt's successor, Mr. Taft, we heard no word of protest. But, as was aptly suggested by Mr. Post in *The Public*, whether one is on top of or under the steam-roller influences somewhat one's point of view.

Throughout the convention, the delegates who were elected to support and who did support me steadfastly to the end, labored for the adoption of a Progressive platform. In this they had no cooperation from the Roosevelt forces. This incident is characteristic: When the Progressive platform was presented to the convention, by Walter C. Owen, the La Follette member of the Committee on Resolutions, in order to obtain a roll call on its adoption, it was necessary under the rules to have a second by two states. La Follette delegates went in every direction, begging for another state to join with Wisconsin and North Dakota in order to get a vote— merely a vote—and every request was met with a flat refusal. Thus through the cooperation of Roosevelt and Taft forces, a record vote upon a definitely Progressive platform of principles was rendered impossible.

The importance of the charge made by Mr. Roosevelt that the nomination was stolen from him, led *La Follette's Weekly Magazine* to engage Mr. Gilbert E. Roe, of New York City, to analyze the evidence and all the proceedings bearing upon the seating of delegates whose title was in dispute. He obtained from the National Committee and the Committee on Credentials all of the evidence presented in every contest to the two committees, and the shorthand notes of the proceedings of both committees. He made an exhaustive study of each one of the contested cases. I submit herewith the results of his work.

There were 1078 delegates to the convention. Five hundred and forty constituted a majority, and was the minimum number of votes necessary to secure the nomination of any candidate. The final vote for President was as follows: Taft, 561; Roosevelt, 107; La Follette, 41; Cummins, 17; Hughes, 2; Absent, 6; not voting, 344. (Five of my 41 votes were cast by the South Dakota delegation.)

Upon the adoption of the majority report of the Committee on Credentials by the convention, Roosevelt in a statement presented by Henry J. Allen of Kansas, said: "I do not release any delegate from his honorable obligation to vote for me if he votes at all, but under the actual conditions, I hope that he will not vote at all." So, in view of this request Mr. Roe, in his analysis, places Roosevelt's actual strength in the convention at 107 plus 344, or 451. In order, however, that there can be no possible question as to the maximum number of Roosevelt votes in the convention, he assumes that the six absent delegates would have voted for Roosevelt, had they been present; that the two who voted for Hughes and the seven from Idaho who voted for the Iowa delegates for Cummins, might also at some time during the proceedings have cast their votes for Roosevelt. This would add 15 more votes to the possible Roosevelt strength, making a total of 466 votes as the maximum which he could have received under any circumstances. The difference between 466 and 540 is 74. Seventy-four additional votes, therefore, must have been obtained from some source in order to have made Roosevelt's nomination in the convention even a possibility.

Mr. Roe then proceeds to analyze the evidence upon which the charge of theft is made. A table which he presents shows the whole number of contests to be 105, the number of seats involved being 248. The actual number of delegates involved was considerably larger than this, as there were sometimes three sets of contesting delegates, and in several instances the same faction of the party had contesting delegates. From the official report it appears that there were 164 Taft delegates seated either by the unanimous vote of the National Committee, or by a viva voce vote when the contest was not regarded by the Roosevelt members of the National Committee as sufficiently serious to require a roll call. To be exact, 26 Taft delegates were seated by a viva voce vote, announced as unanimous and not questioned; 36 were seated by unanimous vote on roll call; contests were withdrawn by 14 Roosevelt contesting delegates after the cases were called, and in the case of 88 delegates, they were seated by a viva voce vote without any request for a roll call. Roosevelt was awarded 19 of the contested delegates.

Deducting from the 248 delegates (the total number in contest) the 19 Roosevelt delegates seated, leaves 229; and deducting the 164 Taft delegates above mentioned, leaves 65, as the only delegates concerning whom there was a substantial contest. The correctness of these figures, Mr. Roe goes on to state, is strikingly verified by the action of the Roosevelt members of the National Committee. Thirteen of those members presented a minority report to the National Committee, in which they set out that the Taft delegates seated from certain states and districts (which Mr. Roe tabulates in his analysis) were improperly seated, and that the Roosevelt delegates contesting these seats, should be placed on the temporary roll. While this table represents that 72 delegates had been seriously contested by the Roosevelt people, the sheet containing the original pencil memoranda which, in some way, became attached to the report, shows that the original number of delegates marked for contest was 66. Enough were afterward added to bring the total up to 72.

On June 19th, Governor Hadley, the leader of the Roosevelt forces, submitted the following motion to the National Convention:

"I move as a substitute for the motion offered by the gentleman from Indiana, Mr. Watson, that the list of delegates, or temporary roll of this convention, be amended by striking therefrom the names of the delegates upon List No. 1, which I hand to the secretary, and that there be substituted in lieu thereof the names upon List No. 2, which I hand to the secretary, and that the temporary roll, when thus amended, become the roll of the convention."

This motion proposed to substitute the Roosevelt delegates for the Taft delegates in the case of the 72 delegates covered by the minority report of the Roosevelt members of the National Committee. The convention refused to adopt the Hadley resolution, and it is this action which the Roosevelt adherents assert made it fraudulent. Since it was in the seating, therefore, of the 72 delegates above mentioned that the Roosevelt followers charge fraud, Mr. Roe reasons that it is not necessary to consider any other contests than the ones involving the seats of the 72 delegates.

After painstaking study of the record evidence he concludes that there was no basis for the claim that a majority of the delegates honestly elected to the National Convention were for Roosevelt; that even if the entire 72 covered by the Hadley Resolution had been given to Roosevelt, he would not have had enough to nominate him; that these 72, after careful investigation of the merits of the contests, and for reasons which he sets forth clearly and in detail, must be reduced by 23, leaving 49 delegates to the National Convention as the maximum number given to Taft by the National Committee which could, on the evidence, fairly have been given to Roosevelt. Mr. Roe does not assert conclusively that these 49 should have been counted as Roosevelt delegates, but that some justification could be found in the evidence for so doing.

Adding to these 49 the 466 which represented the maximum of Roosevelt's strength in the convention, as made up, gives Roosevelt 515. These figures can fairly be reduced. They cannot, with the least show of fairness, be increased. And they show that Roosevelt never had anything like a majority of the honestly elected delegates to the convention. They also show, when the temper of the delegates pledged to the other candidates is considered, that Roosevelt's nomination was impossible, even if every delegate to whom he had any shadow of claim, or who could be regarded as doubtful, be counted for him. The charge of theft against the National Committee for seating Taft delegates where Roosevelt delegates should have been seated, came with bad grace from those who made it. At the worst, the National Committee seated less than 50 Taft delegates on insufficient evidence. Those in charge of the Roosevelt campaign tried to seat more than 150 Roosevelt delegates without any evidence at all. But aside from all this, the knowingly false claims put forward by the Roosevelt managers to more than 150 delegates for weeks prior to the convention, were made, as they were forced to admit while the contests were on trial, with the deliberate purpose of deceiving the Republicans of the country into the belief that Roosevelt's nomination was assured, and that therefore it was better to give him support, hoping that he would prove to be a halfway Progressive, rather than to support a real Progressive candidate, whom the voter personally preferred, but had been led to believe could not be nominated.

Judson C. Welliver is chief political writer on the Washington *Times,* a paper owned by Munsey, who was one of the principal contributors to Roosevelt's campaign and prominent as one of his managers. In an article of Mr. Welliver's in the *Times* of June 9, 1912, is found this startling admission. [The *italics* are mine]:

"The Taft people knew their weakness, and were scared about the situation. They adopted the plan of holding conventions in the South early, because there they had the machinery and could rush matters through with the strong arm procedure and stow away a fine bunch of delegates, while the Roosevelt movement was still unorganized; indeed before Roosevelt *could be announced.*

"This they did, and on the day when Roosevelt formally announced that he was a candidate, something over a hundred delegates had actually been selected. When Senator Dixon (Roosevelt's manager) took charge of the campaign, a tabulated showing of delegates selected to date would have looked hopelessly one-sided. Moreover, a number of southern states had called their conventions for early dates, and there was no chance to develop the real Roosevelt strength in the great northern states till later.

"For *psychological effect, as a move in practical politics,* it was necessary for the Roosevelt people to start contests on these early Taft selections, in order that a tabulation of delegate strength could be put out that would show Roosevelt holding a good hand in the game. A table showing 'Taft, 150; Roosevelt, 19; contested, none,' would not be very much calculated to inspire confidence. Whereas, one showing 'Taft, 23; Roosevelt, 19; contested, 127,' looked very different.

"That is the whole story of the larger number of southern contests that were started early in the game. It was never expected that they would be taken very seriously; *they served a useful purpose,* and now the National Committee is deciding them in favor of Taft; in most cases without any real division."

Beyond any question it is true that during the last few weeks preceding the convention many delegates were elected for Roosevelt because of the false claims put forth by his managers that he had a large lead in the contest—claims which they well know to be false—to the number of at least 150 delegates represented by "fake" contests.

The true psychology of the Roosevelt proceedings at Chicago became perfectly plain. He was there to force his own nomination or to smash the convention. He was not there to preserve the integrity of the Republican Party, and make it an instrument for the promotion of Progressive principles and the restoration of government to the people. Otherwise, he would have directed his managers to contest every inch of the ground for a Progressive platform before the Committee on Resolutions and in the open convention. If he had evidence to prove that Taft could not be honestly and fairly nominated, why did he not direct his lieutenants to present that evidence to the National Committee, and then to the convention and the country, so clearly that the convention would not have dared to nominate Taft and that Taft could not, in honor, have accepted the nomination if made?

The reason is obvious. An analysis of the testimony shows that neither Taft nor Roosevelt had a majority of honestly or regularly elected delegates. This the managers upon both sides well understood. Each candidate was trying to seat a sufficient number of fraudulently credentialed delegates, added to those regularly chosen to support him, to secure control of the convention and steam-roll the nomination. It was a proceeding with which each was acquainted and which each had sanctioned in prior conventions. This explains the extraordinary conduct of Roosevelt. He could not enter upon such an analysis of the evidence as would prove Taft's regularly elected delegates in the minority, without inevitably subjecting his own spuriously credentialed delegates to an examination so critical as to expose the falsity of his own contention that he had an honestly elected majority of the delegates. He therefore deliberately chose to claim everything, to cry fraud, to bully the National Committee and Convention, and sought to create a condition which would make impossible a calm investigation of cases upon merit, and to carry the convention by storm. He filled the public ear with sound and fury. He ruthlessly sacrificed everything to the one idea of his being the one candidate. He gagged his followers in the convention, without putting on record any facts upon which the public could base a definite, intelligent judgment regarding the validity of Taft's nomination. He submitted no suggestion as to a platform of Progressive principles. He clamored loudly for purging the convention roll of "tainted" delegates without purging his own candidacy of his tainted contests, and his tainted trust support. He offered no reason for a third party, except his own overmastering craving for a third term.

Chapter XIII

Why I Continued as a
Candidate—Roosevelt never
a Progressive—His Record

When the men who had supported my candidacy dropped away from me, one by one, and turned to Roosevelt, as "a winner," I weighed, and impersonally too, I think, every phase of the situation. I had gone into the campaign as a candidate, believing that I had been so identified with the Progressive movement that my candidacy was one with it. It is needless to say that having become a candidate, I wanted to win. I should not be frank if I did not admit this to be true. Yet plainly, at any time during the campaign, it would have been my duty to stand aside and support the candidacy of another if, by so doing, I could advance the Progressive cause. It was claimed that Roosevelt had a greater numerical following throughout the country than any other Republican. But that, in itself, was not enough. It is one thing to have a candidate of great popular strength. It is another thing to have a candidate sincerely devoted to the fundamental principles of the cause he is supposed to represent. As I have before stated I could never consent to play a double game with the public; I could not pretend to be a candidate, when in fact I was only a dummy for the real candidate, concerning whose candidacy the people were to be kept in the dark. To withdraw in favor of Roosevelt was quite as impossible, because to surrender the field to him would be to surrender the movement to him.

I have said many times in this narrative, and I had said many times as early as the campaign of 1908, that while giving Roosevelt full credit for all of his preachments for higher ethical standards in our political and social life, what was sorely needed in this critical hour was a real constructive leader with a clear conception of the economic problems of the time. I had tested Roosevelt's

285

public record by the peculiar abilities which manifestly existing conditions demanded, and he had not measured up. Roosevelt at the close of his administration realized himself that in arousing the public conscience to higher civic standards, he had rendered the service for which he was most fitted, and admitted frankly his distaste for the plodding and investigation necessary to a solution of great economic questions. This, indeed, prefaced his appeal for Taft, for whose constructive work Roosevelt believed he had made the ground ready.

In a speech which I delivered at Racine, Wis., in the campaign of 1908, I said:

"President Roosevelt has crystallized public sentiment, and elevated civic standards. He will live in the history of his time, a unique figure. He will not live in history as the author of any great, lasting constructive legislation. He knows his office and his field better than some of his most enthusiastic supporters. He knows that if his name is given to enduring fame, it will be because he has touched the conscience of the foremost nation in the world, lifted its people on to heights, and made them ready for the greatest work that any nation ever did."

In that same speech I commented upon the dangerous precedent which Roosevelt's action, in choosing his successor, tended to establish. I said it was a "wrong thing, a dangerous thing for the President to use the power and all the force of his administration to select his successor."

Repeated experiences with Roosevelt had convinced me that in critical situations his action was often in direct opposition to his utterances; that one could reckon on his doing, not the logical consistent thing to carry out a definite policy, but the expedient thing, the thing that achieves temporary success. These elements in his character were matters of constant disappointment as they revealed themselves to me.

In weighing the course which it was my duty to take when Roosevelt became an open and aggressive candidate, claiming the leadership of the Republican Progressive movement, I reviewed the record of his official life. He had given utterance to many strong Progressive declarations. Taken by themselves, they would persuade the most ardent Progressive. At times this side of the man had led me to be hopeful that he might support our movement, and with his prestige as a former President, if he would but hold fast, give us greatly added strength. But to commit the Progressive cause to his control, to stake all on his remaining steadfast, to "follow, follow, follow, wherever he would lead"—quoting the refrain of those so-called Progressives who did follow him un-questioningly—the thought of doing this always compelled me, whenever this momentous question came up in a serious way, and before taking the final step, to go back along the course over which this man had come, and see whether he had left a straight or a crooked trail.

Important events blazed that trail, and established its general course and direction. More than that—which was the vital thing *now*—they pointed the way he would certainly go in the future. There was his record on the coal land bill; his sponsorship for the Hepburn bill, which was in fact little more than a sham; his shifti-ness on the valuation of railroad property as a basis for rate regu-lation; his aversion to the Anti-Trust Law, and his combination and trust policy which, despite his verbal assaults on trusts, steadily strengthened and encouraged the growth of monopoly; his strong support of the Aldrich-Cannon Standpat tariff program; his criti-cal attitude toward Standard Oil coupled with his confidential re-lations with Morgan, Perkins, Frick, Harriman, and those associated with them, in the interlocking directorates, controlling the Big Business of the country; and his uniform policy of opposition to the Progressive movement in Wisconsin and other states. Each of these, by itself, would shatter for the time being confidence in Roosevelt's integrity of purpose. But it would be followed by such vigorous and apparently sincere denunciation of the evils of privi-lege, as to make one again believe in and trust him. When, how-ever, I reviewed them in their relation one with another, in this great crisis in the life of the Progressive movement, I could not conscientiously accept him as a leader of the Progressive move-ment, and there was no alternative for me but to continue as a candidate.

Roosevelt's attitude with reference to the coal land legislation in 1906, detailed in a previous chapter, is strikingly characteristic. He had encouraged me to believe that he would put back of this important legislation all the power of his administration. That encouragement led me in every speech I made during the recess, and I made many, to tell the story of the coal lands, the correc-tive legislation proposed, and of President Roosevelt's enthusiastic support. Upon my return to Washington at the beginning of the next session I found that, as promised, he had in his message rec-ommended the legislation. After weeks of study and preparation, with the assistance of the Attorney General's department, a broad conservation measure was evolved which, when presented to Roosevelt, received his emphatic approval. But within three days he had receded from his position. Because railroad and special interest Senators bitterly opposed the bill, as they were certain to do, and because they denounced me and my plan as socialistic, the President withdrew his support.

He followed the same course with the Hepburn bill. When this measure was pending in 1906, after the country had anxiously waited for years for legislation to strengthen the Interstate Commerce Law, in conferring with Roosevelt, as I did upon his invitation, I argued the futility of passing the pending bill, which I had carefully studied, and pointed out wherein it failed to touch the basic question—the question which the country had patiently waited to have solved. He had not only tremendous public sentiment back of him in this legislation but the urgent appeal, year after year, of the Interstate Commerce Commission for such amendments to the law as would empower it effectively to deal with this all-important question. But, because he was not sincerely for a thoroughgoing measure, he accepted and gave to the country, as something real, a law which withheld from the commission all authority to correct transportation abuses, all means of determining and enforcing just and reasonable rates, a measure which, in every respect, was fundamentally inadequate.

Subsequent developments have more than justified my criticisms of the Hepburn bill in 1906. Under the Hepburn law, railroad rates steadily increased. Hundreds of millions of dollars have been wrongfully taken from the American people, because Congress and the President failed to give to the Interstate Commerce Commission power to protect the public interest.

One radical defect in the Hepburn bill (and the Interstate Commerce Law is still defective in this regard) was its omission to provide for determining the true value of railroad property as a basis for rate making. Failing to secure the adoption of the valuation amendment which I offered in the Senate, in recording my vote on the passage of the bill I warned the Senate and the country that the measure was fatally defective; that the bill added nothing to the existing law which would enable the commission to determine and enforce reasonable rates; that the country would be sorely disappointed when it understood how little had been achieved after a nine years' struggle to cure the vital defects which the decision of the Supreme Court had made apparent. My frank statement that I could not laud a measure which I felt was, in large degree, a sham, I had reason to know displeased Roosevelt, for the

Hepburn bill was an administration measure and went to the country as a great achievement.

Early in the next session, while filling an engagement in New York, in January, 1907, a long-distance telephone message from William Loeb, Secretary to President Roosevelt, requested me, immediately upon my return to Washington, to call at the White House upon an important matter. The President greeted me cordially when I called. He began his conversation by saying that he had been angered with me for the attacks I had made upon the Hepburn bill, which at the time he thought were unnecessary and unjustifiable; that he had, however, been looking into my criticisms, and the amendments I had offered; that he was now convinced I was right, and that my amendments were important and essential to the bill, particularly the valuation amendment; that he had become satisfied that valuation was necessary to any reasonable regulation of railway rates. He had determined, he said, to take this matter up and push it, and had sent for me to request me to prepare for him the best statement I could, presenting in terse form the importance of valuation. Such statement he proposed to use as the basis of a letter to the Interstate Commerce Commission on the subject of valuation. He said he would give this letter to the press, and would do all he could to awaken public interest in the subject; that he would follow it up in some addresses he intended to make after the adjournment, and when Congress met in December he would urge that the Interstate Commerce Commission be authorized to ascertain the value of the railroad property of the country. He assured me he would make my bill for railway valuation, then pending, an administration measure, and do everything in his power to put it through. I prepared with care the statement he had requested, adding to it some suggestions for improvement of the administrative features of the existing law, and placed it in his hands.

Shortly thereafter I received several calls from newspaper correspondents who came to make inquiry of me as to Roosevelt's taking up the subject of railroad valuation with the Interstate Commerce Commission, and his intention of giving it a prominent place in the administration program of legislation at the next session. The accuracy of their information led me to believe that it had come from White House sources, but I did not feel at liberty to admit any knowledge of what the President proposed to do. Leading newspapers the next day set forth in considerable detail the purpose of the President to address the Interstate Commerce Commission upon the subject of valuation, to present the matter in speeches during the summer, and urgently to Congress in a message at the next session.

Again I experienced great gratification in the belief that Roosevelt really intended to do what he had told me he would do. And I felt perfectly sure that with the power of his administration back of it, the valuation bill would go through, establishing at last the vital principle of scientific rate-making.

But I waited in vain for the appearance of his open letter to the Interstate Commerce Commission, or for some further word. If he wrote such a letter to the commission, I never heard of it. The next expression from him upon the subject of railway valuation was on the occasion of the unveiling of the Lawton statue, at Indianapolis, May 30, 1907. In this address he took the position that, except as to some of the small lines, the railroads of the country generally were not overcapitalized at all, and that railway valuation was not the essential basis for ascertaining and enforcing reasonable rates.

I reviewed also Roosevelt's course upon trusts and combinations. The American people believe private monopoly intolerable. Within the last dozen years trusts and combinations have been organized in nearly every branch of industry. Competition has been ruthlessly crushed, extortionate prices have been exacted from consumers, independent business development has been arrested, invention stifled, and the door of opportunity has been closed, except to large aggregations of capital. The public has not, as a rule, received any of the resultant economies and benefits of combination which have been so abundantly promised. But ordinarily the combinations have demonstrated that the hand of monopoly is deadening, and that business may as easily become too large to be efficient, as remain too small. And as related to government, it is everywhere recognized that trusts and combinations are to-day the gravest danger menacing our institutions.

Since Lincoln's time no man was ever offered such an opportunity to strike an effective blow for his country as was presented to Roosevelt when he became President. Compared with the conditions seven and one half years later, the trusts and combinations at the beginning of his term were but a handful. Limited in number, they stood unsupported, each by itself. They had not yet been fused and welded together with the Morgan system of interlocking directorates. All told, there were but one hundred and forty-nine. This was the most critical time in the whole history of trust formation. It was as though the country were menaced by a fatal plague—as though it had gained a dangerous footing here and there in the most populous districts, where its deadly ravages were beginning to create distress and consternation. It was a case for strict quarantine and extermination; a period when such treatment would not affect the whole community but when those responsible for the conditions could be reached without hardship or suffering to the innocent.

The Sherman Anti-Trust Law, in existence at that time, declared combinations to suppress competition and create or attempt to create monopoly to be criminal.

In plain terms this law provided that:

"Every contract, combination in the form of trust or otherwise, or conspiracy in restraint of trade or commerce among the several states, or with foreign nations, is hereby declared to be illegal."

The law provided further that "every person" making "any such contract" or engaging in "any such combination or conspiracy," and "every person who shall monopolize or attempt to monopolize, or combine, or conspire with any other person to monopolize any part of the trade or commerce among the several states," shall be deemed guilty of a misdemeanor, and subject on conviction to be "punished by a fine not exceeding five thousand dollars or by imprisonment not exceeding one year."

As said by Judge Stewart, of Vermont, in closing the debate in the House of Representatives, when the law was enacted in 1890:

"The provisions of this trust bill are just as broad, sweeping, and explicit as the English language can make them to express the power of Congress on this subject under the Constitution of the United States."

The enactment of this law placed in the hands of the Executive the strongest, most perfect weapon which the ingenuity of man could forge for the protection of the people of this country against the power and sordid greed of monopoly. And its vigorous and sincere enforcement at the time Theodore Roosevelt entered upon his first term of office as President would have crushed and destroyed the comparatively few trusts which were then in existence.

How did President Roosevelt treat conspiracies against the free markets of our country which the law prohibited as criminal combinations? *Not as the law treated them.* The law clearly defined them, and imposed upon the Executive Department of the government the obligation to make an end of them. Instead, in his messages and public addresses, one finds the new President setting himself up as superior to the law. He began by confusing the public mind. He assumed that there was no adequate legislation dealing with the subject of combinations, and attempts on the part of any person or corporation to monopolize trade. In his first message to Congress, he stated it as his judgment that "combination and concentration should be, not prohibited, but *supervised,* and within *reasonable limits* controlled."

The law, in plain terms, *prohibited* even "every attempt to monopolize," and declared "every contract, combination in the form of trust or otherwise, or conspiracy in restraint of trade," *to be illegal.* It said nothing about *supervising* or *controlling* these combinations "within reasonable limits." At that time it would have been a simple matter to execute the law. This it was the President's sworn duty to do. Instead of enforcing obedience to the statute, Roosevelt in his first message warned the country that "the mechanism of modern business is so delicate that extreme care must be taken not to interfere with it in a spirit of rashness or ignorance. "Much of the legislation directed at the trusts," he asserted, "would have been exceedingly mischievous had it not also been entirely ineffective." While admitting the existence of "great industrial combinations," he made no appeal to the public to sustain the law and evinced no disposition to enforce that great statute which the statesmanship of Sherman, Edmunds, Hoar, Turpie, Taylor, Culberson, Stewart, and the ablest men of their time had given us to meet these very changes. Instead he twisted and turned and wound about with words, blurring and smearing the discussion and vaguely suggesting the need of "publicity" and the probable necessity of a "constitutional amendment," finally and emphatically warning Congress and the country against "ignorant and reckless agitators," and pleading throughout for "calm and sober self-restraint."

In an address delivered at Providence on the twenty-third of August, 1902, less than a year after he became President, referring to the "great corporations which we have grown to speak of rather loosely as 'trusts,' " he says:

"Now, the conditions are complicated, and we find it hard to frame national legislation which shall be adequate; while as a matter of practical experience it has been shown that the states either cannot or will not exercise a sufficient control to meet the needs of the case."

And again:

"I believe that the nation must assume this power of control by legislation; if necessary by constitutional amendment. . . . The trust nowadays is a large state corporation which generally does business in other states, often with a tendency toward monopoly. Such a trust is an artificial creature, not wholly responsible to or controllable by any legislation, either by state or nation, and not subject to the jurisdiction of any one court."

The very case he puts comes within the specific terms of the Sherman Act, as quoted above:

"Section 2. Every person (corporation) who shall monopolize or attempt to monopolize . . . any part of the trade or commerce among the several states, shall be deemed guilty," etc.

And then, ignoring the strong statute which he ought to have enforced, and after arguing further the need of conferring additional power upon the national government, he says:

"When it has been given full power, then this full power can be used to *control* any evil influence."

That is, the power which the government already had, but which he was contending had yet to be provided, when supplied, should not be used to destroy the trusts, but "to control any evil influence." He argues further that the government must be very careful not to control too harshly, lest the trust be injured.

In the very next sentence he says:

"When the power has been granted, it would be most unwise to exercise it too much—to begin by too stringent legislation."

Throughout this and later addresses runs the constant admonition that these trusts are great public benefactors, great national assets. We are reminded that we are prospering, and warned against attacks made upon wealth, "not merely individual, but corporate." He says:

"If, in a spirit of sullen envy, they (the people) insist upon pulling down those who have profited most in the years of fatness, they will bury themselves in the crash of the common disaster."

And again:

"The great captain of industry, the man of wealth, who alone or in combination with his fellows, drives through our great business enterprises, is a factor, without whom the civilization that we see round about us here (he was speaking in Senator Aldrich's home city) could not have been built up. Good, not harm, normally comes from the upbuilding of such wealth."

Is it to be marvelled at that the trusts were encouraged to multiply their organizations, and flood the land with watered securities?

In an address delivered at Boston on the twenty-fifth of August, 1902, he reiterated his claim that it was still a mooted question whether the federal government had *any* power to deal with the trust question. He said:

"Now one of the great troubles—I am inclined to think much the greatest trouble—in any immediate handling of the question of the trusts comes from our system of government. Under this system it is difficult to say where the power is lodged to deal with these evils."

The same misleading assertions run through the whole address. Note this:

"Now, *if* we can get adequate control by the nation of these great corporations, then we can pass legislation which will give us the power of regulation and supervision over them. If the nation had that power, mind you, I should advocate as strenuously as I knew how, that the power should be exercised with *extreme caution* and self-restraint."

Five years later he exercised the power to enforce the Sherman Law with "extreme caution and self-restraint" when he permitted Morgan, Gary and Perkins for the Steel Trust to absorb its principal rival, the Tennessee Coal and Iron Company.

At Wheeling, W. Va., September 6, 1902, again he impressed upon his hearers the thought that there was no sufficient remedy for the trust evil, and that they must still suffer the growth and spread of combinations, until further legislation could be enacted; that perhaps they must await the slow process of constitutional amendment. He said:

"But, gentlemen, I firmly believe that in the end power must be given to the national government to exercise in full supervision and regulation of these great enterprises and if necessary, a constitutional amendment must be resorted to for this purpose."

This doctrine when firmly planted in the public mind would excuse and justify shilly-shallying with the trusts throughout his whole term of service.

After his election in 1904, he becomes somewhat more definite. He is more pronounced in his commendation of the great corporations, their benefits to business and society. He rejoices in "the marvellous prosperity we are enjoying" and shows a growing appreciation of the valuable services of the Morgans and the McCormicks, "the industrial leaders of the nation."

In his message, December, 1904, he found it expedient to remind Congress that:

"Great corporations are necessary and only men of great singular mental power can manage such corporations successfully, and such men must have great rewards."

And again he says:

"If the less fortunate man is moved by envy of his more fortunate brother to strike at the conditions under which they have both, though unequally, prospered, the result will assuredly be that while damage may come to the one struck at, it will visit with an even heavier load the one who strikes the blow."

Let it be remembered that this was the same President who later ordered his attorney general not to file a suit against the Harvester Trust until he received "further instructions."

Congress required no restraining influence from the White House to hold it in leash against the combinations which were fast throttling competition. For years it had been the bulwark of privilege for the special interests. But running through all of his utterances as President, we find him warning Congress to hold itself in check, lest it go too far.

Not only was the Cannon-controlled House and the Aldrich-controlled Senate admonished not to take his very general recommendations "to assert the sovereignty of the national government by affirmative action" too seriously, but they were cautioned to beware of the agitator and the demagogue:

"To try to deal with them (the corporations) in an intemperate, destructive, or demagogic spirit would, in all probability, mean that nothing whatever could be accomplished, and, with absolute certainty that if anything were accomplished, it would be of a harmful nature."

It is little less than grotesque to find the President solicitous lest the veterans of privilege, the seasoned bosses of Congress, be swept off their feet by an "intemperate, destructive or demagogic spirit."

Throughout his second administration, having declared that he would not accept a third term, year by year Roosevelt showed his real opposition to the Sherman Anti-Trust Law. It became plain that his failure to vigorously enforce the statute against the competition-destroying trusts was because he was *opposed to the law*. He boldly asserted that "this is an age of combination"; that it was "unfortunate that national laws" on corporations "have sought to prohibit what could not be effectively prohibited."

True enough, combinations "could not be effectively prohibited" if a President was determined that they *should not be prohibited at all*.

By 1907 he apparently believed that the Sherman Law—with which he had played fast and loose for six years—was sufficiently discredited with the public to make its open denunciation timely. And he flatly tells Congress that:

"It is profoundly immoral to put or keep on the statute books a law, nominally in the interest of public morality, that really puts a premium on public immorality, by undertaking to forbid honest men from doing what must be done under modern business conditions, so that the law itself provides that its own infraction must be the condition precedent upon business success."

Here is a frank declaration from Roosevelt that it was immoral to put the Sherman Law on the statute books—that it is immoral to keep it there. Why immoral? Because he says, "it undertakes to forbid honest men from doing what must be done under modern business conditions."

What does the law forbid? It forbids combinations organized to suppress competition and create or attempt to create monopoly. That is exactly what it does and all it does. It is that sort of business that Roosevelt characterized as the business which "honest men" must do under modern business conditions. That is the contention of the Steel Trust, the Beef Trust, the Elevator Trust. It is the trust argument for the trust method. It is the only rule under which the trust can do business, and the "modern business" method under which no one but the trust can do business.

Is it strange that with a President uttering such doctrines in his messages the law was made a dead letter and unlawful trusts and combinations suppressing competition and increasing prices upon the consumer flourished under his administration?

Could United States district attorneys, who wanted to continue in office, or federal judges who might be willing to accept promotion at the hands of this President, be expected to respect or seek to uphold this law when that President would say in a message to Congress that:

"It is a public evil to have on the statute books a law incapable of full enforcement, because both judges and juries realize that its full enforcement would destroy the business of the country."

Thus it was that Roosevelt put the Sherman Anti-Trust Law under the ban of executive disapproval. It was the only federal statute for the protection of the public against these plundering combinations. His denunciation of the law was an executive sanction to violate the law. It opened the floodgates for trust organization, and upon Theodore Roosevelt, more than any other man, must rest the responsibility for the gravest problem which ever menaced the industrial freedom of the American people.

He prosecuted on an average six cases a year against a carefully selected list of these combinations. He went just far enough to give color to the claim that he was upholding the law, but not far enough seriously to injure those prosecuted or deter in the slightest degree the hundreds that were organizing every month throughout his entire administration.

A study of the more important of these cases against combinations under the Sherman Act, shows that the actions were so brought that the government would, at best, win only a nominal victory; and that the decree of the court would be so limited by the allegation of the complaint as to leave the defendant combination in a position, under its existing form or by an easy shift, to continue its wrongdoing.

As stated above, when Roosevelt became President there were 149 combinations and trusts, including railways, the entire 149 having a total stock and bond issue of only $3,784,000,000. When he left the White House there were 10,020 of these monster plants in combination, including, with the combined railroads, a total capitalization amounting to the enormous sum of $31,672,000,000 —more than 70 per cent. of which was water. The power of these combinations was so extensive and so completely did they suppress competition, that they were able to advance prices on transportation, and on the products of the mines and factories to enable them to pay dividends on this fictitious and fraudulent over-capitalization.

The organization of these combinations in transportation, mining, manufacturing, the control of markets and also of money and credit, was largely consummated during the seven years that Roosevelt was President, and in direct violation of the Sherman Anti-Trust Law. Under the terms of that law those engaging in unlawful conspiracies were subject to punishment by both fine and imprisonment. Moreover, under its provisions, every such combination could have been enjoined, and a violation of the injunctive order would have been punishable by imprisonment for contempt. As a rule criminal statutes simply define the offense and prescribe the punishment. But the author of this law, anticipating the powerful influence which such aggregations of wealth might exert to suppress prosecutions, embodied in the statute, in specific terms, a provision making it the duty of the Executive Department to enforce the law. If President Roosevelt, at the beginning of his administration, when there were but 149 trusts and combinations, had used all the power of this great government to enforce the anti-trust law; if he had summoned to Washington every United States district attorney and had called in the Attorney General and his assistants and had said to them: "There are 149 combinations already organized to suppress competition and control the markets; if this law is ever to be enforced, vigorous thoroughgoing action on the part of the government must be no longer delayed; these organizations have been formed in violation of the federal statute; that statute makes it the duty of the United States district attorneys acting under the Attorney General to destroy these criminal conspiracies against the people; it is your duty to enforce this law; it is my duty as President to see that you do enforce it; unless you begin and prosecute criminal actions against every one of these unlawful conspiracies, I will revoke your commissions, and appoint an Attorney General and United States district attorneys who will enforce the law."

Had the President of the United States at that time, I say, taken this strong stand, there would not have been a criminal conspiracy violating this statute in existence at the end of ninety days. It would have saved the people of this country the payment of hundreds of millions of dollars wrongfully taken from them year after year in excessive transportation rates and in extortionate prices which they have had to pay for the necessaries of life. Had this been done before these combined monopolies acquired such absolute mastery, the people would not now be confronted with this momentous question—are these trusts and combinations stronger than the government itself? Can the people free themselves from this mighty power? Can the unjust burden of fraudulent capitalization be lifted from them?

The trusts and combinations, the railroads, the steel trust, the coal trust, all are scheming to secure some action by the government which will legalize their proceedings and sanction their fictitious capitalization. The situation is critical. It may be expected from the attitude of the Supreme Court as shown by the decisions in the Standard Oil and Tobacco cases that any act on the part of the executive or legislative branch of government giving countenance to a trust or combination will be construed as an approval of the thousands of millions of watered stocks and bonds issued, and will fasten upon the people for all time the speculative capitalization of our public service and business corporations.

Roosevelt contends that there is no overcapitalization in the great railroad corporations of the country. And as to other overcapitalized combinations he contends when once they have issued their fictitious capitalization and sold their stocks and bonds to speculators, ever ready to take chances on investments promising enormous returns, regardless of the actual investment underlying these fictitious securities, they shall nevertheless be protected, and the people forever compelled to pay extortionate prices in order to furnish a return to such investors upon these watered stocks and bonds. That this is exactly his position is made clear from the following quotation from his special message to Congress on January 31, 1908:

"When once inflated capitalization has gone upon the market and has become fixed in value, its existence must be recognized. . . . The usual result of such inflation is, therefore, to impose upon the public an unnecessary but everlasting tax."

The fact that the "inflated capitalization has gone upon the market," the fact that a corporation issues watered stocks and that those who trade upon an innocent public buy the watered stocks which can be made to pay large profits only by maintaining an unlawful control of the markets and exacting wrongful prices from the people, according to Roosevelt's theory, gives to these spurious securities "a fixed value" which must be recognized, and that "such inflation" is therefore an "everlasting tax." It is Roosevelt's position that while he is very sorry, nevertheless nothing can be done to relieve the people from the "everlasting tax" due to the billions of dollars of watered stocks which have been wrongfully issued. The innocent public must groan under the burden of paying prices high enough to make a profit to the holders of such stocks upon a grossly inflated capitalization.

It will be the impartial verdict of history that the executive could have saved the people from the appalling conditions which confront us today, if all the power of this great government had been put forth to enforce the Anti-Trust Law. Five or six prosecutions a year, dragging along in the courts at a snail's pace were little more than notice to these business kings that they might proceed to set up their authority against the government and extend their dominion over trade and transportation; that there was no real danger of the law being so enforced as to do much more than to affect the political situation from time to time.

I could not forget in my review of Roosevelt's record that while President he was a reactionary on tariff revision. His constant criticism of the Anti-Trust Law greatly encouraged trust growth and trust activity, which was still further stimulated by his course upon the tariff. Two opportunities presented themselves to him to relieve the people from trust oppression: one, the enforcement of the Sherman Act; the other, a radical reduction of the Dingley tariff duties.

I have already made it plain that from the first he was opposed to enforcing the Anti-Trust Law. Let us see how he behaved regarding the tariff.

The Dingley law was enacted in 1897, with the avowed purpose of excluding, in so far as possible, foreign manufacturers from the American market. With free competition between American manufacturers, prices would have been reduced to the lowest point that could be fixed, still leaving to the American workman fair protection. But with the foreign competition excluded by the high tariff wall, and domestic competition destroyed by the formation of combinations made possible under Roosevelt's treatment of trusts, prices rapidly advanced and very early in Roosevelt's administration the people feeling the burden, and no relief coming to them through the rigid enforcement of the Sherman law, began petitioning for tariff revision. They had begun to understand that if the tariff rates were lowered, foreign competition would reduce the high prices fixed by the trusts and combinations formed by our manufacturers behind the tariff wall. They were quick to see that there was one direct, simple way to reduce the high cost of living and curtail the power of monopoly. And year after year they pled for tariff revision.

Roosevelt was afraid of the tariff issue. He had turned sharp corners on the tariff question from the day he entered public life. He was a member of the Free Trade Club of New York from 1881 until after Blaine's nomination upon a strong protective platform in 1884. He was opposed to Blaine. He was opposed to a protective tariff. But following his natural bent to do the expedient thing, he resigned as a member of the Free Trade Club after Blaine's nomination, and became an ardent advocate of Blaine's election, a Blaine protectionist, a Blaine supporter. In his letter of resignation to the New York Free Trade Club, he said:

"It is impossible to combine the functions of a guerilla chief with those of a colonel in the regular army."

So, he decided to drop his convictions, and be a regular colonel.

As the pressure for tariff revision grew stronger and stronger, Roosevelt's first impulse was to do the popular thing, and yield to the demand for tariff revision. In one of his regular messages to Congress, he inserted a paragraph announcing that later in the session he would send to Congress a special message on tariff revision.

The President's regular messages are prepared long enough before their transmission to Congress to admit of advance copies being sent out by mail to the leading papers of the country, to the end that they may be placed in type, ready to be printed on the day of their delivery. These advance copies are marked "Confidential." They are released for publication on the day they are read in Congress.

After this message was given to the press and before it was released for printing, all newspapers receiving it were notified by

300

wire to strike out the paragraph promising a special message on tariff revision. Whether the interests opposed to tariff reduction learned through reactionary papers of this proposed special message on tariff revision and bore down upon Roosevelt to withdraw the paragraph can only be inferred, but that something happened to persuade Roosevelt to face about on tariff revision is certain, for the paragraph promising revision disappeared from the message before it was transmitted to Congress and printed in the newspapers of the country. It was another instance of the many which mark Roosevelt's public career, when confronted with the alternative of serving the people or privilege, he found it more expedient to serve privilege.

In his first message to Congress, Roosevelt began by discouraging a general revision of the tariff. He said:

"Nothing could be more unwise than to disturb the business interests of the country by any general tariff change at this time."

But the prices were going higher and higher and the people continued to clamor for relief. It was during this period that the strife was so great between the trusts holding on to the high tariff and the people demanding tariff reduction, that the term "standpatter" was coined to describe those who would not yield to the demand for tariff revision downward. And Roosevelt, like Cannon in the House of Representatives and Aldrich in the Senate, stood pat against the public demand.

He admonished the public of the dangers of tariff revision, and defended the standpat policy of Congress, in an address at Minneapolis, Minn., April 7, 1903, saying:

"The tariff affects trusts only as it affects all other interests. It makes all these interests, large or small, profitable; and its benefits can be taken from the large only under the penalty of taking them from the small also."

It is true that legislation upon the tariff or any other subject must come first from Congress before the President is required to approve or veto a measure. But it is also true that the Constitution authorizes the President to recommend legislation to Congress. He may also call an extra session for the consideration of any legislation important enough to warrant it. In all the world there is no position of power comparable to that of the exalted office of President of the United States, and a message from him, setting forth the reasons why the public interest requires legislation upon any subjects for which there is pressing need, if ignored by Congress, at once puts that body upon the defensive before the people.

Did President Roosevelt in all the years of his administration, when these tariff and trust made prices were wrongfully taking hundreds of millions of dollars from the consumers, send a ringing message to Congress recommending tariff revision downward? Did he issue a proclamation calling an extra session for tariff revision, thereby putting the subject up to Congress in a way to compel action? He did neither.

He knew, as all men knew, that the combinations between manufacturers for the control of prices, made tariff revision imperative. Furthermore, he well understood that the Dingley rates when enacted were so high as to be practically prohibitory on nearly all of the necessaries of life; that since the enactment of the Dingley law, through invention, the use of electricity and the adoption of modern methods, the cost of producing the manufactured products had been revolutionized; that the cost to the consumer could have been enormously reduced, still leaving the manufacturer a larger profit than formerly, and for that reason alone duties should have been correspondingly lowered.

He could not altogether ignore the subject. It was too pressing for that. But in his messages he was most guarded in his occasional brief references to the tariff, and you will search the record in vain for any clear, strong declaration favoring a prompt tariff revision to lift the unjust burdens from the people. He gave Cannon and Aldrich the very support they needed to maintain their standpat position, and touched the subject now and then with a deftness that enabled him to escape, for the time, being classed as a standpatter himself.

That he not only was a standpatter, backing and cooperating with standpat leaders in legislation, but gave the great weight of presidential influence to perpetuate their reactionary rule, as late as the middle of his second term, is proven out of his own mouth.

In 1906, when Cannon was at the height of his domination of legislation in the House of Representatives, appointing all the committees, controlling with iron hand all the proceedings, blocking tariff legislation, juggling with labor legislation and with the bill for the publicity of campaign expenses, palming off on the public the Hepburn Railway Rate Bill, with its bushel of chaff and only a grain or two of wheat, Roosevelt on the eighteenth day of August, 1906, wrote from Oyster Bay to Honorable James E. Watson, Member of Congress—the same Watson who was floor manager for the Taft organization in the Chicago convention of 1912—to be used as a campaign appeal for votes, a letter from which I quote the following:

"With Mr. Cannon as speaker, the House has accomplished a literally phenomenal amount of work. It has shown a courage, good sense, and patriotism, such that it would be a real and serious misfortune for the country to fail to recognize. To change the leadership and organization of the House at this time means to bring confusion upon those who have been successfully engaged in the steady working out of a great and comprehensive scheme for the betterment of social, industrial, and civic conditions. Such a change would substitute a purposeless and violent and hurtful oscillation between the positions of the extreme radical and the extreme reactionary, for the present orderly progress along the lines of a carefully thought out policy. . . . It is not too much to say that the courage of Congress within the last few years, *and the hearty agreement* between the executive and legislative departments of the nation, in conducting the needed action each within its own sphere, have resulted with the nation for the first time definitely entering upon the career of proper performance of duty in these matters."

Finally, as he drew on toward the close of his second term, the cumulative effect of years of outcry for a reduction of tariff duties had brought about a situation so tense and critical that Roosevelt felt compelled to deal more at length with the subject, and to indicate that the public might hope for tariff revision in the course of time. In his message of December 2, 1907, he said:

"It is probably well that every dozen years or so the tariff laws should be carefully scrutinized, so as to see that no excessive or improper benefits are conferred thereby."

But however much it might cost the consumer every day, Roosevelt did not propose to disturb his pleasant relations with the big manufacturing trusts. So he made it very plain that Congress ought not to undertake tariff revision under his administration—saying that it was a bad time to revise the tariff on the eve of a presidential election. He had skilfully "staved it off" through all of the years since he became President, and he now had a "good excuse" to offer for its further postponement for the remaining thirteen months of his term. To this end, he added:

"The subject cannot with wisdom be dealt with in the year preceding a presidential election, because as a matter of fact experience has conclusively shown that at such a time it is impossible to get men to treat it from the standpoint of the public good. In my judgment the wise time to deal with the matter is immediately after such election."

And then, when the session of 1907 and '08 was so far advanced that no tariff revision could possibly be undertaken, he transmitted a special message to Congress on the tariff, in which he said:

"The time has come when we should *prepare* for a revision of the tariff."

The time had not come to revise, but only to "prepare" to revise the tariff.

It was inevitable that tariff revision involving tariff reductions such as were vital, especially if it was to result in any relief to the consumer, would incur the hostility of the powerful trusts and combinations. And so, as in all the great emergencies in Roosevelt's public life, we find him carefully steering the middle course. He was determined not to incur the animosity of the standpatters by urging thorough tariff revision; yet he said just enough in its favor at just the right time to leave with the people the impression that he had not wholly ignored their interests.

Nothing better illustrates the Roosevelt method of dealing with public questions than his course upon the tariff while he was President.

No review of Roosevelt's tariff record is complete which does not include his editorial comment on the Payne-Aldrich Law in the *Outlook* of September 17, 1910, quoted in an earlier chapter, in which he said:

"I think that the present tariff is better than the last, and considerably better than the one before the last."

To which must be added his declaration in the New York State platform in 1910 which strongly approved the Payne-Aldrich law, and "enthusiastically endorsed the progressive and statesmanlike leadership of William Howard Taft."

One could not consider Roosevelt as the proposed leader of the Progressive Republican cause without remembering his relations with Morgan, Gary, Frick, Perkins, Harriman, Hill, Gould, Morton and others—the very men who were building up the greatest railroad and trust combinations of the country. In such a crisis, men calling themselves Progressives might ignore the damaging evidence of this connection, but I could not contemplate Roosevelt as the Progressive Republican standard bearer in the face of these disclosures. Who could doubt the meaning of this letter to E. H. Harriman?

"WHITE HOUSE,
"WASHINGTON, October 14, 1904.

"MY DEAR MR. HARRIMAN:

"A suggestion has come to me in a roundabout way that you do not think it wise to come to see me in these closing days of the campaign, but that you are reluctant to refuse, inasmuch as I have asked you.

"Now, my dear sir, you and I are practical men and you are on the ground and know conditions better than I do. If you think there is any danger of your visit to me causing trouble, or if you think there is nothing special I should be informed about, or no matter in which I could give any aid, why, of course, give up the visit for the time being; and then, a few weeks hence, before I write my message, I shall get you to come down to discuss certain government matters not connected with the campaign.

"With great regard, sincerely yours,

"THEODORE ROOSEVELT."

Roosevelt made the claim that this letter was written not with a view of soliciting Harriman's aid for himself, but to secure Harriman's financial assistance to save the New York Republican state ticket in the election of 1904. On that point he is overwhelmed by the letter which Harriman wrote on January 2, 1906, to Mr. Sidney Webster of New York, more than a year afterward.

From this letter it appears that the New York State ticket was not only in danger, but that the state was "doubtful as to Roosevelt himself"; that Roosevelt invited Harriman to come to Washington "to confer on the political conditions in New York State"; that Roosevelt told Harriman that "the campaign could not be successfully carried on without sufficient money," and asked him if he "would help them raise the necessary funds, as the National Committee under the control of Chairman Cortelyou had utterly failed of obtaining them, and there was a large amount due from them [the National Committee] to the New York State committee." Harriman explained to Roosevelt that the difficulty in New York was mainly "caused by the up-state leaders being unwilling to support Depew for re-election to the United States Senate; that if he [Depew] could be taken care of in some other way, matters could be adjusted, and the different contending elements in the party brought into close alliance again." Roosevelt and Harriman talked over what could be done for Depew, and finally Roosevelt agreed that "if found necessary" he "would appoint him Ambassador to Paris."

Harriman says in his letter to Webster:

"With full belief that he, the President, would keep this agreement, I came back to New York, sent for Treasurer Bliss (of the National Committee) who told me I was their last hope and that they had exhausted every other resource. In his presence I called up an intimate friend of Senator Depew, told him that it was necessary in order to carry New York State that $200,000 should be raised at once and that if he would help, I would subscribe $50,000. After a few words over the telephone, the gentleman said he would let me know, which he did probably in three or four hours with the result that the whole amount, including my subscription had been raised. The checks were given to Secretary Bliss who took them to Chairman Cortelyou. If there were any among them of life insurance companies or any other like organizations, of course Cortelyou must have informed the President. . . . This amount enabled the New York State committee to continue to work with the result that at least 50,000 votes were turned in the city of

305

New York alone, making a difference of 100,000 votes in the general result.

"Sometime in November 1904, on my way from Virginia to New York, I stopped and had a short talk with the President. He then told me that he did not think it necessary to appoint Depew as Ambassador to Paris, as agreed, in fact favored him for the Senate. . . ."

It appears from Harriman's letter that Roosevelt preferred to have Depew in the United States Senate rather than appoint him as Ambassador to France. Depew was at that time a director in seventy-four of the combinations controlling the business of the country. For forty years he had been the representative of special interests. He was approaching the close of his first term in the Senate. During that time the record of his votes shows him to be arrayed on every question in favor of special privilege as against the public interest. And in the face of this record, Roosevelt "favored him for the Senate."

This correspondence placed Roosevelt in the position of a solicitor of funds from Harriman and others, representing powerful interests, which became so dominant during Roosevelt's administration, and it is clear that he sought these funds, not only in aid of the state ticket but because, as Harriman says, the state "was doubtful as to Roosevelt himself"; and besides the National Committee was in debt to the New York State Central Committee. Harriman raised this large fund of $200,000, contributing besides $50,000 himself.

But this is not all. Roosevelt's letter of October 14th to Harriman is very significant in many ways. He says: "If you think there is any danger of your visit to me causing trouble, or if you think there is nothing special I should be informed about, or no matter in which I could give any aid, why, of course, give up the visit for the time being." What was there between these two men that led Candidate Roosevelt to think there might be something "special" which Harriman should inform him about? What "matter" was there in which he (Roosevelt) might "give any aid"? And why did he want to see "a few weeks hence, before I write my message," this great master of the highways of commerce, who was also a potential force in the consolidation of the great banking interests for the control of money and credits then under way, and one of the twenty-three directors of the Standard Oil bank, which through various connections then represented more than three hundred and fifty banks, trust companies, railroads, and industrial corporations with an aggregate capitalization of more than $12,000,000,000?

In this connection I remembered that two important suits brought by the Government against the Central Pacific Railroad

Company et al., and the Southern Pacific Railroad Company, et al., and pending when Harriman made his $250,000 contribution were thereafter dismissed in the early part of the year 1905 following Roosevelt's election. Joseph H. Call of California was the special counsel employed to prosecute these cases. Mr. Roosevelt's Attorney-General ordered them dismissed, not through Mr. Call, the special counsel, or upon his advice. Roosevelt's Attorney-General did not appoint Call as special counsel to commence the suit to dissolve the so-called Harriman merger of these two and other lines. This suit was based upon an investigation and report of the Interstate Commerce Commission No. 943 entitled, "In the Matter of Consolidations and Combinations of Carriers," etc. In this report the Commission states that these two lines, the Central Pacific Railroad and the Southern Pacific Railroad, were competing parallel lines across the continent, and had been consolidated together and operated through a holding company called the Southern Pacific Company. This suit was decided against the Government by the Judges of the United States Circuit Court, Eighth Circuit, June 25, 1911. An inspection of this reported case will show that for some mysterious reason the Government *did not join as defendants* these two wrongdoers—the Southern Pacific Railroad Company and the Central Pacific Railroad Company. And moreover, strange as it may seem, the bill *did not charge or allege* that a combination to monopolize commerce or restrain trade had been formed between those two great competing lines; but, on the contrary, the bill admitted that these two lines had been combined in the Southern Pacific Company, the holding corporation, and started out with that fact. The result was that *no decree* could be entered dissolving the combination, as it was not complained of, and because the parties were not before the court a judgment was entered against the Government. That case is now pending upon appeal in the United States Supreme Court; but whatever the outcome, it cannot result in separating these two great lines, because that relief *is not sought by the bill.*

In this suit brought by the Government, under the Roosevelt administration, against Harriman lines, why did his Attorney-General fail to make the Southern Pacific Railroad Company and the Central Pacific Railroad Company parties defendant in that action? Without charging that the contributions made and secured by Mr. Harriman, amounting to $250,000, were for the express purpose of securing a dismissal of the pending suits against the Southern Pacific and the entering of what would appear to be a collusive judgment against the Government in favor of the combi-

307

nation, it would seem that Roosevelt or some one for him ought to explain this whole matter in connection with the contributions.

The proceedings in this case are strikingly analogous to another brought by President Roosevelt's direction on the twenty-eighth of May, 1908, entitled, "The United States of America, Complainant, vs. New York, New Haven & Hartford Railroad Company, Boston & Maine Railroad Company, and the Providence Securities Company, Defendants."

The petition in this case was filed in the Circuit Court of the United States for the District of Massachusetts, and alleged an unlawful combination in restraint of trade, in violation of the Sherman Anti-Trust Law. This case is familiarly known as the New Haven Merger case. The basis of the Government's action was the acquisition by the New Haven, of the Boston & Maine steam railroad, and various New England trolley lines engaged for the most part in conducting intra-state transportation, but which were so connected with one another as to constitute interstate lines, engaged in interstate trade or commerce.

The weakness of the Government's case was the difficulty which it would encounter in proving that the trolley lines were engaged in interstate trade to such an extent as to constitute lines in competition with the New Haven in interstate traffic. Not only had the New Haven acquired the railroad and trolley lines described in the petition, but practically *every steamship line* engaged in interstate commerce, competing against the New Haven's combined steam and trolley lines, between New England and New York. If the complaint had covered the acquisition of the steamship lines by the New Haven Company, through which it suppressed the water competition with its railroad lines, the Government's case would have been absolutely perfect.

Before this action was begun all New England was in ferment over the consolidation, and United States District Attorney French for the District of Massachusetts, assisted by Louis D. Brandeis, conducted an investigation which, after conferences between the District Attorney, Mr. Brandeis, President Roosevelt, and the Department of Justice, resulted in the commencement of the action.

It was made plain to the President and his Attorney-General that the acquisition of the steamship lines by the New Haven constituted a substantial foundation for the action; that while the action might be maintained, if the petition charged only the combination of the railroad and trolley lines, the Government could prove a perfectly plain violation of the Anti-Trust Law if the proper allegations were incorporated in the bill covering the merger of the steamship lines as well.

Before the petition was signed and filed, Morgan's representative, President Mellen of the New Haven, who brought about the whole combination, called upon President Roosevelt, and persuaded him to have omitted from the bill of complaint all reference to the acquisition of the steamship lines.

Roosevelt's compliance with Mellen's request in this regard greatly weakened the case, making it much easier for Attorney-General Wickersham to dismiss the Government's action, which he did within three months after Roosevelt retired, leaving all New England at the mercy of this monster transportation monopoly. This juggling with the Sherman Act resulted in traffic conditions so desperately bad that the Interstate Commerce Commission on its own motion is, at the time of this writing, conducting an investigation which discloses an intolerable situation.

While this obliging concession made by Roosevelt to Morgan's man Mellen took away the strongest prop sustaining the Government's case, nevertheless if Attorney-General Wickersham, in the performance of his plain duty, had amended the Government's petition by proper allegations setting out the facts regarding the steamship lines, and zealously prosecuted instead of dismissing the merger case, he could have fully protected the public interest. But the fact remains that President Roosevelt, through his concessions to President Mellen, opened the way for Wickersham to permit the New Haven merger to escape the penalties of the Sherman Anti-Trust Law.

The Northern Securities case against the Morgan-Hill railroad combination, seems to have pointed the way. This case was brought under the Sherman Law, by Roosevelt's orders in 1902. As his record shows, he was not especially fond of this law, and later openly denounced it, saying its "enforcement would destroy the business of the country." The public was demanding the prosecution of the railroad and other combinations, and some show of compliance with the public demand must be made!

In the Northern Securities case the Government "won," but some way, the victory seemed to be *barren of results*. The railroad combination survived. The poor old Sherman Law was of course "responsible." But let us see why: In this case it was charged that the Northern Pacific and Great Northern railroads, two parallel continental lines, had combined with the Chicago, Burlington and Quincy Railroad to destroy competition and to create a monopoly in transportation. The Government's attorneys in preparing the decree strangely omitted to provide for the dissolution of the combination and conspiracy between the competing and parallel lines; and likewise omitted from the decree the provision that those competing lines be required thereafter to operate independently each through its own board of directors and officers.

The effect of this abortive decree was to leave the combination in full force and operation through a holding company or trust agreement. This defeated the very purpose for which the action was brought and left the Government nothing. Furthermore, the decision entered in that case operated to increase the capital stock of the monopoly one hundred million dollars as a burden upon transportation. That monopoly still exists, with Roosevelt's friend Perkins as one of the directors.

In an earlier chapter I have suggested the opposition encountered throughout my administration as governor, to the enactment of the direct primary, the railroad, and all other Progressive legislation. In considering Roosevelt as the candidate, and a suitable representative of Progressive principles, I could not fail to remember how he had thrown the weight of presidential influence on the side of that opposition throughout our long struggle in Wisconsin. And it was long and bitter. One little word of encouragement, publicly spoken by President Roosevelt, one act of friendly recognition, however slight, would have been as new wine to our battered forces fighting in the gray dawn of this Progressive movement.

But instead, President Roosevelt was then a scoffer, ever ready with expressions of contempt and warning, to be borne back to Wisconsin and planted where they would be most hurtful. And then came the full weight of the administration's appointing power, as a backing to the Standpat-Stalwart reactionary enemy we were fighting, which Roosevelt reinforced with an army of federal officeholders. The representatives of the railroads and combined corporations were very strong, but the support of the Roosevelt administration, meant many more defeats for us and added many a heart-breaking year to our long continued contest.

Henry C. Payne was to Wisconsin what Mark Hanna—with whom he was intimately associated—was to the country. Mark Hanna, representing Big Business, wanted Payne in McKinley's cabinet. I protested. McKinley refused, saying as stated in an earlier chapter, that he would not appoint a man in his cabinet who was known to be a lobbyist. But immediately after McKinley's death, Roosevelt appointed Payne Postmaster-General, placing this adroit manipulator at the head of a force of four thousand postmasters who would take his orders and do his bidding in the Wisconsin fight. In the appointment of Payne, Roosevelt dealt the Progressive cause a body blow.

Joseph W. Babcock, for many years a member of Congress from the Third Wisconsin District, was Chairman of the Congressional Campaign Committee. It was his office to "fry the fat" out of the manufacturers, brewers, railroads, and other special interests, with which to aid in carrying on the campaigns, and thereafter, with Cannon and two or three other members of the inner circle, it was Babcock's business to see to it that no legislation detrimental to special interests should be permitted to go through the House.

Babcock's district was one of the most progressive in Wisconsin. It had a normal majority of eight to ten thousand. The Progressives in his district sought to overthrow him. But with money and offices, the one supplied by the business interests which he served, and the other by the Roosevelt administration, with which he was a favorite, he managed to hold fast to the control of his district. Babcock was not only obnoxious to the Progressive Republicans of his district, but to those of the entire state as well. He took charge of the Standpat campaign against my nomination in 1904. Defeated by the Progressive Republicans in that campaign, Babcock was one of the Standpat leaders who bolted, organized a rump convention, placed a reactionary state ticket in the field, and had himself, Spooner, and two other reactionaries "elected" as delegates to the Republican National Convention, which nominated Roosevelt in 1904. These "delegates" contested the right of the four regularly elected delegates-at-large—of which I was one —to seats in that convention; and without any color of right we were thrown out and they were seated by the National Committee. The Supreme Court of Wisconsin subsequently decided that our convention was the regular Republican Convention.

Babcock's record as a Standpat corporation-serving Congressman was notorious. He was opposed to everything which the Progressive Republican administration in Wisconsin represented, and he fought my renomination and that of every member of our Progressive legislative ticket in 1902. Following this campaign Roosevelt commended Babcock's campaign methods and expressed gratification that they had been able to work so harmoniously, in the following personal letter:

"WHITE HOUSE, WASHINGTON, D. C.
"November 6, 1902.

"Personal.
"MY DEAR BABCOCK:

"I feel that you and your colleagues, Mr. Overstreet, Mr. Hull [both Standpatters], and the others, are entitled to the hearty thanks of every good Republican. I wish to express my appreciation of all that you have done, my delight at the way we have been able to work together, and my astonishment at the accuracy of your forecasts.

"Faithfully yours,
"THEODORE ROOSEVELT."

In 1904 the Progressive Republicans of Babcock's district vigorously contested his renomination, but were unsuccessful. Babcock in this campaign for renomination made effective use of this letter, for which he must have had Roosevelt's special permission, as it was a personal letter from the President, and would not otherwise have been given publicity. It was printed in Wisconsin papers under the heading "Endorsed by Roosevelt." He was nominated, and elected by the scant majority of 326 in a district which he had carried two years before by over eight thousand. Two years later Roosevelt's "influence" did not save him.

The foregoing is given as first hand evidence that Babcock was the kind of Congressman that Roosevelt wanted in control of legislation in the House of Representatives while he was President.

In 1904 Roosevelt wrote a characteristic letter to Chairman Cortelyou of the Republican National Committee, which he has since quoted as evidence that he "took sides" with the Wisconsin Progressives in that campaign. The letter in part ran as follows:

"I think Babcock and his people should be told that, especially in view of the decision of the Supreme Court, there must not be any kind of favoritism shown by us toward the 'Stalwarts.' Under the decision of the Supreme Court any weakening of the La Follette ticket is a *weakening of the national ticket.*"

Nineteen hundred and four was a presidential year, and Roosevelt was a candidate himself. "Any weakening of the La Follette ticket is a weakening of the national ticket," he warns Cortelyou. This letter was in the nature of a reversal of orders to meet the changed conditions. We were no longer in the minority, fighting the fight for principle; we were in the majority, and the decision of the Supreme Court had established our status.

312

Speaker Cannon agreed entirely with Roosevelt's estimate of Babcock's worth. In a letter written in 1903 to Calvert Spensley, Mineral Point, Wis., and published in connection with Roosevelt's as above quoted, Cannon gives it as his judgment that "his (Babcock's) continuance in public life is a matter of concern, not only to his own district and state, but to the whole country." To this he adds: "You will notice from the organization of the House, the responsibility having been placed upon myself to *make the committees,* that Mr. Babcock succeeds himself as a member of the Committee on Ways and Means and as Chairman of the Committee on the District of Columbia."

This surely was a tribute to Babcock's "reliability"!

As further evidence of Roosevelt's aggressive hostility to the Progressive cause in Wisconsin, let the record tell the story: The holder of every important federal office in the state was a persistent lobbyist in close attendance upon the legislature, session after session, using the power and influence of his position under Roosevelt to defeat every Progressive measure. They were bitter in their opposition to direct primaries, to the regulation of railway rates and services, to railway taxation, to the reduction of passenger rates, to the prohibition of rebating, to a corrupt practices act, to pure food legislation—in short, to the entire Progressive program. Members of the legislature pledged to support these measures, betrayed their constituents and were rewarded with lucrative appointments by President Roosevelt in the Treasury Department, the Interior Department, and the foreign service. Federal judgeships were bestowed upon Reactionaries and Standpatters. Owners of newspapers supporting the Progressive state administration faced about, became hostile, and promptly received important appointments abroad.

The opposition of the Roosevelt administration to our Progressive movement in Wisconsin was four years old. We had achieved success despite it, and success can afford to forget. I recalled it at this time only in reviewing Roosevelt's official acts to determine the soundness and sincerity of his late professions as a Progressive Republican.

And at a later date, in 1910, in my campaign for reelection to the United States Senate when, as George W. Perkins afterward admitted to Charles R. Crane, "Wall Street was drained dry" to secure my defeat, Roosevelt, to quote from *The Public,* "skilfully managed to speak in Wisconsin just after the primaries instead of just before." It was the day following the primaries. I had been nominated by more than one hundred thousand majority. All the Progressives of Wisconsin were rejoicing, and messages of congratulation were coming from Progressives of every state. Roosevelt spoke in Milwaukee, and of this speech *The Public* says further: "And when he did speak in Wisconsin after La Follette carried the primaries, why was he so eloquently silent about La Follette?"

Furthermore, it is a fact in political history that Progressive success in every Republican state was secured despite the opposition of the Roosevelt administration, during the seven years that he was President. And during that same period, Progressive Republican Senators and Progressive Republican members of the House of Representatives, as candidates to succeed Standpatters, fought their way to the American Congress against the active influence of Roosevelt, put forth to retain reactionaries in the public service, sometimes by verbal message, sometimes by open letter.

I recite these facts only as a part of the history of the Progressive struggle, and the real attitude of Roosevelt to it, and this too, but a few years ago. Like the flash of a searchlight, they reveal the true relation of his administration to the most hardened types of interest-serving reactionaries. Also they help us to understand why, with outward manifestations of Progressivism, he did so little for the Progressive movement nationally, and so much directly and so much more indirectly for the great combinations of capital during the years that he was President.

Even those who urged Roosevelt's candidacy as the expedient thing, were forced to admit that he was not really Progressive; that he shifted his ground; qualified his positions; compromised important issues; that nobody knew from his record that he would be found to-morrow where he stood to-day. But they justified their course by reasoning that the Progressive movement had become so powerful that, if elected, public opinion would *compel* Roosevelt to be Progressive.

My repeated experiences with him, while he was President had, from time to time, been very trying. Furthermore, his determination to be a candidate for the presidency and to be the *Progressive Republican candidate* had now, for the first time, forced upon me the necessity of making a thorough study of his record upon the issues that were undermining Democracy—the issues which had made the Progressive movement necessary to the preservation of representative government.

I had many times emphasized the good things in Roosevelt's record. On several occasions, when he professed a determination to aid in some fundamentally important Progressive legislation, as for example, the valuation of railroads, I was much impressed, and led to believe that after all he could be relied on, and to feel that if this man with his forcefulness and popular following were once thoroughly enlisted, no one could be more serviceable to the Progressive movement. At such times I gave free expression to my feeling, and then he would disappoint me by doing the expedient thing, yielding the principle or shifting completely to the opposition.

It was one thing, however, to refer generously to the best side of Roosevelt's administration; it was quite another thing to consider Roosevelt as the Progressive candidate for the presidency for a third term, with all that it would mean to the Progressive cause which, when once committed to him, would become responsible for, and bound by everything he said or did. Into this man's hands it was proposed to commit the future of a movement with great national promise, at a critical period in its life that would—as that leadership was loyal to principle or served expediency—establish it as a lasting power for good, or render it merely a transitory and time-serving thing of the hour.

Passing the consideration of the sincerity of his convictions, upon his record alone I could not, in good conscience, accept him as a Progressive candidate for the Republican presidential nomination. His record gave no assurance of profound conviction, or that he was equipped with patience, determination, and experience to deal with great social and economic problems constructively in the public interest.

And lastly, his course in connection with my own candidacy had destroyed my faith in his integrity of character in any matter conflicting with his self-interest.

It was plain to be seen, when Roosevelt rushed into the contest, that he would divide the Progressives and destroy all chance of Progressive control of the Republican convention, as he finally did. But believing that his control of any Progressive movement, independent or otherwise, would be fatal to it, and with supreme confidence that the leadership of the Republican party would ultimately become Progressive as the great body of its rank and file, I determined to fight on for the preservation of the Progressive movement within the Republican party. The reasons for so doing seemed to me to be very strong.

What is known as the Progressive movement had originated within the Republican party, the rank and file of which is not now and never has been subservient to privilege in any form.

While special interests had been increasing their hold upon the administrative side of government at Washington, Progressive Republicans in many staunch Republican states had wrested the control from these interests, and enacted statutes restoring representative government to the people of those states. The reforms wrought out in Wisconsin, Minnesota, North and South Dakota, Iowa, Kansas, Nebraska, Washington, Oregon, and California were secured under Republican leadership and through Republican legislation.

This was a most encouraging situation. But it was not all. In practically every state, except in the South, where there is no real Republican organization, the most of the Republican voters were struggling to overcome reactionary control. This takes time, because a well-organized political machine is able to maintain its rule for a considerable period after an overwhelming majority of the voters of the party are in open revolt against it. But the Progressive element in the Republican party had, in four years, made such strides toward mastery, that it is not too much to say that the national convention of 1912 would have been a genuinely Progressive convention, except for the fact that Roosevelt forced his way into the campaign, divided and demoralized the Progressive forces, swept aside the consideration of issues involving Progressive principles, and converted the contest with Taft into a campaign so bitterly personal that by the time of the Chicago convention the passions aroused upon both sides subordinated everything to a fierce scramble to seat delegates by hook or crook, and secure the nomination. It should not be forgotten that the differences that split the Republican party in two were not based on a platform of principles, but upon the question as to which one of two men should secure the nomination. Fraud and bribery were charged upon both sides. Tempers were at white heat. Threats of personal violence were common. Investigation was baffled. There was no chance for argument. The truth was discounted. Lies were as good as facts. The Roosevelt men charged that the Taft men were stealing the convention. The Taft men charged the Roosevelt men with trying to steal the convention.

And upon this mad squabble for office between Taft and Roosevelt under whose administrations the Republican party had made the trust, tariff, and special interest records for which it was most criticised, Roosevelt proposed to destroy a sound and vital Progressive movement which had already gone far to nationalize itself within a great and powerful organization.

Roosevelt's views respecting the establishment of a third party, a little more than a year before, were disclosed on the occasion of his visit to Madison in the spring of 1911. On his way from the executive residence, where he had been entertained, to the assembly chamber, where he was to speak, he said to Governor McGovern, Lieutenant-Governor Morris, and Speaker Ingram:

"By the way, I wish I could have a chance to talk with you boys about some matters in which I am deeply interested. I am afraid La Follette will start a new party. I do not want to see that happen. I am disappointed with Taft. But I do not want to see La Follette start a new party and create division. You fellows here are in a position to reach him. I wish you would see him and do all you can to prevent his taking that course."

In 1911 Roosevelt thought it would be a great calamity to divide the Republican party. It was a good party then. The only thing that made it so bad as to deserve being riven asunder was that it would not nominate him for a third term in 1912.

Even though a political convention, through passion, intrigue, or corruption, should fail to represent the will of the millions who constitute a political party, with inspiring traditions and Progressive achievement in many states, and real Progressive promise nationally, it seemed very clear to me that such failure should not be permitted to destroy that party.

A political party is not made to order. It is the slow development of powerful forces working in our social life. Sound ideas seize upon the human mind. Opinions ripen into fixed convictions. Masses of men are drawn together by common belief and organized about clearly defined principles. From time to time this organized body expresses its purpose and names candidates to represent its principles. The millions cannot be assembled. Until direct nominations and the rigid control of campaign expenditures shall prevail they must seek to express their will through the imperfect agencies of congressional, state, and national conventions. These agencies are not the party. They are temporarily delegated to represent the millions who constitute the party. If recreant to their trust the party may suffer the temporary defeat of its purposes. But what abject folly to seek upon such a basis to destroy a great political party seven millions strong, with a clear Progressive majority in its ranks, within which there has been built up a Progressive movement that promises to make the Republican party the instrument through which government shall be completely restored to the people.

I would in no degree disparage the good work of Progressive Democrats. Encouraged by Bryan's support of Progressive principles, many Democrats in Wisconsin and other states abandoned their party on state issues and supported the Republican Progressive program. And it was Bryan's superb leadership and courage at Baltimore which nominated a candidate for the presidency who had made a progressive record as governor of New Jersey.

In no partisan spirit, therefore, I have contended that the Progressive movement began within the Republican party. It rapidly advanced its control, shaping policies of state administrations, and stamping its impress upon national legislation as a distinctly Progressive Republican movement. And upon that fact in recent political history I appealed to Progressive Republicans everywhere to maintain their organization within the Republican party. To maintain such organization, blind allegiance to every party nomination and to every party declaration is never essential.

The situation in Congress was supremely important. Democrats had been in the majority in the House of Representatives. That control had been partisan rather than progressive. The leaders in the House and the Democratic majority on the principal committees had not marked out a progressive course. Going just far enough to placate those content to accept form instead of substance, they had never gone far enough to endanger special interest control in legislation.

The crisis in the Republican party, with greater reason than at any time since 1892, had aroused hope of Democratic success nationally. In view of the present control of the House and the attitude of the strong Democratic leaders of the Senate, Democratic victory carried with it small assurance of progressive gains in legislation. Interest control in Congress may change its party label and still be powerful in determining the character of the legislation enacted.

It was time for Progressive Republicans to act with the greatest deliberation.

The course pursued by Roosevelt and Taft in the campaign and at the Chicago convention destroyed all hope of a Progressive Republican victory in the presidential contest for 1912. But there remained a most important service to be rendered by the strong Progressive element in the Republican party. In a large number of Republican states there had been enacted definitely related Progressive statutes based on scientific research which had reconstructed state government, vitalizing it with human interest. There were legislatures to elect, to carry forward this and other creative work. There were Progressive Republican governors and state officers to elect, to administer and safeguard these statutes and lead the way along advancing lines.

In Congress the Progressive Republicans in the Senate and House had furnished the only consistent Progressive program of legislation. The bills offered and pressed for action had shown real constructive statesmanship. This splendid body of fighting Progressive Republicans forced Aldrichism and Cannonism to the last ditch, exposed the iniquities of the Tariff bill of 1909, tore to pieces the pernicious Railroad bill of 1910, recasting it into a measure in the public interest, and, acting in unison, gave Progressive Republican principles a distinct character of commanding importance throughout the country.

After the disaster in 1912 to the Progressive Republican campaign, occasioned by the determination of Roosevelt to be nominated for a third term, or destroy all chance of making the Republican party nationally Progressive, the restoration of the Progressive group in the Senate, as shown by its action on the wool bill and other tariff measures in the closing days of the Second Session of the Sixty-second Congress, attested the validity of its principles. It required only the occasion and the issue to demonstrate the fundamental integrity of the Progressive movement within the Republican party.

It was my contention that this great constructive work, in state and national government, the result of years of patient and intelligent effort within the Republican party, should not be imperilled; that the election of Progressive Republican governors, legislators, Congressmen, and United States Senators should not be jeopardized to make a new party for Roosevelt, who in no sense represented the high ideals of those who made the Republican party Progressive, in many states against his opposition, and who nationalized Progressive policies in his absence from the country.

With Roosevelt and his party, it was solely a question of personal ascendency and control. This was shown by the course taken in various states where true Progressive Republicans were candidates for Congress and for the United States Senate. Unless they followed him and his party, Roosevelt threatened every Progressive Republican United States Senator and Congressman with defeat, by bringing out candidates against them in their districts and states. Likewise, he promised no opposition to the Deneens, the Cannons, and the strongest Standpat types in the Republican party, if they would only declare for him, instead of Taft. To win personally, for the hour, was all in all to Roosevelt.

On him and those who made this war upon Republican Progressive achievement and Republican Progressive candidates rests a grave responsibility.

It was clear to me that the highest obligation of real Progressive Republicans in every state was to maintain their organization and continue to fight within the lines of the Republican party for Progressive principles, policies, and candidates. I felt that no aid or encouragement should be given to a third party plan to divide the Progressive vote and destroy the Progressive Republican movement; that no break should be permitted in the Progressive ranks which would endanger the election of any true Progressive Republican anywhere; that every effort should be put forth to increase the number of thorough-going Progressive Republicans in the United States Senate and the House of Representatives; that the election of a strong body of Progressive Republicans in both branches of Congress might enable them to hold the balance of power in legislation; that that balance would serve as a check upon any President, if reactionary, and if Progressive, would aid him to wring from reactionary opposition in both houses, legislation to protect public interest.

There was every reason for conserving the Progressive Republican organization.

Years before in Wisconsin we had precisely the same condition —the Republican party, with the mass of its membership ready for Progressive legislation, and a leadership bound to the service of special interests. We forced the retirement of the reactionary leaders, and made the Republican party the best possible instrument for achieving representative government.

I believed we could do nationally with the Republican party what we did with it in Wisconsin. I still believe so. Within a few years, such progress has been made in this direction as to justify that belief. It is my conviction that this will sooner bring government back to the people than will be done through the medium of a new and untried party organization. This was most emphatically true when that new party had for its leader the man, under whose administrations, the Republican party made much of the record for which it is most severely condemned.

For these reasons I shall remain in the Republican party at this time. I shall continue to denounce its representatives when they betray public interest. I shall refuse to be bound by its action whenever it fails in its duty to the country, and I shall do all in my power to restore it to the high place in the service and confidence and affection of the American people, which it held when it was the party of Abraham Lincoln. If it shall fail to become thoroughly Progressive as a national party, I shall then stand ready to take such further action as shall seem to serve best the interests of the country.

Through the pages of this autobiography, I have dealt with certain governmental problems, state and national, upon which, during the past twenty-five years, I have studied and reflected. I have touched on these issues only as they were related to my experience, it having been no part of my plan to treat them exhaustively. But my own story could not have been complete without a discussion incidentally, of certain questions of public concern which, from early manhood, have been a part of my daily thinking. With maturer years, the fundamental principles of democracy involved have worked themselves profoundly into my convictions, and the struggle could not have been sustained, year after year, often in the face of disappointment and defeat, had I felt less deeply the eternal justice of the end sought to be attained.

I have never assumed to say that I had worked out to the last conclusion the solution of all these complex problems. But years of plodding investigation convinced me of the economic soundness of my basis, from which I have been content to take the next forward step—always sure of my ground, and sure of my direction.

With the changing phases of a twenty-five-year contest I have been more and more impressed with the deep underlying singleness of the issue. It is not railroad regulation. It is not the tariff, or conservation, or the currency. It is not the trusts. These and other questions are but manifestations of one great struggle. The supreme issue, involving all the others, is *the encroachment of the powerful few upon the rights of the many.* This mighty power has come between the people and their government. Can we free ourselves from this control? Can representative government be restored? Shall we, with statesmanship and constructive legislation, meet these problems, or shall we pass them on, with all the possibilities of conflict and chaos, to future generations?

There never was a higher call to greater service than in this protracted fight for social justice. I believe, with increasing depth of conviction, that we will, in our day, meet our responsibility with fearlessness and faith; that we will reclaim and preserve for our children, not only the form but the spirit of our free institutions. And in our children must we rest our hope for the ultimate democracy.

Speech of
Robert M. La Follette*
Delivered at the
Annual Banquet of the Periodical
Publishers' Association
Philadelphia, February 2, 1912

Mr. Toastmaster, President Curtis, and Gentlemen of the Periodical Publishers' Association:

The great issue before the American people to-day is the control of their own government. In the midst of political struggle, it is not easy to see the historical relations of the present Progressive movement. But it represents a conflict as old as the history of man —the fight to maintain human liberty, the rights of all the people.

A mighty power has been builded up in this country in recent years, so strong, yet so insidious and far-reaching in its influence, that men are gravely inquiring whether its iron grip on government and business can ever be broken. Again and again it has proved strong enough to nominate the candidates of both political parties. It rules in the organization of legislative bodies, state and national, and of the committees which frame legislation. Its influence is felt in cabinets and in the policies of administrations, and is clearly seen in the appointment of prosecuting officers and the selection of judges upon the Bench.

*NOTE: The most important question now before the American people is that of the combined capital represented in trusts, in consolidated railroads, and in the consolidated banking interests, controlling money and credit. I append herewith an address dealing with the history of the growth of this power and some suggestions for meeting its recognized evils.

In business it has crippled or destroyed competition. It has stifled individual initiative. It has fixed limitations in the field of production. It makes prices and imposes its burdens upon the consuming public at will.

In transportation, after a prolonged struggle for government control, it is, with only slight check upon its great power, still master of the highways of commerce.

In finance its power is unlimited. In large affairs it gives or withholds credit, and from time to time contracts or inflates the volume of the money required for the transaction of the business of the country, regardless of everything excepting its own profits.

It has acquired vast areas of the public domain, and is rapidly monopolizing the natural resources—timber, iron, coal, oil.

And this THING has grown up in a country where, under the Constitution and the law, the citizen is sovereign!

The related events which led to this centralized control are essential to a clear understanding of the real danger—the magnitude of this danger now menacing the very existence of every independent concern remaining in the field of business enterprise.

The First Period—The Individual and the Partnership.—For nearly a century after Jefferson declared for a government of "equal rights for all, and special privileges for none," the business of the country was conducted by individuals and partnerships. During this first period business methods were simple, its proportions modest, and there was little call for larger capital than could be readily furnished by the individual or, in the most extreme cases, a partnership of fair size.

From the beginning, when men bartered their products in exchange, down through all the ages, the business of the world had been conducted under the natural laws of trade—demand, supply, competition. Like all natural laws, they were fair and impartial; they favored neither the producer nor the consumer. They had ruled the market and made the prices when the individual and the partnership conducted substantially all commercial enterprises during the first period of our business life.

But as the country developed, as the population poured over the Alleghenies, occupied the Mississippi Valley, pushed on to the Rocky Mountains and down the western slope to California, discovering the boundless wealth of our natural resources—the fields and forests, the mountains of iron and coal and precious metals, there was a pressing call on every hand for larger capital beyond the power of any individual or any partnership to supply. We had outgrown the simple methods; there was a demand for a new business device strong enough to unlock the treasure house of the new world.

The Second Period—The Private Corporation.—The modern corporation was invented to meet that demand, and general statutes for incorporation were soon upon the statute books of every state. Their adoption marked the beginning of the second period of our business life. It was the best machine ever invented for the purpose; simple in organization, effective in operation.

A hundred, a thousand, any number of men could associate their capital, and employing the representative principle upon which our country was based, vote for and elect a president, a general manager, a board of directors, a body of men, no larger than an ordinary partnership, and clothe them with power to conduct the business to the success of which the aggregate capital was contributed.

Men no longer stood baffled by the magnitude of any undertaking, but promptly enlisted an army of contributors, large or small, massed together the required capital and under the direction of the officers and directors of the corporation, a small executive body, seized upon these waiting opportunities, and this second period marked a material development, surpassing anything in the world's history. It was not the era of greatest individual fortune building, but it was the period of greatest general prosperity. And why?

The natural laws of trade—demand, supply and competition—still ruled the market and made the prices in the second period of our business life. The private corporation, in a large measure, supplanted the individual, and the partnership in mining, manufacturing and large commercial enterprises, but each corporation competed with every other in the same line of business. Production was larger, development more rapid, but, under the free play of competition, the resulting prosperity was fairly distributed between the producer and the consumer, the seller and the buyer, because profits and prices were reasonable.

Big capital behind the private corporations drove business at a pace and upon a scale never before witnessed. Competition was at once the spur to the highest efficiency and the check against waste and abuse of power.

In this period of our industrial and commercial progress, America amazed and alarmed our business rivals of the old world. We were soon foremost among the nations of the earth in agriculture, in mines and mining, in manufactures and in commerce as well.

The American market became the greatest thing in all the material world. Its control became the one thing coveted.

The Third Period—The Combination of Corporations.—The evil hour was come upon us. Daring, unscrupulous men plotted in violation of the common law, the criminal statutes and against public right to become masters of that market and take what toll they pleased. To do this thing it was necessary to set aside, abrogate, nullify the natural laws of trade that had ruled in business for centuries. Production was to be limited, competition stifled and prices arbitrarily fixed by selfish decree. And thus we entered upon the third period of our business and commercial life—the period of a combination of the corporations under a single control in each line of business. It was not an evolution; it was a revolution.

And yet certain economists set it down in the literature of the day that the Supreme Ruler of the universe reserved in His great plan a divinely appointed place and time for a Rockefeller, a Morgan, a Carnegie, a Baer, to evolve this new law, which should enable them to appropriate the wealth of the country and Mexicanize its business and its people.

The combination became supreme in each important line, controlling the markets for the raw material and the finished product, largely dictating the price of everything we sell and the price of everything we buy—beef, sugar, woolens, cottons, coal, oil, copper, zinc, iron, steel, agricultural implements, hardware, gas, electric light, food supplies.

Monopoly acquired dominion everywhere.

It brought with it the inevitable results of monopoly—extortionate prices, inferior products. We soon found shoddy in everything we wear, and adulteration in everything we eat.

Did these masters of business stop there? By no means! "Increase of appetite had grown by what it fed on." The floodgates of fictitious capitalization were thrown wide open. These organizations of combinations overcapitalized for a double purpose. The issue of bonds and stocks in excess of investment covered up the exaction of their immense profits, and likewise offered an unlimited field for promotion and speculation.

The establishment of this third period was the beginning of rapidly advancing prices, increasing the cost of living upon people of average earning power until the burden is greater than they can bear.

The Fourth Period—The Combination of Combinations.—The strife for more money, more power—more power, more money—swept everything before it.

It remained only to bring together into a community of interest or ownership the great combinations which controlled, each in its own field—in short, to combine these combinations.

One needs but to study the directory of directories of the great business concerns of the country to determine the extent to which this combination of combinations has been successfully accomplished, thus carrying us over into the fourth period of our industrial and commercial life—the period of complete industrial and commercial servitude in which we now unhappily find ourselves. And this supreme control of the business of the country is the triumph of men who have at every step defied public opinion, the common law and criminal statutes.

This condition is intolerable. It is hostile to every principle of democracy. If maintained it is the end of democracy. We may preserve the form of our representative government and lose the soul, the spirit of our free institutions.

John Sherman, the broadest, clearest visioned statesman of his time, saw this danger away in advance and wisely sought to fortify the government to meet and destroy it.

Of this mighty power he said:

"It is a kingly prerogative, inconsistent with our form of government. If anything is wrong, this is wrong. If we will not endure a king as a political power, we should not endure a king over the production, transportation, and sale of any of the necessities of life. If we would not submit to an emperor, we should not submit to an autocrat of trade with power to prevent competition and to fix the price of any commodity. * * * The remedy should be swift and sure."

Sherman well understood that this government could not exist as a free government with any man or group of men invested with the kingly prerogative over the production, transportation, and sale of any of the necessaries of life. No free people in history very long maintained their political freedom after having once surrendered their industrial and commercial freedom.

The Sherman law placed in the hands of the executive department of this government the most perfect weapon which the ingenuity of man could forge for the protection of the people against the power of monopoly.

It will be the impartial verdict of history that the executive department of government could have saved the people from the appalling conditions which confront us to-day, if all the power of this great government had been put forth to enforce the anti-trust law. Two or three score of prosecutions dragging along in the courts at a snail's pace, from administration to administration, was little more than notice to these business kings that they might proceed to set up their authority against the government and extend their dominion over trade and transportation; that there was no real danger of the law being so enforced as to do much more than to affect the political situation from time to time.

That this was accepted as the government's position by the interests can now be made very plain.

The organization of combinations began quite actively early in 1898. The high tariff rates of the Dingley law encouraged combination and aided in its ultimate purpose.

Between January 1, 1898, and January 1, 1900, 149 trusts were formed to suppress competition and control prices. These combinations were capitalized for $3,784,000,000. The next four years were years of enormous trust growth.

From January 1, 1900, to January 1, 1904, taking account of only the more important trusts, 8,664 great plants were combined, with a total capitalization of $20,379,162,511.

Prices were mounting higher and higher. The people were crying aloud in protest, but protest and denunciation caused no fear on the part of the trust makers, so long as the government was actually prosecuting less than an average of seven cases a year.

Mark what followed: From January 1, 1904, to January 1, 1908, trust consolidation made mighty strides, and the total capitalization reached the astounding sum of $31,672,160,754. In these four years the capitalization increased more than 55 per cent.

The Centralization of Railroad Control.—In the meantime what were the powers doing in the great field of transportation? A swift backward glance reveals the fact that the same system of consolidation, centralized control and suppressed competition had been forced through in violation of law and public right.

The vital interests of organized society in commerce and the public nature of transportation impose upon government the duty to establish and maintain control over common carriers.

To discharge this obligation the government must exact from the common carrier:

(1) Reasonable rates, (2) impartial rates, (3) adequate and impartial services.

The public is interested in adequate and impartial services. The shipper is especially interested in equal and impartial rates. The consumer is especially interested in reasonable rates.

For forty years after railroads were established there was no attempt to invoke governmental control. The public depended solely upon competition between railroads for the protection of public interests.

Finally it learned the elementary lesson that the railroad is a natural monopoly; that there can be no competition excepting at common points, and that at common points the railroads were destroying all competition by pooling agreements.

Then came the demand in 1870 for governmental control—in order to secure reasonable rates. It originated in the upper Mississippi Valley—in Wisconsin, Iowa, Minnesota, and Illinois, for a control of rates within the state.

It spread east and west and became a national movement for controlling interstate commerce.

The supreme courts of the middle western states sustained the state legislation. The Supreme Court of the United States sustained the state courts, and the power of the state and federal governments to control and fix reasonable transportation rates, each in its own sphere, was adjudicated as a public right thirty-eight years ago.

For a generation of time since those decisions the people have struggled to secure an interstate commerce law which would establish and enforce reasonable rates. That was the relief which the consumer, the great body of the people, demanded—reasonable rates.

The shippers have no interest in reasonable rates. They do not pay the freight. The consumer pays the freight. But the shipper is at a disadvantage in supplying his trade unless he has rates relatively equal to those given to other shippers engaged in the same business.

Shippers could easily present concrete cases of injustice. They could readily organize and appear before committees and make their representatives feel their power.

Not so with the consumer, who, in the end, pays all the freight, as a part of the purchase price of everything he buys. He cannot identify the freight charge, because it is a part of the price he pays when he purchases supplies. However small the item, in the aggregate it is important to him. He cannot maintain a lobby. If his United States Senators and his Congressmen do not represent him, he is helpless.

What is the net result of thirty-eight years' struggle with the railroads? Congress enacted the interstate commerce law of 1887; the

Elkins law of 1903; the Hepburn law of 1906; and the recent law of 1910.

Out of all this legislation the shippers have been able to secure a partial enforcement of their contention for an equalization of rates.

The consumers have lost in their long fight for reasonable rates.

After all these years it is not to-day within the power of the interstate commerce commission to take the first step to ascertain a reasonable rate. There is a vast difference between equal rates and reasonable rates.

The consumers are no nearer to securing reasonable rates than they were thirty-eight years ago.

Ninety million people are to-day paying annually to the railroads $2,500,000,000 for transportation—a sum greater than the total cost of maintaining the federal government, the state governments, the county governments, and all the municipal governments of the entire country.

The power of the railroads over Congress has been well-nigh supreme. That their influence was strong enough to defeat legislation is emphatically asserted by a prominent United States Senator, the writer of a letter which I quote:

"UNITED STATES SENATE,
"WASHINGTON, D. C., Feb. 9, 1903.

"DEAR SIR:

"Yours of the 19th ult. came duly to hand. It has happened as I feared: The interstate commerce committee will not report the measure giving power to the interstate commerce commission to fix rates. It is expecting too much from human nature that Senators whose every association is with the great railroad corporations, and whose political lives largely depend upon them, should in good faith approve a measure that would to an extent make the railroads a servant of the people, and to be subject to the decision of the commission when a question of rates is raised. The Senate committee is by a decided majority men who bear these relations to the railroads. I hope that some time in the future the committee will be so constituted that legislation of the character mentioned will issue from it, but I am afraid you and I will be many years older when that occurs.

Yours truly,
"_____"

The control of transportation was achieved through combination. Less than twenty years ago the railroads, overriding the law, secretly combined to suppress every trace of competition and to advance rates.

By 1897, 922 railroad corporations, with 250 allied railroads, having altogether 178,307 miles of road, constituting 95 per cent.

of the vital railway mileage of the country, were organized into six systems, known as the Vanderbilt, Pennsylvania, Morgan-Hill, Gould-Rockefeller, Moore-Leeds and Harriman-Kuhn-Loeb groups and their allies.

Since that time further concentration and control has increased the mileage of these groups to more than 200,000 miles of road. These groups are controlled by eight men, and, as stated by John Moody, in 1904, "the superior dominating influence of Mr. Rockefeller and Mr. Morgan is felt in a greater or less degree in all of the groups."

But an even greater danger was in waiting—the control of capital and credit, the very life of all business.

The Centralized Control of Banking, Capital, and Credits.—The country is only just beginning to understand how completely great banking institutions in the principal money centres have become bound up with the control of industrial institutions, the railroads and franchise combinations.

That there was a tendency on the part of great banking associations to merge and combine could not be overlooked. But while financial and economic writers had directed public attention to the fact, and had even pointed out the opportunity and temptation for the use of this augmented power, in connection with the promotion of the speculative side of business organization, they were slow to believe that banking institutions could be so prostituted. Certain critical observers had, however, as long as five or six years ago, suggested the dangerous tendencies in this direction.

Thus early an English economist, writing in *Littell's Living Age,* said:

"The recent extreme stringency of money in New York would probably never have arisen if the banks, instead of preparing for the autumn demands, had not locked up their funds in the financiering of Wall Street. That the banks are, to a large extent, under the domination of the big financiers is well known, and the recent insurance investigations have shown how, under such domination, private interests may be made to prevail over those of the public."

Addressing the Minnesota Bankers' Association at Lake Minnetonka about this time, Thomas F. Woodlock, formerly editor of the Wall Street *Journal,* author of "The Anatomy of Railroad Reports," and now a member of the New York Exchange, sounded this note of warning:

"The one thing that stands out most prominent, in my judgment, with reference to Wall Street banking, is the danger of the concentration of banking powers in the hands of a few great speculative interests. We have clearly defined tendencies in Wall Street, the ultimate effect of which is likely to be the creation of two or three powerful groups of banks. There is, for example, the so-called 'Standard Oil' group of banks headed by the National City; there is the so-called 'Morgan Life Insurance' group, with the National Bank of Commerce and the First National Bank at its head. These two groups contain many of the most powerful banks in New York City, and together account for a very large proportion of the total volume of credit at the disposal of the public. * * * The connection between the management of the banks in New York City and the great financial and speculative interests is very close, and if we ever have serious banking trouble it will come from this fact."

In an article on the "Concentration of Banking Interests in the United States" (written in 1905), Charles J. Bullock, formerly professor of economics, Williams College, now at Harvard, said:

"Unlike the central banks of other countries, our largest institutions are closely connected with various industrial interests, so that they do not occupy an independent position. Their policy is not controlled with sole regard for the general welfare of our banking system; but they have been drawn into vast enterprises, into promotion or reorganization, often of a speculative character, and have displayed less, not more, than ordinary conservatism. The National City Bank stood sponsor for the Amalgamated Copper Company, and the First National Bank has lent its aid to the various undertakings with which Mr. Morgan has been identified."

Under the title "Perils of the Money Trust," the Wall Street *Journal* (1903) editorially pointed out these dangers in the following language:

"What is taking place is a concentration of banking that is not merely a normal growth, but concentration that comes from combination, consolidation and other methods employed to secure monopolistic power. Not only this, but this concentration has not been along the lines of commercial banking. The great banks of concentration are in close alliance with financial interests intimately connected with promotion of immense enterprises, many of them being largely speculative. The bank credits of the country are being rapidly concentrated in the hands of a few bankers who are more interested in banking on its financial (watered stock) side than in banking on its commercial side.

"Such concentration as this is dangerous in a political sense. The people have already been greatly disturbed by the concentration that has taken place in the industrial world. * * * But concentration in the industrial world is a far less menacing condition than concentration in banking. The men or set of men who control the credits of the country control the country.

"And if this concentration continues at the rapid rate with which it has progressed in the past ten years there will surely come a time when the people, alarmed at the growth, will rise up in some vigorous measure to assert their power. Such an uprising would involve the most serious consequences and would likely be carried to the most unreasonable limits. There can be no doubt that further concentration of banking power in New York is the end in view of some of our leading bankers. They believe that there will be a further reduction in the number of banks and a further increase in the power of the big banks. That is one reason why this banking concentration needs to be studied and its consequences carefully weighed.

"But there is still another reason why this development in modern banking is open to criticism. It is largely a departure from commercial banking. It is turning the power over bank credits into financial (stock promotion) channels. So long as the country is prosperous no immediate danger may be apprehended from such a development as that. * * * But it is always the unexpected that happens, and our panics are commonly ushered in by some unforeseen calamity and it is a fair inquiry to make whether banking conducted on a "department-store" principle, with credits concentrated in a few great institutions, and with these institutions having large interests in financial and speculative enterprises, would be in a position in such a moment of unexpected calamity to do more than to protect the financial and speculative interests with which it is allied. In such a contingency what protection would be left for the great commercial interests of the country?"

The plain truth is that legitimate commercial banking is being eaten up by speculative banking. The greatest banks of the financial centre of the country have ceased to be agents of commerce and have become primarily agencies of promotion and speculation. By merging the largest banks, trust companies, and insurance companies masses of capital have been brought under one management, to be employed not as the servant of commerce, but as its master; not to supply legitimate business and to facilitate exchange, but to subordinate the commercial demands of the country upon the banks to call loans in Wall Street and to finance industrial organizations, always speculative, and often unlawful in character. Trained men, who a dozen years ago stood first among the bankers of the world as heads of the greatest banks of New York City, are, in the main, either displaced or do the bidding of men who are not bankers, but masters of organization.

The banks which were then managed by bankers as independent commercial institutions are now owned in groups by a few men, whose principal interests are in railroads, traction, telegraph, cable, shipping, iron and steel, copper, coal, oil, gas, insurance, etc.

This subversion of banking by alliance with promotion and stock speculation is easily traced.

There was every inducement for those who controlled transportation and a few great basic industries to achieve control of money in the financial centre of the country.

The centralization of the banking power in New York City would not only open the way for financing the reorganization and consolidation of industrial enterprises and of public utilities throughout the country, but would place those in authority where they could control the markets on stocks and bonds almost at will.

With this enormous concentration of business it is possible to create, artificially, periods of prosperity and periods of panic. Prices can be lowered or advanced at the will of the "System." When the farmer must move his crops a scarcity of money may be created and prices lowered. When the crop passes into the control of the speculator the artificial stringency may be relieved and prices advanced, and the illegitimate profit raked off the agricultural industry may be pocketed in Wall Street.

If an effort is made to compel any one of these great "Interests" to obey the law, it is easy for them to enter into a conspiracy to destroy whoever may be responsible for the undertaking.

The bare names of the directors of two great bank groups—the Standard Oil group and the Morgan group—given in connection with their other business associations is all the evidence that need be offered of the absolute community of interest between banks, railroads, and all the great industries.

There are twenty-three directors of the National City Bank (Standard Oil). There are forty directors of the National Bank of Commerce (Morgan). Examination of these directorates shows that the two groups are being knit together in business associations, suggesting their ultimate unification.

Subject to personal differences which may arise between powerful individuals of these different groups, resulting in occasional collision, they are practically a monopoly, and as far as the public is concerned, practically one group. The business partner of the head of the Morgan group is found on the directorate of the chief financial institution which heads the Standard Oil group. And one of the leading directors of the National City Bank (Standard Oil) is a member of the board of directors of the principal financial institution in the Morgan group. The directors of the leading organizations comprising the two principal groups are bound together in mutual interest as shareholders in the various transportation franchise, and industrial concerns which have been financed by one or the other of the group in recent years.

Fourteen of the directors of the National City Bank are at the head of fourteen great combinations representing 38 per cent. of the capitalization of all the industrial trusts of the country.

The railroad lines represented on the board of this one bank cover the country like a network. Chief among them are the Lackawanna, the Chicago, Burlington and Quincy, the Union Pacific, the Alton, the Missouri Pacific, the Chicago, Milwaukee and St. Paul, the Chicago and Northwestern, the Rock Island, the Denver and Rio Grande, the Mexican National, the Baltimore and Ohio, the Northern Pacific, the New York Central, the Texas and Pacific, the Erie, the New York, New Haven and Hartford, the Delaware and Hudson, the Illinois Central, the Manhattan Elevated of New York City, and the rapid-transit lines of Brooklyn. These same twenty-three directors, through their various connections, represent more than 350 other banks, trust companies, railroads, and industrial corporations, with an aggregate capitalization of more than twelve thousand million dollars.

That is a part only of what is behind the directorate of the National City Bank of New York, the head of only one of these groups.

The twenty-three directors of the National City Bank, the head of the Standard Oil group, and the directors of the National Bank of Commerce, forty in number, hold 1,007 directorships on the great transportation, industrial, and commercial institutions of this country.

The ability of these group banks of New York through their connected interests to engage in underwriting, to finance promotion schemes, where the profits resulting from overcapitalization represent hundreds of millions of dollars, places them beyond let or hindrance from competitors elsewhere in the country. Their ability to take advantage of conditions in Wall Street, even if they did not create these conditions, forcing interest rates on call loans as high as 150 per cent., would enable them to command, almost at will, the capital of the country for these speculative purposes.

But one result could follow. Floating the stocks and bonds in overcapitalized transportation, traction, mining and industrial organizations does not create wealth, but it does absorb capital. Through the agency of these great groups hundreds of millions of dollars of the wealth of the country have been tied up. Other hundreds of millions have been drawn upon to supply these great speculating groups in their steadily increasing Wall Street business.

I would not unjustly decry Wall Street or ignore the necessity of a great central market to provide capital for the large business undertakings of this country. I recognize the rights of capital and the service which capital can render to a great producing nation such as ours. But this government guarantees equality of opportunity for all men, and it likewise guarantees equality of opportunity for all capital. And corporations and combinations of corporations, with their centralized banking and extending branch connections from state to state, are not entitled to special favors in legislation.

The whole course of banking and currency legislation has steadily favored the great banking institutions, especially those having community of interest with the industrial and transportation companies of the country.

The committees of Congress controlling this legislation are chargeable with this neglect of public interest. Since the enactment of the National Banking Law, with each recurring Congress the Comptroller of the Currency has recommended legislation needful for the better protection of the depositors and the commercial interests generally, as against the speculative interests of Wall Street. These recommendations have been uniformly ignored. In proof of this, I cite an extract from a public statement of Deputy Comptroller of the Currency Kane, issued March 31, 1908, as follows:

"While numerous have been the recommendations of the eleven comptrollers who have presided over the affairs of the Currency Bureau since its establishment, which, in the judgment of each, would have increased the security of the depositors and creditors of the banks, practically none has been enacted into law or has received the serious consideration of the legislative branch of the government. No one has had better opportunities to observe from an impartial and disinterested standpoint the practical operations of the banking laws and to note their weak features in regard to the security of creditors than the respective Comptrollers of the Currency. Notwithstanding the many recommendations made by the several comptrollers, there has been practically no amendment of the law since the passage of the original bank act of February 25, 1863, which can be said to have had for its object the particular welfare of the depositor.

"Of the fifty-four acts amendatory of the original enactment which have been adopted since that date, practically all have been in the interest of greater latitude or privileges to the banks.

*   *   *   *   *   *   *

"The responsibility should rest where it properly belongs—upon the law and the lawmakers, and not upon the administrative officials."

This is but the barest outline of the upbuilding of the power which now controls.

Is there a way out? Let us consider.

By its decisions in the Standard Oil and Tobacco cases the Supreme Court has all at once created itself into a legislature, an interstate commerce commission and a supreme court, combined in one.

The "rule of reason" gives it legislative power, the power to determine according to its own opinion that some restraints of trade are lawful and other restraints unlawful. The power to carry out

335

the dissolution and reorganization of the trusts and to work out the details is exactly the power that a legislature turns over to a commission. Punishment for contempt is the court's substitute for the criminal penalty that the legislature attaches to the violation of its statutes.

The supreme court has amended the anti-trust act in exactly the way that Congress repeatedly refused to amend it, and has usurped both legislative and executive power in doing it. Whether we wish it or not, Congress is now compelled to create an inter-state trade commission to control the trusts, or else leave the control to the federal courts, acting as a commission.

Such a commission should not fix prices. Price regulation assumes that we are dealing with a necessary monopoly, as in the case of railroads and public utilities. But the commercial monopolies are based on unfair and discriminatory practices and special privileges. These can be abolished in several ways.

Amend the Sherman law by enacting specific prohibitions against well-known practices that constitute unreasonable restraints of trade. One of these is the brutal method of the Standard Oil Company of cutting prices in any place where there is a competitor in order to kill him off, while keeping up prices in other places. Another is the club wielded by the tobacco trust, which put the jobbers in a position where, unless they refrained from buying of a competitor, they could not get from the trust the brands which were indispensable to the successful conduct of their business. These and several other obviously unreasonable restraints of trade are definitely prohibited in the bill which I have introduced in the Senate.

The bill also places the burden of proof on the trust to show that any restraint of trade which it practices is reasonable—that is, that it benefits the community.

It also provides that when the court has once entered its final decree and declared a trust illegal, any person who has suffered damages may come in under that decree and simply petition that his damages be paid without proving anything except the amount of the damages. If this had been law when the Standard Oil and Tobacco decisions were rendered, those decisions would have meant something more than mere victories on paper.

In addition to these amendments to the anti-trust law, there is need of a commission to stand between the people and the courts in order to investigate the facts and to prohibit all unreasonable

336

restraints not specifically described in the law. This commission should have full power to ascertain the actual cost of reproduction, or physical value of the property; the reasonable value that the intangible property, such as good will, would have under conditions of fair competition, and to distinguish this from the illegal values that have been built up in violation of law. It should ascertain the value that depend on patents, monopoly of natural resources and all other forms of special privilege; the amount of property that has been paid for out of illegal profits taken from the public, distinguished from the property paid for out of legitimate profits and true investment. It should in this way ascertain the true cost of production and whether the prices charged are yielding extortionate profits or only the reasonable profits that competitors could earn. These are the facts that the people must know before they will consent to any legislation that treats illegal values as though they were legal.

With these facts ascertained and made *prima facie* evidence in court, these illegal values cannot be permanently fastened on the American people. It will take time to pull down this false structure of illegal capitalization of the trusts, but it is now the greatest menace to prosperity.

If these laws are adopted, then every business man, as well as the courts, will know definitely what is meant by the "rule of reason." Legitimate business will have its course laid out clear and certain before it, and every investor will know precisely what the law allows and what it prohibits.

The trust problem has become so interwoven in our legal and industrial system that no single measure or group of measures can reach all of it. It must be picked off at every point where it shows its head.

Every combination of a manufacturing business with the control of transportation, including pipe lines, should be prohibited, in order that competitors may have equal facilities for reaching markets.

The control of limited sources of raw material, like coal, iron ore, or timber, by a manufacturing corporation, should be broken up and these resources should be opened to all manufacturers on equal terms.

It is claimed on all sides that competition has failed. I deny it. Fair competition has not failed. It has been suppressed. When competitors are shut out from markets by discrimination, and denied either transportation, raw material or credit on equal terms, we do not have competition. We have the modern form of highway robbery. The great problem of legislation before us is first for the people to resume control of their government, and then to protect themselves against those who are throttling competition by the aid of government.

I do not say that competition does not have its evils. Labor organizations are the struggling protest against cut-throat competition. The anti-trust law was not intended or understood to apply to them. They should be exempt from its operation.

The tariff should be brought down to the difference in labor cost of the more efficient plants and the foreign competitor, and where there is no difference the tariff should be removed. Where the protective tariff is retained its advantages must be passed along to labor, for whose benefit the manufacturer contends it is necessary.

The patent laws should be so amended that the owners of patents will be compelled to develop them fully or permit their use on equal terms by others.

More vital and menacing then any other power that supports trusts is the control of credit through the control of the people's savings and deposits. When the Emergency Currency Bill was before Congress in 1908, Senator Aldrich slipped into the conference report certain provisions which he had withdrawn in the Senate, and withdrew provisions which he had first included. He eliminated protection against promotion schemes, excluded penalties for false reporting, dropped provisions for safeguarding reserves, inserted provisions for accepting railroad bonds as security. Now he comes with another plausible measure to remedy the admitted evils of our inelastic banking system.

When we realize that the control of credit and banking is the greatest power that the trusts possess to keep out competitors, we may well question their sincerity in offering a patriotic measure to dispossess themselves of that power. It is the people's money that is expected to give security to this plan and the people must and shall control it.

The proposed Aldrich Currency plan is the product of a commission composed of men who are or have been members of the committees of the two houses of Congress, which have controlled all legislation relating to currency and banking. With such a record it behooves the public to examine with the utmost care any plan which they recommend, however plausible it may appear upon its face. A critical study of the scheme of this commission will convince any student of government finance, that under the guise of providing elasticity to our currency system, it is in reality an adroit means of further concentration and control of the money and credits of the United States under a fifty-year franchise, augmenting the power of those who already dominate the banking and insurance resources of the country.

Our National Banking Law is a patchwork of legislation. It should be thoroughly revised. And all authorities agree that a comprehensive plan for an emergency currency is vitally important. When the basic principle of such a plan is once determined, when it is settled that government controlled banks are to be, *in fact*, controlled by the government *in the public interest*, the details can easily be worked out.

An emergency currency circulation should be backed by proper reserves, issued only against commercial paper that represents actual and legitimate business transactions. No plan should be adopted which admits of control by banking interests which, under existing conditions, means, in the end, control by the great speculative banking groups.

In all our plans for progressive legislation, it must not be forgotten that we are only just beginning to get control of the railroads. The present law is an improvement, but the Interstate Commerce Commission requires to be greatly strengthened. It should have a much larger appropriation, enabling it to prosecute investigations in all parts of the country. It should make physical valuations of the railroads, eliminating watered stock, monopoly values and the unwarranted inflation of railway terminals to conceal monopoly values. And the Commerce Court should be abolished as a mere subterfuge interposed to handicap the commission.

As a first necessary step for the regulation of interstate commerce, we *must* ascertain the reasonable value of the physical property of railroads, justly inventoried, upon a sound economic basis, distinguishing *actual* values from *monopoly* values derived from violations of law, and must make such discriminating values the *base line* for determining rates. The country should know how much of the eighteen billions of capitalization was contributed by those who own the railroads, and how much by the people themselves. We should also provide for the extension of the powers and the administrative control of the Interstate Commerce Commission.

A word to the Magazines.—I have sketched the growth and power of the great interests that to-day control our property and our governments. I have shown how subtle and elusive, yet relentless, they are. Rising up against them is the confused voice of the people. Their heart is true but their eyes do not yet see all the intricate sources of power. Who shall show them? There are only two agencies that in any way can reach the whole people. These are the press and the platform. But the platform in no way compares with the press in its power of continuous repeated instruction.

One would think that in a democracy like ours, people seeking the truth, able to read and understand, would find the press their eager and willing instructors. Such was the press of Horace Greeley, Henry Raymond, Charles A. Dana, Joseph Medill, and Horace Rublee.

But what do we find has occurred in the past few years since the money power has gained control of our industry and government? It controls the newspaper press. The people know this. Their confidence is weakened and destroyed. No longer are the editorial columns of newspapers a potent force in educating public opinion. The newspapers, of course, are still patronized for news. But even as to news, the public is fast coming to understand that wherever news items bear in any way upon the control of government by business, the news is colored; so confidence in the newspaper as a newspaper is being undermined.

Cultured and able men are still to be found upon the editorial staffs of all great dailies, but the public understands them to be hired men who no longer express honest judgments and sincere conviction, who write what they are told to write, and whose judgments are salaried.

To the subserviency of the press to special interests in no small degree is due the power and influence and prosperity of the weekly and monthly magazines. A decade ago young men trained in journalism came to see this control of the newspapers of the country. They saw also an unoccupied field. And they went out and built up great periodicals and magazines. They were free.

Their pages were open to publicists and scholars and liberty, and justice and equal rights found a free press beyond the reach of the corrupt influence of consolidated business and machine politics. We entered upon a new era.

The periodical, reduced in price, attractive and artistic in dress, strode like a young giant into the arena of public service. Filled with this spirit, quickened with human interest, it assailed social and political evils in high places and low. It found the power of the public service corporation and the evil influences of money in the municipal government of every large city. It found franchises worth millions of dollars secured by bribery; police in partnership with thieves and crooks and prostitutes. It found juries "fixed" and established business plying its trade between litigants and the back door of blinking justice.

It found Philadelphia giving away franchises, franchises not supposedly or estimated to be worth $2,500,000, but for which she had been openly offered and refused $2,500,000. Milwaukee they found giving away street-car franchises worth $8,000,000 against the protests of her indignant citizens. It found Chicago robbed in tax-payments of immense value by corporate owners of property through fraud and forgery on a gigantic scale; it found the aldermen of St. Louis, organized to boodle the city with a criminal compact, on file in the dark corner of a safety deposit vault.

The free and independent periodical turned her searchlight on state legislatures, and made plain as the sun at noonday the absolute control of the corrupt lobby. She opened the closed doors of the secret caucus, the secret committee, the secret conference, behind which United States Senators and Members of Congress betrayed the public interest into the hands of railroads, the trusts, the tariff mongers, and the centralized banking power of the country. She revealed the same influences back of judicial and other appointments. She took the public through the great steel plants and into the homes of the men who toil twelve hours a day and seven days in the week. And the public heard their cry of despair. She turned her camera into the mills and shops where little children are robbed of every chance of life that nourishes vigorous bodies and sound minds, and the pinched faces and dwarfed figures told their pathetic story on her clean white pages.

The control of the newspaper press is not the simple and expensive one of ownership and investment. There is here and there a "kept sheet" owned by a man of great wealth to further his own interests. But the papers of this class are few. The control comes through that community of interests, that interdependence of investments and credits which ties the publisher up to the banks, the advertisers and the special interests.

We may expect this same kind of control, sooner or later, to reach out for the magazines. But more than this: I warn you of a subtle new peril, the centralization of advertising, that will in time seek to gag you. What has occurred on the small scale in almost every city in the country will extend to the national scale, and will ere long close in on the magazines. No men ever faced graver responsibilities. None have ever been called to a more unselfish, patriotic service. I believe that when the final test comes, you will not be found wanting; you will not desert and leave the people to depend upon the public platform alone, but you will hold aloft the lamp of Truth, lighting the way for the preservation of representative government and the liberty of the American people.

Index

Van Hise, Charles R., 13, 14, 15, 71
Van Valkenberg, E. A., 215, 216, 217, 220, 222, 224
Vilas, William F., 5, 17, 54–55, 62
Voter's Handbook, 120–21
Vreeland Bill, 199

Wall Street, 248, 313
Wanamaker, R. M., 239–40, 245, 246
Warner, William, 178
Warren, F. E., 170
Warren, Lansing, 109
Water-Power Legislation, 155
Watson, James E., 281, 302
Webster, Sidney, 305

Wellborn, Olin, 27
Welliver, Judson C., 283
Wheeler, William G., 111
White, William Allen, 247
Whittier, John G., 132
Wickersham, G. W., 180, 309
Wilson-Gorman Law, 87
Wisconsin "Machine," 78, 79, 81, 83, 98
Women and Public Service, 134–36
Wood, Joseph, 37–38
Works, John D., 222
Wright, Nathaniel, 230

Youmans, Theodora W., 136